THE ENVIRONMENT AND WORLD HISTORY

THE CALIFORNIA WORLD
HISTORY LIBRARY

*Edited by Edmund Burke III, Kenneth Pomeranz,
and Patricia Seed*

THE ENVIRONMENT
AND WORLD HISTORY

Edited by

Edmund Burke III
and Kenneth Pomeranz

University of California Press

Berkeley   Los Angeles   London

University of California Press, one of the most
distinguished university presses in the United States,
enriches lives around the world by advancing
scholarship in the humanities, social sciences, and
natural sciences. Its activities are supported by the UC
Press Foundation and by philanthropic contributions
from individuals and institutions. For more information,
visit www.ucpress.edu.

University of California Press
Berkeley and Los Angeles, California

University of California Press, Ltd.
London, England

Library of Congress Cataloging-in-Publication Data

Burke, Edmund.
    The environment and world history / edited by
Edmund Burke III and Kenneth Pomeranz.
        p.   cm.
    Includes bibliographical references and index.
    ISBN 978-0-520-25687-3 (cloth : alk. paper)
    ISBN 978-0-520-25688-0 (pbk. : alk. paper)
    1. Environmental sciences—History.   I. Pomeranz,
Kenneth.   II. Title.
GE50.B87   2009
304.2—dc22   2008040826

Manufactured in the United States of America

17   16   15   14   13   12   11   10   09
10   9   8   7   6   5   4   3   2   1

This book is printed on Natures Book, which contains
50% postconsumer waste and meets the minimum
requirements of ANSI/NISO Z39.48–1992 (R 1997)
(Permanence of Paper).

To the memory of John Richards

CONTENTS

FIGURES, MAPS,
AND TABLES

PREFACE

Environmental history has the potential to transform our understanding of the human past. Like the perspective of gender history, an environmental perspective is not readily contained within existing subdisciplines of history. By focusing on the impact of human activity on the biosphere, the environmental perspective not only opens new topics for investigation but also changes our understanding of the emergence of the modern world. Environmental history has developed its own distinctive vocabulary and methodologies. Yet most environmental historians, while aware that ecology is a global and holistic science, have tended to frame their work more narrowly and to focus on the impact of anthropogenic change on ecological regions or even particular eco-niches. Few have sought to make broader connections to world-historical forces. Perhaps as a result, most world history textbooks relegate environmental history to a polite few paragraphs, if that much. Recently some environmental historians, among them Alfred Crosby, Richard Drayton, Richard Grove, John McNeill, Carolyn Merchant, John Richards, and Richard Tucker, have been seeking to inscribe their work in larger, even global, contexts. Yet such large perspectives remain atypical.[1]

Moreover, because of the geographic origins of the field, environmental history has been strongly dominated by accounts of the experience of the United States and Western Europe. United States environmental historians, in particular, have been slow to recognize that the emerging environmental histories of other areas might cast American events in a different light. However, a recent survey by Paul

Sutter provides a good example of what might be gained from a wider perspective.[2] Viewed from the perspective of South Asia, Sutter argues, the environmental history of the United States appears preoccupied with the impact of capitalism on wild nature, and with conservation movements as the means of redressing the balance. By contrast, historians of the South Asian environment have emphasized the impact of colonialism on their societies and the agency of peasant social movements against both the colonial and postcolonial states.[3]

Here the American unconsciousness of the presence of empire in westward expansion is suddenly visible. Whereas U.S. settlers regarded North America (and particularly the U.S. West) as an unpopulated space, the realm of "nature," and the home of the "ecological" Indian, British colonialists in South Asia could not miss the fact that they were intruding into a landscape crowded with preexisting local uses and claims, and so they made explicit their goals and rationales for subordinating those claims.[4] From the South Asian perspective, U.S. conservation and preservationist movements resemble nineteenth- and twentieth-century British colonial policies that sought to police marginal (often indigenous) people and delegitimize their modes of land use on behalf of major agricultural interests. Confirmation of this insight is provided by Mark Spence, whose study of U.S. national parks suggests that the creation of national parks was shaped not only by preservationist imperatives but also by struggles with the indigenous populations and American dominion over the continent.[5] The comparative gaze we find in Sutter's stimulating essay has much to offer those interested in constructing an environmental history of the United States that integrates the history of colonialism. A central purpose of this book is to encourage precisely this type of comparative thinking, which results in reframing and deprovincializing familiar national or regional narratives.

Meanwhile, the new world history that has emerged over the last thirty years also has the potential to reframe the way we think about history in general, rather than simply becoming another discrete subfield. In particular, it challenges us to rethink modern history not as the history of Europe at large, but as a shared history of conflict and collaboration in which Asians, Africans, and Americans have also participated.[6] Notable strides have been made in some areas, such as understanding the early modern emergence of a world economy and the crucial roles of non-European collaborators in the formation of what became formal European empires.[7] In this enterprise, world history, like environmental history, can help us revisit the significance of any particular history—including that of Europe, whose entry into modernity is often represented as independent of events anywhere else on the globe. Thus far, however, civilizations, states, and cultures have remained the dominant units of analysis, even in world history—both because of the need to maintain dialogue with historians who are deeply attached to those units and because of the intrinsic difficulties of imagining and implementing alternatives. Thus, despite its promise, world history has thus far done better at comparing regional-scale phenomena than at providing new narratives in which the globe itself is the unit under consideration. We do not argue for privileging either of these levels of analysis at the expense of the other, but we suggest that both are necessary if either global or environmental history is to influence how we think, both about history and about our current global dilemmas.

Given the shared intellectual potential of environmental history and world history, as well as the parallel intellectual agendas that call for reframing the relationship of parts and wholes, it is surprising that a global environmental history, incorporating the strengths of both perspectives, has been slow to emerge. Instead, the two disciplines have tended to proceed down separate tracks. Most world historians have relegated the environment to the margins of actually existing world histories as a kind of afterthought, rather than considering it as a factor informing the analysis from the outset.[8] At a time when the consequences of human environmental impacts are becoming increasingly evident, a more global environmental history and a more environmentally conscious world history have much to offer us. Environmental histories, with their attention to global, regional, and local ecologies, offer world history the possibility of breaking out of its traditional civilizational and national frameworks. The knowledge that human development has real, and increasingly ascertainable, limits, and that these are in large measure ecological, must inevitably shape the kinds of histories we write and the kinds of shared lives we imagine. We do not know just when a particular species will expire, or particular ecological niches will be terminally polluted, or the atmosphere irrevocably poisoned; we do know, however, that imagining these limits is not fanciful but a vital necessity. Putting the environment into world history is therefore an urgent intellectual project.

Edmund Burke III

NOTES TO PREFACE

1. See, for example, Alfred W. Crosby, *Ecological Imperialism* (Cambridge: Cambridge University Press, 1987); Richard Drayton, *Nature's Government: Science, Imperial Britain, and the "Improvement" of the World* (New Haven: Yale University Press, 2000); Richard H. Grove, *Green Imperialism: Colonial Expansion, Tropical Island Edens and the Origins of Environmentalism, 1600–1860* (Cambridge: Cambridge University Press,

1995); John R. McNeill, *Something New under the Sun: An Environmental History of the Twentieth Century* (New York: W. W. Norton, 2000); Carolyn Merchant, *The Death of Nature: Women, Ecology, and the Scientific Revolution* (New York: Harper & Row, 1980); John F. Richards, *The Unending Frontier: An Environmental History of the Early Modern World* (Berkeley: University of California Press, 2003); and Richard P. Tucker, *Insatiable Appetite: The United States and the Ecological Degradation of the Tropical World* (Berkeley: University of California Press, 2000).

2. Paul Sutter, "Reflections: What Can U.S. Environmental Historians Learn From Non-environmental Historiography?" *Environmental History* 8, no. 1 (2003): 109–29.

3. See, for example, Ramachandra Guha and Madhav Gadgil, *This Fissured Land: An Ecological History of India* (Delhi: Oxford University Press, 1992).

4. For a critique of this position, see Shepard Krech III, *The Ecological Indian: Myth and History* (New York: W. W. Norton, 1999). For a more balanced view, see Andrew C. Isenberg, *The Destruction of the Bison: An Environmental History, 1750–1920* (Cambridge: Cambridge University Press, 2001).

5. Mark David Spence, *Dispossessing the Wilderness: Indian Removal and the Making of the National Parks* (New York: Oxford, 2000).

6. For a stimulating recent overview, see Robert Marks, *The Origins of the Modern World: A Global and Ecological Narrative* (Lanham, MD: Rowman & Littlefield, 2002).

7. On the world economy, see, for example, R. Bin Wong, *China Transformed: Historical Change and the Limits of European Experience* (Ithaca, NY: Cornell University Press, 1997); Kenneth Pomeranz, *The Great Divergence: China, Europe and the Making of the Modern World Economy* (Princeton: Princeton University Press, 2000); and Kaoru Sugihara, "The East Asian Path of Economic Development: A Long-term Perspective," in *The Resurgence of East Asia: 500, 150 and 50 Year Perspectives*, ed. Giovanni Arrighi, Takeshi Hamashita, and Mark Selden (London: Routledge, 2003), 78–123. At least two large collaborative projects have emerged from this rethinking so far: the Global Price and Income History Group (headquartered at the University of California, Davis) and the Global Economic History network (headquartered at the London School of Economics).

For three of the many works that have helped reframe the emergence of European empires in ways that allow more agency to non-European actors—each dealing with a different period—see Sanjay Subrahmanyam, *The Portuguese Empire in Asia, 1500–1700* (London: Longman, 1993); C. A. Bayly, *Imperial Meridian: The British Empire and the World, 1780–1830* (London: Longman, 1989); and Frederick Cooper and Ann Laura Stoler, eds., *Tensions of Empire: Colonial Culture in a Bourgeois World* (Berkeley: University of California Press, 1997).

8. In an otherwise impressive recent survey, C. A. Bayly's *The Birth of the Modern World, 1780–1914: Global Connections and Comparisons* (Malden, MA: Blackwell, 2004), the environment is still missing in action.

ACKNOWLEDGMENTS

The idea for this volume derived from Edmund Burke's 1998 National Endowment for the Humanities Institute for College Teachers, "The Environment and World History." The lively questions and comments raised by the participants and presenters in the institute encouraged us to proceed with publication of some of the presentations. Drafts of five of the chapters included here were originally presented to the institute (those by Michael Adas, Edmund Burke, Mark Cioc, Kenneth Pomeranz, and John Richards). Subsequently, in an effort to broaden coverage, we invited additional submissions and are pleased to include the essays by William Beinart, Mahesh Rangarajan, Lise Sedrez, and Douglas Weiner. We thank White Horse Press for permission to reprint portions of an article by Rangarajan, "Environmental Histories of South Asia: A Review Essay," originally published in *Environment and History* 2, no. 2 (1996): 129–44; and *African Affairs* for permission to reprint portions of an essay by Beinart, "African History and Environmental History," *African Affairs* 99, no. 395 (2000): 269–302. Finally, we thank ICS Press for permission to reprint John Richards's essay "Toward a Global System of Property Rights in Land," from *Land, Property, and the Environment*, ed. John F. Richards (Oakland, CA: Institute for Contemporary Studies Press, 2002), 13–27.

Many individuals read and critiqued different versions of this book, and we thank them here. They include David G. Christian, Ross E. Dunn, Jason W. Moore, Ravi Rajan, David G. Sweet, and Mary Wilson. Without Jane Arons,

Urmi Engineer, and Patricia Sanders, who helped prepare the manuscript for publication, this book would never have seen the light of day, and we thank them for their assistance. Finally, we are especially grateful to Alissa Roedig, who did the final editing of the entire manuscript before submission, and to the contributors themselves, who waited patiently while the manuscript came together from its various sources.

PART ONE · OVERVIEW

ONE · Introduction

World History and Environmental History

KENNETH POMERANZ

LOOKING FOR GLOBAL FRAMEWORKS

This book's preface argues that a closer integration of world history and environmental history is "an urgent intellectual project." This idea is hardly new, but scholars still have a long way to go in implementing it. In certain obvious ways, the perspectives of world history and environmental history seem to fit together readily: land formations, wind patterns, and other geophysical phenomena pay no attention to borders, and the environmental effects of sheep, sugar production, and nuclear waste are temptingly easy to compare across cultural settings. Yet as a result of the linguistic and national boundaries that constrain scholarship, an environmental history with a truly global perspective has been slow to emerge. Research has proceeded down regional tracks, each largely unaware of the others. Meanwhile, most world history has continued to include the environment haphazardly and to foreground it only when it cannot be avoided—as in the conquest of the Americas—rather than to integrate it consistently into world-history narratives. By providing a survey of recent work from which a truly global and integrative environmental world history may eventually emerge, this volume seeks to contribute to a sustained dialogue between the two fields. By bringing environmental and world historians together, it hopes to encourage the construction of a more methodologically self-conscious and integrative environmental world history: one that also bears on such staple issues of "mainstream" history as state formation, imperialism, economic development, and the defining characteristics of both early modernity and modernity.

We take the last five hundred years as our time frame, paying particular attention to continuities between the early modern and modern periods. In this respect we depart from two landmark works that aim at a reasonably comprehensive global environmental history—John McNeill's *Something New under the Sun: An Environmental History of the Twentieth Century* (2000) and John Richards's *The Unending Frontier: An Environmental History of the Early Modern World* (2003). Each of these works focuses on one side of the divide between early modern and modern, a divide which they, like many environmental historians, place at the nineteenth-century boom in fossil-fuel use, industrialization, and power-driven transport. Indeed, because most of Richards's stories end around 1800 and most of McNeill's begin around 1900, even these two works together leave this transition largely unexamined. This book notes many important nineteenth-century discontinuities, but it nonetheless tries to tell stories that span that divide.

Most of these stories are about regions that are familiar from area studies: China, Africa, Latin America, Russia, the Middle East and North Africa, Southeast Asia, and India. Bringing together a number of people initially trained as area experts, but now framing their topics in global terms, has obvious advantages. But building a world history book out of mostly area-focused chapters still needs some justification; moreover, our list of areas is far from comprehensive. (There is no essay on Australia, North America, or Japan, for instance, and the one essay on Europe makes its point through a case study of the Rhine. Our principal focus is on today's poorer countries.) Politically and culturally defined areas are not the only possible units of analysis; several essays define other alternatives. My own essay, for instance, notes that in some periods (perhaps including the present), the flows of people and resources between China's littoral and the rest of maritime Asia are more important than those between the coast and China's own interior of the same country.[1]

We have tried, in short, to use both national and broader regional units while remaining conscious of their provisional nature. Those units remain essential points of departure for addressing three recurrent themes of this volume. One is the relationship between state formation and environmental history. A second is the need to place modern developments in the context of deep histories of human interactions with particular environments. The third, which follows from the others, is that regionally specific political economies and cultural practices continue to shape the local instantiations of a global transformation in the management of nature and society, which we call the developmentalist project.

John Richards's essay highlights two interrelated trends evident across much of Eurasia since roughly 1450. First, as populations recovered from plague, wars of Mongol succession, and other fourteenth-century crises, land use intensified. Formerly nomadic areas were converted to settled farming or ranching; slash-and-burn agriculture gave way to higher-yielding (and more laborious) practices; forests and marshes were reclaimed for uses that allowed humans to appropriate more of the biomass they produced, thereby restricting the domains of competing flora and fauna. Meanwhile, state organizations grew larger and stronger. A relatively small number of large states grew by swallowing their neighbors, and certain kinds of polities (e.g., independent city-states) all but vanished. The winners were also increasingly paramount within their own borders, raising centrally commanded armies that dwarfed other armed forces, asserting direct authority to settle a wider range of their subjects' disputes, collecting and maintaining more thorough records, and collecting ever more revenues. These two kinds of consolidation were linked by the growing costs of war, which ruthlessly eliminated those with inadequate resources. Thus war drove an ongoing fiscal transformation, which encouraged (among other things) more intensive land use.

Though most extensively studied in Europe, these processes also occurred elsewhere.[2] Victor Lieberman has shown them at work in mainland Southeast Asia;[3] another example is the bloody century that led Japan from the Onin war (1467–77) to the Tokugawa regime. In China and (less fully and less lastingly) India, where one huge state eliminated competition among near equals, these tendencies were less obvious, but still present. The Qing (1644–1912) ruled far more territory than any previous dynasty, mapped it more precisely, raised more revenues, and (at least in the eighteenth century) intervened at the grass-roots level more effectively than its predecessors in areas from agriculture to religion.

Insofar as state-making processes drove the global intensification of land use, the latter cannot simply be ascribed to capitalism, much less to an Enlightenment that emerged when these processes were already in full swing. (Attributing this intensification to population pressure is erroneous for the same reason.) Even if we identify the main cause as commercialization, for a long time the most important networks for this development were intra-Asian ones, which do not fit easily under the rubric of capitalism.[4]

Instead, we treat European capitalism and science as culturally specific variants of patterns found much more broadly: drives to create stronger, territorially defined states, to transform the physical environment for the sake of state power and (often secondarily) the welfare of the realm's people, and to "tame" or "conquer" nature, making it more predictable and controllable. Success required increasingly reliable (though often tense) relationships between states and owners of capital: groups of merchants that could provide revenue (and sometimes organization) that states needed, and people willing to invest in transforming the land.

Not surprisingly, these efforts often disregarded the interests of people who lacked a fixed relationship to any territory. Population growth (especially after 1700) further tipped the balance of power against nomadic peoples. Nomads did not disappear (as contemporary resistance to dam building, mining, and other attempts to appropriate remote resources remind us), and they occasionally threatened settled people and states even in the late eighteenth century (e.g., with the rise of the Sa'uds or Afghan incursions into India); but densely settled areas faced fewer such threats after about 1700, and settled peoples were on the offensive from Xinjiang and Siberia to the Brazilian and North American interiors. As I have argued elsewhere, even regimes descended from nomadic conquerors often changed their policies and self-presentation during this period.[5] The Manchu Qing dynasty for instance, was inclined during its first century to emphasize the decadence of the Han Chinese it had conquered and to claim for itself the Spartan virtues of a rough frontier people (though they also laid claim to Confucian refinement); meanwhile, in Central Asia, they often presented themselves as the heirs of the Mongols. By 1800, however, they were much more likely to present themselves within China as civilized rulers indistinguishable from other good Confucians, and to legitimize their rule in inner Asia with a classically Han Chinese rhetoric of uplifting barbarians.

Ideologically, successful regimes across Eurasia (and later elsewhere) generally portrayed the good person as one who had a stable relationship to some property (as owner or fixed tenant, for example) and participated in "improving" it. Such ideas were not new, of course: the Biblical association of nomads with the children of Cain and the ancient Chinese concern with fixing people in place as an essential step in civilizing them are just two examples.[6] Holy men, whether from Sufi, Daoist, or other traditions, sometimes claimed the privilege of movement for themselves; and some ethical traditions (including certain strands of Buddhism and Christianity) advocated renouncing the material world entirely. But these countertendencies rarely enjoyed state support for long, and they became more marginal as time went on.

South Asian statecraft—in which, as Mahesh Rangarajan notes in his essay, sparsely populated regions were valued as sources of fodder, and nonsedentary groups associated with those ecologies were seen as "key elements in the precolonial polity"—provide contrasting traditions that endured into the nineteenth century; but even there, states often encouraged sedentarization at the expense of nomads and shifting cultivators, even before colonialism.[7] Edmund Burke's essay on the Middle East notes the strategic importance of nonsettled groups who provided both cavalry and warhorses for export from Ottoman and Safavid lands and were long accorded special privileges, but he also notes the tension between these privileges and "full exploitation" of the potential agricultural surplus—a goal that increasingly won out in the nineteenth and twentieth centuries. Overall, ethical and political traditions that treated nonsedentary people inclusively faced increasing pressures even where they were strongest, and were more and more exceptional in Eurasian terms. (The story in most of sub-Saharan Africa and the pre-Columbian Americas is different: pressures to intensify cultivation were generally weaker, but ruling classes of cavalry experts were relatively scarce south of the Sahel and non-existent in the pre-Columbian Americas.)

THE DEVELOPMENTALIST PROJECT: A SCHEMATIC OUTLINE AND HISTORY

It is these commitments to state-building, sedentarization, and intensifying the exploitation of resources that we have designated the developmentalist project. It did not begin as an ideology or set of ideologies subsequently put into practice: on the contrary, growth-promoting practices, often created ad hoc, generally predated explicit and detailed schemas that linked and justified them. The most influential such synthesis was liberalism—itself a set of ideas that could be assembled in many different ways, with different emphases. (Benjamin Schwartz, for instance, has shown that the early twentieth-century Chinese thinker and translator Yan Fu, who gave a decidedly statist cast to Smith, Mill, and other classic liberals, did not misunderstand them so much as build on their thought along lines that seemed important in his time and place—much as we might say that John Rawls or Amartya Sen has done.)[8] But there were other lines of argument that upheld many similar goals and actions, whether within Europe (mercantilism, and much later, some kinds of socialism), East Asia ("national prosperity thought" in Tokugawa Japan, some elements of "statecraft" thinking in China), the Ottoman world, Muhammad Ali's Egypt, or South Asia (as in Tipu Sultan's Mysore).[9]

Whatever one calls it, developmentalism and resistance to it frame much of the environmental history of the last several centuries. This pattern imparts a family resemblance to many far-flung stories of frontier settlement, intensive cropping regimes, irrigation and flood-control schemes, and so on; this resemblance is reinforced by frequent imitation of techniques that succeeded elsewhere. In the nineteenth and especially the twentieth centuries, the widespread development of factories, railroads, and airports—and the increasingly universal acceptance of GNP per capita as a measure of human welfare and regime success (despite its rather loose relationship to both)—have further strengthened these resemblances, though differences remain. We do not invoke the concept of a shared developmentalist project to efface these differences or suggest that environmental histories everywhere are necessarily converging, but to establish a baseline of rough similarity that also allows us to discuss meaningful differences.

The concept of a shared developmentalist project has implications for some frequently invoked narratives in environmental history (and in economic history, which is so often environment's flip side). It reinforces the still-contested point that the modern world was not simply born in Europe. Capitalism as a mode of production—particularly the creation of a huge workforce with nothing to sell but its labor power, and private owners of land and capital who purchased labor power rather than rely on extramarket coercion—may remain central to stories of European development, but it has become increasingly clear that the absence of that particular configuration does not mean an absence of development or its environmental consequences.

This observation is not new: Robert Marks and Mark Elvin, for instance, have eloquently described how Chinese "commercialism without capitalism" produced many of the same environmental tendencies (toward intensification and monoculture, for example)[10]—but it bears repeating. The much more capital-intensive development of the industrial era—including railways, huge amounts of paved road, and eventually large factories—did require special institutions for gathering and deploying massive sums of financial capital, but this was a separate story, in which government borrowing for war brought forth most of the major innovations. Financing war was a problem by no means unique to Europe, and these needs created complex financial institutions in, for instance, South Asia as well; nor does this Braudelian kind of capitalism require a capitalist mode of production in the stricter Marxian sense. And if one measures industrialization not by the market value of the output but by the quantities of land and people that become involved— probably more relevant criteria for environmental historians—then noncapitalist (or at most semicapitalist) regimes have presided over most of the spread of industrialization: for example, the USSR, Eastern Europe, China, and India under Jawaharlal Nehru.

By the same token, although the attitude of Renaissance and Enlightenment science toward nature—summed up for many environmentalists in Francis Bacon's determination to "torture Nature until she gives up her secrets"—may have been unusually aggressive (Mark Cioc's essay provides telling examples), we now know better than to assume that non-Europeans lived in harmony with nature. William Beinart's essay points out that although the emphasis on indigenous environmental wisdom in much African historiography is a useful corrective to the assumptions of many colonial (and contemporary) experts about native "profligacy," it can be overdone: indigenous ideas often did not prize preservation, or led to ineffective prescriptions. Mahesh Rangarajan also warns us against too sharp a division between an assumed precolonial ecological harmony and subsequent exploitation. Indigenous people often embraced foreign techniques: for better or worse, their ideas about land management sometimes resembled foreign ones. Moreover, any dichotomy between native and foreign experts obscures the range of actors on the scene: where, for instance, would one place the Egyptian engineers described in Edmund Burke's essay, trained in schools established by Muhammad Ali on the model of the French École Polytechnique?

This point is not wholly new either: North American environmental history, for instance, has long since moved beyond the myth of the ecological Indian.[11] Nor does questioning the dichotomy between the heedless Westerner and the self-controlled non-Westerner undermine the point—also made by Beinart—that there are genuine, experientially verified alternatives to Western-style developmentalism. In Africa, Latin America, and South Asia, for instance, resources held in common have sometimes continued to meet economic needs without being overexploited (as models based on individual self-interest would predict); and labor-intensive multicropping, based on traditional knowledge, has sometimes generated higher per capita output and food security than Green Revolution projects in the same area.[12] But exploring the "environmentalism of the poor"[13] is very different from attributing a special environmental sensitivity or indifference to growth to non-Westerners: indeed, what makes the above examples so compelling is that the local solutions produce *both* economic benefits and environmental sustainability, and so make sense in "Western" terms, too. They may not be profit-maximizing, if we assume that each peasant calculates like a capitalist firm, mentally deducting from his or her output the implicit cost of every hour of labor at the market-wage rate: but such a calculus was probably rare among the millions of producers who nonetheless helped power development around the world, including parts of Europe.[14] If we think in terms of the developmentalist project rather than a more stringently defined capitalism, it is much easier to include these actors in a unified environmental history.

What, then, were the concrete manifestations of the developmentalist project? Perhaps the most basic is a continuing increase in incentives and pressures to expand economic production. Often these came in liberal form: private rights to property specified with increasing detail and given expanded protection (from community sanctions, other private parties, and the state itself), and the development of markets for both products and factors of production. These features are evident in many places, especially from the eighteenth century onward. But incentives did not always take the same form: Soviet production quotas, for instance, certainly increased output for quite a while. And especially (though not exclusively) in the early modern period, property rights and market incentives for some people often meant coercion for others, whether in the cases of South Asian concessionaires granted monopsonies on local textiles for export, chartered colonial companies granted statelike power over pepper producers, slaveholders producing for European markets, or monopolist tax farmers in many places whose growing cash exactions forced peasants to produce more for the market.

The increased commodification that resulted had many dimensions. Increasingly, natural objects, including animals, were regarded primarily as sources of wealth, obstacles to economic tasks, or both (live foxes raided farms; dead foxes yielded fur). Sacred taboos and notions of magical efficacy became less prevalent. We should not assume that this disenchantment with nature was a new process. Nor should we see it as simply a matter of the rise of European science, or as necessarily entailing secularization. For centuries, processes of migration and conquest, such as Chinese settlement of the area south of the Yangzi, had involved a taming of strange landscapes, including swamps, rivers, and wild animals, whose spirits had previously demanded sacrifices to prevent disasters but who now became either self-controlled or objects of control. Such processes might or might not involve importing new religions, as European conquests in the Americas did; what matters for our purposes is that the new religious configurations imagined ruling nature, not fearfully propitiating it.[15]

Both the spread of "world" religions in the early modern period and changes within those religions certainly marked an acceleration in these processes.[16] As the Mughals and Indian Ocean commerce pushed back the Bengal frontier, for instance, cults emerged around Indian Muslim holy men specifically associated with forest clearing and land reclamation: they protected woodcutters from tigers, designated areas for clearance, invited settlers, and even fixed tax rates.[17] Even in

AGAINST / IDOLATRY

long-settled areas that nobody would call frontiers, campaigns by centralizing authorities against enthusiastic religiosity often combined attacks on local cults with desacralizing local landscapes.[18] Relatively naturalistic—if not, by our standards, scientific—explanations of droughts, disease, and other calamities were often promoted to replace those that empowered unlettered but charismatic local figures. In China, where the imperial state had claimed for centuries to mediate between heaven and earth and thereby influence disasters, "moral meteorology" was in decline by the mid-eighteenth century.[19] The age of high imperialism would accelerate these trends further, but did not create them.

Other environmental manifestations of early modern state and market expansion are well known. Long-distance trade and missionary work brought many plant, animal, and microbial species to new places; some, with no natural enemies in their new environments, spread spectacularly. The expansion of long-distance trade also increased the vulnerability of various resources to demand from people far away and enabled some people and societies to appropriate resources while insulating themselves from the environmental impact of this appropriation. The devastation of the area around the Potosí silver mines and the ecological devastation of sugar islands may be the best-known early modern examples, but others abound. Moreover, the consumers responsible for these ecological earthquakes were not always European: Chinese demand devastated seals and otters from California to Alaska, stripped sandalwood from Pacific islands, and consumed perhaps one-third of the early modern world's internationally traded silver.[20]

Several eighteenth-century societies stretched the limits of what Fernand Braudel calls the "biological old regime," transcending long-standing population ceilings. More land was cultivated more intensively, and more farms produced yields matching the historical highs for their areas. (Most early modern agricultural progress consisted not of improving the best yields but of finding ways to reach those yields on more and more plots, each with its own idiosyncrasies of soil, drainage, and microclimate.)[21] One factor in raising yields was a large increase in labor inputs: this change was propelled both by population growth and by families' needing to work more hours as real wages fell or stagnated in most societies (in part, presumably, in response to that population growth) to support a growing number of children. In England, the only society for which we have studies so far, hours worked per year per person seem to have peaked around 1800 (despite real-wage trends that were better than most places).[22] The growth of double cropping, of handicraft output, and various other indicators suggest that people elsewhere also worked unusually long hours in the eighteenth and nineteenth centuries. In

INDUSTRIOUSNESS

relatively fortunate places, a growing availability of consumer goods for ordinary people—some of them ecological exotica, such as sugar and tobacco in Europe—may also have stimulated increased labor for the market: part of what Jan de Vries has called the "industrious revolution."[23] But whatever the mix of reasons, the outcome is clear: more people were working harder and coordinated across larger spaces, usually by merchants. The sea as well as the land felt the impact: North Atlantic fishing boomed, and late in the eighteenth century, Japanese fishing followed suit.[24]

If the eighteenth century pushed the limits of the biological old regime, the nineteenth and especially the twentieth century shattered them. New technologies and energy sources (discussed further below) led the way. Despite continuities in the developmentalist project across this technological divide, its later manifestations were qualitatively different. Having half of the growth in human population since 10,000 B.C.E. occur in the past thirty years, and half of all net water withdrawals in the past fifty, and a fifteenfold increase in annual energy consumption since 1900 (seventy-five-fold since 1800), in addition to unprecedented kinds of environmental impact (including nuclear wastes, ozone depletion, and anthropogenic climate change), has marked a distinct era.[25]

New levels of environmental peril eventually led to newly resourceful efforts at cleanup. Whether increased concern with our environmental impact suggests a break with developmentalist thinking is beyond our scope here. Some instead see cleanup as continuing the developmentalist project, with increased wealth making people less disposed to treasure each dollar of additional income regardless of environmental cost, and better technology making continued growth sustainable.

Certainly the twentieth century has seen both unprecedented environmental degradation and some remarkably successful cleanups, primarily in richer areas. London, Tokyo, Pittsburgh, and many other first-world cities have much cleaner air than they did fifty or one hundred years ago. Old species have been reintroduced to some intensely polluted rivers (though, as Mark Cioc's chapter on the Rhine shows, these recoveries are far from complete). Forest covers about as much of Europe as it did 150 to 200 years ago, and more of the United States than it did 100 years ago.[26] Some of these changes reflect regulations and limits on development, but others reflect the developmentalist project itself. (Examples of the latter include the replacement of coal by cleaner-burning oil and natural gas, and increasing long-distance trade in food and lumber, allowing marginal farmland near big markets to revert to forest.) Various endangered species have increased their numbers within protected habitats, mostly but not exclusively in wealthier countries.

INEVITABLE ?

Thus we cannot assume that the developmentalist project invariably leads to environmental degradation. Moreover, a broader perspective on environmental history reminds us that *environmental disaster* is itself a subjective term. If land that supports less biodiversity than before feeds more humans, at what point does that become a bad trade-off? If "traditional" landscapes prized by tourists and residents are in fact modern creations built on the wreckage of older landscapes, does that change their value?[27]

Nonetheless, twentieth-century environmental history is still mostly about deterioration, particularly in places that industrialized a bit later, or have not done so to any great extent. They have often been prone to particularly careless forms of development, whether because control was far away (in colonial cases), or because national governments sought to catch up quickly at any cost. Many such countries have also had particularly authoritarian governments, making it hard to translate environmentalist dissent into action. The Russian case, outlined by Douglas Weiner in this volume, is especially disturbing, but other examples abound.

Unprecedented economic growth has created unprecedented economic inequality in the past two centuries. It has also created unprecedented environmental inequalities, with the world's poor far more exposed to unhealthy air and dangerous wastes than the rich, and far less likely to have access to clean water. In fact, the environmental cleanups mentioned above were often facilitated by relocating polluting activities. Pittsburgh is cleaner in part because it is no longer Steeltown, and forests in the richer nations have stopped shrinking because forests elsewhere are shrinking faster.[28] This trend can, of course, be said to dovetail with developmentalism elsewhere, with poorer areas happily accepting smokestack industries; whether they will ever get rich and clean up their own environments remains to be seen.

Moreover, this kind of cleanup does not address our era's truly global environmental problems. Displacing heavy industry may clean up Stuttgart or Sheffield, but it will not make the world any cooler. Nor is it clear how well the powerful national states built on centuries of developmentalism can address these issues. As John McNeill has argued, thus far even fairly democratic polities have been much better at addressing environmental problems that are immediately and locally present (e.g., cleaning up the water that current citizens drink) than at addressing problems like global warming, which are more diffuse and unfold more slowly.[29] It is easy to explain this trend through a framework of interest-group liberalism but not obvious

Copenhagen · Kyoto?

what to do about it. Meanwhile, international organizations, while potentially a great help in addressing such problems, can also be part of the problem (e.g., by striking down national environmental regulations as barriers to trade). Mark Cioc's essay shows how cooperative governance of the Rhine—probably the world's longest-running example of multinational environmental management—eventually embraced goals beyond simply promoting growth. But that case involves one medium-sized river and six wealthy countries. Despite urgent needs, the future environmental role of organizations on various geographic scales remains unclear.

EMPIRES, INDUSTRY, TIME, AND PLACE: PERIODIZING WORLD ENVIRONMENTAL HISTORY

A synthetic volume can highlight often-overlooked continuities across time and similarities across space. Yet stitching together early modern and modern trajectories calls attention to the discontinuities and uneven effects of two hugely important phenomena emerging in the nineteenth century: industrialization and the new imperialism. Here, assembling regional case studies instead of topical essays crossing regions serves us well. Whether we are dealing with settler colonialisms that remade the flora, fauna, and disease pools of the neo-Europes, new property rights and head taxes that effectively outlawed nomadism, or the creation of mining and plantation enclaves, these essays repeatedly show imperialism leaving its mark on specific environments. Together, they also let us do something less common: use environmental history as a lens through which to examine imperialism.

Alfred Crosby's classic *Ecological Imperialism* begins with environmental history as the thing to be explained, memorably asking why the sun never sets on the empire of the dandelion. But it is perhaps even more powerful in using environmental history to explain empire, with domesticated animals, plants, and above all microbes providing the most compelling explanation we have of how so few early modern Europeans conquered such vast areas in the temperate Americas and Oceania.[30] And one common (though usually implicit) way of framing the new imperialism of the late nineteenth century is by seeing it as a period in which industrialization briefly created power differentials within Africa and Eurasia comparable to those which biology had previously created between the Old and New worlds.

But the vast imperial expansion of circa 1750 to 1850—especially, but not only, Britain's presence in India—could not have depended on the broad-based industrialization of the metropoles, because that happened later. (More specific advances in iron and steel manufacture, gun making, and shipbuilding were certainly important, however, as were such advantages as cheap printing and precision navigational instruments.) In addition, recent literature has made it clear that even around 1900, when the West's military advantage was at its peak, imperial relationships were never as one-sided as many participants (and scholars) have imagined.

The idea of a developmentalist project also reminds us that in many of the larger European colonies, the gap in intentions between colonizers and colonized was never as wide in reality as it was in the minds of some Europeans, who imagined themselves introducing dynamism to "inert" societies. The history of mainland Southeast Asia's great river deltas (the Mekong, Chao Phraya, and Irrawaddy), discussed in Michael Adas's essay, is a good example. Events in British Burma and French Vietnam did not differ radically from those in independent (albeit British-influenced) Thailand. Moreover, all of these projects built on drainage and settlement efforts that had begun well before colonization, and they continued long-term processes of increasing control of the river deltas by states and ethnic groups expanding from centers on the interior plains.[31] All three also involved many people (mostly Indian and Chinese) who were neither Europeans nor indigenous peoples.

Certainly some people did not undertake any developmentalist project of their own, and they were dragged by the new imperialism into a world they never wanted. Nomadic peoples probably suffered the most devastating shocks; Rangarajan's point that such groups had often been part of state-making projects in precolonial India (as soldiers, for instance, or as groups that traveled and provisioned armies), but became external objects of post-1857 British colonial state formation, is an important one, with parallels elsewhere. Likewise, he and other scholars have rightly emphasized the novelty (in most, though not all regions) of colonial plantations as a way of organizing both labor and landscape. But those who dragged others into such arrangements often included not only imperialists but also local elites and diasporic entrepreneurs who had pursued developmental projects before the Europeans came and continued doing so after independence. Finally, to draw again from Rangarajan's essay, it is also important to remember that "tribal" resistance sometimes succeeded against these coalitions, whether before, during, or after colonialism.

Through an environmental lens, then, imperialism often looks different in degree but not in kind from the "civilizing" projects that states carried out on their own populations and landscapes. The difference blurs even more when we include under this rubric various projects undertaken by China and Russia (both pre- and postrevolution) in their respective parts of inner Asia; when we consider the long-term continuities in the Middle East discussed in Burke's essay; when we look at periods when the European subjects of major Western European empires had not yet won rights radically different from those of overseas subjects; and when we point to continuing imperialism after formal decolonization.

This is emphatically not to say that imperialism was unimportant. Imperialism often marked a major acceleration of home-grown developmentalist projects, with far stronger centralizing states, more doctrinaire opponents of collective property (or of customary restrictions on the use of private property), and more voracious appetites for local resources held by people even more distant from the environmental fallout of mines, dams, and other projects. It shifted state priorities, sometimes disastrously (as shown in my discussion of how inland north China flood control suffered as the state concentrated on defending its coast and paying off foreign indemnities) and brought both new diseases and (later) new cures. As Rangarajan points out, seeing a process (such as state-encouraged land clearance) under way in a particular place before a colonial power began to encourage it does not necessarily mean that the foreigners made no difference; in some places, land had been cleared many times before, often with government encouragement, only to revert to forest when economic or political forces shifted. But it does suggest that there are reasons to insert imperialism into long-running stories of developmentalism, and still longer-running stories of natural processes, rather than to grant automatic primacy to a scheme that divides histories into periods such as precolonial, colonial, and postcolonial, or to assume that either the onset or the end of colonialism marks the onset of modernity. Thus looking through an environmental history lens offers support, for instance, to the Cambridge School's attempt to place the history of the British empire in South Asia into both global and long-term regional narratives, rather than isolate the period of British rule.[32]

There is also controversy over how to understand industrialization from the viewpoint of world history and environmental history. Environmental historians—especially those working on a grand scale—are generally more inclined than some other kinds of historians to see a dramatic industrial revolution, and to place the transition to fossil fuels and high energy use at its heart. This classic view of the significance of energy is central, for instance, to the big-picture work of John Richards and John McNeill and the still-larger perspective of "big history." It has also made a comeback in recent years among historians influenced by E. A. Wrigley's distinction between organic and inorganic economies, especially those in the "California school" trying to write global or comparative history.[33] But a strong emphasis on energy is a somewhat eccentric position in economic and social history these days, and it is worth briefly discussing why environmental and world historians, who tend to work on large scales that sometimes obscure discontinuities, here seem particularly eager to emphasize a watershed.

One reason is banal but important: because early engines converted fuel to work very inefficiently, their contribution to GNP was often smaller than their environmental impact. Figure 1.1, showing the soaring amount of energy consumed per dollar of GDP during the first several decades of industrialization in several nations, is instructive; if we had reliable data for the USSR or post-1949 China, the peaks of energy consumed per dollar earned would be even higher. Thus, growth in energy consumed was considerably faster than even the unprecedented GDP growth of early industrial societies.

These soaring rates of energy consumption per dollar began to decline after a few decades, often almost as sharply as they had risen; and thereby hangs another tale. Looking at this chart without knowing the price history of twentieth-century energy, an economist could be forgiven for assuming that economies had become less profligate with energy because it became expensive; indeed, in a few episodes (particularly in the 1970s), that was the case. But most of the story has been quite different: energy has been generally growing cheaper for the past two centuries (until very recently), while engines have become more efficient for other reasons. Often the goal was to make the engine smaller, so that it would not need expensive building specifications, such as reinforced floors, or so that it would be cheaper or more portable. Fuel efficiency, though certainly welcome (fuel became cheap, but not free), was often incidental. For an economist, a resource that was used more sparingly per dollar of overall economic activity while it also became cheaper adds up to a sector of shrinking importance, as it represents a smaller share of the market value of total output: measured this way, all raw materials, including farm products, account for only 10 percent of the U.S. economy today. An environmental historian, however, might be more inclined to look at still-rising gross output of energy, its increasingly effective use, and at the increasing number of settings and activities in which people used fossil-fuel (or hydroelectric) power as it became both cheaper and better targeted to the tasks at hand. Certainly, despite the declining share GDP spent on energy, today's economies are inconceivable without cheap energy. And much of the increased productivity of the twentieth century—the ability to produce more with the same amount of inputs—is probably due to the increased efficiency of energy use.[34]

Energy use also increased in early modern times, but much less so than in the past two centuries; and in most early modern times and places, energy was not

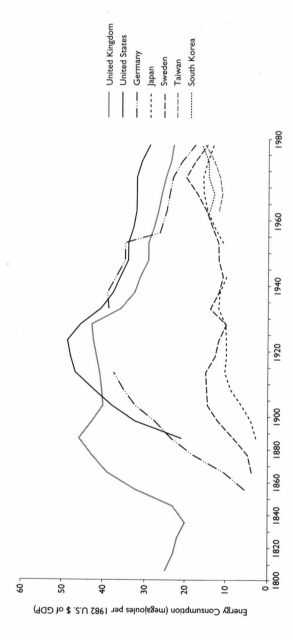

FIGURE 1.1.

Megajoules of energy consumed per 1982 U.S. dollar of GDP (some values interpolated). *Sources:* Data for the United States, United Kingdom, Sweden, and Japan through the early 1890s are taken from a similar graph in Vaclav Smil, *Energy, Food, Environment* (Oxford: Oxford University Press, 1987), p. 67. I have created roughly comparable estimates for fossil-fuel consumption in Germany (1850–1938) and West Germany (1949–80) and for Taiwan and South Korea using data from the following sources: Thelma Liesner, ed., *One Hundred Years of Economic Statistics* (New York: Facts on File, 1987); B.R. Mitchell, *European Historical Statistics, 1750–1975* (New York: Facts on File, 1980); United Nations, *National Accounts Statistics: Analysis of Main Aggregates, 1982* (New York: United Nations, 1982); and Joseph A. Yager, *The Energy Balance in Northeast Asia* (Washington, DC: Brookings Institution, 1984).

becoming cheaper, nor was conversion necessarily growing more efficient.[35] On the contrary, both price series (where we have them) and literary evidence (where we do not) attest to the rising price of wood, the most important source of heat energy in most of the densely populated parts of the pre-nineteenth-century world. At least in Europe, prices for animal fodder—the fuel for the most important engines of the period, other than human muscle—also generally rose throughout the early modern period.[36] Societies that relied heavily on animal power confronted a low and essentially unchangeable rate of energy conversion: horses and mules, for instance are about 10 percent efficient, whereas humans are about 18 percent efficient, and some modern power sources have conversion efficiencies close to 40 percent.[37] (Pre-1800 steam engines were even more profligate, with conversion ratios of 1 to 2 percent; the original Newcomen engine was only 0.7 percent efficient.)[38] Thus, although the growing energy consumption of early modern times looks familiar, it had much less economic benefit than modern increases and none of their self-reinforcing quality. Therefore an environmental perspective seems to vindicate our intuition—and that of earlier world historians—that a fairly sudden fossil-fuel revolution really did inaugurate a new era.

A final thread that runs through this essay—and this volume—is the importance of state-making in environmental history. States—"coercion-wielding organizations that are distinct from households and kinship groups and exercise clear priority in some respects over all other organizations within substantial territories," in Charles Tilly's phrase—reach into the lives of virtually every person on earth, and do so far more deeply and continuously than their predecessors five hundred years ago; they regulate access to and use of virtually all the land on this planet, much of the water, and some of the atmosphere.[39] Their pursuit of greater powers—relative to their own populations and relative to each other—has led them to change people's relationships to their particular parts of the biosphere, usually by encouraging greater human appropriation of what we now call natural resources. This mutually reinforcing relationship between increased state capabilities and increasingly forceful (if not always successful) human interventions in the environment is central to the notion of a developmentalist project, and, while not quite a universal, is more widespread around the world, and across the last five centuries, than either capitalism or modern science. Perhaps only commercialization—the growing scale of commercial transactions and the growing range of items treated as commodities—has been equally omnipresent, and often these two phenomena are hard to disentangle. But precisely because the state is so ubiquitous in these stories, it may be best to discuss this subject as part of a preview of the chapters that follow.

PLAN OF THE CHAPTERS

We begin with two essays that are global in scope: one by Edmund Burke on the *very* long-run history of the environment and developmentalism, and one by John Richards on convergent systems of property rights and land use around the world. They are followed by eight case studies with specific geographic foci. All of them speak to the themes above as well as to regionally specific issues and historiographies.

Edmund Burke's essay, "The Big Story: Human History, Energy Regimes, and the Environment," is actually even broader than that title suggests. Burke argues that the environmental history of the past five centuries is best understood in the context of a ten-thousand-year history (since the last ice age) of humans trying to render their environments reliable. He then charts the intensification of struggles for ecological security as population growth accelerated across much of Africa and Eurasia after roughly 1400. At the same time, increasingly sophisticated organizations and transfers of plants, animals, and microbes across vast distances (especially the "Columbian exchange") created massive local disequilibria and diversified the tools available for (re)conquering particular landscapes. One result was massive deforestation, creating early modern energy crises. This trend set the stage for the fossil-fuel revolution, which he also sees as an epochal shift. He particularly emphasizes the centrality of cheap energy to agricultural transformations that have made it possible to escape the Malthusian constraint that available land could not grow as fast as population while simultaneously shedding labor from farms, thus propelling the urbanization and mass migration central to modern social history.

This succession of agricultural revolutions is part of the commodification and increasingly intensive use of land at the heart of John Richards's "Toward a Global System of Property Rights in Land." For Richards, it is above all growing states—and not only European ones—that propel this process. Whereas many accounts focus exclusively on the increased rights of private proprietors, Richards reminds us that behind these proprietors stand states that make themselves the final arbiters of property rights. Most often, states have added rights to the bundle enjoyed by private owners, reducing those of communities (e.g., rights to gleaning) and tenants (e.g., permanent or hereditary tenancies). But states have also asserted their ultimate control over owners with such measures as banning the private use of fire to manage land, or regulating or forbidding hunting. Some states have also set certain lands aside as "potent symbols of national identity," off-limits to private exploitation—often against considerable resistance.[40]

Meanwhile, in cities—especially the many twentieth-century cities surrounded by squatter settlements—states have often confirmed some of the rights sought by tenants; those rights have themselves often become commodities in very active (if not always legal) markets. Although these are often fiercely contested processes, with states raiding or even razing illicit settlements, Richards points to a tendency to grant recognition to squatters, who then cease agitating for better housing elsewhere. He thus sees at least three different kinds of land rights which, although not universal, have become increasingly common, and all of which have had multiple points of origin around the globe.

Edmund Burke's chapter on the Middle East provides a deep historical account of the region's changing environment. It focuses primarily on water. Middle Eastern states since ancient times have been unusually dependent on water management, as irrigation was vital to producing the agricultural surpluses which (until the recent rise of petroleum revenues) were the only source of revenues sufficient to sustain a powerful state in this region. Many of the techniques developed not only supported large Middle Eastern populations but were also exported to various parts of Asia and Africa, Iberia, and (through Spain) the Americas. But they required high levels of maintenance, and so they were politically fragile; recurrent problems contributed to a prolonged (and much-debated) agricultural decline from perhaps 1300 to 1750.

Sometime after 1750 recovery began, allowing the Middle East's population to grow even faster than the global average (by well over 1,000 percent between 1750 and 2000). Burke finds that the policies pursued by the Ottoman Empire, by Egypt under Muhammad Ali and his successors, and by areas that came under foreign (especially French) rule were similar; differences among ecologies were far more important than those between places ruled by "the West" and "the rest." The Ottoman *tanzimat* reforms, in particular, displaced pastoralists and encouraged commercial agriculture in ways quite familiar from other settings, and with a similar range of environmental results. The same was true of late nineteenth-century initiatives in mining and industry.

Burke then turns to modern hydraulic engineering in the Middle East, beginning with attempts to increase cotton production in the Nile delta. He shows how nineteenth-century decisions—particularly the switch to perennial rather than periodic irrigation—all but necessitated some sort of high dam on the Nile, as was constructed under Gamal Abdel Nasser. He is thereby able to connect the complex gains and losses from the dam both to twentieth-century ideas about dams, economic development, state power, and national identity and to more deeply seated dynamics set in motion by Muhammad Ali, late nineteenth-century British governors, and other figures. After quickly surveying modern water management on the Tigris and Euphrates as well, he turns to Morocco, examining attempts to create large-scale, export-oriented farms. This last dream drew on models ranging from ancient Rome to French colonial plans to irrigated commercial farming in California; ultimately, it was undone by the environmental damage caused to marginal lands and vital aquifers through intensive chemical usage. Today, development in the Middle East seems unable to keep up with population growth, in no small part because it depends on water-management techniques with limited capacities and serious side effects. Middle Eastern agriculture continues to grow by using increased inputs of labor land and capital, as it has for centuries, but modern technologies have not produced a breakthrough to yield sustained productivity growth.

My chapter on the history of China's environment also focuses on water, especially in north China, where flood control has historically been especially difficult and water supply fickle. Thus it may seem obvious that state involvement would focus on managing the environment of this region, but that outcome was far from inevitable: many logics of state formation would have suggested letting north China simply be a backwater and concentrating state efforts where revenue potential was much higher. That this did not happen—on the contrary, wealthy areas in the Yangzi valley were forced to subsidize the north and various other ecologically fragile zones throughout the Ming and most of the Qing dynasties—tells us much about Chinese political economy and its particular kind of developmentalism. The essay then describes how this older statecraft unraveled amid nineteenth-century imperialism, new domestic political dynamics, and internally generated environmental stresses. After describing the environmental and social crises that followed, the essay looks at technocratic and populist responses and how the People's Republic has oscillated between them. The last section argues that despite post-1978 marketization and urbanization, the PRC still has a distinctive political economy of water, and that contemporary dilemmas of growth still reflect both the positive and the negative legacies of late imperial statecraft.

Mark Cioc's essay—the only one here focused on an "advanced" region—presents the developmentalist project in undiluted form. The Rhine, as he shows, has been the object of almost continuous reengineering since 1815, when what the chief engineer called a "general operational plan" for "defense against a Rhine attack" was combined with a plan for free trade that emerged from the French Revolution, and a multinational administration for the river that emerged from the Vienna settlement. The result was a river-cum-canal—almost perfectly straight, as narrow as possible, and eventually contained within cement walls. This artificial Rhine epitomized Renaissance and Enlightenment ideas about how to use nature. Even if it had not become badly polluted, it could not have supported much life, as the bends, braids, and other niches that fish use for feeding, spawning, and egg-laying were eliminated. When the adjacent Ruhr coalfields boomed and major chemical companies clustered along the Rhine, it was essentially converted into a massive sewer pipe: of the 165 species found in the river in 1900 (no doubt already far fewer than a century before), 138 were gone by 1971. A perfect servant of industry in one of the world's most productive regions—never flooding, easy to navigate, useful for heating, cooling, and dumping—the river was all but destroyed as a habitat. Over the past forty years, restoration efforts have brought back a few species (now dependent on artificial propagation). But fundamentally, Renaissance- and Enlightenment-era engineering is now a permanent feature of the Rhine. Although such complete disregard for biology is no longer in favor, its effects here are largely irreversible.

Michael Adas's essay, "Continuity and Transformation: Colonial Rice Frontiers and Their Environmental Impact on the Great River Deltas of Mainland Southeast Asia," also focuses on water. It echoes Burke's Middle Eastern story by emphasizing the similarities between events in colonized Burma and Vietnam and uncolonized Siam/Thailand. But Adas's is also a different kind of colonial story, with Chinese and Indian immigrants—people neither indigenous nor conquering—playing central roles.

Although Adas points to continuities between precolonial and colonial development efforts, he also notes equally striking continuities in the environment itself. The development of these great rice frontiers parallels the extension of wheat frontiers in the Americas and Australia, which also involved massive immigration, staple grain exports (often back to the immigrants' countries of origin), massive land clearance, and the driving off of indigenous large mammals (bison in North America, elephants in Southeast Asia) and nomadic peoples. Yet Adas shows that the Southeast Asian changes did not break with older ecologies as sharply as the neo-European wheat frontiers, the advance of peanuts and cotton into the African Sahel, or forest clearance in Brazil. Water was controlled in new ways, but it came from the monsoons and rivers that had flooded these areas for ages. New rice varieties were imported, but they were planted side by side with old varieties rather than displacing them. Cultivation methods also mixed old and new; basic seasonal cycles did not change. Staggering agricultural surpluses were generated with less ecological disruption than on other great agricultural frontiers.

But the rice boom was hardly without cost. As swamps vanished, so did fish and shellfish that had provided important dietary supplements—which were especially missed when world rice prices collapsed in the 1930s, devastating tenants (who paid fixed cash rents) and landless laborers. New dikes blocked the arrival of the fresh silt once carried by rivers (as the Aswan Dam did in Egypt), depleting delta soils; firewood became scarce. Most subtly and most surprisingly, the widespread cultivation of rice paddies led to enormous increases in the production of methane, a very potent greenhouse gas. (Ironically, tropical rice may be particularly vulnerable to global warming, as the plant needs cool evenings for proper growth.)[41] As Adas notes, the world is far too dependent on paddy rice production to abandon it, but production methods need to change. Even when development projects seem to have delivered great benefits with relatively little disruption, there may be (literally) invisible environmental complications.

William Beinart's "Beyond the Colonial Paradigm: African History and Environmental History in Large-Scale Perspective" takes us deeper into specifically colonial settings, with more of the sharp discontinuities and traumatic introduction of alien projects and species that form our classic images of imperialism. Discontinuities abounded, as one would expect when nineteenth-century imperialism met areas with many shifting cultivators, forest peoples, and others who had little motivation to intensify land use or to accept proletarianization. Catastrophes were common, and not only in exceptionally brutal colonies like the Belgian Congo: for instance, colonialism spread smallpox, trypanosomiasis, and other devastating diseases.

Yet Beinart detects a historiographic trend away from apocalyptic treatments of African environmental history, which resonate strongly with the activism of many early environmental historians and postindependence desires to correct the biases of colonizers' histories. The more recent literature does not deny the arrogance, greed, and ignorance that often animated colonial policy making, but it does argue that precolonial environmental trends were more complex than we often realize. They included both surprising successes (for instance, settlement sometimes promoted afforestation in the savannah) and ecological degradation caused by expanding political units, much like what occurred elsewhere: Great Zimbabwe, for instance, seems to have exhausted its soils and forests.

Looking at the period since independence, Beinart argues that "science and the state remain potentially powerful allies for poor people." Skepticism about states—especially in Africa—solving problems is routine today. But Beinart reminds us that the environmentalism of the poor often emphasizes demands for environmental services, such as clean water at affordable rates. Such services require a state role and often large-scale engineering projects. Failures in planning and scientific miscalculations make for spectacular and genuinely important stories, but, Beinart argues, a preference for such tales often obscures "the rapidity with which scientists in Africa grappled with, sometimes grasped, complex diseases, ecologies, and natural phenomena." AIDS, he reminds us, is unlikely to be conquered by traditional knowledge.

Beinart also reminds us that though independent African states have often pushed through environmentally insensitive and unsuccessful development plans, Africans and their environments have also suffered acutely from state weakness. Cash-hungry contenders in violent conflicts (often exacerbated by foreign meddling) have often lacked a secure long-term stake in the areas they occupy: they have stripped forests and other resources, killed elephants for ivory, and created refugees who have done further environmental damage. States too weak to secure good lending terms from Western governments, banks, and multilateral agencies have often been forced by debt repayment to be almost as predatory to their environments as transient warlords. In conclusion, Beinart speaks of the "profound ambivalence" in recent writings that still emphasize the asymmetry of global relations but recognize the need to explore "the shared human capacity to wield power for ill as well as good, over nature as well as people."

Mahesh Rangarajan also focuses on the colonial period, but in the context of longer-running trends, bringing both continuities and discontinuities into focus. He notes at least three reasons why British rule marked an important and negative milestone for South Asia's environment. First, the British (especially after 1870) reconfigured politics to marginalize pastoralists and shifting cultivators: this move in turn freed them to maximize arable land and land revenues more single-mindedly. Second, imperial foresters gained control of close to one-fifth of the Indian subcontinent. Although these forests served various purposes—from generating foreign exchange to providing railroad ties to preventing desiccation—the needs of local communities were rarely considered, much less those of elephants and tigers. Third, though state-sponsored irrigation projects sometimes improved water security, they caused other problems, from malaria to salinization to drought itself (when older systems were not properly maintained).

Yet Rangarajan also modifies this well-known story. India's diversity confounds simple blanket assessments at any historical moment. Regional labor shortages often helped people resist full-fledged sedentarization. Divisions within the colonial state gave other groups room to maneuver. The science that forestry officials and others invoked was multifaceted, and was not always transferred from core to periphery; to assume it was, Rangarajan warns, is to indulge in "Occidentalism," creating an artificially inflexible West to serve as foil to the constructed East. Thus, like Beinart, he insists that one must draw on diverse knowledge systems to make sense of, and ameliorate, South Asia's environmental problems.

Lisa Sedrez's "Latin American Environmental History: A Shifting Old/New Field" notes historiographic trends similar to those observed by Beinart and Rangarajan. Classic early works on Latin American environmental history were mostly tales of decline, whereas recent works see more complex patterns. But Sedrez argues against abandoning the declensionist framework, preferring to supplement it with enough discussion of attempted alternatives to show that decline is not inevitable. She also notes a robust intellectual environmental history (tracing changing conceptions of nature), environmentally informed history of natural resources, and histories of what she calls "landscapes and places." This last genre attempts a synthesis of intellectual and material environmental history, focusing on understandings of particular landscapes, rather than on conceptions of abstract nature. It traces the changing meanings communities attach to their homes and work sites and shows how those meanings have reshaped social practices. Sedrez cites John Soluri's work on banana plantations and reactions to the emergence of monoculture in Honduras as one example, but she suggests that this kind of environmental history may be the most illuminating in studying urban environments, where 80 percent of Latin Americans now live. She also suggests that studying cultural adjustments to environmental problems could provide an important complement to studies of environmental-justice movements, and to studies of the effects of large projects such as dams and highways.

Our final essay, Douglas Weiner's "The Predatory Tribute-Taking State: A Framework for Understanding Russian Environmental History," links a particular form of governance to an environmental trajectory. Like several other scholars, Weiner connects the Soviet Union's wildly unrealistic plans for conquering nature—from creating new animal species to warming the Arctic to irrigating the steppe—to its attempts to create a new type of person: Maxim Gorky's apologia for the Baltic–White Sea Canal was tellingly titled "In Transforming Nature, Man Transforms Himself." But for Weiner this utopianism is rooted not only in Communist ideology but also in conundrums the Soviets inherited from their "tribute-taking" predecessors. Russian rulers led militarized regimes largely unconstrained by law and sought to maintain armies larger than their economy could really support. They saw their people and territory as resources to be exploited as much as possible. Meanwhile, the czarist gentry adopted a similar attitude toward their private domains. Both were committed to maintaining their power over others and saw agronomic miracles as a quick way to obtain wealth without risking social change. Thus, although Communism may have provided new justifications, Weiner suggests that preexisting commitments to suppressing labor and to competing with more efficient societies had already produced a need to believe in technological quick fixes that would turn nature into capital, making pre-Soviet Russian elites Lysenkoists avant la lettre.

Although the Soviet commitment to science had some potential to nurture a more far-sighted approach to nature, this view proved no match for the celebration of standardization, a succession of military emergencies, and officials' continued tribute taking. These tendencies continue today, exacerbated by economic crisis and desperate dependence on resource exports. In closing, Weiner argues that, given the thousand-year reign of the tribute-taking state, policies that were (and are) deeply irrational in economic and ecological terms made a certain political sense; moreover, numerous historical traumas, including devastating invasions, often made stable authoritarianism seem relatively attractive.

Thus Weiner suggests that the Russian commitment to an all-out war on nature may have been paradoxically linked both to a Marxian belief in the capacity to remake everything, including humans, and to a deep unwillingness to risk changing the power relationships among humans. Russian society and ecology have thus been deeply shaped by interactions with other developmentalist projects (and the failure to imitate them successfully), but at the same time Russia has carried to an extreme tendencies very much present in developmentalist projects elsewhere: the worship of growth and of state power; the tendency to see nature as an enemy to be conquered, and to insist that technological change will make risky social change unnecessary; the use of international resource sales as a crutch for regimes unable to gain consent and revenues adequate to their ambitions from their own citizens; and claims of both technocratic competence and external threats as a means to avoid accountability.

As we have seen, "liberals" and nationalists who learned from the West about how new institutions could make their countries powerful, while putting much less emphasis on freedom for its own sake, were not necessarily misreading Western ideas: they were emphasizing elements of those ideas that seemed particularly salient to those threatened by the West's own aggressiveness. By the same token, each element of Russia's tragic environmental history has its counterparts in other versions of the developmentalist project, including more successful ones. Noting these family resemblances is part of the approach Weiner calls for in his (and the book's) final sentence: "In the process [of thinking about Russia's current dilemmas], the global West might even begin to take a look in the mirror, where the outlines of a sinister convergence have become more pronounced of late." Without necessarily being equally pessimistic, we hope that bringing together the stories we have chosen encourages just those kinds of comparisons: not studies that contrast a "successful," usually Western, case with another that somehow failed to match it, but those that recognize shared problems, imperfect responses, and powerful mutual influences across time and space.

NOTES

1. For two interesting (and different) perspectives on the formation of a coastal zone reaching from northeast to southeast Asia, see Hamashita Takeshi, "The Tribute Trade System and Modern Asia," *Memoirs of the Research Department of the Tōyō Bunko* 46 (1988): 7–25; and François Gipouloux, "Integration or Disintegration: The Spatial Effects of Foreign Direct Investment in China," *China Perspectives* 17 (May–June 1998): 6–13.

2. See Charles Tilly, *Coercion, Capital, and European States, A.D. 990–1990* (London: Basil Blackwell, 1990).

3. Victor Lieberman, *Strange Parallels: Southeast Asia in Global Context, c. 800–1800* (Cambridge: Cambridge University Press, 2003).

4. Consider, for instance, the very low rate of proletarianization—probably under 10 percent of the labor force—in China's most developed region (the lower Yangzi) even in the eighteenth century, and the absence of land and labor markets in Southeast Asia.

5. Kenneth Pomeranz, "Imperialism, Development, and 'Civilizing' Missions, Past and Present," *Daedalus*, April 2005, 34–45.

6. Mark Elvin, *The Retreat of the Elephants: An Environmental History of China* (New Haven: Yale University Press, 2004), 90–93, 101–5, 228–30, and 244.

7. See also David Ludden, *An Agrarian History of South Asia* (Cambridge: Cambridge University Press, 1999), 96, 132–33, 136–240; Mahesh Rangarajan, "Colonialism, Ecology and Environment, Departures and Beginnings," in *India and the British Empire*, ed. Nandini Gooptu and Douglas Peers (Oxford: Oxford University Press, in press).

8. Benjamin Schwartz, *In Search of Wealth and Power: Yen Fu and the West* (Cambridge, MA: Harvard University Press, 1964), 242–47.

9. Luke Roberts, *Mercantilism in a Japanese Domain: The Merchant Origins of Economic Nationalism in Eighteenth-Century Tosa* (Cambridge: Cambridge University Press, 1998). Helen Dunstan, *Conflicting Counsels to Confuse the Age: A Documentary Study of Political Economy in Qing China, 1644–1840* (Ann Arbor: Center for Chinese Studies, University of Michigan, 1996), esp. 293–327; Pierre Étienne-Will, "Discussions about the Market-Place and the Market Principle in Eighteenth-Century Guangdong," in

Zhongguo haiyang fazhan shi lunwen ji, ed. Tang Xiyong (Taibei: Zhongying yanjiu-yuan Zhongshan renwen shehui kexue yanjiusuo, 1999), 323–89. Donald Quataert, "The Age of Reforms, 1812–1914," in *An Economic and Social History of the Ottoman Empire*, ed. Suraiya Faroqhi, Bruce McGowan, Donald Quataert, and Şevket Pamuk (Cambridge: Cambridge University Press, 1994), esp. 761–77. Afaf Lutfi Al-Sayyid Marsot, *Egypt in the Reign of Muhammad Ali* (Cambridge: Cambridge University Press, 1984), 100–110, 122–25, 137–97, 231; Roger Owen, *The Middle East and the World Economy, 1800–1914* (London: Methuen, 1981), 64–67. C.A. Bayly, *Imperial Meridian: The British Empire and the World, 1780–1830* (London: Longman, 1989), 47, 53, 69, 157, 173, 186.

10. Elvin, *Retreat of the Elephants*, esp. 167–216; Mark Elvin, "The Environmental Legacy of Imperial China," *China Quarterly* 156 (December 1998): 733–56. Robert Marks, "Commercialization without Capitalism: Processes of Environmental Change in South China, 1550–1850," *Environmental History* 1, no. 1 (January 1996): 56–82; Robert Marks, *Tigers, Rice, Silk and Silt* (Cambridge: Cambridge University Press, 1998).

11. For an early example of skepticism, see William Cronon, *Changes in the Land* (New York: Hill & Wang, 1983), 19–53.

12. Paul Richards, *Indigenous Agricultural Revolution: Ecology and Food Production in West Africa* (Boulder, CO: Westview Press, 1985), 142.

13. The phrase is most often associated with Joan Martínez-Alier, *The Environmentalism of the Poor: A Study of Ecological Conflicts and Valuation* (Cheltenham, U.K.: Edward Elgar, 2002).

14. For some East Asian cases, see Penelope Francks, "Rural Industry, Growth Linkages, and Economic Development in Nineteenth-Century Japan," *Journal of Asian Studies* 61, no. 1 (2002): 33–55; and Harry Oshima, "The Transition from an Agricultural to an Industrial Economy in East Asia," *Economic Development and Cultural Change* 34 (1986): 783–809. For continental Europe, see, for instance, George Grantham, "Agricultural Supply During the Industrial Revolution," *Journal of Economic History* 49, no. 1 (March, 1989): 44, 48, 51, 64, 66, which notes an increased concentration on labor-intensive preferred grains for sale near growing cities (because such grains commanded a high price, and densely populated peri-urban farms had plenty of labor available) and a sharp decline in land left fallow (because cities provided plenty of manure), which also led to an increase in the demand for labor. This was increasingly provided by previously "underemployed" family members. Meanwhile, the same farmers were becoming more dependent on inferior foods (e.g., chestnut flour, potatoes, and oatmeal); this trend suggests that, despite improvements in other aspects of their material lives, it is unlikely that their "profit," had they calculated it the way a firm does, was being maximized. English farmers, who were maximizing not yields but profits were, by contrast, generally shedding labor.

15. For cases connected to the Chinese colonization of the south, see Rolf Stein, "Religious Taoism and Popular Religion from the Second to the Seventh Centuries," in *Facets of Taoism: Essays in Chinese Religion,* ed. Holmes Welch and Anna Seidel (New Haven: Yale University Press, 1979), 53–81; David Johnson, "City God Cults in T'ang and Sung China," *Harvard Journal of Asiatic Studies* 45, no. 2 (1985): 363–455.

16. For two among many examples (and with very different interpretations), see Keith Thomas, *Religion and the Decline of Magic* (New York: Scribner's, 1971), 641–68; and Michael Taussig, *The Devil and Commodity Fetishism in Latin America* (Chapel Hill: University of North Carolina Press, 1980), 155–68.

17. Richard Eaton, *The Rise of Islam and the Bengal Frontier* (Berkeley: University of California Press, 1993), 207–19, provides some examples; but see Mahesh Rangarajan, "Colonialism, Ecology and Environment," for the continued importance into the nineteenth century of ideas that "saw the forest not as a place of primeval chaos, but as a place at the heart of power."

18. An interesting exception to the pattern is the Ottoman defense of local cults against Wahabi insurgents seeking to "purify" Islam by eliminating them. In the nineteenth century, however, the Ottoman state itself often suppressed local cults in semi-wild areas. On the latter period, see Selim Derengil, *The Well-Protected Domains* (London: I. B. Tauris, 1998), 44–84.

19. Elvin, *Retreat of the Elephants,* 198.

20. John R. McNeill, "Of Rats and Men: A Synoptic Environmental History of the Island Pacific," *Journal of World History* 5, no. 2 (Fall 1994): 319–26; Jim Hardee, "Soft Gold: Animals Skins and the Early Economy of California," in Dennis O. Flynn, Arturo Giráldez, and James Sobredo, *Studies in Pacific History* (Aldershot, U.K.: Ashgate, 2002), 23–40. On silver, Andre Gunder Frank, *ReOrient: Global Economy in the Asian Age* (Berkeley: University of California Press, 1998), 142–49, surveys a variety of estimates, ranging as high as 50 percent of all silver produced in this period winding up in China; he prefers the higher estimates, but the point stands even with the figure I use here.

21. See, for instance, Kenneth Pomeranz, "Beyond the East-West Binary: Resituating Development Paths in the Eighteenth-Century World," *Journal of Asian Studies* 61, no. 2 (May 2002): 554–55 and accompanying notes; Grantham, "Agricultural Supply," 56–57.

22. Hans-Joachim Voth, *Time and Work in England, 1750–1830* (Oxford: Clarendon Press, 2000), 129.

23. Jan de Vries, "The Industrious Revolution and the Industrial Revolution," *Journal of Economic History* 54, no. 2 (June 1994): 249–70.

24. Though human impact on the oceans is of great importance, it is not much discussed in this book; for a useful survey, see Richard Ellis, *The Empty Ocean* (Washington, DC: Island Press, 2003).

25. For one among many such lists, see David Christian, *Maps of Time* (Berkeley: University of California Press, 2004), 462. For the energy figures, see John McNeill, *Something New under the Sun: An Environmental History of the Twentieth-Century World* (New York: W. W. Norton, 2000), 15.

26. On Europe, see John Richards, "Land Transformation," in *The Earth as Transformed by Human Action*, ed. B. L. Turner et al. (Cambridge: Cambridge University Press, 1990), 164; on the United States, see Michael Williams, *Deforesting the Earth: From Prehistory to Global Crisis* (Chicago: University of Chicago Press, 2003), 409.

27. Examples might include birch and aspen forests in parts of the upper Midwest, which took over from white pine forests, which were clearcut because they make far better lumber; dense stands of pineapple trees in Hawaii, whose thick skins enabled them to survive attacks by imported insects that killed many other species; and Danish hedges, created as part of a desperate struggle against the deforestation, erosion, and sandstorms that followed a boom in early modern shipbuilding. For the Midwestern case, see William Cronon, *Nature's Metropolis: Chicago and the Great West* (New York: W. W. Norton, 1992), 202–3. On Denmark, see Thorkild Kjaergaard, *The Danish Revolution, 1500–1800* (Cambridge: Cambridge University Press, 1994), 1–2.

28. Williams, *Deforesting the Earth*, 393–493.

29. McNeill, *Something New under the Sun*, 248–49.

30. On biology and the conquest of the Americas (and other "neo-Europes"), see Alfred W. Crosby, *Ecological Imperialism: The Biological Expansion of Europe, 900–1900*, 2nd ed. (Cambridge: Cambridge University Press, 2004); but for a view putting much less emphasis on epidemics, see Robert McCaa et al., "Why Blame Smallpox? The Death of the Inca Huayna Capac and the Demographic Destruction of Tawantinsuyu (Ancient Peru)," www.hist.umn.edu/~rmccaa/aha2004/whypox.doc, accessed July 2, 2008.

31. Lieberman, *Strange Parallels*, 126–31, 258, 293–94, and 409–10.

32. For a specifically environmental argument to the contrary, see Madhav Gadgil and Ramachandra Guha, whose history of the Indian environment, *This Fissured Land* (Berkeley: University of California Press, 1993), jumps from the formation of caste (an allegedly environmentally conservative system) to the effect of British resource hunger, as if no significant changes had occurred in the centuries between.

33. E. A. Wrigley, *Continuity, Chance and Change: The Character of the Industrial Revolution in England* (Cambridge: Cambridge University Press, 1988); Kenneth Pomeranz, *The Great Divergence: China, Europe, and the Making of a Modern World Economy* (Princeton: Princeton University Press, 2000); R. Bin Wong, *China Transformed: Historical Change and the Limits of European Experience* (Ithaca: Cornell University Press, 1997); Jack Goldstone, "Efflorescences and Economic Growth in

World History: Rethinking 'the Rise of the West' and the Industrial Revolution," *Journal of World History* 13, no. 2 (2002): 323–89.

34. In fact, Robert Ayres and Benjamin Warr argue that increases in "useful work"— energy consumed times the efficiency of the converters—account for almost all of the productivity increases in the U.S. economy in the twentieth century. See Ayres and Warr, "Accounting for Growth: the Role of Physical Work," homepage of the International Energy Agency (Fontainebleau: Center for the Management of Environmental Resources; www.iea.org/dbtw-wpd/Textbase/work/2004/eewp/Ayres-paper1.pdf, accessed August 2, 2005). There are, however, methodological problems in their analysis: the effective energy use series and the GDP series do have a strong correlation, but so might various other series that tended to increase steadily over the century.

35. In the Netherlands, for instance, per capita energy use in 1650 was between double and triple the figure for 1560, but then fell by 15–20 percent by 1750. This would make the overall increase probably about 100 percent over two hundred years (Jan de Vries and Ad van der Woude, *The First Modern Economy: Success, Failure, and Perseverance of the Dutch Economy, 1500–1815* [Cambridge: Cambridge University Press, 1997], 709–10). By contrast, global per capita energy use rose more than tenfold between the late nineteenth century and the end of the twentieth: see Vaclav Smil, *Energy in World History* (Boulder, CO: Westview Press, 1994), 187.

36. Fernand Braudel, *The Structures of Everyday Life* (New York: Harper and Row, 1981), 196–97.

37. For humans and animals, see McNeill, *Something New under the Sun,* 10–11. These figures naturally vary with circumstances. For modern electrical plants, see Smil, *Energy in World History,* 174. One irony here is that the machines that used essentially free energy—wind and running water—improved their technical efficiency first.

38. Smil, *Energy in World History,* 161, 164. Twentieth-century steam engines were typically between 10 percent and 20 percent efficient.

39. Charles Tilly, *Coercion, Capital, and European States,* 1.

40. For U.S. examples, see Karl Jacoby, *Crimes against Nature: Squatters, Poachers, Thieves, and the Hidden History of American Conservation* (Berkeley: University of California Press, 2001); for southern African ones, see William Beinart, "Introduction: The Politics of Colonial Conservation," *Journal of Southern African Studies* 15, no. 2 (January 1989): 149–51, 156–57.

41. See "Rice Yields Plunging Due to Balmy Nights," *New Scientist* 10, no. 23, www.newscientist.com/article/dn6082.html, accessed June 29, 2004.

TWO · The Big Story

Human History, Energy Regimes,
and the Environment

EDMUND BURKE III

Most histories depict the present as the endpoint of an ascending trajectory that links the agricultural revolution, classical Greece, the Renaissance, the Industrial Revolution, and modern times. This may make for good teleology, but is such a graph plausible? There are several reasons to think not. First, we have no evidence that modernity is a permanent stage in human history, particularly when we consider the human impact on the biosphere—deforestation, species extinctions, and other forms of environmental damage. It is unlikely that modern levels of consumption can be generalized for all humans or last indefinitely into the future. Indeed, humanity's talent for fouling its own nest is not uniquely modern, and the world economy and the state are the product of millennia of experimentation and interaction.

In this chapter I examine the environmental consequences of human development over the very long term as a way of providing a different perspective on the environmental quandary we currently face. The other essays in this book address the environmental legacies of world civilizations and regions over the more recent past or survey different regions' environmental histories. Here I examine the deep history of humanity, energy regimes, and the environment. My purpose is threefold. First, by placing modernity in the larger context of the flow, conversion, and storage of planetary bioenergy, I want to call into question the conventional historical narrative, which views the Industrial Revolution as a natural outcome of human development, and instead insist on the ways in which it constituted an unprecedented break in human relations with nature and the environment. Second, by focusing on the history of energy regimes, I want to disaggregate the Industrial Revolution into analytically distinct processes in order to argue for the decisive importance of the fossil-fuel revolution. Third, by studying energy regimes throughout world history, I seek to contextualize current concerns. At a time of renewed anxiety about the end of oil, the current moment seems an especially appropriate one in which to conduct such an exercise.

The close connection between humans and the environment was mediated first and foremost by fire. The Big Bang of course provides the ultimate fire story: its concentrated energy is still expanding. At the moment of the Big Bang, 13.7 billion years ago, incomprehensibly enormous amounts of energy were released, illuminating billions of stars and setting all in motion, including the history of Earth and of our species. The second law of thermodynamics tells us that, infinitely gradually and imperceptibly, this energy is being exhausted. Once created, the stars provided stable, long-lived stores of free energy. Energy is thus central to the universe.

But what is energy? Authorities have no single, specific answer to this question. Richard Feynman, for one, famously cautioned that "we have no knowledge of what energy *is*. We do not have a picture that energy comes in little blobs of a definite amount."[1] Conventionally, energy is defined as the capacity to do work. In our solar system, the temperature differential between our sun and the Earth provides the free energy necessary to create most forms of complexity. (Free energy is energy available to do work.) Complex entities, such as the life forms on Earth, absorb huge flows of energy and dissipate large amounts of free energy. Complex structures thus constantly increase disequilibrium and entropy in the universe.[2]

The mastery of fire provides a way of framing the relations of humans and the biosphere. Stephen J. Pyne has powerfully argued that at some early point in the history of the species, this mastery distinguished humans from other mammals.[3] The ability to manipulate fire allowed early humans to tap the solar energy stored in wood (biomass) and to transform the natural environment; it thus gave humans a crucial advantage over other megafauna. The systematic use of fire by humans to open clearings in the forest propitious to human settlement is one of the earliest signs of the emergence of *Homo sapiens,* apparently predating even the development of language. It may also have marked the origins of agriculture. For this reason, Johan Goudsblom has seen in fire the source of civilization.[4]

Vaclav Smil's *General Energetics* provides an integrated approach to forms of energy flow, storage, and conversion that links the geosphere, the biosphere, and human society.[5] The primary source of all forms of energy on this planet is the sun. (The molten core of the earth—itself stemming from the origins of the solar system—is a secondary source.) Energy conversions at all levels are driven by solar energy. Scientists recognize four forms of energy in the universe: nuclear, chemical, thermal, and mechanical (kinetic). The last three especially have, in different combinations, been important in the emergence of life on earth.

Central to life on earth is photosynthesis, the process by which solar energy is captured and stored by plants. All complex life forms have devised methods of accessing the solar energy stored in plants. Human metabolism allows us to unlock this store of energy either directly, by consuming plants, or indirectly, by consuming animals. Alone among other complex life forms on earth, humans have been able to devise means of storing and using solar energy. Seen in the light of energy conversions, human history assumes a rather different, indeed remarkable shape.

In the context of the deep history of humans and the flows of energy on this planet, some historians see the Industrial Revolution as a breakthrough that allowed first Western Europeans and then others to transcend the previously existing material limits on growth. For them, the Industrial Revolution is only the most recent phase in the development of our species. These historians emphasize its scientific and technological dimensions and neglect its energetic aspects. But if we rethink modernity in terms of its bioenergetics, we see that there have been only two major energy regimes in human history: the age of solar energy (a renewable resource) from 10,000 B.C.E. to 1800 C.E., and the age of fossil fuels (a nonrenewable resource) from 1800 C.E. to the present. This latter category includes coal, petroleum, and natural gas. Nuclear power constitutes an additional, if problematic, source of energy.[6] This unprecedented transformation lies at the heart of any history of humans and their relationship to the environment.

For one thing, this view suggests a rather different chronology of human history from the one we are used to. Organizing this alternative history in tabular form yields something like table 2.1. Both the age of solar energy and the age of fossil fuels can be further subdivided. Our story begins in the Paleolithic era (250,000–100,000 B.C.E. to 10,000 B.C.E.) when early human hunter-gatherers first incorporated the use of fire into processing a diet of wild grains, fruits, nuts, and plants and hunting. By roughly 20,000 B.C.E., their enormous success had resulted in the distribution of hunter-gatherers all around the world (dates on the peopling of the Americas lag but have been consistently revised backward).[7] Over the ensuing thousands of years, humans, plants, and animals underwent imperceptible but cumulatively important genetic changes in interaction with one another. The culmination of this process of coevolution was the Neolithic revolution (ca. 5000 B.C.E.), when, as a result of ever-increasing human populations, hunter-gatherers

TABLE 2.1   Human Energy Regimes through History

The Age of Solar Energy (origins to c. 1800 C.E.)	
Hunter-gatherers; mastery of fire	2.5 million B.C.E.–10,000 B.C.E.[1]
Early farming	10,000 B.C.E.
Early agrarian age under regional empires	5000 B.C.E.–1400 C.E.
Late agrarian age under conditions of globality	1400 C.E.–1800 C.E.

The Age of Fossil Fuels (c. 1800 C.E.–present)	
Early fossil-fuel era; coal and steam	1800 C.E.–present[2]
Late fossil-fuel era; petroleum, natural gas, and atomic power	1800 C.E.–present

[1]Hunter-gatherer lifestyles have continued in isolated locales to the present.
[2]Coal continues to be a major source of energy.

discovered a means of obtaining a reliable food supply: farming. Although Neolithic peoples adopted farming with reluctance, once they had done so there was no going back. Farming transformed the relationship of humans to the bioenergetic system of the planet by allowing them to extract much greater energy yields from animal husbandry and agriculture. Farming had one huge advantage: it supported more people in a given area and thus encouraged the development of more densely packed settlements with an increased capacity for cooperation and mutual learning (as well as conflict). Over the next several millennia, agriculture emerged in various locations around the world, including Egypt, Mesopotamia, the Ethiopian highlands, West Africa, the valley of the Yellow River, the Indus valley, and—somewhat later—the highlands of Mesoamerica and the Andes.[8] Thus began the agrarian age, which lasted from around 5000 B.C.E. until 1800 C.E. (The agrarian age can in turn be divided into two unequal periods: the classic agrarian age, 5000 B.C.E. to 1400 C.E., and the late agrarian age, 1400 C.E. to 1800 C.E.)

This agricultural revolution transformed the relations between humans and the environment. Agriculture can be viewed as a solar-energy system controlled by humans, in which the energy output of selected plants is monopolized for human purposes. Humans can be regarded by states as ambulatory solar-energy storage systems, and cities containing many humans can be seen as complex energy machines. Over the next several millennia, a species-level step up the energy-conversion staircase occurred as complex societies and cities emerged across Eurasia. Humans developed additional methods of energy conversion as well as a greater need for stored energy.[9] Agriculture encouraged the clearing of land for farming. Civilizations emerged, and with them trade, warfare, and religion. These developments established the basic rules of the energy conversion game that shaped the relations of humans to the environment until the dawn of the Age of Fossil Fuels around 1800 C.E. The ability of societies to mobilize large numbers of people to perform specific tasks greatly multiplied the ability of humans to access the solar energy embedded in crops (as well as to construct walls, pyramids, canals, and cities). Cities organized and transformed the energy of urban artisans, merchants, religious specialists, bureaucrats, military personnel, and other specialists. We can thus think of cities as complex energy machines.

Control over people was therefore a central feature of the energy strategy of most states and societies in the age of solar energy. Those able to organize large numbers of humans gained a major energy premium. To execute an important project, much human labor would have been required, as humans are quite inefficient machines.[10]

A second type of energy leveraging that occurred more or less simultaneously with the rise of agriculture was the domestication of horses and other traction animals (another type of ambulatory solar-energy storage system). Animal power was especially important for basic agricultural tasks such as plowing and harvesting, as a horse generates roughly six times the power of a man and has much greater endurance. Because horses could only do certain types of work, however, a mix of human and animal power was needed for most purposes. The use of animal power became widespread across much of Afroeurasia (but not the Americas).

Finally, technological invention enabled humans to leverage additional energy. Simple technologies (such as water-lifting devices, pulleys, and levers) developed early in the agrarian age multiplied the energy available from human power. Further technical innovations over the centuries provided solutions to a host of energy bottlenecks. By the early agricultural era, the use of fire had progressed beyond cooking food and providing warmth to propel advances in metallurgy for making tools and weapons, firing ceramics, brewing, and dyeing textiles. However, these technologies were prone to environmental "overshoot" because of large-scale deforestation.[11] Succeeding millennia saw the development of technologies for water management, mining, writing systems, maritime communications, textiles, mathematics, and astronomy. Important as these inventions were in enabling humans to maximize their use of the solar energy, their overall contribution was relatively modest, given their relatively low efficiency. New inventions and the modification of old ones, along with their gradual diffusion, continued to provide incremental advantages.

Although agrarian-age societies might under favorable conditions press against their ecological limits through the complex linking of demographic increase, technological change, the expansion of the economy, and the reach of the state, they were inherently unstable and prone to sudden collapse from famine, disease, and warfare.[12] In the ensuing centuries, control over people (and animals), as well as control over croplands, defined the bioenergetic limits of human development. The size of ancient empires therefore provides a crude measure of their energy capabilities.[13] Anthropogenic damage to the environment (deforestation, for example) was sometimes extensive, but agrarian-age systems were essentially self-correcting and self-limiting, as the consequences of environmental overshoot were readily apparent within a generation or two. The transition to agriculture thus provides a powerful way of visualizing the environmental feedback loops that occurred with the onset of modernity.[14] The rules of the energy game of the agrarian age remained in effect during the six and a half millennia of the classic agrarian age (5000 B.C.E. to 1400 C.E.).

The remarkable stability of human population levels in this period provides a powerful demonstration of this point. Empires rose and fell, to be sure. But the energy calculations remained much the same. The only way populations could increase significantly was through improved technology and agricultural cropping practices. Around 100 C.E. the world population peaked at about 250 million (see figure 2.1). Between ca. 300 C.E. and 650 C.E. there was a hemispheric-wide dip, before human populations began once again to increase across Afroeurasia. Not until ca. 1000 C.E. did they again reach 250 million.[15]

Agrarian societies always had a tendency to push their ecological limits. Peasant families tended to maximize births as a survival strategy. States and entrepreneurs tended to seek a technological edge over local competitors by modifying existing technologies. Mining, in particular, tended to stimulate technological innovations, as its high energy demands continually provoked crises and bottlenecks requiring solutions. Trade and migration provided access to goods, ideas, and people not locally available, but introducing these could have unforeseen destabilizing consequences.

Improvements in existing technologies and the diffusion of new technologies stimulated population growth as well. For example, according to Andrew Watson, with the spread of Islam, a "medieval Islamic green revolution" occurred, spurred by the diffusion of new crops, irrigation systems, and agricultural technologies, which led to the rebuilding of old cities (and the construction of new ones) both in the old Middle Eastern core areas and in Central and South Asia, North Africa, and

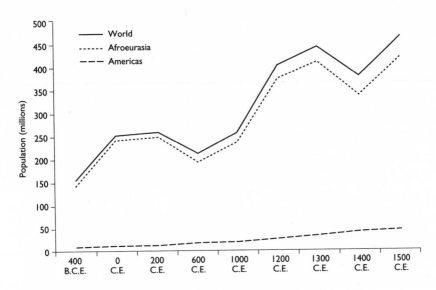

FIGURE 2.1.

World population, 400 B.C.E.–1500 C.E. *Source:* Adapted from Massimo Livi-Bacci, *A Concise History of World Population* (Cambridge, MA: Blackwell, 1992), 31.

Spain.[16] A similar burgeoning of populations occurred in China under the Song dynasty (960–1279). There, as a result of internal colonization and the construction of the Grand Canal, the center of gravity of the Chinese empire gradually shifted from the northern China plain, where dry farming had dominated, to the southern Chinese rice-growing areas (see Kenneth Pomeranz's essay on China in this volume).[17] In roughly the same period, new technologies such as the mold-board plow and the horse collar enabled European peasants to farm the heavy soils of Eastern Europe and led to significant population increases there. In South Asia, the big push started somewhat earlier. The opening of the vast delta of the Ganges valley to rice cultivation decisively shifted the focus of Indian civilization to Bengal (see the essay by Mahesh Rangarajan in this volume).[18] By the tenth century the regional empires of Africa, Europe, and Asia had become more densely networked, and commercial exchanges were becoming more important.

From about 1000 C.E. onward, an unprecedented population increase defied the old limits on growth and pushed the global population to around 350 million by 1400 C.E. This period can be seen as a culmination of the potentialities of the old-style agrarian empires, even though its advances were in some ways obscured by the Mongol conquests of the thirteenth century and the Black Death of the 1340s.

TABLE 2.2   Estimated World Regional Populations

(millions)

	1400 C.E.	*1500 C.E.*	*1600 C.E.*	*1700 C.E.*	*1800 C.E.*
China	70	84	110	150	330
India	74	95	145	175	180
Europe	52	67	89	95	146
Sub-Saharan Africa	60	78	104	97	92
Latin America	36	39	10	10	19
World totals	375	476	578	680	954

SOURCE: J. R. Biraben, "Essai sur l'évolution du nombre des hommes," *Population* 34 (1979): 16.

Three developments in this period enabled humans to improve on the energy calculus of the age of solar energy: the diffusion and perfection of basic technologies and concepts that enhanced the efficiency and productivity of Eurasian societies; the growing efficiency and wider application of wind energy (which enabled ocean navigation); and the development and adoption of more powerful and reliable gunpowder weapons. By 1400, it was clear that the terms of the energy equation were shifting throughout the hemisphere, provoking wars of conquest, more efficient exploitation of old territories, and the encouragement of trade. Nonetheless, the underlying energy equation of the age of solar energy remained in place.

One sign that humanity was entering a new energy context was the expansion of world population from 375 million to 954 million between 1400 and 1800 (table 2.2).[19] These changes especially affected the interlinked societies of North Africa, Europe, and Asia (where the vast majority of humans lived). Between 1400 and 1800 the Chinese population increased from 70 million to 330 million; India's population grew from 74 million to 180 million; and Western Europe saw growth from 52 million to 146 million. Only the Americas, which suffered an unparalleled demographic catastrophe following the arrival of Europeans, constitute an exception to this pattern. The Great Dying was the most devastating epidemiological event known in world history.[20]

In response to the new conditions of incipient globality, new agrarian empires emerged across Eurasia, reflecting their greater efficiency in mobilizing people and energy resources. States and empires such as Spain, France, the Hapsburg Empire, imperial Russia, the Ottoman Empire, the Safavid Empire, the Mughal Empire, Ming and Qing China, and Tokugawa Japan attained unprecedented power.

Although statistical measures are lacking, it seems evident that early modern empires wielded significantly greater power than their predecessors because of their mastery of new military and mining technologies, and techniques of shipbuilding and navigation. Early modern societies also showed an increased capacity for social organization and political management. Long-distance trade and oceanic fishing brought protein (herring and cod), basic food grains (rice, maize, and manioc), precious metals, stimulants (spices, sugar, coffee, tea, and cacao), and textile fibers (silk and cotton) across oceans. The diffusion of new agricultural technologies, know-how, and crops brought vastly increased production and profits for some, and also made it possible to feed unprecedented numbers of people worldwide. As John F. Richards argues in the next chapter, the land-use policies put into place between 1400 and 1800 encouraged the establishment of state-enforced property rights in land, as well as more specialized and more capitalist uses of land. As a result, the local property regimes of indigenous peoples, and the community property rights of peasant communities, came under increasing challenge.

By 1800 complex social organizations, including larger and more elaborate bureaucratic state structures and systems of economic exchange, technology, and communication had emerged all around Eurasia as well as in parts of Africa. As centralizing states sought to maximize the productivity of their lands, they also tried to devise policies that would channel the energies of local agrarian elites and entrepreneurs. Between 1400 and 1800, agriculture in early modern Europe became increasingly delocalized as agricultural products became commodified.[21] Many states deployed increasingly well-tuned systems of exploitation and more effective technologies that strengthened their power in agrarian core areas and along internal frontiers. More particularly, Western European states were able to exploit their external frontier regions (the Americas, Africa, and the Indian Ocean zone), notably for silver, spices, sugar, silk, and cotton. One consequence, as Richards has argued, was a sharp increase in environmental degradation of all kinds.[22]

Indeed, the increased environmental degradation of this period can be seen as a sign that the energy dynamics of the late agrarian age had shifted into a new phase. The huge increase in global population between 1400 and 1800 sent the price of fuel and wood soaring, and global energy demands began to push against the existing local and regional ecological limits. The consumption of wood for mining, shipbuilding, industrial uses, and domestic heating reached unprecedented levels, especially in Europe, the Mediterranean, and Japan. By around 1800 (earlier in Britain), Western Europe, Japan, much of China, and parts of the Americas found themselves in an energy crisis. As world population increased, the clearance of forest land for agricultural purposes accelerated. Simultaneously, the principal industrial fuels (wood and charcoal) fell into increasingly short supply. In addition, the expansion of mining and metallurgy led to the deforestation of entire regions around the major mining sites. Silver and mercury mining in Japan and Latin America (and in Potosí and Huancavelica in the Peruvian Andes, and Zacatecas in central Mexico) were especially destructive. Mining also significantly decreased forest cover in England, northern France, and central Europe. The wood crisis was further exacerbated by the boom in naval construction. The demands for ship's timbers, masts, and spars strained the forests of the Baltic and New England, as well as the Indian Ocean rim, where vessels for the Asian trade were constructed. Finally, in Brazil and the Caribbean, the sugar industry, which consumed vast quantities of wood and charcoal to fire sugar boilers, was another cause of local deforestation.[23]

At this point, something unprecedented occurred: the transition from biomass (wood and charcoal) to fossil fuels (initially coal, later petroleum and natural gas) as the principal source of heat energy. Thus began the age of fossil fuels. Thus far there have been two major phases: the age of coal (1800–1914) and the age of petroleum and natural gas (1880–present). Although coal had been known for centuries, it was little used as a fuel. Burning coal produced a nasty smell, gave off clouds of inky smoke, and had evident health consequences. As a result, there was enormous resistance to employing it. The shift began first in Britain, whose economy was the most severely affected by the wood shortage. By a lucky circumstance, moreover, Britain was well endowed with coal, and the coalfields were conveniently located near rivers (thus making coal easier to transport).[24] The transition from wood and charcoal to fossil fuels marks a fundamental shift in human and planetary history. Like the transition from the hunter-gatherer lifestyle to farming, it was neither desired nor sought after. With the availability of vast quantities of coal, the amount of heat energy accessible to humans became virtually limitless (although, as coal deposits are not universally distributed around the world, some societies inevitably profited more than others).

The advent of the age of fossil fuels released humans from their dependence on organic materials and from the trade-offs between heat, food, and raw materials. Previously, wood had been the main building material worldwide, and brick making had been very expensive because of the prodigious quantities of wood it required. With coal, it became possible to produce bricks cheaply and in quantity. This development lessened the demands on local wood resources both as fuel and as building material. Finally, the shift to coal lessened the dependency of its users on human and animal labor. As increasingly efficient technologies were developed, previously labor-intensive sectors such as agriculture and transport began to shed labor, freeing up workers for other purposes.

The effect of the coal revolution was multiplied exponentially by the development of the steam engine. Steam engines made it possible to capture the heat energy from burning coal, to concentrate it, and to use it to power machinery. The development of steam engines thus deserves to be considered analytically as separable from and as significant as the transition to coal itself.

Mechanization and steam engines transformed British (and subsequently European, U.S., and Japanese) industrial production in the nineteenth century in three important ways. One was the revolution in transport brought about by railroads and steamships. Steam power enormously increased the ability of humans to transport bulky, heavy goods like coal and iron over long distances. Previously, mining operations had tended almost literally to burn out once they had exhausted the fuel potential of nearby forests. With steam engines and railroads, coal could be moved long distances for pennies a ton, stimulating industries far from the mineshaft. Beginning in the early nineteenth century, railroads soon linked local communities to distant cities and countries, with accelerating economic and social consequences.[25] Steamships fueled by coal sounded the death knell for sailing ships following their introduction in the 1840s. Cheaper, more reliable, and faster than sail, steamships stimulated an unprecedented increase in trade and human migration.[26] In sum, steam power made possible a revolution in global communication, shrinking the globe and facilitating both European imperialism and nationalism.

At first, steam engines were restricted to powering the pumps that removed water from the mines. (The original Newcomen engine was bulky and immovable, consumed coal at prodigious rates, and was only 0.7 percent efficient.) But as efficiency increased, coal came to power the steam locomotives that moved the coal and iron ore to the foundries and factories of Europe. Soon coal and steam power were being used to power the Industrial Revolution. Steam engines and machines of all kinds gave humans an ability to produce far greater quantities of goods of all kinds than ever before, decisively altering the balance between man and nature. Coal (and its more energy-intensive derivative, coke) made it possible to produce vastly greater quantities of iron and steel while sparing the forests. It also allowed blast furnaces to reach much higher temperatures and to produce steel of much higher quality. (The fact that coal was a nonrenewable energy source was not yet widely recognized.) By 1812 coal gas was being used to light public streets, factories, and homes in London, and by midcentury it was widely used in Europe and America.[27]

From an environmental perspective, the availability of fossil fuels dramatically transformed the energy equation for societies all over the world. In the nineteenth century, energy consumption per capita rose rapidly in Europe, and later in other parts of the colonial developing world. Today, a nation's energy consumption correlates closely with its position in the world economy.

Although there is no denying that the Industrial Revolution was a remarkable event, the way we tell its history has tended to skip over the centrality of the energy transformation. We trace its origins instead to ineluctable processes of economic change fortuitously hard-wired into the DNA of "the West" (all those amazing technical inventions and that capitalist entrepreneurial zeal).[28] However, this perspective misconstrues a central element of the transition. The epochal move from solar-fueled to fossil-fueled economies depended crucially on the presence of coal in apparently unlimited quantities and readily exploitable forms. From an energy perspective, we might say that without fossil fuels, there would have been no Industrial Revolution, or at most a much-reduced and self-limiting one.

But if there had been no coal, then, too, Europe would look more like sub-Saharan Africa, much of the Mediterranean world prior to the twentieth century, or Latin America. These regions have little or no coal and depend heavily on external energy sources. If European coal were not conveniently located near water, then Europe would have had a history like China or South Asia (which have lots of coal, most of it difficult to access). The geography of the distribution of coal seems to map the developed world. Another way of thinking about this is to say that Britain's coal consumption in 1800 made available an additional 15 million acres to agricultural purposes that had previously been dedicated to producing wood for fuel.[29] If British factories had been dependent on wood (or more likely, charcoal) for fuel, there would not have been enough wood in all of Britain to fuel the boilers of the "dark Satanic Mills." The consequences of what Vaclav Smil calls the "Great Transition" from wood to coal was therefore momentous.[30]

This transition involved many trade-offs. Although it spared the forests, it caused terrible air pollution. Carbon dioxide emissions increased greatly, as did pollution of rivers and streams, and acid rain. By the nineteenth century, the killer fogs that bedeviled Charles Dickens's London had their counterparts everywhere in the industrial world. Inky black clouds enveloped cities and their hinterlands for weeks at a time, causing epidemics of respiratory diseases, shortening lives, and poisoning the atmosphere. The transition to fossil fuels shattered all previous human expectations of how much was too much. Previously, the overuse of resources was readily apparent: now resources could be consumed without regard for the environmental consequences.

Another major step up the energy-consumption ladder occurred with the invention of electric power. The principles behind electricity had been known since the end of the eighteenth century, and several important discoveries in the nineteenth century (notably by Michael Faraday) showed that electricity could be produced from mechanical energy. The first electrical generating plants (developed by Thomas A. Edison) came on line in 1882 and were at first used to generate electric lighting. But Edison was wedded to direct current, which was more costly to produce and of limited applicability. Nicola Tesla's 1887 discovery of alternating current (which, unlike direct current, could be transmitted over long distances at high voltages) and its successful commercial production by Westinghouse in 1893 (using hydropower generated by Niagara Falls) set the stage for the electrification of the United States. By 1900 dynamos and steam turbines were being used to generate electricity for use in factories and households and to power railroad locomotives. Coal-fired steam generators were for a long time the standard for most electrical utilities providers. With the coming of electricity, world human energy consumption soared to record levels. As the applications of electricity mushroomed in the twentieth century, its use spread around the globe. Engines of all types became ubiquitous. Our modern world is unimaginable without electricity.

By 1900, the consumption of fossil fuels began to shift from coal to oil. Oil was first exploited commercially in Pennsylvania in 1859 and was primarily used for lighting and heating, in the form of kerosene. The technical challenges of transporting and refining oil were eventually solved, as pipelines and oil tankers were developed. With the development of the internal combustion engine, the place of petroleum as a source of energy was assured. The transport sector remained the primary consumer of oil until after World War II.

Since the early nineteenth century, there has been a thousandfold increase in the consumption of fossil fuels. Figure 2.2 provides figures for a sample of world societies in different periods. Global per capita energy consumption was about 5 billion joules per year in the Neolithic period (ca. 10,000 B.C.E.). With the coming of the agrarian-age empires, per capita energy use increased notably. For example, the Han Chinese empire (206 B.C.E.–20 C.E.) consumed around 20 billion joules per year, about half of it being used for food-production and household needs. By 1300 C.E. European societies had doubled their energy consumption in all categories.

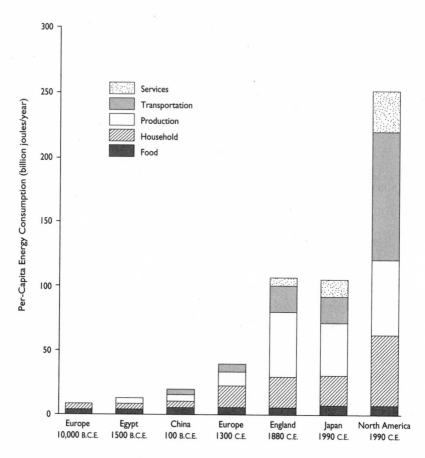

FIGURE 2.2.

Per-capita energy consumption in world history, selected societies. *Source:* Vaclav Smil, *Energy in World History* (Boulder, CO: Westview Press, 1994), 236.

Unfortunately, this figure does not include data on the late agrarian age, when we know that both energy consumption and energy efficiency increased significantly. As a result, it exaggerates the rapidity of the transition to fossil fuels. Between 1330 and 1880, British per capita energy consumption more than doubled. The portion of energy consumption devoted to production and transportation increased dramatically, both in absolute terms and per capita. This marks the apex of the coal phase of the age of fossil fuels. Indeed, in 1990 Japanese per capita energy consumption had still not reached the levels enjoyed by Britain in 1880. By this time, however, North American per capita energy consumption was more than double that of Britain in 1880. In the United States, an unprecedented pro-portion of this total was devoted to transportation and services. Overall, per capita energy consumption increased more than twenty-five-fold between the Neolithic period and the present.

Table 2.3 offers an even more stunning demonstration of increases in energy use, showing average energy consumption in different historical eras. For most of human history, from the Paleolithic period to the advent of industrial society, human energy consumption was barely adequate to fulfill basic metabolic needs. There was a slight increase in energy use with the coming of advanced agrarian societies. Then, about a century ago, global energy use suddenly shot up to around 123.2 billion calories per day. This reflects the larger food and domestic usage figures seen in figure 2.2. But the greatest expansion of energy use occurred in the most recent period, which I. G. Simmons calls advanced technological society, where it rose to a truly extraordinary 1,380 billion calories per day.[31] Since the early nineteenth century, there has been a thousandfold increase in the consumption of fossil fuels worldwide.[32]

The importance of oil and natural gas to human energy consumption has increased remarkably. Figures compiled by the Worldwatch Institute for the second half of the twentieth century show that total world fossil-fuel consumption has increased from less than 2 billion tons in 1950 to 8 billion tons in 2000 (figure 2.3). These are extraordinary figures: both the 1950 total by itself, and the 2000 figure, which reflects a fourfold increase in energy consumption worldwide in fifty years.

These figures may conceal a somewhat paradoxical trend: a rise in the consump-tion of coal. In 2005, those best placed to know suggested that global coal resources should last for 250 years, at current levels of consumption. (Because coal consump-tion has been rising, this assumption may need to be reexamined.)[33] Geologists estimate petroleum and natural gas reserves at 5 percent of coal reserves. With world oil consumption currently rising, coal may become far more important in the future. China and India, the two most populous countries in the world, each with populations exceeding one billion, are petroleum-poor and coal-rich and have rapidly increasing energy requirements. Coal production has been increasing in recent decades, even in North America and Europe.

The age of fossil fuels has also seen the rise of an entirely different source of energy: nuclear power. The use of nuclear energy now seems likely to increase as well, even though there has been no solution to the key bottleneck, the disposal of highly toxic nuclear wastes. European states such as Britain and France have recently begun planning the next generation of reactors to replace the aging reactors

TABLE 2.3   Average Daily Per-Capita Energy Consumption in Different Historical Eras

	Food (including animal feed)	Home and Commerce	Industry and Agriculture	Transportation	Total per Capita	World Population (millions)	Total
Protohumans	2*				2		
Hunters' society (12,000 B.C.E.)	3	2			5	6	30
Early agricultural society (3000 B.C.E.)	4	4	4		12	50	600
Advanced agricultural society (1000 C.E.)	6	12	7	1	26	250	6,500
Industrial society (1900 C.E.)	7	32	24	14	77	1,600	123,000
Present era	10	66	91	63	230	6,000	1,380,000

SOURCE: Adapted from David Christian, *Maps of Time: An Introduction to Big History* (Berkeley: University of California Press, 2004), 141.
*Units of energy = 1,000 calories/day.

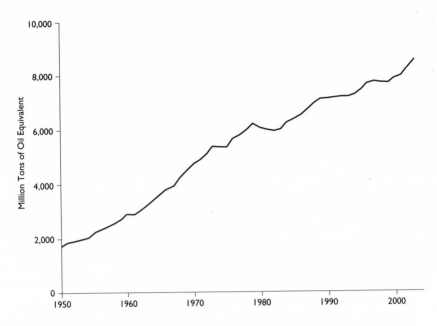

FIGURE 2.3.
World fossil-fuel consumption, 1950–2003. *Source:* Worldwatch Institute.

now in service. Nuclear power provides 7 percent of the world's energy and 17 percent of its electricity.[34] France, which closed its last coal mine in April 2004, currently produces more than 80 percent of its energy from nuclear reactors, making it the world leader in nuclear-energy consumption. The United States produces about 20 percent of its energy from nuclear sources.

Viewing human history in terms of energy consumption allows us to recognize the basic ecological trade-offs involved in choosing energy sources. It also provides a basis for reevaluating the significance of the Industrial Revolution and the current energy bottleneck in which humanity finds itself. Can we draw on our collective learning to find a solution? The environmental and energetic balance is not reassuring. Certainly the rest of the planet cannot increase its levels of energy consumption to match the levels of Europe, North America, Australasia, and Japan; nor can these levels be sustained indefinitely. Indeed, viewed against the background of all of human history, present levels of energy consumption appear deeply aberrant.

Is it possible to devise a sustainable fossil-fuel strategy?[35] Most experts agree that the discovery of additional quantities of petroleum on the scale of the oilfields of Saudi Arabia is most unlikely. Although coal reserves are larger, current methods of using coal do not hold out great hope for the long run. Most of the other remedies proposed (such as shale oil or alternative sources, such as solar, wind, and nuclear energy) have significant limitations. No single solution to the current impasse is apparent. But then the discovery of fossil fuels was itself improbable and at first stoutly resisted: other solutions may emerge that are implausible or unimaginable today.

Thomas Malthus (1766–1834) observed that the four human needs—food, clothing, shelter, and fuel—were in direct competition. An increase in one need necessitated reducing consumption of the others, and as population increased, difficult trade-offs were the inevitable result. These trade-offs had constrained the possibilities for economic growth since the early agrarian age and could be deferred only for brief periods. Although the enormous economic growth of the early nineteenth century impressed Malthus and his contemporary Adam Smith, both men were haunted by fears of a return to the cycles of demographic growth, overshoot, and population crash that had been the pattern throughout human history. Neither man ever recognized that he lived at the dawn of the Industrial Revolution and that the exploitation of fossil fuels had shattered the old limits on growth.[36] The current moment is freighted with a similar indeterminacy. So Malthus and Smith were wrong about the future. Or, in view of the new circumstances, prematurely pessimistic—by two and a half centuries. Today, with global population levels approaching seven billion human beings, although there are some grounds for guarded optimism, we can for the first time begin to contemplate the end of the age of fossil fuel. Some authorities suggest that given current rates of population increase and consumption patterns, we may actually be entering the down phase of a modern Malthusian cycle.[37]

NOTES

1. Richard Feynman, *The Feynman Lectures on Physics* (Reading, MA: Addison-Wesley, 1988), 4.2.

2. David Christian, *Maps of Time: An Introduction to Big History* (Berkeley: University of California Press, 2004), appendix 2.

3. Stephen J. Pyne, *World Fire: The Culture of Fire on Earth* (New York: Holt, 1995). See also, by the same author, *Vestal Fire: An Environmental History, Told through Fire,*

of Europe and Europe's Encounter with the World (Seattle: University of Washington Press, 1997); *Fire in America: A Cultural History of Wildland and Rural Fire* (Princeton: Princeton University Press, 1982); and *Burning Bush: A Fire History of Australia* (New York: Holt, 1991).

4. Johan Goudsblom, *Fire and Civilization* (London: Penguin, 1992).

5. Vaclav Smil, *General Energetics: Energy in the Biosphere and Civilization* (New York: John Wiley and Sons, 1991). See also his *Energies* (Cambridge, MA: MIT Press, 1999).

6. Rolf Peter Sieferle, *The Subterranean Forest: Energy Systems and the Industrial Revolution* (Cambridge, U.K.: White Horse Press, 2001).

7. For a convenient summary of the new chronology for the settlement of the Americas, see Charles C. Mann, *1491: New Revelations of the Americas before Columbus* (New York, Alfred A. Knopf, 2005).

8. On the origins of agriculture, the best guide is B. D. Smith, *The Emergence of Agriculture* (New York: Scientific American Library, 1995). See also Jared Diamond, *Guns, Germs and Steel* (New York: Vintage, 1998).

9. An excellent summary of the debate on the origins of agriculture can be found in Christian, *Maps of Time,* chapter 8.

10. Stephen Boyden, *Patterns in Biohistory* (Oxford: Oxford University Press, 1987), 196. See also Charles A. S. Hall, Cutler J. Cleveland, and Robert Kaufmann, *Energy and Resource Quality: The Ecology of the Economic Process* (New York: John Wiley and Sons, 1986).

11. John R. McNeill, "Woods and Warfare in World History," *Environmental History* 9, no. 3 (2004): 388–410.

12. Infrahistorical factors such as bolide impacts, earthquakes, floods, droughts, volcanism, and El Niño and La Niña events, are also nontrivial sources of environmental change. They are not considered here because they lie outside the realm of human causality.

13. Christian, *Maps of Time,* 316–24.

14. For one approach, see Jason W. Moore, "The Modern World System as Environmental History: Ecology and the Rise of Capitalism," *Theory and Society* 32 (2003): 307–77.

15. Peter Christensen, *The Decline of Iranshahr: Irrigation and Environments in the History of the Middle East, 500 B.C. to A.D. 1500* (Copenhagen: Museum Tusculanum Press, 1993), 65–70.

16. Andrew Watson, *Agricultural Innovation in the Early Islamic World* (Cambridge: Cambridge University Press, 1983).

17. Mark Elvin, *Patterns of the Chinese Past* (Stanford, CA: Stanford University Press, 1973), chapter 9. The classic work remains Joseph Needham et al., *Science and Civilization in China,* vol. 6, part 2, *Agriculture* (Cambridge: Cambridge University Press, 1984).

18. On the environmental history of India, see Madhav Gadgil and Ramachandra Guha, *This Fissured Land: An Ecological History of India* (Berkeley: University of California Press, 1993). See also the introduction to Richard Grove, Vinita Damodaran, and Satpal Sangwan, eds., *Nature and the Orient: An Environmental History of India and Southeast Asia* (Delhi: Oxford University Press, 1998).

19. Colin McEvedy and Richard Jones, *An Atlas of World Population History* (New York: Facts on File, 1978).

20. On the Great Dying and the Columbian exchange, Henry F. Dobyns, "Estimating Aboriginal American Population: An Appraisal of Techniques with a New Hemispheric Estimate," *Current Anthropology* 7 (1966): 395–415, is fundamental. Mann provides some recent population estimates in *1491*.

21. Jason W. Moore, "Environmental Crisis and the Metabolic Rift in World-Historical Perspective," *Organization and Environment* 13, no. 2 (2000): 126.

22. John F. Richards, *The Unending Frontier: An Environmental History of the Early Modern World* (Berkeley: University of California Press, 2005).

23. For an overview of global deforestation in this period, see the magisterial study by Michael Williams, *Deforesting the Earth: From Prehistory to Global Crisis* (Chicago: University of Chicago Press, 2006), chapters 6–8. See also Richards, *Unending Frontier*.

24. John U. Nef, *The History of the British Coal Industry* (London: Cass, 1932), 2 vols.

25. Patrick O'Brien, ed., *Railroads and the Economic Development of Western Europe, 1830–1914* (New York: St. Martin's, 1983).

26. Henry Fry, *The History of North Atlantic Steam Navigation* (London: Sampson, Low, Marston & Co., 1896); James Croil, *Steam Navigation* (Toronto: William Briggs, 1898).

27. Vaclav Smil, *Energy in World History* (Boulder, CO: Westview Press, 1994), 160. Wolfgang Schivelbusch, *Disenchanted Night: The Industrialization of Light in the Nineteenth Century* (Berkeley: University of California Press, 1995), provides a convenient history of gas lighting.

28. For example, Eric Jones, *The European Miracle: Environments, Economies and Geopolitics in the History of Europe and Asia*, 3rd ed. (Cambridge: Cambridge University Press, 2003).

29. E. A. Wrigley, *Continuity, Chance and Change: The Character of the Industrial Revolution in England* (Cambridge: Cambridge University Press, 1988), 54–55.

30. Smil, *Energy in World History*, 156, 138. Five kilograms of wood are equivalent to one kilogram of charcoal.

31. Ian G. Simmons, *Environmental History: A Concise Introduction* (Oxford: Blackwell, 1993).

32. On the fossil-fuel revolution, see Clive Ponting, *A Green History of the World: The Environment and the Collapse of Civilizations* (London: Penguin, 1993), chapter 13. On the European dimensions, see Williams, *Deforesting the Earth*, chapter 6.

Table 2.3 masks a huge divergence between richer, industrialized societies and poorer, nonindustrialized societies worldwide and similarly impressive differences between rich and poor within individual societies. Indeed, what is striking about the last century of energy use is the massive advantage it has offered to the favored few, whether in rich or poor societies, at the expense of the poor. By 1900, the United States was consuming more than 50 percent of all of the energy used in the world. In 1950, despite the industrialization of other parts of the world and a global increase in energy use, U.S. energy consumption was still 30 percent of total world consumption. Because the U.S. population then represented 3 percent of the global population, this decline reflects its decline relative to other countries.

33. Worldwatch Institute, *Vital Signs* 2004, www.worldwatch.org

34. Worldwatch Institute, *Vital Signs,* 2004, www.worldwatch.org

35. See Mark Jaccard, *Sustainable Fossil Fuels* (Cambridge: Cambridge University Press, 2005).

36. Wrigley, *Continuity,* 47–51, 66–67.

37. Christian, *Maps of Time,* 471–81, especially 471. See also David Kennedy, *Preparing for the Twenty-First Century* (London: Fontana Books, 1994).

THREE · Toward a Global System
of Property Rights in Land

JOHN F. RICHARDS

Since the late fifteenth century, the global landscape has been transformed by human action.[1] Land, formerly abundant in most parts of the world, has become relatively scarce and valuable as human numbers have increased twelvefold (from 0.5 to 6 billion people). Land use for agriculture, pastoralism, resource extraction, industrial production, commerce, and human settlement has become more specialized and capital-intensive. Intensified land use, in conjunction with the discovery and use of fossil-fuel energy, has caused massive changes in the natural environment. The total standing biomass in the world today is considerably less than it was in 1500, and biodiversity has been much reduced in each region of the world.

Over the past six centuries, humans have raised their knowledge, control, and use of the world's lands to an unprecedented level. By the late 1990s, every hectare of the world's land surface was known, recorded, demarcated, mapped, and claimed as part of the territory of a particular nation-state (or of a consortium of states, as in Antarctica). Cascading technical advances in astronomy, navigation, mathematics, geography, and cartography, as well as dramatic improvements in transportation, have made possible unprecedented territorial control and access. Today's world is truly a unified and largely inhabited unit divided into precisely measured tracts of land.

Over the past few centuries, every human society has moved toward a similar regime of rights in landed property. Bewilderingly complex, particularized, local systems of property rights in land have been altered, transformed, or replaced by simplified, more uniform sets of rules in a remarkably similar fashion across all world regions. Paradoxically, however, these converging property rules have helped to establish more precise, exact, nuanced, and complex rights over individual parcels of land. This trend reflects the intensifying manipulation and use of smaller and smaller units of land, within land markets of increasing transparency and efficiency.

How do we detect and analyze the processes and structural changes that have produced these converging property-rights regimes? My approach here is to look for similar large-scale processes of change over longer periods.[2] In this effort, I seek to detect similarities across comparative cases rather than to identify differences. This essay examines three massive changes in land use and property rights over the past six centuries: first, the displacement or extinction of indigenous peoples and the consequent obliteration of localized property-rights regimes; second, the erosion of community property rights in land exercised by peasants in agrarian societies; and third, as part of the massive process of global urbanization in the past two centuries, the struggle of an ever more compressed and ever-growing urban lower class for stable property rights in urban land. Although the last change began later than the others, all three processes proceed simultaneously today.

THE CENTRALIZING STATE

Early modern and modern states have been the principal agents of intensified human land use and land management. Intensifying land use is essential to state centralization and modernization. Today all land areas are ultimately claimed as property by a nation-state (or sometimes more than one). Each state does its best to demarcate and defend its national boundaries, which are located precisely on maps and on the ground.[3] Behind these lines, each state exercises territorial strategies to control its national land area. Some portion, often quite large, remains under active ownership and management by official agencies. In most nation-states, the remaining land is relinquished to the active ownership of private individual or corporate landowners. Part of the nation-state's credibility rests with its guarantee of predictable and stable private property rights in land. The modern state, as ultimate owner, can and does take private property by right of eminent domain, usually with compensation, for public purposes such as constructing highways and creating artificial lakes. In times of emergency or crisis, states act ruthlessly to seize land for purposes of national defense and survival. However, confidence in private property depends upon assurances that the state will not arbitrarily or needlessly seize lands. The state itself must be constrained by rules and statutes that guarantee land ownership.

The state's assertion of complete property rights over all land within its boundaries is an essential aspect of modern nationalism, national identity, and the nation-state. The growth of nationalism has been coterminous with growth in state control over land. Construction of a national territory is vital to national identity and community. The nation-state uses territoriality to define membership (e.g., by birthright citizenship) and to build a shared national culture aimed at uniformity everywhere within its boundaries. Lacking a secure national territory, nationalisms remain incomplete and unfulfilled movements. Ultimate land ownership, expressed in sovereign control over a fixed territory, is an essential step in nation building. Simultaneously, nationalism validates the sweeping property claims of the nation-state as ultimate landlord. Every bit of land within the national boundaries is the inheritance of the national community. The nation-state has a solemn responsibility to manage its lands for the present and the future. Which vision informs this stewardship and how lands are to be managed remain matters of dispute and controversy.

Centralizing states—both early modern monarchies and modern nation-states—with their ever-extending territorial reach, have destroyed or swept aside hundreds, perhaps thousands, of indigenous peoples.[4] From the Tupi Indians of coastal Brazil in the sixteenth century to the Meratus Dayaks of South Kalimantan to the peoples of Indonesia in the late twentieth century, every era has claimed its roster of victims.[5] Hunter-gatherer, shifting cultivator, or nomadic pastoralist peoples have never been satisfactory revenue-producing subjects for aggrandizing states. Often such "primitive" or "savage" peoples have been elusive and difficult to count and tax; usually they are subsistence producers who generate little usable surplus; often they are the inconvenient occupants of lands bearing resources of great value; and generally they are objects of great suspicion, fear, and hatred. Deficient in numbers, technology, and literacy, these marginal peoples can resist only for a time the onslaught of "civilized" powers.

A state opens frontiers to expand into space designated as wild, empty, or desolate, inhabited by groups identified as savages or nonpersons. As it does so, the state announces new, overriding claims of ownership over lands viewed as waste or wilderness. State-encouraged frontier expansion destroys systems of landholding and land use employed by indigenous groups. Newly defined property rights in land support more intensive, market-oriented production by the new settlers. Population density increases with settlement and sedentary cultivation. In the most common scenario, the conquering state gives or sells settlers individual property rights over arbitrarily assigned tracts of land. These lands are seized from the indigenous peoples, whose rights of occupancy and use are disregarded, taken by force, or bartered for trivial compensation. Whether these pioneer owners have only smallholdings or are allowed to claim large estates largely depends on the structural forces and ideology dominant in the period and region. Depending on local ecology, the settlers may engage in plow agriculture, commercial pastoralism (ranching), or mining. Forests are cleared, swamps drained, grasslands plowed, and purportedly dangerous wildlife killed off as the frontier presses forward.

Frontier expansion confiscates loosely demarcated, community-managed land employed by indigenous peoples for shared hunting and gathering, for grazing, or for shifting horticulture.[6] If they survive the initial shock of contact, indigenous groups may remain on their original settlements or habitations and retain their individually occupied homesteads and garden plots and community space, but the total lands accessible to their use are sharply reduced and compressed. Moving to new, undepleted lands for horticulture, grazing, or hunting becomes difficult as those lands are occupied and claimed by settlers. Often new diseases accompany political and cultural pressures to further weaken indigenous resistance to settler pressure. As the frontier moves forward, new lands are surveyed and demarcated.

As early as the sixteenth century, the governments of the Netherlands revived cadastral mapping as a tool of state land management.[7] Techniques employed by professional surveyors improved to the point that land could be precisely named, located, and represented on a map. Surveyors became more proficient at determining their exact positions from published astronomical observations. From known locations and heights, they could do transects over previously unmapped lands and obtain the data for accurate topographical mapping. After baselines were established, surveyors could begin detailed cadastral mapping of the new lands. (Of course, detailed cadastral mapping did not depend on precise location by longitude and latitude; it was used to divide lands long before this period.) Land maps are intended, as James Scott reminds us, to be "a geometric representation of the borders or frontiers between parcels of land."[8] They are intended to link landowners precisely with their property, primarily for tax purposes. Often in frontier circumstances, surveyors map and lay out parcels of land in anticipation of occupation and ownership by settlers. Their official land maps establish a new, usually gridded landscape comprehensible to arriving settlers but opaque to indigenous peoples.

The state, as ultimate landowner, confirms the property rights of the new settlers by written documentation preserved in official archives. The original claims for land, with their crude bounds marked by natural features, trees, or streams, are gradually superseded by new, precisely measured plats from cadastral surveys. In most instances, these new settlers hold individual proprietary rights over their lands. For a time at least, the state is willing to concede virtually the full bundle of ownership rights to its hardy pioneers. It will, if necessary, adjudicate disputes over ownership and use in the courts and will back up properly registered ownership claims by force.

Most centralizing states encourage the development of an open land market in agricultural land in these newly settled areas. The state frees land from the constraints of community and the slow-paced, cyclical pattern of indigenous land use. The new property-rights system is aimed at speeding ownership transfers and easing changes in land use. As land becomes a commodity with a price, it is readily transferred from one owner to another and subject to the most productive use determined by the market. As villages and towns are settled and expand, suburban and urban lands become fungible and available for any urbanized use. Urban land-use changes become even faster and easier as transaction costs decrease in booming land markets.

States also retain active ownership and management of portions of newly annexed lands. A common practice has been to establish territories for indigenous peoples—usually less desirable and productive tracts—so that they may be more easily controlled and kept from contact with settlers. On these tracts, often referred to as reservations or native lands, group property rights over land may be tolerated by the conquest state. Generally, however, these rights are also determined, measured, recorded in written documents, and thereby frozen in place in a newly static system of land tenure. Keeping them out of any form of land market preserves native lands. Outsiders are prohibited from acquiring property rights on these reservations. Native peoples caught up in these territorial systems face the worst of both worlds: their older systems of production are less effective under the new conditions, and they have no capital and often no legal way to improve production on their reserved lands. Not surprisingly, state demarcation of reserved lands has contributed to new, more unified composite identities and far greater cohesion among the peoples so bounded.[9]

The centralizing state often bars pioneer settlement in large areas of potentially valuable natural resources—especially forests. Continually rising timber prices in the early modern and modern world economy have encouraged states to retain at least some portion of unsettled forest lands for revenue purposes. In defining such spaces, the universal tendency has been to discourage and remove indigenous peoples living on these lands. Fear of the use of fire as an ecological tool by shifting cultivators has been one of the primary motives for removals, along with stereotypical concerns about savage violence. The effect has been to depopulate forests designated as state property. Punitive military expeditions have been followed by creation of quasi-military patrol and guard systems to keep people away from forest resources. Under some regimes and in some periods, however, local people living adjacent to the forest were permitted to graze animals, gather fuelwood, thatch, berries, and other forest products, and even hunt and fish to a limited extent. Access was always contingent and regulated by the state as landowner.

In some forested lands, little or no management occurred, as officials simply leased timber-cutting rights to private contractors (often for illegal compensation and bribes) with scarcely any thought for sustainable development. Often an influx of settlers—either legally or illegally as squatters—followed. Elsewhere in national or state forestlands, forestry agencies have employed professionally trained foresters and scientists as land managers. Globally accepted standards for forest science and management have been coalescing since the eighteenth century.[10] Timber harvesting on state forestland, usually by leases and permits to private contractors, generated a revenue stream for the treasury. Foresters have, however, consistently fought for the territorial integrity of their bounded state-owned forestlands. Sometimes they have prevailed against powerful public and private groups seeking to clear and develop state forestlands for profit, sometimes not.

By and large, foresters have been more concerned with generating usable timber supplies than with maintaining the ecological integrity of forests. Concern for sustainable use and for replanting has tended to vary according to the morale, political support, financial, and timber needs of the regime. For example, under wartime supply pressures, state-run forests universally suffer intense cutting and exploitation. Generally, even in normal circumstances, the pressures for overexploitation have led to overcutting in most state-owned forests worldwide.[11] Scientific theories and threats of financial loss have encouraged obsessive concerns with wildfire in forest, brush, and grassland settings.[12] One way to measure intensifying land management around the world is to look at the steadily growing effort and resources put into suppressing fires that occur naturally or by human action. Fire has changed from a commonly employed tool to a hazard that must be suppressed. The use of fire has been stripped from the bundle of ownership rights by the centralizing state. In most twentieth-century societies, firing state-owned lands is a criminal offense. Employing fire on private property is strictly regulated and often prohibited by official edict.

It is primarily the state, rather than local society, that condemns the use of fire as a threat to order and suppresses burning. Because firing the woods is an essential process for shifting cultivators, this practice puts them on a collision course with officials. Foresters, engineers, and scientists have universally condemned the use of fire by indigenous peoples as a tool of ecological management to encourage game or to promote soil fertility. That intimate ecological knowledge and sense of place that permitted local peoples to employ fire successfully is disparaged and ignored.

State claims to ultimate land ownership extend to nearly all natural resources. Rights to consume wildlife, for example, are extracted from the bundle of property rights attached to land. Wildlife—animals, birds, fish—are claimed as property by the state, which may or may not permit individuals to hunt, fish, trap, or otherwise make use of these resources. (Of course, state interest in regulating hunting is mixed with its concern to regulate the use of weapons by its citizenry.) Even on lands long conceded to private or corporate ownership, the state regulates treatment of wildlife by its rules regarding hunting, taking, or disturbance of animal, fish, and bird populations. Specialized wildlife and fishery agencies evolve that regulate the taking of wildlife and often intervene in natural processes by breeding and stocking favored species, by manipulating the physical environment, and by exterminating species considered vermin because they harm preferred wildlife. Frequently these agencies fix bounded territories whose sole purpose is to protect wildlife from human depredation. In these reserves, humans may be excluded, save for regulated excursions to view wildlife and flora.

Some state-owned lands become potent symbols of national identity. The monuments, sites, gardens, and walks of the national capital, the carefully maintained terrain of major battles, and the grounds of a vast military cemetery are all bounded areas sacred to the nation and its history. So are the state-owned natural parks that surround and protect dramatically appealing natural features such as active volcanoes, steam geysers, river canyons, glaciers, mountains, and coral reefs. Such features have come to be viewed as part of the national property and are made accessible to all by the nation-state. The national parks system in the United States is among the most developed and extensive in the world, but other nations have their own versions of this territorial definition of nature. The nation-state's proprietorial rights in these areas are to be maintained in perpetuity. Citizens have tightly controlled rights of access to these sites, but no further rights. Almost all forms of natural-resource exploitation and economic production on these sites— save tourism—are generally prohibited. The land's sacral qualities are to be retained by preservation, by preventing change. The transformations of the market and capitalist development are excluded and restrained by this categorization.

PEASANT SOCIETIES AND LAND MARKETS

Freely transferable landed property rights often threaten community identity, social stability, and sense of place—especially if these rights permit outsiders to capture control of community land. On the other hand, market forces may serve to open up opportunities for members of local elites to acquire land and hence gain more power within their community.

Community struggles with land markets have been a central theme in the recent history of the agrarian societies of Europe and Asia. During the late medieval and early modern periods, peasant communities across Europe, Asia, and parts of Africa developed strong, resilient organizational structures that controlled land use and restricted membership. The village and its lands constituted a defined territorial unit. In these hierarchical societies, village elites or notables held dominant power—power that early modern states found useful to foster and support. Headmen and councils from dominant families and households gathered and paid land taxes, negotiated with landlords and tax collectors, kept order, dispensed justice, and organized village defenses when regimes collapsed. Kinship ties between dominant peasant households, expressed in shared lineage or caste idioms, facilitated operation of these institutions.

Depending on the intensity of land use and modes of cultivation, individual property rights in land remained with individual families or households in peasant societies. These rights did not depend on prior recognition from the state but emerged when, in Robert Netting's words, "land is a scarce good that can be made to yield continuously and reliably over the long term by intensive methods."[13] Well-tended, irrigated, manured garden plots, for example, were passed down from one generation to the next in most peasant societies. Individual property rights did not generally confer the right of alienation beyond the community or lineage but did permit temporary use, borrowing, or leasing among households of the same lineage or community.

Dominant peasant elites acted as managers of village lands and natural resources under common property-ownership institutions. As population densities increased in areas of sedentary cultivation, individual communities found it useful to restrict access and control resource extraction from village pastures, irrigation works, forests, and wastes. Local elites devised organizational structures: rules and enforcement mechanisms that ensured sustained land use and provided access (usually unequal) to all members of the community. Access to these lands was an important income supplement to all, but especially to the poorer members of each community.

Market forces, in general, have tended to weaken and ultimately destroy common-property regimes and to erode the territorial powers of village elites. Vigorous demand and efficient land markets have made it more difficult for village elites to regulate land ownership and occupancy. This change has not occurred without contestation, protest, and sometimes violence. The pace and scope of transition to individualized property rights in community lands have varied in different regions. Promarket policies by states have hastened this transition; antimarket policies sometimes have slowed the process but never stopped it completely. Today, local common-property regimes are vestigial and close to extinction.[14]

Descriptions of this process form a staple of the literature on the history of agrarian societies. The questions of enclosure and the commons informed the theorizing of the classical economists. In early modern Europe, common property controls over village lands and resources were ubiquitous. The protracted process of peasant emancipation involved commutation, or freedom from manorial obligations; partition of common lands among those who had previously held rights of access; and consolidation of scattered plots of arable land under one owner.[15] As these legal reforms occurred, markets in land penetrated the countryside, and commercialization of agriculture followed. As early as the sixteenth century, the peasant communal institutions in the manorial villages of southern England felt market pressures and began to be subject to enclosure.[16] On the continent, it was not until the early nineteenth century that the French Revolution triggered legal reforms in France; similar reforms were occurring by midcentury in Germany.[17]

The major exception to this trend is Russia. By the seventeenth century the Russian *mir* or commune had evolved, according to Werner Rösener, into "the most extreme form of communal control over agrarian terrain anywhere in Europe."[18] Nothing resembling enclosure occurred in Russia. The abolition of serfdom in 1861 left legal control of land in the hands of the commune, which periodically repartitioned land among its members. Challenges to the collective authority of the commune over its members and lands came with new migratory labor opportunities and with some modest consolidation of lands by upper peasants who could control repartition. However, the *mir* remained impervious to land markets until the Stolypin reforms of 1909.[19]

Asian agrarian societies went through similar processes. In the mid-seventeenth century, the victorious Manchus who founded the Qing dynasty dismantled the manorial social formation of the Ming dynasty, with its landlords and serfs, and reapportioned land to newly enfranchised village communities of smallholding peasants.[20] To increase rural production and state revenues, the Qing regime actively supported and encouraged peasant smallholding ownership rights. The state also actively encouraged land reclamation to increase production. Nevertheless, in the later Qing regime, corporate landholdings of lineages and village common-property lands became increasingly vulnerable to active land markets as internal settlement frontiers closed.[21] A brisk land market emerged, despite continuing rights of preemption on sales of land. Sellers retained the right to recover the land by repayment of the sale price or, if the value of the land had gone up, to seek an additional payment from the buyer. This practice was a reflection of the deep-seated Chinese belief that land was held in trust for a family. There was also a long-standing division of subsoil and surface rights, each of which could be pawned, sold, or mortgaged.[22]

In Tokugawa Japan, where land was formally inalienable, one estimate puts communally managed village forests and meadows at twelve million hectares. When formal rights of alienation in land were introduced, village lands were steadily reduced and stand at approximately three million hectares today.[23]

In early modern India, sedentary peasant communities vigorously expanded cultivation throughout the subcontinent.[24] As they did so, they constructed village communities that actively managed village lands and resources. Rural land markets for rights of occupancy and cultivation remained relatively undeveloped and village common-property institutions unchallenged until the British colonial period. Thereafter, brisk markets in land developed in nearly every region of sedentary cultivation in the subcontinent, and communal property rights declined accordingly.[25]

In North Africa, the same patterns are apparent. In early modern lower Egypt, for example, land markets, circumscribed by tight elite control over the transfer and working of cultivated lands in each village, were freed and extended by liberal reforms under Khedive Ismail in the 1860s.[26]

Sub-Saharan East Africa followed a slightly different path in the absence of strong, centralizing, early modern nation-states. Population growth, land-use intensification, and peasantization took place under more loosely organized chieftaincies and patrilineages. Only after colonial conquest in the late nineteenth century did land markets emerge. Patterns in land use of the cattle-keeping, horticulturalist Chagga peoples on the slopes of Mount Kilimanjaro or the Kipsigis of western Kenya illustrate this process.[27] The loss of community-managed lands to expanding cultivation and private land ownership in modern agrarian societies removed an important asset for all, but especially for poorer peasant families. Peasant communities lost a significant buffer against scarcity. Commodities and amenities found beyond the cultivated fields of the village, in woods, grassland, and wetland, were a significant part of household resources. Readily gathered fuelwood for domestic cooking and heating is but one of the many resources that were accessible to the poorest rural family. Supplemental foodstuffs, medicines, and building materials were literally at hand.[28] These products, coupled with grazing for a few animals and the produce of small plots of land, offered a modest subsistence despite the vagaries of the local labor market.

LAND, PROPERTY RIGHTS, AND URBAN SPACE

One of the most significant global social processes since 1800 has been massive growth in the size and number of large cities. Rural-to-urban migration and natural increase have turned a rising percentage of the world's population into city dwellers. Since 1950, this trend has accelerated. In 1985 the number of people living in urban areas had reached 2 billion, or just over 43 percent of the total world population (up from 726 million and 29 percent in 1950).[29] At present, several metropolises have populations of more than 10 million and one, Mexico City, is approaching 20 million. The number of cities with populations of more than half a million has risen to nearly a thousand.

The world's cities have also expanded steadily in territory, although not proportionally with their growth in population. A continuing compression of urban space has resulted, as more and more people crowd into less space. Urban land has been increasingly needed simply for buildings, with a consequent decline in open or green space. In Mexico City, with its huge population crowded into 2,700 square kilometers of land, only 6 percent of the land area is not occupied by buildings and roads. The average amount of green space per inhabitant is just five square meters.[30]

This compression has had obvious implications for global land use and for converging systems of property rights in urban land. Property-rights regimes in cities, despite local peculiarities, are remarkably alike. Cities have expanded in territory, although not proportionally with their growth in human numbers. In every growing city, urban land has risen sharply in value as demand for urban space has increased; and land markets have proved to be extraordinarily powerful forces. Access to and control of urban lands has become one of the most contested areas in modern life. Speculation in land just prior to urban expansion or improvement has been a primary avenue to the accumulation of wealth and capital. Ownership of prime urban properties is generally a guarantee of rising revenue streams and appreciating capital values for both buildings and land. The twin forces of capitalism and industrialism require a continuing, creative process of construction, alteration, destruction, and movement in the use and configuration of urban space.

Nevertheless, cities are resistant to change in land use. Capital invested in the built environment with its fixed buildings, streets, and other infrastructural elements has its own inertia and trajectory once established. As David Harvey puts it, the contemporary city "forms what we might call a *palimpsest,* a composite landscape made up of different built forms superimposed upon each other with the passage of time."[31] Cities become more and more "sclerotic" as incremental changes are made in their physical fabric, generation after generation. Occasionally, extraordinary political consensus permits radical changes in cityscapes. Examples of such moments include the British Indian colonial regime's authoritarian power to drive wide boulevards through crowded lower-class neighborhoods (slums) in early twentieth-century Mumbai and Calcutta. Rhetorical appeal to the sanitary virtues of opening up the densely crowded slums of the city to light and air were coupled with fears of Indian political unrest in slum areas.[32]

Population growth arising from economic growth in cities exacerbates the problem of land markets. Urban elites invariably are torn between the temptations to profit from unrestricted operation of land markets—as rentiers, as developers, as speculators—and the need to resist and control market forces. Elites in every postindustrial city have resorted to territorial strategies to control land use and to tame the urban land market. Their continuing effort to attain social and political stability and to foster a sense of place and urban identity leads to the sequestering of some urban land from the market. As with national territory and the nation-state, cities retain control of municipal property to meet the space needs of city government, to create streets and other spaces for public transit, and to reserve land for monuments and other sacred sites.

The new nineteenth-century sciences of urban planning, city management, and public health drew their strength from the practice of zoning urban land for specific purposes.[33] Within each zoned area, municipal codes set out detailed rules for land use and buildings that are consistent with that use and with public welfare. Particular attention is paid to segregating and securing residential space for upper-class and elite residents of the city from intrusion by the lower classes.

The greatest strain on urban land use and property rights has been caused by poor migrants to the cities. Aside from earning a living, their greatest struggle has been to obtain tolerable, affordable housing within reasonable proximity to their work. Access to housing involves some form of property rights in urban space—whether as tolerated squatters or as tenants, or even eventually as owners. Tenement and slum dwellers who organize themselves can and do press for concessions from landlords and the municipality. These may include due-process protections for tenants, the provision of basic amenities, occupancy rights, and rent control. In other words, these residents seek protection from the untrammeled land market. In this struggle, a sense of place and strong community identities may emerge over time. These ties are reinforced by the tendency of migrants to cluster in areas according to ethnic and regional origin.

Somewhat paradoxically, the interests of poor, lower-class urbanites in gaining rights to a modicum of living space coincide with the interests of most members of urban elites. The economic health of the city demands cheap labor in the industry and service sectors. The political health of the city requires relative contentment among the lower classes. Extreme poverty and inadequate sanitation among its poorer inhabitants threaten the public health of the city. Crowding and crime among the urban poor threaten the physical security of the upper classes.

Between 1850 and 1950, the cities of the industrial age absorbed vast numbers of migrants, put them to work, and provided housing in tenements. Across Europe, Asia, Africa, and the Americas, the migratory flow began. Industrializing cities took in migrants from the surrounding countryside. In primary cities like New York as well as provincial centers like Cleveland, steady inflows of migrants had to be accommodated.[34]

Slowly, municipal reformers and lower-class residents themselves generated a series of entitlements and reforms that gave meaningful property rights to tenants of the urban lower class.[35] Rights of occupancy and standards of amenities began to coalesce in municipal codes. Various municipal projects to build and subsidize workers' housing came to fruition by the 1920s. Driven in part by the concern for public health, slum-clearance projects often preceded the construction of new public-housing schemes. Under varying mixes of private and public ownership, lower-class dwellers in the industrial cities of the world obtained legally recognized rights to urban living space.

Mumbai illustrates this global process. The founding of what proved to be profitable cotton textile mills in the city by Indian entrepreneurs launched its industrial base as early as the 1860s. Rural migrants in search of work poured into the city from its surrounding agricultural districts. Between the first census in 1872 and that in 1941, the population increased from 644,000 to 1.5 million.[36] Often, rural migrants worked seasonally, between the busiest times of the agricultural year, and returned home. To keep a good job, however, required full-time residence in the city. Many migrants practiced circular migration. Male workers from as far away as two hundred miles from Mumbai kept their families in their villages, remitted their surplus pay, returned on holidays, and later retired to the village.[37] The pattern of circular migration from the countryside encouraged retention of strong intercaste ties with fellow villagers in Mumbai. Groups of single men from the same village rented living space and ate together.[38]

Because land in colonial Mumbai was limited by its island configuration (about the size of Manhattan), living space near the textile mills was scarce. Wealthy property owners had already constructed five- to seven-story dwellings, many of which were converted into tenements with one-room accommodations for families. The textile mills built additional multistory tenements to rent to their workers. Private developers built two-story structures to accommodate shops on the ground level and tightly packed tenants on the second floor. These tenement buildings, known as *chawls*, might have as many as five hundred people living in a single structure. Each family had a room about ten feet square opening onto a communal veranda, with shared privies on each level connected to a single shaft, and a single standpipe for water. Late nineteenth-century population densities in these slum districts were as high as 1,200 per acre. The 1911 census reported that more than 80 percent of Mumbai's population lived in *chawls*.[39]

Housing for textile workers was concentrated in a working-class neighborhood known as Girangaon. In spite of intense rural ties, working class life in Mumbai developed its own distinctive character. Community organizations, such as *chawl* committees, wrestling gymnasiums *(akhadas)*, and Muslim neighborhood societies *(melas)* flourished. Neighborhood bosses *(dadas)* headed gangs and operated protection rackets, but they also protected their neighborhoods from street violence and rioting. Jobbers who contracted with the mills for labor and trade-union leaders became spokesmen for community interests.[40]

Rent control, imposed as early as 1918, and retained permanently after World War II, gave protected tenants substantial property rights. The mills and other owners of rent-controlled *chawls* abandoned any investment in the buildings because the rents were so low. As a result, sitting tenants were free to sell their rights for thousands of rupees to new tenants, who then paid minuscule rents to the mills or other landlords.[41]

As populations stabilized in these neighborhoods, residents developed a strong sense of place and an attachment to the intimacy and community life of the *chawl*.[42] As Norma Evenson comments: "Over the years the chawl was to become part of the image and legend of Bombay, even spawning writers who celebrated the intimate and supportive social life engendered by shared balconies and courtyards. Like many city neighborhoods despised by planners, the chawl districts could inspire deep affection and loyalty among their inhabitants."[43]

After World War II, as the colonial world disintegrated, these relatively harmonious arrangements in Mumbai and other industrial cities around the world were superseded by vast new waves of urban migration. Only in North America and Europe have suburbanization, upper-class and elite flight, and the automobile culture caused the relative decline of many industrial cities, such as Baltimore and Liverpool.[44] Most world cities have grown in size at a pace unprecedented in human history.

In present-day Mumbai, for example, close to half of the inhabitants of the city, an estimated 6 million or more people, live in squatter settlements or slums, not *chawls*. These people are not destitute, like the hundred thousand or more pavement dwellers so visible in the city; rather, they have some resources and income. Most are immigrants, some recent, some going back two or even three generations.[45] Almost all are employed in either service or industry. They work as servants in the high-rise buildings for the middle- and upper-class residents of the city. They are carpenters, mechanics, orderlies, clerks in offices, and factory workers. Many work in industrial establishments within the slum itself, such as small metal-fabricating shops, welding or paint-mixing operations, metal foundries, leather tanneries, or plastic-recycling operations (to make the plastic sheets sold to slum dwellers). Men, women, and children work long hours. Many women do handwork, sewing, and assembling in the home. These are working-class and lower-middle class people who have dignity and aspirations for the future.

As soon as a family occupies a few square meters of land and puts up a few flimsy wooden sticks, plastic sheets, and a few boards, it has established informal ownership rights to that plot. Formal landowners find it impossible to evict hut dwellers, once established, by legal action. Their only recourse is informal coercion. Often the easiest course of action is to employ criminal gangs in the slums, who collect regular rent from each slum dweller. Payment of protection money permits the slum family to remain and to improve its home. Frequently, absentee landowners simply ignore the situation and cede control of the land to the gangs, who have no formal legal title.

Mumbai slums are crowded; the slum dweller has only the space occupied by his or her hut. Connecting lanes are really footpaths so narrow that even motor scooters cannot be ridden, but have to be pushed. Lacking storm-water drainage, the slums are often flooded in the rainy season. As time passes, however, the inhabitants make improvements: They build dwellings of corrugated iron and brick; they connect to the electricity supply legally or, more often, illegally; they pay to have water piped to their homes. They decorate their space and buy appliances, TVs and video players, and electric fans. In the older Mumbai slums, the majority of the inhabitants have electricity.

Over time, slum dwellers develop informal property rights that can be bought and sold on an emerging land and housing market. In established Mumbai slums, an improved house can be sold for more than one hundred thousand rupees (roughly US$2,500 at official exchange rates, but equivalent to much more in local purchasing power). A continuing threat to their tenure lies in a potentially more valuable use for the land. Determined private owners can buy off the gangsters, drive off the slum dwellers, and sell or convert the land to another use. Or the state can clear a slum in the name of urban improvement. Generally, however, older slums serve as massive vote banks for Indian politicians, who therefore prevent demolition. Indian social reformers also campaign against slum clearance.[46] In a final stage, an improved slum can be recognized as fit for human habitation by action of the state of Maharashtra, and its dwellers then receive formal rights and recognition of their property. When this happens, community latrines, water taps, public lighting, schools, and welfare centers eventually appear.

Mumbai's experience has been shared by other cities in Latin America, Africa, the Middle East, and Asia. The sheer volume of migration to the cities has overwhelmed previous arrangements for creating and sustaining rights to urban living space. By and large, urban elites in these postcolonial cities have been unable and unwilling to accommodate or control the vast numbers of newcomers. Migrants have acted spontaneously to move beyond the territorial constraints of bounded neighborhoods, house lots, and the formal land market. Instead, they have built audacious squatter settlements—without tenure or permission—on any accessible urban land and created their own property regimes.[47]

Although subject to sporadic demolition and removal, most squatter settlements survive over decades to develop coherent community identities and consciousness. Residents make incremental improvements in their homes, improve water supplies, and even find ways to obtain electrical power. As time passes, an informal property market emerges in which prices paid for improved dwellings and lots can rise to substantial heights. The state may formally recognize and record the property rights of slum dwellers.[48] Often slum dwellers gain a political voice that helps to stabilize their tenure by enabling them to resist slum-clearance measures. Social reformers, rather than supporting destruction of working-class slums and rebuilding of public projects as in the older industrial-city model, organize slum dwellers to fight off such attempts and to press for incremental improvements in their situation.[49]

This pattern has been observed even in socialist states that have attempted to control migration and that, in theory, have permitted no land markets or private property. Nascent land markets have appeared in Russia, China, and Eastern Europe. In Soviet Russia, the industrialization and collectivization of agriculture unleashed twenty-three million Soviet peasants to move to cities between 1926 and

1939. Despite the imposition of internal passports, the Soviet authorities failed to control and direct this flow. Soviet urban planners failed to build anywhere near enough workers' housing, provide transport, or regulate the shantytowns that sprang up around Soviet cities. Peasant migrants to the cities retained their communal organization in workers' *artels* despite heavy official indoctrination aimed at creating a workers' consciousness.[50] Migrants living in shantytowns developed their own occupancy rights over urban space.

For the first three decades or so of its existence, the People's Republic of China succeeded in controlling urban growth and migration from the countryside to the city. The post-1949 government planned and built uniform, extensive, low-rise cityscapes consisting of three- to five-story buildings with mixed residential, health, educational, industrial, and commercial activities in each unit. These walled wards, organized by work units, offered facilities for living, recreation, shopping, and work within walking distance. The guarded and gated inhabitants were tightly controlled and monitored. Without work permits that also provided registration and a place to live, rural dwellers could not easily migrate to the city.[51] After 1980, however, these controls were relaxed. Since then, between fifty and one hundred million peasants officially domiciled in the countryside have moved to the cities illegally and formed a "floating population." Earning their living in the most arduous and ill-paid kinds of urban work, these migrants are still not able to obtain urban certification and are denied access to official housing. They live with relatives, in small workers' hotels, and in various shanties and shantytowns. In other words, contemporary China has some of the same sorts of slums found in other countries around the world.[52]

PLACE, ELITES, AND THE NATION-STATE

Since the fifteenth century, land markets in every world region have dissolved the constraints imposed by states and local communities and converged toward a shared world system. Steady population increases, economic growth, and technological advances over these centuries have imparted economic value to a greater and greater share of the earth's land surface. In spite of the vicissitudes of political struggles and shifting ideologies, the long-term trend is toward more transparent, accessible markets in private property rights in land. In these markets, land use shifts rapidly and suddenly to meet economic incentives. A unified, price-fixing world market in land is still subject to the obstacles of nation-state territorial control, but the number of transnational land transactions continues to rise.

Nation-states, and behind them the international order, provide guarantees for long-term stability of ownership, for the validity of contracts, and for monetary stability. Scarcities of suitable lands lead to rising prices and rising demand. Landed property rights permit rapidly changing land use, aimed at obtaining the highest economic benefit for each parcel of land bought or sold. This is by no means a solely Western idea or a process driven solely by Westerners, but a global phenomenon.[53] From one perspective, human management of land everywhere has become more centralized, more intrusive, and more instrumentally effective. Large-scale capitalist forms of agriculture and resource extraction are prominent throughout the world. Land-use decisions increasingly reflect the narrow interests of large-scale, complex organizations and the professional interests of the land managers they employ. Often these managers have little or no direct knowledge of the tracts that they control. Over the early modern and modern periods the intimate, personal ties often seen between land managers and their lands (even on the largest estates) have been altered, attenuated, or eliminated altogether.[54]

Intensifying land markets have fostered ambivalent reactions. The centralizing state as ultimate owner has acted decisively to set aside bounded tracts of land from the market to meet national objectives. Simultaneously, political elites in both early modern and modern states have concluded that relatively unconstricted land markets stimulate economic growth. (The twentieth-century socialist attempt to suppress land markets and private property in the former Soviet Union, Eastern Europe, Cuba, and the People's Republic of China have demonstrated the costs of this policy.) A surprising number of sharply contested national issues arise from conflicting notions of appropriate land use.

All nation-states concern themselves with the long-term stability of land rights and their recording and demarcation. But more than this, ultimate control of land use is absolutely fundamental to the centralizing state and helps to define national values and character. Print and new electronic communications permit the deployment of visual images of land use. They engender an intimate sense of shared management and concern for the national territory. It is at this juncture that the interests of local elites and the territorial state coincide. National identities and local identities are formed from converging territorial interests.

The triumph of converging forms of alienable private land ownership does not end the preoccupation of local elites—both rural and urban—with land. They struggle to control the allocation of property and the rules by which it is to be used. The worldwide tension between the local community and land markets, and between the local community and the state, continues. Property rights in land remain a central point of conflict, negotiation, compromise, and tension in every community. The formal arena for this struggle is the law, litigation, and courts or the administrative offices of the nation-state. Modern land use is controlled by territorial strategies of planning, classification by area (i.e., zoning) and development codes. Local governments, guided and limited by state and national laws and regulations, try to control and tame land markets by demarcation of both urban and rural lands for specific purposes: residential, commercial, recreational, industrial, and municipal, among others. Zoning of course also permits various forms of social, political, and ethnic segregation by territory. These approaches mirror territorial segregation as practiced by the nation-state. The informal arena for conflict lies in devices such as social and economic pressure, extralegal violence, or other coercive measures undertaken by elites.

Behind this territorial strategy lies the deeply emotional connection of people with their physical environment. The sense of place engendered by the occupancy and use of land is an important source of community identity. Landscape and cityscape are part of the power of place. Nothing is so disorienting as physical displacement. The pathology of displacement and refugeeism includes "disorientation, memory loss, homelessness, depression and various modes of estrangement from self and others."[55] Land is one of our most deeply felt concerns, one that affects our immediate sense of security and resonates with our deepest moral, aesthetic, and religious attitudes. The physical environment of early childhood imprints a profound and indelible impression on the individual. Our earliest memories contain images of space and of land use that are part of our identity. Nostalgia for a past land use and configuration of space is an important, often unacknowledged force in human affairs.[56] Of course, strong emotive ties to place are not necessarily a product of childhood memories or long residence. In today's mobile societies, new residents frequently find themselves rapidly invested in a sense of place as they engage with issues of land use.

Those most deeply involved in the struggle over property rights in land continue to be the elites who control land and its uses. Elites engage in personal interaction in various circumscribed social spaces under accepted rules. Local elites, despite the size of the territorial unit—even a very large city—by and large have face-to-face contact. These conflicts elicit a discourse, based on varying ideologies of belief and morality, in which desirable land uses are debated. The stability of the local elite rests in large measure on its capacity to control and dominate this discourse. Nevertheless, local notables are constrained from applying a pure calculus of rational advantage or profit to land transactions. Their calculations are shaped by the prevailing ideologies and metaphors by which they legitimate their power. The long-term health and interest of the community must be a consideration. Far-sighted policies are often the privilege of the privileged when it comes to land.

Improved communications have made the boundaries of the community more permeable than ever before. New ideologies and new values intrude easily and quickly into the community and contribute to the debate and struggle. Increasingly, elite struggles over land use and management spill over into public debate and assessment. Participatory politics force expansion of local elites to accommodate new members in a more diverse and enlarged dominant group. Simultaneously, prices in modern land markets are fixed by ever widening and enlarging market areas.

Perhaps the most typical conflict over property rights in land—evoked in numerous literary accounts—is that over the exploitation of a natural resource that has become valuable and marketable. Prices for certain tracts of land soar. Should this exploitation be permitted? Issues of stability, tradition, and nostalgia are pitted against the excitement of new wealth and productivity in internecine elite conflict. In recent decades a new environmental or ecological ethic has entered the ideology of appropriate land use among elites.

NOTES

1. See John F. Richards, "Land Transformation," in *The Earth as Transformed by Human Action: Global and Regional Changes in the Biosphere over the Past 300 Years*, ed. B. L. Turner (Cambridge: Cambridge University Press, 1990); and John F. Richards, "World Environmental History and Economic Development," in *Sustainable Development of the Biosphere*, ed. R. E. Munn and William C. Clark (Cambridge: Cambridge University Press, 1986).

2. For a similar approach to world history, see David Hackett Fischer, *The Great Wave: Price Revolutions and the Rhythm of History* (New York: Oxford University Press, 1996). Fischer's appendix O, "Economics and History," contains a stimulating discussion of the value of descriptive history and the benefits of framing a *problématique* or a set of empirical questions.

3. For an example of renewed interest in territoriality, nationalism and the nation-state, see Winichakul Thongchai, *Siam Mapped: A History of the Geo-body of a Nation* (Honolulu: University of Hawaii Press, 1994).

4. For a recent comparative treatment of this process, see Richard John Perry, *From Time Immemorial: Indigenous Peoples and State Systems* (Austin: University of Texas Press, 1996). See also John F. Richards, "Only a World Perspective Is Significant: Settlement Frontiers and Property Rights in Early Modern World History," in *The*

Humanities and the Environment, ed. Jill Conway, Kenneth Keniston, and Leo Marx (Cambridge, MA: MIT Press, 1998). Fernand Braudel, in *The Structures of Everyday Life* (Berkeley: University of California Press, 1992), 98–103, makes a similar point.

5. On the Tupi, see John Hemming, *Red Gold: The Conquest of the Brazilian Indians,* rev. ed. (London: Papermac, 1995); on the present-day Dayak, see Anna Lowenhaupt Tsing, *In the Realm of the Diamond Queen: Marginality in an Out-of-the-Way Place* (Princeton: Princeton University Press, 1993).

6. See, for example, Linda S. Parker, *Native American Estate: The Struggle over Indian and Hawaiian Lands* (Honolulu: University of Hawaii Press, 1989).

7. R. J. P. Kain and Elizabeth Baigent, *The Cadastral Map in the Service of the State: A History of Property Mapping* (Chicago: University of Chicago Press, 1992).

8. James C. Scott, "State Simplifications: Nature, Space and People," *Journal of Political Philosophy* 3 (1995): 191–233.

9. For one example of this process, see Peter Robb, "The Colonial State and Constructions of Indian Identity: An Example on the Northeast Frontier in the 1880s," *Modern Asian Studies* 31 (1997): 245–83. In this essay Robb describes the demarcation of the Naga Hills of southeastern Assam by British administrators and the subsequent definition of the Nagas as imperial subjects.

10. Henry E. Lowood, "The Calculating Forester: Quantification, Cameral Science, and the Emergence of Scientific Forestry Management in Germany," in *The Quantifying Spirit in the Eighteenth Century,* ed. Tore Frängsmyr, Robin E. Rider, and J. L. Heilbron (Berkeley: University of California Press, 1990), 315–42.

11. See Paul W. Hirt, *A Conspiracy of Optimism: Management of the National Forests since World War Two* (Lincoln: University of Nebraska Press, 1994), on the United States national forests.

12. The scholar most responsible for bringing the issue of fire to our attention is Stephen Pyne. His global synthesis is *Vestal Fire: An Environmental History, Told through Fire, of Europe and Europe's Encounter with the World* (Seattle: University of Washington Press, 1997).

13. Robert M. Netting, *Smallholders, Householders: Farm Families and the Ecology of Intensive, Sustainable Agriculture* (Stanford, CA: Stanford University Press, 1993), 158.

14. This is not to deny that those peasant-run systems that have survived—high mountain pastures and local irrigation systems—cannot teach us important lessons. See Elinor Ostrom, *Governing the Commons: The Evolution of Institutions for Collective Action* (Cambridge: Cambridge University Press, 1990).

15. Werner Rösener, "Neighbors and Village Communities," in *The Peasantry of Europe* (Oxford: Blackwell, 1994): 157–70, 172. Rösener maintains that the authoritarian regimes of the estates east of the Elbe River did not succeed in eliminating a resilient village community in Eastern Europe.

16. The literature on enclosure and the commons in early modern England is gigantic. See Robert C. Allen, *Enclosure and the Yeoman* (Oxford: Clarendon Press, 1992); and J. M. Neeson, *Commoners: Common Right, Enclosure and Social Change in England, 1700–1820* (Cambridge: Cambridge University Press, 1993).

17. Rösener, "Neighbors," 174–84.

18. Rösener, "Neighbors," 168.

19. The clearest description of the commune is to be found in Christine Worobec, *Peasant Russia: Family and Community in the Post-emancipation Period* (Princeton: Princeton University Press, 1991). See also Esther Kingston-Mann, Timothy Mixter, and Jeffrey Burds, eds., *Peasant Economy, Culture, and Politics of European Russia, 1800–1921* (Princeton: Princeton University Press, 1991); Ben Eklof and Stephen Frank, *The World to the Russian Peasant: Post-emancipation Culture and Society* (Boston: Unwin Hyman, 1990); Roger P. Bartlett, *Land Commune and Peasant Community in Russia: Communal Forms in Imperial and Early Soviet Society* (New York: St. Martin's Press, 1990).

20. Sucheta Mazumdar, *Sugar and Society in China: Peasants, Technology, and the World Market* (Cambridge, MA: Harvard University Asia Center, 1998), 216–17.

21. Mazumdar, 217–30; Peter C. Perdue, *Exhausting the Earth: State and Peasant in Hunan, 1500–1850* (Cambridge, MA: Harvard University Press, 1987).

22. Perdue, *Exhausting the Earth*, 136–40. See also Anne Osborne, "The Local Politics of Land Reclamation in the Lower Yangzi Highlands," *Late Imperial China* 15 (1994): 1–46; Anne Osborne, "Highlands and Lowlands: Economic and Ecological Interactions in the Lower Yangzi Region under the Qing," in *Sediments of Time: Environment and Society in Chinese History*, ed. Mark Elvin and Liu Ts'ui-jung (Cambridge: Cambridge University Press, 1998), 203–34; and Tai-Shun Yang, "Property Rights and Constitutional Order in Imperial China" (PhD diss., Indiana University, 1987).

23. M. A. McKean, "Management of Traditional Common Lands *(Iriachi)* in Japan," in *Proceedings of the Conference on Common Property Resource Management, April 21–26, 1985* (Washington, DC: National Academy Press, 1986), 533–89; J. Mark Ramseyer, *Odd Markets in Japanese History: Law and Economic Growth, Political Economy of Institutions and Decisions* (Cambridge: Cambridge University Press, 1996).

24. For an example of an early modern settlement frontier, see Richard Eaton, *The Rise of Islam and the Bengal Frontier, 1204–1760* (Berkeley: University of California Press, 1993).

25. See Minoti Chakravarty-Kaul, *Common Lands and Customary Law: Institutional Change in North India over the Past Two Centuries* (Delhi: Oxford University Press, 1996). For a discussion of the colonial state's destruction of communal lands in nineteenth-century Sri Lanka, see Nihal Perera, *Society and Space: Colonialism, Nationalism, and Postcolonial Identity in Sri Lanka* (Boulder, CO: Westview Press, 1998).

26. See Kenneth M. Cuno, *The Pasha's Peasants: Land, Society, and Economy in Lower Egypt, 1740–1858* (Cambridge: Cambridge University Press, 1992).

27. Sally Falk Moore, *Social Facts and Fabrications: "Customary" Law on Kilimanjaro, 1880–1980* (Cambridge: Cambridge University Press, 1986); Michael Donovan, "Capturing the Land: Kipsigis Narratives of Progress," *Comparative Studies in Society and History* 36 (1996): 658–86.

28. For an eloquent argument to this effect for England, see Neeson, *Commoners,* especially 158–84, "The Uses of Waste."

29. Brian J. Berry, "Urbanization," in Turner, *The Earth as Transformed by Human Action,* table 7.5, "The World's Urban Population, 1950–1985," 116. See Ali Madanipour, *Tehran: The Making of a Metropolis* (Chichester: John Wiley, 1998), 137–40, on the disappearance of green space in Tehran in the second half of the twentieth century.

30. Adrian Guillermo Aguilar, Execquiel Excurra, Teresa Garcia, Marisa Mazair Hiriart, and Irene Pisanty, "The Basin of Mexico," in *Regions at Risk: Comparisons of Threatened Environments,* ed. Jeanne X. Kasperson, Roger E. Kasperson, and B. L. Turner II (Tokyo: United Nations University Press, 1995), 327.

31. David Harvey, *Justice, Nature, and the Geography of Difference* (Cambridge, MA: Blackwell Publishers, 1996), 417.

32. Norma Evenson, *The Indian Metropolis: A View toward the West* (New Haven: Yale University Press, 1989), 113–45.

33. Brian Ladd, in *Urban Planning and Civic Order in Germany, 1860–1914* (Cambridge, MA: Harvard University Press, 1990), discusses Germany's lead in this innovation.

34. Kenneth A. Scherzer, *The Unbounded Community: Neighborhood Life and Social Structure in New York City, 1830–1875* (Durham, NC: Duke University Press, 1992); and W. Dennis Keating, Norman Krumholz, and David C. Perry, *Cleveland: A Metropolitan Reader* (Kent, OH: Kent State University Press, 1995).

35. See, for example, J. A. Yelling, *Slums and Slum Clearance in Victorian London* (London: Allen & Unwin, 1986).

36. Rajnarayan Chandravarkar, *The Origins of Industrial Capitalism in India: Business Strategies and the Working Classes in Bombay, 1900–1940* (Cambridge: Cambridge University Press, 1994), 30.

37. Hemlata C. Dandekar, *Men to Bombay, Women at Home: Urban Influence on Sugao Village, Deccan, Maharashtra, India, 1942–1982* (Ann Arbor: University of Michigan Center for South and Southeast Asian Studies, 1986), 219–21.

38. Dandekar, *Men to Bombay,* 233.

39. Evenson, *Indian Metropolis,* 139–42. In less-crowded Calcutta, by contrast, jute-mill owners bought up empty land adjacent to their factories and leased large plots to their Indian labor contractors so that they could build lines of thatched-roof,

mud-packed bamboo huts clustered around ponds for water. The labor contractors rented cubicles in these huts to the factory workers they recruited for work in the jute mills. These settlements became the *bustee*s of Calcutta. Frederic C. Thomas, *Calcutta Poor: Elegies on a City above Pretense* (Armonk, N.Y.: M.E. Sharpe, 1997), 63–65.

40. Chandravarkar, *Origins of Industrial Capitalism*, 168–238.

41. V.S. Naipaul interviewed a *chawl* resident who in 1985 paid 35,000 rupees for the lease to a unit and whose rent was only 12.5 rupees per month. V.S. Naipaul, *India: A Million Mutinies Now* (New York: Viking, 1991).

42. Naipaul, *India*, 60–69.

43. Evenson, *Indian Metropolis*, 142.

44. Harvey, *Justice, Nature*, 404.

45. Jeremy Seabrook, *Life and Labour in a Bombay Slum* (London: Quartet, 1987).

46. See Seabrook, *Life and Labour*, 84–110, for a description of one protest against slum clearing. A documentary film made by Anand Patwardhan, *Bombay, Our City* (First Run Icarus Films, 1990), interprets these events.

47. Joe Lugalla, *Crisis, Urbanization, and Urban Poverty in Tanzania: A Study of Urban Poverty and Survival Politics* (Lanham, MD: University Press of America, 1995), 43, reports that 70 percent of the total population of Dar es Salaam consists of squatters.

48. For example, in 1979 Tunis revised its urban code and gave formal approval to established illegal settlements around the city. Elizabeth Vasile, "Devotion as Distinction, Piety as Power: Religious Revival and the Transformation of Space in the Illegal Settlements of Tunis," in *Population, Poverty, and Politics in Middle East Cities*, ed. Michael E. Bonine, 113–40 (Gainesville: University Press of Florida, 1997), 125.

49. See Robert Gay, *Popular Organization and Democracy in Rio de Janeiro: A Tale of Two Favelas* (Philadelphia: Temple University Press, 1994).

50. David L. Hoffmann, *Peasant Metropolis: Social Identities in Moscow, 1929–1941* (Ithaca, NY: Cornell University Press, 1994).

51. Piper Rae Gaubatz, "Urban Transformation in Post-Mao China: Impacts of the Reform Era on China's Urban Form," in *Urban Spaces in Contemporary China: The Potential for Autonomy and Community in Post-Mao China*, ed. Deborah Davis, Richard Kraus, Barry Naughton, and Elizabeth J. Perry (Washington, DC: Woodrow Wilson Center Press, 1995), 28–60.

52. Dorothy J. Solinger, "The Floating Population in the Cities: Chances for Assimilation?" in *Urban Spaces in Contemporary China*, 113–39.

53. Douglass North and Paul Thomas make a similar point regarding property rights in land in Europe and its dominions in *Rise of the Western World: A New Economic History* (Cambridge: Cambridge University Press, 1973).

54. See Piers M. Blaikie and H. C. Brookfield, *Land Degradation and Society* (London: Methuen, 1987), for a discussion of this point.

55. Edward S. Casey, *Getting Back into Place: Toward a Renewed Understanding of the Place-World* (Bloomington: Indiana University Press, 1993), 38.

56. M. H. Matthews, *Making Sense of Place: Children's Understanding of Large-scale Environments* (Hemel Hempstead, U.K.: Harvester Wheatsheaf, 1992).

FOUR · The Transformation of the
Middle Eastern Environment,
1500 B.C.E.–2000 C.E.

EDMUND BURKE III

DEEP HISTORY: 1500 B.C.E.–1450 C.E.

The environment is rarely mentioned in most histories of the modern Middle East. It tends to hover on the margins of discussions of other, presumably more important topics, such as the onset of imperialism and nationalism and the region's political and economic transformation. Indeed, most histories of the modern Middle East regard the environment as a source of backwardness, which only the application of modern science and technology can overcome. Such modernist fables are, of course, uplifting to a degree. The introduction of modern technology (regardless of the auspices under which it took place) certainly transformed the relations between humans and the Middle Eastern environment. However, if we consider the deep history of the region, the ability of humans to alter the environment profoundly is hardly new, and the choices made by elites have always had consequences (often unforeseen) further down the line.

I use the term *Middle East* to include all of southwest Asia and northern Africa, from Iran to Morocco, while my chronological scope is from 1500 B.C.E. to the present. The Middle Eastern region is vast (more than six thousand kilometers across) and ecologically diverse (although predominantly arid and semiarid). Located in the center of the Great Arid Zone, it extends from the Sahara in the west to the deserts of China and Central Asia in the east. Focusing on the environment provides the basis for a new comparative history of the region along ecological lines: the river valleys; the Mediterranean areas of dry farming; and the deserts, oases, and waste lands where pastoralism was predominant. Each of these three zones had its own prevailing flora and fauna, patterns of agriculture, and forms of social and political organization.

Because of its location at the juncture of Africa, Europe, and Asia, the Middle Eastern climate is shaped by the complex interaction of four different wind systems. These are the seasonal monsoons that govern the climate of the Indian Ocean region, including southern Arabia, East Africa, and southern Iran; the inner Asian wind system that brings snow and bitter cold from the steppe in winter; the summer thermals that arise in the deserts of Arabia and the Sahara; and the Atlantic system that brings fall and winter rains. Rainfall is a function of both altitude (the higher the elevation, the more rain the land receives) and location (regions facing the prevailing winds have much higher rainfall than those in the rain shadow on the lee side of the mountains). Climatological records reveal an enormous variability in the timing and amounts of annual rainfall, as well as in different locales in any given year. For example, although annual rainfall averages 30 inches (approximately 750 millimeters) across the region, there is virtually no rainfall in the Empty Quarter of southeastern Arabia, but in excess of 60 inches (1,500 mm) a year between the southern coast of the Caspian Sea and the Alburz Mountains of Iran.

Most Middle Eastern people have always lived in the river valleys (of the Nile, the Tigris-Euphrates-Karun, the Amu Darya, and the Hilmand), which were central to the fate of ancient Middle Eastern empires.[1] It was here that the first cities and the first agrarian empires developed. The Mediterranean zone and adjacent steppes, where dry farming was predominant, have also been well studied. Their history has been shaped by the actions of states and empires originating in the river valleys, as well as by longer time climatic cycles (such as El Niño and the so-called Little Ice Age). The third environment I discuss—that of the deserts, waste lands, and oases—was primarily inhabited by pastoral nomadic groups. Pastoralism emerged in the first millennium B.C.E. as an adaptation to the harsh conditions of the desert steppe. Pastoralists have played a disproportionate role in the history of the region, repeatedly conquering the agrarian empires in the river valleys. Historically, pastoralists have also facilitated exchanges (both material and cultural) between the societies and civilizations that surround them. The Silk Road that connected China and the West is but the most vivid example. The relationship between the agrarian world of the river valleys, the merchants of the urban centers, and the pastoral nomads of the steppe constitutes a leitmotif in the history of the region.[2]

By placing the history of the Middle Eastern region in a global, ecohistorical context, I seek to uncover larger processes of interaction between humans and the environment. The specific features of the Middle Eastern environment distinguish it from other world regions, which have in turn prompted distinctive solutions to its environmental problems. While operating on a world-historical scale has evident disadvantages—details tend to blur into the background—it has compensations as well. We can perceive larger patterns the existence of which we might otherwise have missed.

Archaeologists and ancient historians have long been aware of the great environmental changes brought about by ancient water-management projects. However, in their efforts to record the achievements of ancient empires, they have failed for the most part to accord the Middle Eastern environment the attention it deserves. A significant exception is Robert M. Adams's classic survey *The Land behind Baghdad*, on the successive transformations of the Diyala plain of southern Iraq.[3] Adams argues that it is only by viewing them over the very long term that the creation of territorially defined states in the ancient Middle East and the subsequent transformation of the physical environment become legible to the archaeologist.

From this perspective, one can observe a family resemblance among the states and empires of the premodern period from China to the Mediterranean. All were based on irrigation, intense cropping, and large flood-control schemes. All sought to displace the negative consequences of these methods onto those outside the society. The drive to make nature predictable and controllable goes back to the origins of civilization itself. The modern world was not simply born in Europe but was the result of long-term processes of accumulation, organization, and control of people and of the environment. World historians are beginning to speak of a "developmentalist project" as a kind of shorthand for the slow genesis of the modern state (see the introduction to this volume by Kenneth Pomeranz).

I begin with a brief review of the legacy of Middle Eastern water management—clearly a centerpiece of any environmental history of the region. Next, I explore the remarkable transformations brought about by the rise of Islam, which culminated in what one scholar has called a "medieval Islamic green revolution."[4] I conclude this section with a review of current scholarly opinion on the causes of the environmental decline of the region.

THE LEGACY OF MIDDLE EASTERN WATER MANAGEMENT

Archaeologists inform us that water-management technologies were being used by the early states in the Fertile Crescent as early as 5000 B.C.E. Distinctively different approaches developed in the valley of the Nile and the Tigris-Euphrates basin, shaped by the different characteristics of the two floodplains. In Egypt, a state based on agricultural production first emerged in the Nile valley in the fifth millennium B.C.E. The Nile flood is especially propitious for agriculture. It originates in the Ethiopian highlands with the onset of the monsoon rains in East Africa. In early summer, the Nile's major tributaries—the White Nile and the Blue Nile—reach flood stage. Until the construction of the Aswan High Dam disrupted this pattern in 1972, the water arrived in Egypt in early August, where it inundated the valley floor. By the end of the month, it retreated just in time for the fall planting, leaving a deposit of silt coating the fields. The early Egyptian dynasties learned to harness the Nile flood and to time the planting of crops according to its rhythms. Under the pharaohs, a system of basin irrigation was developed that ensured a regular grain crop. Openings were made in the river banks to permit the floodwaters to cover the adjacent agricultural areas. When the floods retreated, water was drawn from the Nile by a variety of water-lifting devices. These included the *shaduf,* a device for dipping water; the Archimedean screw; and the *noria,* a kind of water wheel.[5] These devices, which could be powered either by humans or by harness animals, were well suited to the specific characteristics of the Nile River.

The circumstances in the Tigris and Euphrates valleys were significantly different. Instead of coming to flood stage in the late summer, the Tigris peaks in April, when it jeopardizes the spring harvest. Its steep banks and fast, rushing waters posed a constant challenge to hydraulic engineers. By contrast, the Euphrates trickles slowly through an arid floodplain and loses much of its water to evaporation. There is evidence of irrigation works in the Tigris-Euphrates basin as early as 5000 B.C.E. By 1500 B.C.E., humans were able to dramatically redirect the flow of waters in the floodplain. Through a systematic, politically directed process lasting more than a millennium, five major transverse canals were constructed that diverted the waters of the Euphrates across the floodplain to the Tigris.[6] A second major engineering feat that greatly extended the zone of irrigation was the construction between the first millennium B.C.E. and 1000 C.E. of two huge, interconnected, parallel diversion canals (artificial rivers, really) off the Tigris—the Nahrawan and the Katul al-Kisrawi—which were among the greatest engineering projects of their time. To slow and divert fast-moving waters, weirs were constructed. Finally, reservoirs were built throughout the region, making possible such major works as the royal gardens of the Assyrians and the Sasanids.[7]

As a result of more than a millennium of warring against the rivers, the Mesopotamian floodplain was substantially transformed. Under the Sasanids (234–634 C.E.), an extensive canal complex, including five large dams, was constructed on the

Karun River and its tributaries in Kuhzistan, northeast of the Tigris-Euphrates delta. At the height of the Sasanid Empire, it is estimated, the floodplain contributed almost 50 percent of the land-tax revenues.[8] The huge increase in the area under irrigation made it possible to cultivate a summer crop as well, which significantly increased the food supply. As a result, the human population of Mesopotamia reached an all-time high under the Sasanids.[9] Already in ancient times, the Mesopotamian floodplain was no longer a natural environment.[10]

Despite the impressive engineering works of successive Persian dynasties, it proved impossible to sustain these high levels of agricultural productivity. As Adams has shown, the Euphrates shifted its course by more than three hundred kilometers in the first millennium B.C.E., leaving much of the central floodplain high and dry. These shifts were to become a recurrent pattern.[11] Persistent flooding and hydrological changes in the sixth and seventh centuries further undermined the prosperity of the Tigris-Euphrates delta region. The Tigris shifted dramatically again in the early seventh century (around 628 C.E.), turning sections of the Diyala floodplain from prime agricultural land to desert and weakening the Sasanids at a critical phase in their struggle with the Byzantines.[12] To the north, siltation and salinization gradually choked the transverse canals, weirs, and floodgates. Although the Arab conquerors made heroic efforts to restore and revive the system from the mid-seventh century onward, and revived agriculture for a time, in the end it was to no avail. By the time of the Mongol conquest, the Nahrawan and Katul al-Kisrawi complexes were no longer functional.[13]

Moving from Mesopotamia to the Iranian plateau, we discover a very different environment. Extending more than sixteen hundred kilometers from the borders of geographical Iraq in the west to Afghanistan and India in the east and surrounded by mountains, this vast, semiarid upland plateau initially appears unpropitious for agriculture. Because farming normally requires at least 400 millimeters of rainfall per year and the Iranian plateau receives barely 350 millimeters per year (with important local and annual variations, of course), irrigation was a necessity. With irrigation, areas receiving as little as 150 millimeters per year were rendered arable.[14] On the eastern edges of the Iranian plateau, the Amu Darya basin to the north and the Hilmand river valley to the south, environmental conditions resemble those of the Tigris and Euphrates river valleys. By 500 B.C.E. the Mesopotamian irrigation toolkit of dams, canals, and weirs had been deployed in the Amu Darya and the Hilmand river valleys as well, and vast agricultural estates had emerged.

The irrigation technology that most facilitated the extension of agriculture in the Iranian plateau was the *qanat* (Arabic) system. *Qanat*s (known in Persian as *kariz*) were gravity-flow tunnel wells (also known as filtration galleries). They first appeared more or less simultaneously around 2500 B.C.E. in eastern Turkey, Kurdistan (northwestern Iran), and Sistan (southeastern Iran). It has been suggested that *qanat*s emerged as an offshoot of the ancient mining industry in the region. Expertise in tunneling was readily transferable, and miners often unintentionally tapped into underground streams.[15] By the sixth century B.C.E., *qanat*s were found across the Iranian plateau. Their diffusion facilitated the consolidation of Persian authority and the establishment of cities and towns. Under the Achaemenids (550–331 B.C.E.), whose empire at its zenith encompassed the land from the Nile to the Indus, *qanat* technology spread throughout the Middle East. *Qanat*s used only local materials, they employed no energy to tap underground aquifers, and they transported water great distances (up to fifty kilometers) with little loss from evaporation. Although they were expensive to build and maintain, they were a sustainable technology well adapted to the semiarid environment of the Iranian plateau.[16] Under the Sasanians, agriculture reached its height in the Iranian plateau, and human populations rose, largely as a result of the diffusion of *qanat* technology. *Qanat*s were also widely employed in Afghanistan, South Asia, Central Asia, and even around the Saharan fringes of Africa. As late as the 1960s, *qanat*s supplied 50 percent of the irrigation water used in Iran.

AN ISLAMIC GREEN REVOLUTION?

The rise of Islam appears to have facilitated a great expansion of agriculture throughout the Middle East. Andrew Watson has called this phenomenon the "medieval Islamic green revolution."[17] With the coming of Islam, the ancient world was united for the first time under one government; with one religion, Islam; and with one main written language, Arabic. As a result, Watson contends, the establishment of the Abbasid empire in 750 C.E. greatly increased the movement and interaction of peoples (and the spread of ideas) throughout the region. The emergence of a vast Islamic trading zone facilitated the spread of new crops, most of which originated outside the Middle East. Most were food crops: Watson lists rice, sorghum, watermelon, lemon, lime, orange, artichoke, plantain, spinach, sugar cane, eggplant, mango, coconut palm, hard wheat, and banana). Cotton, an important fiber crop, was also included. Although Watson's claims that some crops (rice, sugar, and cotton among them) were introduced under Islamic auspices are surely wrong (these crops were already known in Sasanid Persia before the Muslim conquest), his broader argument, which encompasses the diffusion of water-management devices, crops, and agricultural techniques throughout the lands of Islam, seems generally valid.

Central to Watson's argument is the emergence of an identifiable water-management toolkit. It incorporated earlier regionally based hydraulic macrotechnologies (including dams, canals, weirs, reservoirs, aqueducts, and *qanat*s) and microtechnologies (water-lifting devices such as the *noria*, the *shaduf*, the Archimedean screw, the cistern, and the horizontal windmill). The diffusion of these technologies, together with new crops and techniques, throughout the Islamic world was encouraged both by the policies of Islamic governments and by the practices of private landowners, including the establishment of royal gardens and the diffusion of agricultural manuals and seed stock. Perennial irrigation cumulatively led to increased yields, new crop rotations, the expansion of the area under cultivation, and, most important, the emergence of an additional growing season (summer) for irrigated crops. Moreover, because the labor requirements of crops under irrigation were greater than those of dry farming, the demand for labor expanded as the area under cultivation increased. Watson argues plausibly that this trend facilitated population increase, the construction of new cities, and the rebuilding of old ones.

Although many, if not all, of the crops and the irrigation technologies mentioned by Watson were already present in the Iranian plateau before the rise of Islam, the idea of an Islamic green revolution still seems essentially correct.[18] Thomas Glick provides solid evidence for the deliberate adoption of new irrigation technologies and crops from the Iranian plateau by the peoples of the Saharan fringes of southeast Morocco and the Iberian peninsula. He has traced the diffusion of the *qanat* system and other irrigation technologies from the Middle Eastern core areas to the Spain of the Umayyads.[19] This was one of the most important technology transfers in premodern times. Glick notes that "the Arabs and Berbers did not bring canals, *qanat*s, dams or *noria*s with them; they only brought ideas. In assessing the hydraulic technologies of al-Andalus [Iberia], therefore, the physical origin of canals is irrelevant: whatever the Muslims found they integrated into a quite different social, cultural and economic system than that prevailing before, according to norms they brought with them."[20]

Glick usefully distinguishes between the macrosystems of Spain (regional systems, for which the Muslims built on a Roman foundation), the mesosystems (which operated at the village level), and microsystems (which operated at local levels, such as tank, cistern, or *noria* irrigation of the family parcel). The latter two were profoundly shaped by the water-management tools that arrived in Spain with the Muslims in 711. In the fourteenth century, the construction of *qanat*s in southeastern Morocco tapped into underground aquifers in the Sahara. The *khattara* (as *qanat*s are called in the Maghreb) facilitated the expansion of the existing date-palm oasis of Sijilmasa (present-day Tafilalt) and facilitated its emergence as the northern entrepôt for the trans-Saharan gold trade.[21]

I have argued elsewhere that under the aegis of Islam, the diverse regional irrigation traditions of ancient Persia, India, and the Mediterranean came together as a suite of water management technologies, or what I have been calling here a water-management toolkit.[22] Although the prevailing historiography emphasizes China's uniqueness, a historian acquainted with Persian hydraulic engineering and irrigation accomplishments can draw inferences suggesting an eastward transfer of technology.[23] For example, the construction of China's Grand Canal postdates by some two millennia the hydraulic engineering projects that transformed the Mesopotamian floodplain.[24] Arnold Pacey has suggested a "dialogue of Asia" whereby Mesopotamian canal expertise diffused eastward to China.[25] It is also likely that Chinese irrigation devices such as *noria*s and horizontal windmills were first developed in the Iranian plateau and subsequently exported to East Asia by the twelfth century or later.[26]

Less clear is the history of water-management technology in South and Southeast Asia, where irrigation systems appear to have emerged autonomously as adaptations to local ecologies. For example, the Deccan plateau in southern India has an indigenous and ancient system of man-made reservoirs (referred to in English as *tanks*), well adapted to the monsoons and regional conditions. The South Asian tank system subsequently diffused with Hinduism to Southeast Asia.[27] Was it also the model for the royal gardens of the Assyrians and Sasanids? Because northern India and the Indus and Ganges plains had long been in contact with Mesopotamian civilizations, there seems no need to force an answer. With the rise of Islam, the tank system of reservoirs was widely adopted outside the Middle Eastern core region. For example, the Ghuta oasis of Damascus, the large reservoirs of Kairouan in Tunisia, and the *sahrijayn* of fourteenth-century Almohad Marrakech all show the influence of the tank system.[28]

The diffusion of these water-management techniques did not stop in the lands of Islam. Iberian hydraulic systems and irrigation technologies were transplanted to the colonial Americas (via the Canary Islands), where they have left an enduring legacy in the water systems of Mexico and the southwestern United States.[29] After the incorporation of Holland into the Spanish Hapsburg empire, Iberian hydraulic technology also informed Dutch land-reclamation projects.[30] Caesare Maffioli suggests that Middle Eastern hydraulic technologies were incorporated into Venetian strategies of managing the marshlands of the Po estuary.[31] Finally, there is evidence that Iberian communal irrigation technologies were transferred to British India in the nineteenth century.[32]

RETHINKING THE DECLINE OF MIDDLE EASTERN AGRICULTURE TO 1500 C.E.

Until recently, scholars have agreed that the environment of the Middle East suffered an irreversible decline in the premodern past, although they differed over its timing and its causes. Indeed, this narrative of decline has constituted the orthodox scholarly view since the time of the ancient Greeks. At different times, Middle Eastern backwardness has been attributed to the activities of specific agents—early metallurgists, the omnivorous Mediterranean goat, nomadic invasions (by the Arabs and the Mongols), and (especially by colonial authors) the baleful influence of Islam. Indeed, to take up the history of the Middle Eastern environment is to confront a host of stereotypes and biases, both indigenous and Western, which have systematically obscured the larger story from view.

One of the best-known theories of decline is found in Karl Wittfogel's book *Oriental Despotism*.[33] First put forward in 1957, Wittfogel's theory asserted the allegedly despotic nature of the government of "hydraulic" civilizations. He claimed that the construction and maintenance of an extensive irrigation system fostered the emergence of states that exercised complete control over society. Without government control, complicated irrigation systems were fated to break down and the empires they sustained to disappear. Wittfogel's examples of hydraulic societies included ancient (and modern) China, ancient Egypt, Mesopotamia, and, more improbably, the Soviet Union. His theory no longer carries much weight because of both its conflation of inherently dissimilar societies and its blatant ideological loading (it was formulated during the Cold War). More fundamentally, as scholars have come to recognize the crucial importance of local political networks in maintaining large-scale irrigation systems, the inherent implausibility of Wittfogel's ideas has become increasingly evident.

A second explanation of the environmental decline is deforestation and related land degradation. Most authorities agree that although significant deforestation of the Middle Eastern forests occurred in the modern era, it was already well under way in ancient times. In his survey of the environmental practices of ancient Greece and Rome, Donald Hughes concludes that neither the Greeks nor the Romans were the responsible stewards of nature they have sometimes been painted as.[34] Rather, their economic and military needs led ineluctably to deforestation and landscape degradation.

Theodore Wertime has suggested that deforestation was caused by the wood-energy (biomass) demands of ancient metallurgy.[35] Iron smelting required vast quantities of fuel. Wertime has speculated that the production of the 70 to 90 million tons of Iron Age slag found around the Mediterranean would have required the felling of 50 to 70 million acres of trees. Wertime's argument does not stop with metallurgy but takes in the amount of fuel required for the fabrication of bricks, the production of quicklime from limestone, the making of pottery, and household cooking fires. (By one estimate, each household in the ancient Mediterranean required one to two tons of firewood per year.)[36] Taking the subject further, John Perlin has proposed that as the demands of inefficient Bronze Age (and Iron Age) furnaces progressively denuded hinterlands of their forest cover, patterns of deforestation in the Middle East tended to chart the rise and decline of ancient civilizations, but this view is contested.[37]

A third theory locates the source of the decline in the depredations of pastoral nomads, especially the Arabs. J. V. Thirgood has argued that although the Greeks and Romans restrained the grazing of their sheep and goats, things changed after the Arab conquests of the seventh century, when pastoralist herders dominated the Middle East.[38] Thirgood's views echo those of French colonial authors about the Maghreb (as well as some postcolonial range-management experts).[39] However, although archaeological excavations in Mesopotamia substantiate that the recession of agriculture roughly coincided with the Arab conquests, the specific timing of the Arab invasions does not match the process of decline. Finally, those who seek to blame the nomads fail to recognize that the process of decline was not irreversible: irrigation systems could be restored to their former productivity by sustained investment of political will, labor, and money (as the Sawad region in southern Iraq was revived under the Abbasids).[40]

A final theory blames the decline of agriculture in the Middle East on the depredations of the Mongols. Although there is evidence of decline in the period following the Mongol conquest, in some areas the decline actually preceded the conquest. In any event, the current view is that the Mongol impact was localized and of relatively limited duration. Oleg Petruchevsky has argued that the fiscal policy of the Mongols, which favored pastoral production at the expense of agriculture, caused sharp population declines in Khurasan and Transoxiana, as seen in census counts and tax records.[41] Other studies have shown, however, that the Iranian plateau and Mesopotamia, which were also governed by the Ilkhan Mongol rulers, were not permanently affected. Indeed under the Ilkhans (1256–1336), trade expanded, local economic activity increased, and there was renewed investment in agriculture.[42]

Moreover, a determination can be noted among the post-Mongol elites of the region to reestablish agrarian bureaucratic states from the late fifteenth century.

A more satisfactory explanation of the decline of Middle Eastern agriculture requires a more complex analysis of causality. Middle Eastern agriculture suffered from inherent environmental constraints, including the vulnerability of the environment to infrahistorical change (tectonic activity and severe flooding) and political disarray (which undermined the capacity of elites to carry out long-term agricultural policies).[43] Endemic disease must also be taken into account. Peter Christensen has suggested that, from a Eurasian perspective, Mesopotamia was a massive disease pool, the focus of chronic and acute infections that periodically spread throughout the Mediterranean world. With each visitation of plague, tax revenues plunged and the work force was depleted. As the population declined, it became increasingly difficult to maintain the intricate system of dikes, weirs, and canals. The plague of 749 C.E., which struck on the eve of the Abbasid revolution, may have killed as much as 40 percent of the population in the Mesopotamian floodplain.[44] Plague is also the likely culprit for the progressive abandonment of the transverse canals from 1350 to 1550. Steven Borsch's recent study of the effect of plague on the Nile irrigation system reinforces this line of argument. As population levels plummeted, the state became less able to maintain the system, and production declined sharply. Whereas in England, sharp population declines from plague created opportunity spaces for new growth, in the Middle East, complex irrigation systems failed to recover rapidly.[45] Agriculture was more resilient in the Iranian plateau, where endemic diseases were much less of a factor.[46]

The consequences of human action and naturally occurring events were neither irreversible nor inevitable. To view the decline of Middle Eastern agriculture as the unavoidable result of environmental conditions is an unnecessarily reductive view. The environment itself was shaped by long-term historical processes. Neither the huge canal systems in the Tigris-Euphrates basin nor the artificial oases in the deserts and plateaus were necessary for human survival. Rulers made choices. The environmental costs, as always, were borne by later generations.

THE MIDDLE EAST ENVIRONMENTAL CRISIS, 1450–2000

To understand why the Middle East was economically marginalized during the long sixteenth century, relative to Europe and China, we need to view it in a global context. From 1450 to 1750, with the incorporation of the Americas, human population growth began to accelerate all across Eurasia; states developed new military and organizational capabilities; a truly global world economy emerged for the first time; and communications capabilities (printing as well as transportation) developed in unprecedented ways. As the changes compounded, states that were able to adapt to the new conditions of warfare, commerce, and communications achieved exceptional power. These changes were particularly important in China, where the Ming dynasty (1367–1644) replaced the Mongol Yuan (1280–1367), and in Western Europe, which was just emerging from the Black Death. The Middle East was unable to keep up with this expansion. To fully comprehend the reasons, it is useful to compare the ecohistorical predicament and specific strategies of Middle Eastern states with those of China and Europe.[47]

By 1450, all across Eurasia, states had begun to experience significant economic contractions as population growth met the constraints of ecological limitations. As Kenneth Pomeranz has argued, China and Western Europe pursued contrasting approaches to overcoming these constraints. Europe's solution was to exploit its maritime advantage through overseas expansion, as a result of which it achieved levels of wealth and power well beyond agrarian-age norms.[48] Europe's overseas colonies provided a strategic advantage in the struggle for lands and resources, and the availability of colonial raw materials (above all the silver of the Americas) allowed it to participate in the new global market from a position of strength. First Europe muscled in on the Asian spice trade; then, as the sugar revolution (1650–1800) transformed the Atlantic economy by linking Africa, the Americas, and Europe, it realized enormous profits from the slave trade and sugar production in the Caribbean. The emergence of a truly global market in spices, sugar, and other commodities did not lead to a definitive break with the material limitations on growth (notably the shortage of fuelwood) that had characterized the agrarian age; but it did allow Europe to transcend at least some of the limitations of its ecological situation.

Faced with a similar population crunch, ecological constraints, and increasing deforestation in its old core zone, China devised a different strategy. Under the Ming dynasty, the Chinese economy became increasingly marketized; it switched from paper money to a silver-based currency, propelled by its dynamic agricultural sector and growing population. However, because China lacked significant deposits of silver, it was compelled to enter the Asian trade to acquire silver in the vast quantities required. Chinese porcelains, silks, and other manufactured products found ready markets in maritime Asia and Mediterranean Europe. Instead of pursuing an overseas empire, however, China under the Qing (1644–1911) chose to deal with its environmental constraints by encouraging expansion into southern and western China.[49] For a time this strategy of internal colonization brought levels of growth and per capita consumption that rivaled or even exceeded those of Western Europe. Although Europe and China pursued different paths to modernity in response to similar demographic and ecological constraints, until 1750, both strategies were equally successful in increasing the standard of living and growth rates. Both were able to dodge basic contradictions by externalizing their environmental problems. But as its internal resources became exhausted, Chinese rates of growth gradually declined, and its basic ecological contradictions reasserted themselves.[50]

The Middle East case sheds further light on the strategies of Europe and China. The discovery of the Americas and the emergence of a global market in the sixteenth century transformed the topology of the global networks of the Middle East. First, the Middle East became increasingly marginal to the global exchange of goods, ideas, and people. Its land-transport advantages became redundant, and its fading dominance of the internal seas of Eurasia made it increasingly irrelevant in the age of ocean transport. Second, when Europeans acquired direct access to American silver and West African gold, they marginalized the Muslim-dominated trans-Saharan routes that had been an important source of gold for Europe. Finally, in a period of sharpened competition between Europeans (especially the Hapsburgs) and the Ottomans, the discovery of the Americas provided Europeans with untrammeled access to New World resources, including mineral resources, forests, and vast tracts of arable land. As a Mediterranean but not an oceanic power, the Ottoman Empire was precluded from externalizing its environmental contradictions in the same way. Moreover, as the legatee of ancient empires that had exploited the same resource base for millennia with diminishing returns, it could not pursue the Chinese option of intensive colonization of a resource-rich and demographically weak interior.

From 1450 to 1750, the areas between the Nile and the Oxus were marked by a renewed commitment to the agrarian bureaucratic state under the Ottomans (1280–1922) and the Safavids (1501–1722). Although we have no information on the environmental consequences of these projects, a brief review is in order. Under Shah Abbas (1588–1629), Persia sought to revive the agricultural potential of Iraq through the reconstruction of irrigation canals and associated infrastructure. Isfahan was endowed with gardens and vast royal irrigation tanks and made a center of carpet production by the Safavid state, as well as receiving significant state investment in agricultural production.[51] The environmental consequences of Ottoman military and political policies have also been little explored. Certainly

Ottoman strategic ambitions were on a par with those of other major Asian land empires of the period. In the early sixteenth century, Ottoman engineers embarked on the construction of two major canals that sought to link the Volga River with the Don and the Nile with the Mediterranean.[52] In the end both were abandoned. Ottoman needs for raw materials for the manufacture of swords, cannons, and other weapons must have stimulated the mining industry of Anatolia and the Balkans. Similarly, the environmental impact of the Ottoman army and navy on the forests of the Black Sea region and the Caucasus must have been considerable.[53]

The vulnerability of the Middle Eastern "gunpowder empires" (the term is Marshall Hodgson's) was not initially apparent.[54] Europeans did not decisively dominate the Ottomans and other western Asian powers until after 1750. (Until then, the European empire in maritime Asia was mostly based in enclaves and islands.) In 1500, the Ottoman empire controlled European access to Asian commodities like spices, sugar, coffee, tea, and cotton, and Ottoman luxury goods like silk carpets, porcelains, and Damascus steel were still competitive in Eurasian markets.[55] Gradually, despite Ottoman efforts to preserve their monopoly of the spice trade, the advantage passed increasingly to the Europeans.[56] Demand for new commodities like coffee and tobacco compensated for the gradual decline of the spice trade. By 1800 Middle Eastern manufactured products (especially woolens, silks, and sugar) were facing greatly increased competition as well.[57]

Central to the economic strategy of both the Ottomans and Safavids was the expansion of silk production. Silk carpets and clothing were produced for both the luxury and domestic markets and made the fortunes of many entrepreneurs as well as of the royal households that patronized them.[58] Bursa, Tabriz, Isfahan, and Shiraz became major silk-producing centers with large artisan populations and a network of provincial suppliers with important investments in mulberry trees (on which the silkworms fed). The ecological impact of the silk industry was significant, although it has been little studied. Two effects can be mentioned here: the land-use implications of mulberry tree monoculture, and the considerable fuel-wood requirements for processing the cocoons.[59]

The recent historical literature on the Ottoman empire makes it clear that there are no grounds for viewing the period as a dark age.[60] Ottoman and (to a lesser extent) Safavid state elites were as deeply committed to the developmentalist project (see introduction) as the elites of any other Eurasian empire in the period, even if the results did not always meet expectations.

Both the Ottoman and the Safavid empires originally drew support from predominantly Turkish-speaking pastoralist groups whose presence in eastern

Anatolia and the Iranian plateau had significant environmental consequences. They maintained vast flocks of sheep, the wool of which was used to produce carpets as well as woolen items for domestic use, including clothing, embroidered saddlebags, blankets, and tents. Much as in Spain, where the guild of wool producers was organized as the Mesta and sheep migration routes were sanctioned by the state, wool producers had an important role in the Ottoman economy.[61]

The Middle East (and especially the Ottoman empire) was also a center for horse breeding for the European and Indian markets.[62] The commercial breeding of horses for elite and cavalry stables was a lucrative affair. Both the Ottomans and the Safavids adopted policies that preserved vast areas for horse pasturage and sheltered them from taxation. The political and economic clout of pastoralists affected the balance between agrarian, mercantile, and pastoralist powers well into the twentieth century throughout the Middle East. By inhibiting the expansion of agriculture, it also weakened the ability of Middle Eastern states to exploit their agrarian resources.

All across Eurasia, the period 1450–1750 was marked by the rise of huge cities. The largest city in Europe was Istanbul, which at its peak in the seventeenth century had a population of 750,000. The system for provisioning Istanbul, which required the close organization of the grain trade of the Danube basin, undoubtedly had environmental consequences, though these have been little studied.[63] The same is true of the substantial urban construction boom that occurred in most of the provincial capitals of the empire. Moreover, the expansion of Isfahan under the Safavids represented a parallel initiative, with clear environmental consequences. The expansion of cities and the general economy also led to enormous new demands for wood, both as a building material and as a source of energy. Although Western Europe faced the same difficulty, it found a relatively convenient, enormously rich source of energy ready to hand that led to unprecedented growth, power, and change.

By 1700, Western Europe faced a looming energy crisis caused by rapidly increasing deforestation. The crisis jeopardized the remarkable economic growth that had accompanied the establishment of the colonial empires in the Americas, maritime Asia, and Africa. Just at this point, the fortuitous discovery of abundant deposits of coal near Europe's water-transport network sparked the transition from biomass energy to fossil fuels. As a result, the previous environmental limits on economic growth were overcome, and humans adopted an entirely new relationship to the environment.

The new global energy regime was as significant for humanity as the mastery of fire, the discovery of farming, and the emergence of a truly global market around

1500.[64] Access to fossil fuels was fundamental to the Industrial Revolution (which is unimaginable without them). No longer limited by the availability of biomass energy, states and economies acquired vast new capabilities.

Already poorly endowed in wood, the Middle East's transition to industrialization in the nineteenth century was greatly handicapped by the absence of significant deposits of coal. Only in the twentieth century did the Middle East become a major energy player, as the fossil fuel revolution moved on from coal to petroleum and natural gas. The Middle East lacked both the ecological resources and the strategic position to make the transition to the age of fossil fuels.

Coal and colonies thus provided an ecohistorical strategic advantage that enabled Europe to dominate the globe after 1750. While Western Europe went from strength to strength, most of the rest of Eurasia, including the Middle East, experienced increasing difficulties. By 1918 the Ottoman Empire was no more, and European imperialists controlled the region and its resources.

The Ottoman adoption of the developmentalist project dates from the nineteenth century, although its roots go back to the end of the eighteenth century, when Russian expansionism into the Black Sea region under the empress Catherine and her successors directly threatened the territorial integrity of the empire. In response, Ottoman elites proposed a broad range of reforms, just as Peter the Great had done earlier in czarist Russia. After several false starts, under Sultan Mahmud II (1807–39), the reform process finally took hold. European military advisers were hired and advanced military technologies imported: the result was the creation of a modern army, the *nizam jedid*.[65] The *tanzimat* state-modernization reforms marked the evolution of the developmentalist project into a set of political and economic policy choices—now, because of the influence of Enlightenment thought, separable from Christianity and thus available. In the course of the long nineteenth century, this shift was to spread throughout the world. The *tanzimat* reforms provided a vision of how the Ottoman state and its economy might be transformed and how its enemies at home and abroad might be vanquished.

In the Ottoman Empire, the developmentalist project strengthened the state in numerous ways. One was through military modernization and associated administrative and fiscal changes.[66] The *tanzimat* era reforms thus had a far-reaching effect on the environment of the Middle East and North Africa. In its economic guise, the *tanzimat* focused on retrofitting the Ottoman legal and administrative system (including the adoption of a modern land code) to attract foreign trade and investment. In tandem with this effort, internal communications (including port facilities, urban infrastructure, railways, and telegraph) were modernized.

Politically, the reforms increased state power and thereby enabled the forced sedentarization of pastoralists (the Turkomen, Bedouin, and Kurdish peoples). At a stroke, age-old land-use patterns and relationships between pastoral nomadic peoples and sedentary populations were transformed. The displacement of pastoralists from marginal lands favored the expansion of commercial agriculture. This shift was to become a key theme in the modernization of Middle Eastern societies. Finally, the reform process manifested itself in ambitious engineering projects, including the Suez Canal (1867) and the construction of major dams on the Tigris and the Nile, permitting the state to mold nature to its will.

Under Muhammad Ali Pasha (1805–41, also known as Mehmet Ali), Egypt vigorously pursued a parallel self-strengthening program, and the developmentalist project soon transformed the rest of the adjacent regions. In Arabia, Iran, Afghanistan, and Morocco the reform impulse was weaker, and its implementation had for the most part to await the twentieth century.

The incorporation of the Middle East into the world market after 1750 had important consequences for its environment. In general, it accelerated deforestation (as a result of greater demand for timber for ships, houses, improvements and fortifications, and mining) and land degradation. The adoption of modern systems of communications had evident long-term environmental effects as well. Although the new technologies and forms of organization were perfected and systematized in Western Europe, they were not culturally specific and so were readily adopted elsewhere. Taken together, the economic reforms worked in contradictory ways and unevenly benefited different social groups. Over time they undermined the old society without fully bringing a new one into being. Here the Ottoman experience essentially replicates that of the rest of the world outside Western Europe.

The concept of the developmentalist project enables us to see the continuities in environmental history. Changes were not simply imposed from without. Middle Eastern governing elites took an active role in shaping the forms modernity has taken in the region. The essential similarity of the modernizing policies imposed in different nations, despite the deeply differing motivations of the reformers, is striking. Consider, for example, the experiences of Turkey and Algeria. Turkey pursued a route of self-initiated reform, whereas Algeria was colonized by France in 1830; but Turkish reformers and French colonial officials adopted broadly similar policies. These included the establishment of a modern bureaucracy, a legal system based on the French legal code, modern systems of communications, and administrative policies that favored commercial agriculture at the expense of pastoralists.

Despite these continuities, however, these changes had distinctive and specific consequences for the relations of humans and the environment in the Middle East.[67] In the rest of this chapter I examine, first, how the changes of the long nineteenth century affected the river valleys. I examine the role of engineers in the transformation of the Middle Eastern environment before going on to survey the role of hydraulic engineering in the transformation of these valleys in the fossil-fuel era. I then survey the consequences of the developmentalist project for rural populations and environments in the Mediterranean areas of the Middle East as well as the deserts and oases. Finally, I seek to draw some lessons from the history of the Middle Eastern environment for the rest of the world.

ENGINEERS AND THE MIDDLE EASTERN ENVIRONMENT

The period known as the long nineteenth century (roughly 1800–1918) was marked by the fossil-fuel revolution and the Industrial Revolution. However, it was also the century of engineers. Middle Eastern engineering projects (including the Suez Canal and ambitious railroad and telegraph lines) were emblems of global modernity. They demonstrated the ability of humans to tame nature through the application of steam power and electricity. Environmental historians have not paid much attention to the role of engineers in this period. Yet they were crucial to the environmental transformations that ensued after 1750. Engineers were the leading purveyors of the idea of progress and mastery over nature that was central to the developmentalist project.

In the Middle East, the French model of engineering in the service of the state was particularly influential. French graduates of the École Polytechnique, the École des Ponts et Chaussées, and the École des Mines played a central role in the modernization of French infrastructure in the nineteenth century.[68] The prestige of French engineering prowess extended even to British colonial India, where irrigation officers were trained according to French standards.[69]

In the first half of the nineteenth century, the École Polytechnique was heavily influenced by an ideology of social progress connected to the thought of Henri de Saint-Simon (1760–1825). Under the influence of Saint-Simon's leading disciple, Barthélemy Prosper Enfantin (1796–1864), a faculty member at the École Polytechnique, many students were attracted to Saint-Simonism, which evolved into a cult of progress adapted to the needs of an industrial age. In an 1832 article, "Le système de la Méditerrannée," Michel Chevalier (1806–79), a leading Saint-Simonian theorist, developed a vision of the Mediterranean as an economic and political hub.[70]

The goal of French industrial policy, he proposed, should be the unification of the Mediterranean under French leadership and its integration into the new global political economy. Chevalier called for the construction of a large network of railroads and canals under the leadership of French technocrats and capitalists. Saint-Simonians were among the founders of leading French banks of the period, including the Crédit Mobilier, the Crédit Foncier, and the Crédit Lyonnais. Saint-Simonian ideas about the French path to development emphasized the construction of a modern railroad grid that would link the Atlantic and Mediterranean worlds.

Under the leadership of the Saint-Simonians, the Middle East (and the entire Mediterranean) came to modernity. Most of the prestige projects in the Middle East, including the two principal icons of Egyptian modernity—the Suez Canal and the Aswan High Dam—were the result of French engineering prowess and Saint-Simonian inspiration. Ferdinand de Lesseps, the father of the Suez Canal, was a dissident Saint-Simonian. There was also a proposal for the construction of a major dam across the Nile, though it was never constructed.[71] Saint-Simonians were also involved in all aspects of the conquest of Algeria (1830–48), where they provided the only coherent vision of how colonization might be linked to a larger strategic vision.[72] The radiating influence of the Saint-Simonian technocratic vision, like the light of a dying star, continued to shape the transformation of the Mediterranean environment long after it had run its course in France.

In Egypt, engineering schools have an almost unbroken history dating from the early Muhammad Ali period, when an École Polytechnique was established in Cairo by Charles Lambert, a Saint-Simonian graduate of the original École.[73] As elsewhere in the Mediterranean and Latin America, the title of Engineer (Arabic *muhandis*) became a much-coveted honorific. By 1882 most irrigation engineers in Egypt were Egyptian nationals. In the 1920s a quarter of modern Cairo—Muhandisin—was constructed according to the latest urban-planning standards to house engineers and their families. Between the two world wars, Egyptian engineering schools produced more than one hundred graduates a year. By 1945, the faculty at the modern university engineering schools was almost entirely Egyptianized. Under the presidency of Gamal Abdel Nasser (1956–70), engineers constituted a large, prestigious, and powerful component of the political administrative elite. Indeed, Egypt, alone among the countries in the region, produced engineers far in excess of positions available locally. By 1918 there were several hundred European-trained engineers in the Ottoman domains (including Egypt). By the 1970s, Egyptian engineering schools were producing more than five thousand engineering graduates a year.[74]

After World War I, the École Polytechnique was opened to foreign and colonial applicants (who had previously been admitted only as external students), although it was not until after 1945 that they were able to secure adequate employment in their home countries. In Iran, following the rise to power of Reza Shah (1925–41), more than 640 student engineers were sent to Paris to study at the École Polytechnique. On their return to Iran, they played an important role in devising and implementing the modernization policies of the Pahlavi regime. In 1945, French-trained engineers took the lead in establishing the Association of Iranian Engineers, which later played a role in the politics of the postwar era, notably under Mohamed Mossadegh. After World War II, graduates of the École Polytechnique and the École des Mines helped found professional associations of engineers in Lebanon, Tunisia, and Morocco. French-trained engineers took the lead in establishing national engineering schools in the newly independent states.[75] A more complete history of the engineering profession in the Middle East might shed much light on the development policies of post-1945 states and thereby enable us better to understand the connections between colonial and postcolonial policies and their effects on the environment.

HYDRAULIC ENGINEERING
IN THE MIDDLE EASTERN RIVER VALLEYS

Egypt is central to a study of irrigation and water-management regimes in the Middle East. The continuity of water management in the Nile valley over more than five millennia is unmatched anywhere. Large-scale irrigation projects did not begin with the developmentalist project but with the pharaohs. In the modern period, Egypt has offered the best example of successful agricultural modernization, starting with Muhammad Ali, under whose rule a plan to construct a dam on the Nile at Aswan was developed in 1834, with French assistance, though not implemented.[76] The Suez Canal remains a showcase of the progress-oriented ideology of the developmentalist project. Since the 1980s, however, the stagnation of Egyptian agriculture has exposed the limits of this particular development strategy.

A pioneer of the developmentalist project, Muhammad Ali adopted policies that dramatically transformed Egypt in the nineteenth century.[77] Under his rule, the Egyptian economy was opened to the world market and converted to the production of cotton for export.[78] In the first half of the nineteenth century, the mechanized production of cotton textiles was the world's leading industry, and cotton supplies were inadequate. Egypt was well positioned to take advantage of the situation because of its strategic location, abundant fertile land, and industrious work force. At the outset, however, Egypt faced problems with the existing irrigation system, the variable quality and numerous varieties of cotton produced, and the social organization of labor. Under Muhammad Ali, efforts were made to address each of these bottlenecks.

The discovery of long-staple cotton by a French technical adviser, Louis Alexis Jumel (1785–1823), was crucial to what came next.[79] The fibers of the Jumel variety of cotton, which were longer and stronger than those of other common varieties, could be readily processed by machine. By standardizing on the production of Jumel cotton, Egypt became the leading producer of premium cotton for British mills.[80] Egyptian cotton soon set the world standard. French experts laid down strict rules on how to grow Jumel cotton and devised a hierarchical labor organization to enforce its cultivation. Egypt was turned into a vast cotton plantation, and peasants were not permitted to grow subsistence crops on land allocated to cotton production.[81]

To maximize production, it was necessary to end the centuries-old system of irrigation, which relied on the annual floods, and move to a system of perennial irrigation. By adding a summer growing season, this scheme enabled cotton production to continue year-round. By 1833, 144 kilometers of new canals had been constructed, notably the Mahmudiya Canal in the delta (1817), and existing canals were deepened so that they would be below the level of the river even in the dry season. Barrages were built on the main Nile delta canals to retain water and facilitate the provision of water to secondary and tertiary irrigation networks.[82] As a result of perennial irrigation, the area devoted to cotton production was expanded, and output increased dramatically. Production rose from 135 million kilograms in 1880 to 328.5 million in 1914. The intensification of land use led to new cultivation practices, notably the widespread plowing of fields (not practiced under the old irrigation system, in which the silt laid down by the annual flood fertilized the fields). The confirmation of the state's responsibility for the development of the irrigation infrastructure was perhaps the most important consequence of the widespread adoption of perennial irrigation.

Under British rule (1882–1952), the water-management system was upgraded several times. In the 1880s, three major off-take canals were built in the delta, and in 1902 the first Aswan dam was constructed under the direction of Sir Colin Moncrieff. The height of the dam was raised several times by the British, and by 1933 the storage capacity of the reservoir was 5.7 billion cubic feet.[83] To facilitate the movement of cotton to the world market, railroads were constructed along the Nile corridor (1,519 kilometers by 1877).

The Egyptian environment was affected in important ways by these innovations. To begin with, the advent of perennial irrigation was accompanied by human health problems, notably an increase in schistosomiasis and other water-borne diseases. More crucial was the inadequate investment in drainage. If irrigation water is not regularly flushed and drained away, mineral salts tend to accumulate in the soil. Over time this problem led to the loss of much productive land to agriculture. The problem of drainage is as old as the pharaohs. Before the Muslim era, more than 600,000 hectares in the northern Delta are estimated to have been lost to salt intrusion.[84] In mitigation, perennial cultivation (especially after the construction of the 1902 Aswan dam) lessened a second age-old problem, the irregularities of the Nile flood, which had caused severe shortfalls in cereal production and induced periodic famines.

The British approach to irrigation also had regressive social consequences. The consolidation of private property rights in land and labor, together with the transformation to perennial irrigation, worked to the advantage of wealthy landowners. Besides greatly increasing the area of cultivated land, it intensified pressures on landless peasants, igniting the endemic peasant land hunger that is featured in Abdel Rahman Sharkawi's classic 1930s novel of social protest, *Egyptian Earth*.[85] By the interwar period, the stark contrast between the small class of wealthy landowners (known as *umdah*s) and the vast numbers of landless peasants had begun to have political consequences. The adoption of perennial irrigation under the British eventually generated the social tinder that led to the Free Officers coup in 1952 and brought Nasser to power.

After World War I, petroleum and natural gas supplanted coal as the primary energy source for most societies, and the human capacity to manipulate the environment again accelerated dramatically. While the state acquired far-reaching new powers of intervention, the entire Middle East became more closely linked to the world economy, as other regions came to depend heavily on its oil and gas. These energy sources provided humans with unprecedented capacities to manipulate the environment, in Egypt as well as elsewhere. Massive engineering projects such as the Aswan High Dam, while consistent with the logic of nineteenth-century hydrological engineering, greatly surpassed it in scope. The dam provided cheap and abundant supplies of electrical power to a state not otherwise well endowed with energy resources. It also made possible perennial irrigation that increased the cultivated land area and greatly reduced Egypt's exposure to El Niño–induced famines, like the 1877 famine witnessed by Ulysses S. Grant.[86] Without the Aswan High Dam, there is little doubt that the 1980s Sahel famine that devastated the fringes of the Sahara would have hit Egypt hard as well. Given the relentless demographic pressures to which Egypt is exposed, preventing this disaster was no small achievement. Only in the past few years has Egypt once again had to turn to the international grain market to supplement its domestic food supply. In this sense, it can be said that the dam bought Egypt thirty years' respite from population pressures.

However, the dam has also had negative environmental effects. A lack of investment in drainage has led to increasing salinization, which causes a decline in productivity and eventually the loss of cultivated land. Siltation has also become a major problem: no longer deposited along the Nile flood plain, silt has accumulated in the vast man-made Lake Nasser upstream of the dam, where it has threatened to obstruct the outlets of the dam and the lake itself. In the absence of the annual deposit of silt on their fields, Egyptian farmers have become dependent on commercial fertilizers. The gains from productivity stem primarily from increases in the area under cultivation, as yields per hectare have remained substantially constant. Finally, as silt no longer flows into the Mediterranean through the Nile delta, the fisheries of the eastern Mediterranean have been deprived of their principal source of nutrients, and as a result fish stocks have declined precipitously (although overfishing no doubt has also been a factor).[87]

Since 1918, a number of other ambitious water-management schemes have been planned in the Middle East, consistent with the aims of the developmentalist project. One involves the attempts of the three riparian states (Turkey, Syria, and Iraq) to erect dams across the Euphrates River. The absence of coordination between the three states (despite international agreements) has thus far not led to conflict, but the highly political nature of the dam projects in each state does not augur well for future cooperation. In Turkey, the Southeast Anatolia Project (SEAP) led to the construction of more than eighty dams and sixty-six hydroelectric power stations and costs in excess of US$20 billion, partly subsidized by the World Bank.[88] The project's centerpiece, the Ataturk Dam on the Euphrates, was completed in 1992. It was intended to jump-start the economic development of eastern Anatolia as well as increase government control over separatists in Turkish Kurdistan.

Syria's dependence on the Euphrates is equally crucial to national development objectives, as the Euphrates is by far the largest river in Syria. The Tabaqa Dam, begun in 1973, was conceived by Soviet engineers and built as a kind of Syrian counterpart to the Aswan Dam. It has a planned storage capacity of 12 billion cubic meters but has been plagued by numerous technical problems (including land subsidence, seepage, and evaporation). In the droughts of the 1980s, Syria's insistence on taking its full water rights provoked major conflicts with both Iraq and Turkey, the other riparian states. Conflicts are only expected to increase as the Turkish Southeast Anatolia Project is completed. Already there have been difficulties caused by Syrian objections to the levels of waters impounded by Turkish dams. Unless there is a negotiated solution, the reduction in the flow of the Euphrates is likely to compromise the Syrian irrigation projects.[89]

Since the period of the Ottoman *tanẓimat,* repeated attempts have been made to restore Iraqi irrigation to the levels of water supply in ancient Persia.[90] The construction of the Hindiyah barrage prior to World War I was followed by the building of numerous dams, canals, and artificial lakes under the British and Iraqi governments in the years that followed. As in Egypt, the modernization of Iraqi irrigation was undermined by insufficient investment in drainage (which led to salinization and the loss of agricultural land). The Third River project, completed under the government of Saddam Hussein, sought to open a vast canal to collect and drain saline waters from irrigation canals fed by the Tigris and Euphrates. It originated in studies conducted in the 1950s by American engineers and was completed by the Iraqi government in 1994. The Third River project represents a classic form of developmentalist thinking about rivers as drains (see Mark Cioc's study of the Rhine in this volume). Since the downfall of the Hussein regime and U.S. occupation, Iraqi plans for the Tigris and Euphrates have remained in limbo.

DRY FARMING AND PASTORALISM SINCE 1918

In the river valleys of the Middle East, the environment has been shaped by major engineering projects since 1918. The experience of the dry-farming and pastoralist regions has been different. A more complete survey would discuss the Iranian plateau, geographic Syria, and the Arabian peninsula; here I confine my discussion to North Africa.

Like other parts of the Middle Eastern region dependent on rain-fed agriculture, the Maghreb (the region encompassing Tunisia, Algeria, and Morocco) has an average rainfall of 10 inches (250 mm) per year, with considerable local variation; Libya's is much lower. In precolonial times, water-management schemes focused on small-scale projects.[91] Examples include the *qanat*-style irrigation tunnels in the Tafilalt oasis area and the tank system of irrigated gardens. The precolonial North African economy focused on the production of cereals (barley and wheat) and cultivation with the scratch plow. This style of agriculture was relatively drought tolerant, and at precolonial population levels it was largely in balance with the environment.

The coming of the French marked a major change in the agrarian economy of the Maghreb and brought about a gradual shift to forms of high-input agriculture aimed at production for an export market rather than self-sufficiency. French colonial rule in North Africa began in 1830 in Algeria, 1881 in Tunisia, and 1912 in Morocco. Evoking the history of the Roman Empire, when North Africa was allegedly the granary of Rome, the French colonial government fashioned a progressive narrative in which it would restore the Maghreb to its former agricultural wealth through enlightened colonial rule. The French sought to make the desert bloom by fostering the dry farming of grain in the central regions. By the 1880s the high plateaus of the Algerian interior, long a zone of pastoral transhumance, had been opened to grain farmers using tractors and combine harvesters to grow wheat and barley for the French market. Mechanized production was encouraged by a program of subsidies and bonuses and high crop prices in France, despite greater actual costs. Throughout colonial North Africa, environmentally anomalous modern high-input agriculture was accompanied by extreme concentration of land ownership. Europeans farmed roughly 30 percent of Algeria's arable land, 20 percent of Tunisia's, and 13 percent of Morocco's. This shift devastated the flocks and herds of the pastoralists while exposing the thin soils of the Tellian Atlas to erosion.[92]

In Morocco, French authorities similarly encouraged wheat farming by a select group of wealthy French and Moroccan farmers in the central coastal plains known as *le Maroc utile*. As a result, areas under cultivation for cereal production increased significantly, from 1.9 million hectares in 1918 to nearly 3 million hectares in 1929. Although cereal production increased correspondingly, so did vulnerability to drought. The favoring of wheat over barley, which is more drought tolerant, exacerbated the effects of drought. A major crisis in 1929–1933 coincided with the Great Depression to devastate French cereal farmers in Morocco and Algeria. Only later did agronomists recognize that the "granary of Rome" ideology had blinded the French to the environmental realities of the Maghreb: rain-fed agriculture is an environmentally perilous undertaking. According to one recent study, serious droughts in the region have been recorded in twenty-five of the past one hundred years.[93]

After the failure of the agricultural experiment in Morocco, French authorities sought to tap the hydrological resources of the Atlas mountains, the westward slopes of which received seasonal rainfall averaging 750 millimeters annually. Dams were constructed with the goal of boosting Morocco's irrigated land to one million hectares. In the exalted language of the moment, engineers vowed, "Not a single drop of water to the sea!" By 1949, land under irrigation in the Kasba Tadla and Beni Amir areas had expanded from two thousand to thirteen thousand hectares. By the 1950s, the French had completely reorganized production in the modern sector of the Moroccan agricultural economy and devised a new strategy to produce fruits and early vegetables for the European market. In this undertaking they were heavily influenced by the California model of agriculture, using irrigation, synthetic pesticides, and scientific agricultural methods. The Organisation Cherifien de Controle et d'Exportation, modeled on the California Fruit Growers Exchange, was charged with setting quality standards, researching new varieties, analyzing market conditions, and establishing the Moroccan "brand" in the European market.[94]

The French decision to modernize Moroccan agriculture in the 1940s and 1950s left a permanent legacy. Since the 1960s, the independent North African states have continued to push cereal production into increasingly marginal agricultural lands despite the evident environmental folly of such a strategy.

In the world of pastoralist stock raising, too, the coming of the French represented a major transformation. Whereas contemporary range ecologists are apt to see a fluctuating balance between pastoralism, agriculture, and forest ecology, French colonial attitudes had long reflected environmentalist concerns with deforestation, overgrazing, and conservation that viewed pastoralists as a baleful influence. George Perkins Marsh's focus on forests echoed French scientific concern with the environment of the Middle East and North Africa.[95] An early expression of this concern was the French Forest Code of 1827, which was subsequently exported unchanged to the very different environment of North Africa.[96] Arid environments, unlike tropical ones, are well adapted to drought and disturbance and recover well from dramatic vegetation changes. Whereas the North African environment was well adapted to fire and grazing, the code imposed strict limits on both.

The attitudes of the contemporary Maghreb states toward their pastoralist populations have regrettably tended to replicate French colonial views, ascribing land degradation to overgrazing. Recent work on range ecology in Africa has sharply challenged these negative views of pastoralist behavior, instead representing pastoralism as a sustainable way of life. Range ecologists view the arid and semiarid rangelands of the Maghreb as being in disequilibrium because of the harsh nature of the climate, population increase, and the draining of aquifers as a result of the proliferation of tube wells.[97]

Influenced by French colonial visions of agricultural plenty, postindependence Morocco launched a project that sought to increase the reach of modern agriculture by creating tractor cooperatives and establishing model farms. Drawing on French colonial plans, it aimed at irrigating one million hectares of land. That there have been some successes is evident from the record. By 1986 Morocco was the second largest exporter of oranges in the world (claiming 13 percent of the world market), and 80 percent of all its agricultural exports were fruits and vegetables. However, only a portion of Moroccan agricultural land is suited to California-style agriculture. The Moroccan state has lacked the means to implement the California model fully.[98] Neither the French nor the government of independent Morocco was able to counter the influence of the vested interests that are a legacy of the colonial land system. Crucially, the strategy of concentrating on modern irrigated agriculture has failed to address Morocco's dramatic demographic increase (more than 3 percent per annum). Instead of fostering a self-sufficient peasantry, the adoption of the California model has worsened existing inequalities. Most of the investment has gone to enrich the already wealthy, while poor peasants have continued to lag. In the opinion of some experts, the California model has been as big a failure as the French grain experiment.[99] It has failed to provide food security, raise rural standards of living, or provide adequate foreign exchange earnings. Although land under cereal cultivation has increased considerably, yields per hectare have not kept pace. Given the environmental realities, the new goal of food security is, in the opinion of many agronomists, equally mythical. Only the driving myth has changed. Yet, paradoxically, faith in modern high-input agriculture persists.

In the nineteenth century, farmers on the central plains of the United States believed that "rain follows the plow." Family farms were planted on the prairie, and for a time bumper crops rolled in. Farmers were disabused of this notion only by the devastating droughts of the 1920s that created the Dust Bowl. Nothing daunted, a generation of developmental economists and agronomists exported much the same ideology to the Third World after World War II. For a time, it seemed as though the strategy was working, as high-input agriculture—heavily dependent on synthetic pesticides and fertilizers and hybrid seeds—led to record harvests and soaring hopes of food security throughout the Third World. But a darker side soon became evident. The gains, largely derived from the extension of agriculture into marginal land, were eclipsed by the costs, which included pesticide-fouled aquifers and wealth for some at the ruin of many. But by the 1970s, record famines (sometimes intensified by El Niño events) in the Sahel, northeast Brazil, East Africa, and a host of other places prompted a reassessment. The new slogan from some agronomists was "drought follows the plow."[100]

Because of the failure of high-input agriculture, planners of the development strategies of Third World countries have been left in a quandary. Confronted by unrelenting demographic pressures, some believe they have little option but to persist with the same methods. These problems are especially acute for regions lacking major river systems, such as the Maghreb. Even Egypt and states along the riparian corridor of the Euphrates like Turkey, Syria, and Iraq, although they are more fortunately situated, are facing similar pressures. Egypt is no longer self-sufficient in food production. Most of the rest of the region has not been for some time, and the food deficits grow with each passing year. At the beginning of the twenty-first century, the Middle East is showing signs of exceeding the carrying capacity of the land. Large-scale engineering solutions seem unlikely to provide the solution. Here the words of Peter Christensen, referring to Iran, can be applied to the Middle East region as a whole: "In spite of considerable investments and the transfer of modern, western agrarian technology, [Iran] has not increased productivity—rather the opposite, if we look at productivity per unit area. The point is that resource scarcity, primarily lack of water, has imposed fundamental limits on production, limits which until now neither more capital nor improved technology nor alternative forms of social organization have been able to transcend. In this sense Iran differs from both pre-industrial Europe and the wet-rice societies of Asia."[101]

This long-term perspective radically challenges cherished developmentalist beliefs. If output per hectare has not increased over the very long run, then something is wrong with their expectations. Heroic efforts like the Aswan High Dam have added to the total area under the plow throughout the region (and in the process expanded the irrigated areas at the expense of the other ecologies), but they can no longer forestall the inevitable decline. The pattern of agricultural outputs in the United States serves as a warning for the Middle East: despite ever-increasing energy inputs in the form of fertilizers and other additives, agricultural outputs relative to energy inputs have stagnated or even regressed over the past fifty years.[102] Environmental catastrophe looms throughout the Middle East as aquifers are depleted, rivers and seas are increasingly polluted, and land degradation accelerates.[103]

CONCLUSION

From the perspective of the deep history of the Middle Eastern environment, its modern history looks substantially different. States and peoples have been transforming the regional environment for millennia, not just since the onset of modern times. Already by the first millennium B.C.E., if not before, human actions had substantially remolded the Mesopotamian environment with a series of major hydraulic engineering projects, including massive dams, canals, and artificial rivers. In this context, modern engineering marvels like the Aswan High Dam no longer seem so original, and the assumption that modern people are unique in their capacity to adversely affect the environment seems questionable. The graph of environmental degradation needs to be redrawn. Instead of a curve rising sharply to mark the onset of the modern era, the new shape would show spikes in anthropogenic environmental damage with the origins of civilization and the age of metallurgy, and then a sharp upswing starting around 1450. Around 1750, as the fossil-fuel revolution completely altered the game, the curve would rise steeply. Perhaps not surprisingly, the graph of environmental degradation closely conforms to that of human demographic trends.

If we pay attention to the deep history of the Middle East, we can also see that modernity is not just Western. Rather, its roots lie deep in the common past of northern Africa, Europe, and Asia. Not only have humans been altering the environment in which they live for millennia, but states and economies have been gradually knitting webs of connection between humans for at least as long.[104] From a world-historical perspective, a central element of the modern state, the military and fiscal revolution was already in place in East Asia. It subsequently diffused across Afroeurasia, and in the process transformed warfare and the organization of the state through the introduction of new tactics, strategy, and weaponry. Muslim rulers were quick to see the advantages of gunpowder weapons and were among the first to deploy them on a large scale.[105]

Putting the Middle Eastern environment at the center of the frame allows us to see that the environmental policies pursued by indigenous and colonial rulers since 1750 are essentially similar. Both built paved roads, railroads, dams, canals, and modern irrigation schemes. Both invested in capital- (and technology-) intensive mining; both greatly increased their consumption of wood (both as a construction material and as fuel) and fossil fuels. The fossil-fuel revolution has only deepened these similarities. Since the end of colonialism, no Third World state has elected to forgo the benefits of modern medicine, military weapons, or communications technologies. In this sense, we are all modern.

The developmentalist project has short-circuited social processes by pursuing macrolevel policies and procedures without linking them to meso- and microlevel processes. The results have been mixed. On the plus side, the Middle East is able to feed a significant proportion of its citizens, despite dramatically higher populations (although food security remains an important issue), to provide great quantities of relatively cheap petroleum and natural gas to the world market (with one-time revenue gains for the producing states and state elites, and economic benefits for many), and to bring about greater economic integration of the region into the world market (with incidental advantages for the region). On the negative side, environmental degradation has increased dramatically, with higher levels of deforestation, irreversible land degradation, spoilage of fisheries, depletion of aquifers, and pollution of water resources. Given the fragility of the Middle Eastern environment, the cumulative, irreversible impacts of these changes pose a significant challenge for the future.

As a consequence of its fragile and overburdened environment and its long history of human intervention, today the Middle East finds itself confronting unprecedented challenges. Because the legacy of squandered water resources, deforestation, and pollution of all kinds is far longer in the Middle Eastern region, and because the vulnerability of Middle Eastern semiarid and arid landscapes is more evident, their cumulative consequences are also particularly visible. The flayed Middle Eastern environment epitomizes the world as it will be. For this reason, it is of relevance to all those who are concerned about the global environment. Like the proverbial canary in the miner's cage, the Middle East provides a warning for the rest of the planet. Will the future bring a desperate struggle over water and other basic resources? Or will human ingenuity once again find a way out of the mess it has created?

NOTES

1. Peter Christensen, *The Decline of Iranshahr: Irrigation and Environments in the History of the Middle East, 500 B.C. to A.D. 1500* (Copenhagen: Museum Tusculanum Press, 1993).

2. Marshall Hodgson, *The Venture of Islam,* vol. 2 (Chicago: University of Chicago Press, 1974), 62–151.

3. Robert M. Adams, *The Land behind Baghdad: A History of Settlement on the Diyala Plains* (Chicago: University of Chicago Press, 1965).

4. Andrew Watson, *Agricultural Innovation in the Early Islamic World* (Cambridge: Cambridge University Press, 1983).

5. On Islamic water-lifting devices, see Ahmad Y. Hassan and Donald J. Hill, *Islamic Technology: An Illustrated History* (Cambridge: Cambridge University Press, 1986), 37–55.

6. J.M. Wagstaff, *The Evolution of Middle Eastern Landscapes: An Outline to A.D. 1840* (London: Croom Helm, 1985), 93–97, 148–51.

7. Attilio Petruccioli, "Rethinking the Islamic Garden," in *Transformations of Middle Eastern Natural Environments: Legacies and Lessons,* ed. Jane Coppock and Joseph A. Miller (New Haven: Yale University Press, 1998), 349–63. See also Karen Foster

Pollinger, "Gardens of Eden: Exotic Flora and Fauna in the Ancient Near East," in Coppock and Miller, *Transformations*, 320–29.

8. Peter Christensen, "Middle Eastern Irrigation: Legacies and Lessons," in Coppock and Miller, *Transformations*, 15–30.

9. Christensen, *Decline of Iranshahr*, 73.

10. On early Islamic irrigation techniques, see Hassan and Hill, *Islamic Technology*, 80–91.

11. Christensen, *Decline of Iranshahr*, 72.

12. Adams, *Land behind Baghdad*.

13. Christensen, "Middle Eastern Irrigation," 19.

14. Christensen, *Decline of Iranshahr*, 19.

15. Paul Ward English, "Qanats and Lifeworlds in Iranian Plateau Villages," in Coppock and Miller, *Transformations*, 187–205.

16. English, "Qanats and Lifeworlds," 194.

17. Watson, *Agricultural Innovation*. See also Andrew Watson, "The Arab Agricultural Revolution, 700–1100," *Journal of Economic History* 34, no. 4 (1974): 8–35.

18. Eliahu Ashtor, *The Social and Economic History of the Near East in the Middle Ages* (London: Collins, 1976); Christensen, *Decline of Iranshahr* and "Middle Eastern Irrigation," 19.

19. Thomas Glick, "Hydraulic Technology in al-Andalus," in *The Legacy of Muslim Spain* (Leiden: Brill, 1992), 974–86. For a more complete discussion, see Thomas Glick, *Irrigation and Society in Medieval Valencia* (Cambridge, MA: Harvard University Press, 1973).

20. Thomas Glick, "The Attempt to Adopt the Valencian Communal System in British India," in *Irrigation and Hydraulic Technology: Medieval Spain and Its Legacy* (Aldershot, U.K.: Variorum, 1996), 978.

21. Ronald A. Messier and Neil D. MacKenzie, *Archaeological Survey of Sijilmasa, 1988* (Rabat: Institut National des Sciences de l'Archéologie et du Patrimoine, 1989); James A. Miller, "Sustained Past and Risky Present: The Tafilalt Oasis of Southeastern Morocco," in *The North African Environment at Risk*, ed. Will D. Swearingen and Abdellatif Bencherifa (Boulder, CO: Westview, 1996), 55–69; E. W. Bovill, *The Golden Trade of the Moors* (London: Oxford University Press, 1958); Mohammed El Faiz, *Jardins de Marrakech* (Arles: Actes Sud, 2002).

22. Edmund Burke III, "The Middle East at the Center," keynote address to World History Association annual meeting, Atlanta, GA, June 2003.

23. See Joseph Needham, *Science and Civilization in China*, vol. 4, *Physics and Physical Technology* (Cambridge: Cambridge University Press, 1971), especially part 3, *Civil Engineering and Nautics*. See also Mark Elvin, *The Pattern of the Chinese Past: A Social and Economic Interpretation* (Stanford, CA: Stanford University Press, 1973).

24. Needham (*Science and Civilization,* 4:282) dates the Grand Canal from the Sui dynasty (580–618 C.E.).

25. Arnold Pacey, *Technology in World Civilization: A Thousand-Year History* (Oxford: Basil Blackwell, 1990), 8. On the development of lateral derivate irrigation canals in China from the fifth century B.C.E., Needham comments: "Thus was the Babylonian pattern transplanted to Chinese soil" (*Science and Civilization,* 4:374).

26. Elvin, *Pattern of the Chinese Past,* 126–28.

27. Madhav Gadgil and Ramachandra Guha, *This Fissured Land: An Ecological History of India* (Berkeley: University of California Press, 1993). See also David Ludden, *An Agrarian History of South Asia* (Cambridge: Cambridge University Press, 1999).

28. El Faiz, *Jardins de Marrakech,* 30–42.

29. Thomas Glick, *The Old World Background of the Irrigation System of San Antonio, Texas* (San Antonio: Texas Western Press, 1972), 3–67.

30. H. F. M. van de Ven, ed., *Hydrology for the Water Management of Large River Basins* (Wallingford, U.K.: International Association of Hydrological Sciences, 1991); Johan van Veen, *Drain, Dredge, Reclaim: The Art of a Nation* (The Hague: Martinus Nijhoff, 1962).

31. Caesare S. Maffioli, *Out of Galileo: The Science of Waters, 1628–1718* (Rotterdam: Erasmus Publishing, 1994).

32. Glick, "Attempt to Adopt the Valencian Communal System."

33. Karl Wittfogel, *Oriental Despotism: a Comparative Study of Total Power* (New Haven: Yale University Press, 1957).

34. Donald Hughes, *Pan's Travails: Environmental Problems of the Ancient Greeks and Romans* (Baltimore: Johns Hopkins University Press, 1994).

35. Theodore A. Wertime, "The Furnace versus the Goat? Pyrotechnologic Industries and Mediterranean Deforestation," *Journal of Field Archeology* 10 (1983): 445–52; Theodore A. Wertime and James D. Muhly, *The Coming of the Age of Iron* (New Haven: Yale University Press, 1980).

36. Wertime, "The Furnace versus the Goat," 446.

37. John Perlin, *A Forest Journey: The Role of Wood in the Development of Civilization* (New York: W. W. Norton, 1989).

38. J. V. Thirgood, *Man and the Mediterranean Forest* (New York: Academic Press, 1981), 67–69, 74.

39. Jean Despois, *L'Afrique du nord* (Paris: Presses Universitaires de France, 1949); Augustin Bernard, *Afrique septentrionale et occidentale* (Paris: Armand Colin, 1937).

40. Christensen, *Decline of Iranshahr.*

41. Oleg Petruchevsky, "Iran under the Il-Khans," in *The Cambridge History of Islam,* vol. 5, ed. J. A. Boyle (Cambridge: Cambridge University Press, 1988).

42. Christensen, *Decline of Iranshahr.*

43. Adams, *Land behind Baghdad.*

44. Christensen, *Decline of Iranshahr,* 75–80.

45. Stuart J. Borsch, "Environment and Population: The Decline of Large Irrigation Systems Reconsidered," *Comparative Studies in Society and History* (2004): 451–68.

46. Christensen, *Decline of Iranshahr,* 120–23.

47. For Bernard Lewis, the answer was Islam. See his *What Went Wrong? The Clash between Islam and Modernity in the Middle East* (New York: Oxford University Press, 2002).

48. See Kenneth Pomeranz, "The Transformation of China's Environment, 1500–2000," in this volume. See, more generally, Andre Gunder Frank, *ReOrient: Global Economy in the Asian Age* (Berkeley: University of California Press, 1998) and Kenneth Pomeranz, *The Great Divergence: China, Europe, and the Making of the Modern World Economy* (Princeton: Princeton University Press, 2002).

49. Pomeranz, *Great Divergence;* Frank, *ReOrient.* See also Robert Marks, *The Origins of the Modern World* (New York: Rowman and Littlefield, 2002).

50. Pomeranz, "Transformation of the Chinese Environment."

51. Christensen, *Decline of Iranshahr;* Roger Savory, *Iran under the Safavids* (Cambridge: Cambridge University Press, 1980).

52. W. E. D. Allen, *Problems of Turkish Power in the Sixteenth Century* (London: Central Asian Research Centre, 1963).

53. Bruce McGowan, *Economic Life in Ottoman Europe: Taxation, Trade and the Struggle for Land, 1600–1800* (Cambridge: Cambridge University Press, 1981).

54. Marshall G. S. Hodgson, *The Venture of Islam* (Chicago: University of Chicago Press, 1974), 3: 16–22.

55. On the economic history of the Ottoman Empire from 1500 to 1800, see Suraiya Faroqhi, Bruce McGowan, Donald Quataert, and Şevket Pamuk, *An Economic and Social History of the Ottoman Empire,* vol. 1 (Cambridge: Cambridge University Press, 1994).

56. Giancarlo Casale, "The Ottoman Age of Exploration: Spices, Maps and Conquest in the Sixteenth-century Indian Ocean" (Ph.D. diss., Harvard University, 2004).

57. For an overview of the eighteenth century, see Bruce McGowan, "The Age of the Ayans," in Faroqhi et al., *Economic and Social History of the Ottoman Empire,* 637–758.

58. On Iran, see Leonard Helfgott, *Ties That Bind: A Social History of the Iranian Carpet* (Washington, DC: Smithsonian Institution Press, 1994). On the Ottoman Empire, see Faroqhi et al., *Economic and Social History of the Ottoman Empire.*

59. On the Lebanese silk industry, see Boutros Labaki, *La soie dans l'économie du Mont Liban, 1840–1914* (Beirut: Publications de l'Université Libanaise, 1979).

60. Huri Islamoghlu-Inan, *The Ottoman Empire and the World Economy* (Cambridge: Cambridge University Press, 1987).

61. On the Mesta in Spain, see David Ringrose, *Spain, Europe, and the "Spanish Miracle," 1700–1900* (Cambridge: Cambridge University Press, 1996). On Italy, see John Marino, *Pastoral Economics in the Kingdom of Naples* (Baltimore: Johns Hopkins University Press, 1988). For the Ottoman case, see Suraiya Faroqhi, *Towns and Townsmen of Ottoman Anatolia: Trade, Crafts and Food Production in an Urban Setting* (Cambridge: Cambridge University Press, 1984).

62. Fernand Braudel, *The Mediterranean and the Mediterranean World in the Age of Philip II*, 2 vols. (New York: Harper and Row, 1973).

63. Halil Inalcik, *The Ottoman Empire: The Classical Age, 1300–1600* (London: Weidenfeld and Nicolson, 1973). Robert Mantran, *Istanbul dans la seconde moitié du XVIIe siècle: Essai d'histoire institutionnelle, économique et sociale* (Paris: A. Maisonneuve, 1962).

64. The concept of the energy regime is developed by Johan Goudsblom, *Fire and Civilization* (London: Allen Lane, 1992) and Fred Spier, *The Structure of Big History* (Amsterdam: Amsterdam University Press, 1996). See also David Christian, *Maps of Time: An Introduction to Big History* (Berkeley: University of California Press, 2003).

65. Bernard Lewis, *The Emergence of Modern Turkey* (Oxford: Oxford University Press, 1961); Niyazi Berkes, *The Rise of Secularism in Turkey* (Montreal: McGill University Press, 1964); Donald Quataert, *The Ottoman Empire to 1922* (Cambridge: Cambridge University Press, 2001).

66. Specialists generally reserve the term *tanzimat* to denote the military reforms of 1839 to 1856. Here I employ it to refer more broadly to the nineteenth century as a whole (see below).

67. On the nineteenth century, see Resat Kesaba, *The Ottoman Empire and the World Economy: The Nineteenth Century* (Albany: State University of New York Press, 1988); Şevket Pamuk, *The Ottoman Empire and European Capitalism, 1820–1913* (Cambridge: Cambridge University Press, 1987); Charles Issawi, *An Economic History of the Middle East and North Africa* (New York: Columbia University Press, 1982); Roger Owen, *The Middle East in the World Economy* (London: Methuen, 1981). See also William R. Polk and Richard Chambers, *The Beginnings of Modernization in the Middle East* (Chicago: University of Chicago Press, 1968).

68. Antoine Picon, *L'invention de l'ingénieur moderne: L'École des Ponts et Chaussées, 1747–1851* (Paris: Presses de l'École des Ponts et Chaussées, 1992); Jean-Pierre Callot, *Histoire de l'École Polytechnique* (Paris: Charles Lavauzelle, 1982); Terry Shinn, *Savoir scientifique et pouvoir sociale: L'École Polytechnique, 1794–1914* (Paris: Presses de la Fondation Nationale des Sciences Politiques, 1980).

69. William Willcocks, *Sixty Years in the East* (Edinburgh: William Blackwood & Sons Ltd., 1935). The United States Military Academy at West Point was also originally modeled on the École Polytechnique.

70. Philippe Régnier, *Les saint-simoniens et Égypte, 1833–1851* (Cairo: Banque de l'Union Européenne, 1989).

71. Magali Morsy, ed., *Les saint-simoniens et l'Orient: Vers la modernité* (Aix-en-Provence: Edisud, 1989).

72. Morsy, *Les saint-simoniens et l'Orient.*

73. On the history of the engineering profession in Egypt, see J. Heyworth-Dunne, *An Introduction to the History of Education in Modern Egypt* (London: Cass, 1968); Clement Henry Moore, *Images of Development: Egyptian Engineers in Search of Industry* (Cambridge, MA: MIT Press, 1980); Joseph Szyliowicz, *Education and Modernization in the Middle East* (Ithaca, NY: Cornell University Press, 1973); and Bill Williamson, *Education and Social Change in Egypt and Turkey* (London: Macmillan, 1987). See also Ghislaine Alleaume, "Linant de Bellefonds (1799–1883) et le Saint-Simonisme en Égypte," in Morsy, *Les saint-simoniens et l'Orient,* 113–32; and *L'École Polytechnique du Caire et ses élèves: La formation d'une élite technique dans l'Égypte du XIXe siècle* (PhD diss., Université de Lyon II, 1993).

74. Moore, *Images of Development,* 4–11.

75. Anousheh Karvar, "Les polytechniciens étrangers et les mouvements nationaux," *Revue de l'Occident musulman et de la Méditerrannée* 73–74 (1994): 120–26.

76. Alleaume, "Linant de Bellefonds," 125–27.

77. Afaf Lutfi al-Sayyid Marsot, *Egypt in the Reign of Muhammad Ali* (Cambridge: Cambridge University Press, 1984).

78. Roger Owen, *Cotton and the Egyptian Economy, 1820–1914* (Oxford: Oxford University Press, 1969); Alan Richards, *Egypt's Agricultural Development, 1800–1980* (Boulder, CO: Westview Press, 1982).

79. Owen, *Cotton and the Egyptian Economy,* 28–57.

80. On the restructuring of the global cotton market in the nineteenth century, see Sven Beckert, "Emancipation and Empire: Reconstructing the World Wide Web of Cotton Production in the Age of the American Civil War," *American Historical Review* 109, no. 5 (December 2004): 1405–38.

81. Richards, *Egypt's Agricultural Development.* For an attempt to situate these changes in a global perspective, see Beckert, "Emancipation and Empire."

82. Richards, *Egypt's Agricultural Development;* John Waterbury, *Hydropolitics of the Nile Valley* (Syracuse, NY: Syracuse University Press, 1979), 31–33.

83. William Willcocks, *Egyptian Irrigation* (London: E. & F.N. Spon, 1913).

84. Waterbury, *Hydropolitics,* 35–37.

85. Abdel Rahman Sharkawi, *Egyptian Earth* (Austin: University of Texas Press, 1990).

86. Thousands of Egyptians perished in the 1877 drought. See Mike Davis, *Late Victorian Holocausts: El Niño Famines and the Making of the Third World* (London: Verso, 2001), 103–5.

87. On the effect of the Aswan Dam, see J. Donald Hughes, "Ripples in Clio's Pond: The Dams at Aswan; Does Environmental History Inform Decisions?" *Capitalism, Nature, Socialism* 11 (December 2000): 73–81. On the decline of Egyptian fisheries, see Ray Bush and Amal Sabri, "Mining for Fish: Privatization of the 'Commons' along Egypt's Northern Coastline," *Middle East Report* 216 (Fall 2000): 20–23, 45.

88. Daniel Hillel, *Rivers of Eden: The Struggle for Water and the Quest for Peace in the Middle East* (Oxford: Oxford University Press, 1994).

89. Hillel, *Rivers of Eden.*

90. For a long view of Iraqi irrigation schemes, see Willcocks, *Sixty Years in the East,* and Hillel, *Rivers of Eden.*

91. Paul Berthier, *Les anciennes sucreries du Maroc et leurs reseaux hydrauliques,* 2 vols. (Rabat: Imprimeries Françaises et Marocaines, 1966); Will D. Swearingen, *Moroccan Mirages: Agrarian Dreams and Deceptions, 1912–1986* (Princeton: Princeton University Press, 1987).

92. Will D. Swearingen, "Is Drought Increasing in Northwest Africa? A Historical Analysis," in Swearingen and Bencherifa, *North African Environment,* 117–33.

93. Swearingen ("Is Drought Increasing?" 127) notes that barley, the predominant native cereal, has a 30 percent lower soil-moisture requirement than wheat, ripens faster, and can be harvested earlier, and is therefore less vulnerable to summer heat and drought.

94. Swearingen, *Moroccan Mirages.*

95. George Perkins Marsh, *Man and Nature* (Cambridge, MA: Harvard University Press, 1965).

96. Theodore Woolsey and William Greeley, *Studies in French Forestry* (New York: John Wiley & Sons, Inc., 1920); Richard H. Grove, *Green Imperialism: Colonial Expansion, Tropical Island Edens and the Origins of Environmentalism, 1600–1860* (Cambridge, U.K.: White Horse Press, 1995); S. Ravi Rajan, "Foresters and the Politics of Colonial Agroecology: The Case of Shifting Cultivation and Soil Erosion, 1920–1950," *Studies in History* 14, no. 2, n.s. 1 (1998): 218–36.

97. Diana Davis, "Environmentalism as Social Control? An Exploration of the Transformation of Pastoral Nomadic Societies," *Arab World Geographer* 3, no. 3 (2000): 182–98.

98. More recently, the California model has come to look increasingly like a Faustian bargain, as siltation and salinization in the southwestern United States have led to a long-term pattern of decreased yields in large areas of the Colorado River basin. See Marc Reisner, *Cadillac Desert: The American West and Its Disappearing Water* (New York: Viking, 1986).

99. Swearingen, *Moroccan Mirages* and "Is Drought Increasing?"

100. Michael H. Glantz, ed., *Drought Follows the Plow: Cultivating Marginal Areas* (Cambridge: Cambridge University Press, 1994).

101. Christensen, *Decline of Iranshahr*, 249.

102. Richard Manning, *Against the Grain: How Agriculture Has Hijacked Civilization* (New York: North Point Press, 2004), provides a particularly tonic polemic. See also David Pimentel et al., "Food Production and the Energy Crisis," *Science* 182 (November 1973): 443–49, and Barry Commoner, *The Closing Circle* (New York: Bantam, 1971).

103. For recent surveys of the Middle East environment, see the home pages of the World Resource Institute (www.wri.org), and Worldwatch Institute (www.worldwatch.org). See also the reports of RAED, the Arab Network of NGOs for Development, which copublishes the *Sustainable Mediterranean Newsletter* with the Mediterranean Information Office (www.mio-ecsde.org).

104. For the very long-term perspective, see John R. McNeill and William McNeill, *The Human Web* (New York: W. W. Norton, 2002); and Christian, *Maps of Time*.

105. The first recorded instance of the large-scale use of gunpowder weapons in the Mediterranean occurred in the twelfth century, when they were employed by the Almoravids against their Iberian Christian rivals. Later, using this technology, the Ottomans were able to lay siege to Vienna twice between 1500 and 1800. Hassan and Hill, *Islamic Technology*, 106–20.

FIVE

The Transformation of China's
Environment, 1500–2000

KENNETH POMERANZ

CHINA'S ENVIRONMENT AND THE
DEVELOPMENTALIST PROJECT

China has often served as the supposed antithesis of Western environmental trends.
Sometimes it has been praised (for example, for careful, loving attention to the soil
or for Maoist indifference to materialism); at other times it has been damned (for
improvident pronatalism or for a Stalinist obsession with heavy industry). More
recently, writers have argued that China has not proved very different in the long
run: it has adopted Western-style, consumerist notions of the good life, and a combination of foreign technologies, market discipline, and a role for the state that
emphasizes fostering economic growth. Its environmental challenges are therefore
held to be much like those faced by the West—though more severe because of its
large population—and its responses to them will be shaped largely by engineers,
economists, and other technocrats, guided by essentially the same algorithms that
are used elsewhere. The rise of that elite in the twentieth century is thus the big
story of environmental management in China, and most of the rest of Chinese
history—both before the emergence of modern industry and during the Maoist
period—is seen as either largely irrelevant to how these issues are now addressed
or relevant only as a set of costly detours.

This essay takes a different view. I argue for long-term continuities that shaped
Chinese approaches to economic development and environmental management or

have done so until the very recent past. These include: (1) a preference for keeping large numbers of people in the countryside, and for encouraging rural industry (whether manual or mechanized), rather than separating a purely agricultural countryside from industrial cities; (2) notions of statecraft in which the central government actively props up regions in which the ability to live a normative family life is economically and ecologically vulnerable, while intervening less in the economies of richer areas (except to tax them); and (3) a set of material conditions powerfully shaped by these notions that has given environmental protection a rather different significance in China than in liberal traditions. Much of the liberal version of the developmentalist project (see the introduction to this volume) has indeed been adopted in China over the past century—and some components of it, such as widespread reliance on price-setting markets, date from centuries earlier (without, of course, having been part of any self-conscious liberalism until recently). Nonetheless, the long-term continuities I list above have always colored China's version of this project in environmentally significant ways. Overall, then, Chinese development in the imperial past was not as radically different from stylized Western paths as has often been suggested, and it has not become as similar to them in recent years as many people claim.

THE LIBERAL/DEVELOPMENTALIST PROJECT AND ITS CHINESE MODIFICATIONS: A VIEW FROM THE LATE EMPIRE

The "liberal project" at issue here does not describe the totality of any actual historical experience; it is a model invoked (often unconsciously) by many historical actors and modern scholars, encompassing certain goals and processes that have surfaced around the world in recent centuries. It emphasizes the economic, "developmental" facets of liberalism that became especially prominent in the nineteenth and twentieth centuries, and the idea that useful knowledge creates power that can be mobilized to transform nature in pursuit of material benefit for people. "Material benefit" is measured largely by levels of individual consumption, and to a lesser extent by the political status and security of a national state in which people are presumed to have a stake. (Late nineteenth-century Chinese, drawing on an ancient vocabulary to translate these goals as they found them in the works of various Western liberal thinkers, reduced them to *fu qiang*, or "wealth and power.")[1]

Aside from these goals, this version of liberalism has little to say about what the good life is: it does not favor particular gender roles, forms of worship, or concepts of beauty except as they are related to these economic and political ends. (By taking no stance on the relative merits of what people choose to consume, this form of liberalism also makes it harder to justify any particular distributional claims: for instance, the argument that adding a dollar to one person's income will do more good that adding it to that of somebody else, except insofar as different actors may have different propensities to invest their resources in ways that further advance the accumulation of wealth or national goals, such as military defense.) Moreover, political values that were axiomatic to classical liberalism—self-determination, public discussion, and the consent of the governed—are at best secondary, and are often sacrificed to the growth-oriented calculations of technocrats. Only with this very substantial proviso can one speak of any modern Chinese regime—or of many others around the world—as being influenced by a "liberal project." It is for this reason, that, in the introduction to this volume, I speak instead of a less specific, older, and more widely pursued "developmentalist project." However, with the growth of Western power from the late eighteenth century onward, specifically liberal versions of developmentalism have become especially important, often in places far outside liberalism's historic home. In what follows, I continue to refer to a *developmentalist* project when describing a more general commitment to increasing production, state revenues, and so on, that dates back to (at least) early modern times, but I use the more specific *liberal project* to provide a point of comparison for various Chinese strategies and dilemmas, particularly in the past two centuries.

Put crudely, this liberal project's account of its own environmental history goes something like this: "First people learn how to run roughshod over nature; then they get rich; then they clean up." Further, the argument suggests that after increased technological power and the decline of old taboos (often linked to religious life purposes that liberalism displaces) allow people to achieve material prosperity, people's preferences shift; they become more willing and able to pay for preserving and restoring nature. But because the pressures from both a revenue-hungry state and self-interested, market-oriented individuals to use resources profitably are so powerful, these other values can be served only by creating legal preserves from which market mechanisms are excluded. Thus the state, which had previously helped to break down customary barriers to the complete commodification of resources, later intervenes (usually in the name of the nation) to decommodify some resources and remove them from regular use; it also insists that those who degrade resources that are in regular use (such as the air and water in populated areas) pay at least some of the costs of restoring their quality.

By contrast with this imagined sequence, the Chinese state has long intervened for environmental purposes. Moreover, those purposes were generally seen as part of sustaining particular kinds of economic activity, rather than either making resources available for whatever use the market might dictate or removing them from the market entirely. The creation of barriers to any intensive use has generally occurred only in border regions with large minority populations, where it was felt that more intensive development might be culturally and strategically destabilizing. In China proper, environmental policy has focused on supporting access for all to some resources considered central to subsistence and on setting priorities among competing uses that promote specific kinds of production felt to be socially and culturally uplifting. These considerations have interacted with each other, with both liberal and other forms of the developmentalist project, and with the needs of the state itself in constantly shifting ways; but they have never become irrelevant.

The Chinese state has been involved in ecological management for many centuries. Karl Wittfogel's theory of "oriental despotism," based on government control of a "hydraulic society," has long been discredited, but it retains some kernels of truth. Water control has been a consistent concern, especially in north China, where limited and irregular rainfall makes agriculture risky without irrigation, and the Yellow River poses a chronic flood threat. (Other ecological problems have also been significant, but this essay concentrates on water.) Although the state has not been nearly as consistently or deeply involved in water control as historians once believed, it has always been involved in some important projects, and its visions of a good environmental and economic order have often set the tone for other actors.

Through much of the late imperial period, those visions involved economic development, but along lines very different from those of the "liberal project." Essentially, Ming and Qing leaders saw economic activity as providing the material underpinnings for the social and cultural practices through which people fulfilled their essential nature. This undertaking required stable family life and could be most broadly realized in a world of independent farming households. Agriculture not only provided material sustenance but also involved people in bringing to fruition processes initiated by heaven—an essential part of the role of humans in the cosmos, which in a sense made work and worship one. This agrarianism did not imply a vision of complete local self-sufficiency, as it sometimes did elsewhere; Ming and especially Qing statesmen understood the advantages of the division of labor and often gave markets a considerable role in securing subsistence for the largest possible number of people. Nevertheless, the market and economic production were not ends in themselves: they helped facilitate the Confucian good life for as many people as possible. Sustained per capita growth was therefore of much less interest than some combination of aggregate growth and distributive guarantees that would ensure everyone sufficient economic means to live in accordance with certain values: accumulation in itself was not a measure of human fulfillment or the merits of a society.

This economic vision created a particular idea of environmental management in which the central task within China proper was the reproduction of the material basis of modest agrarian prosperity in ever-more precarious ecological conditions, as Chinese settlers moved up hillsides, pressed closer to riverbanks, lowered water tables, and moved onto marginal lands. Meanwhile, environmental policy for many (though not all) non-Han areas sought to ensure that any reshaping of the landscape and economy occurred gradually, if at all.[2] Chinese economic and environmental policy still bears the stamp of these ideas.

There are at least two other ways of conceptualizing the intersection of the Chinese environment, economy, and state. The first assumes a long-standing interest in manipulating both environment and economy to increase state power, particularly military power. One example of such efforts is the Grand Canal, more than one thousand miles long. It was built, at considerable cost to the normal drainage of some rivers, to carry southern grain to capitals placed, for strategic reasons, on a northern plain too poor to feed large urban populations. Other examples include the colonies of farmer-soldiers (and supporting irrigation works) created on marginal lands that might otherwise fall to nomads in the northwest; the insistence on local self-sufficiency in grain (at enormous cost to the soil in some places) from the late 1950s through mid-1970s; and the drive to build inland industrial complexes at various points in the twentieth century. Although at times extremely destructive, these priorities have sometimes interacted more positively with the "reproductionist" emphasis on maintaining the bases of Chinese life in ecologically vulnerable areas, even if doing so required subsidies from richer areas.

In the second view, over the past century, the statist project and (less often) the reproductionist project have merged into the global "liberal project." As Chinese officials became increasingly aware of how industry increased state power in Europe, North America, and Japan, heavy industrial development became increasingly important in strategies for protecting the sovereignty of the state and (theoretically) the Chinese people. Slightly later, ideas of what was economically desirable for "the people" were altered by the liberal notion of limitless consumption creating ever-increasing utility, and environmental policy has increasingly reflected that end. With the increased prominence of the liberal project has come an increased role for technocrats and a diminished role for generalists chosen on grounds of supposed moral excellence, both in government per se and in the less-formal local bodies that often conceive and carry out water projects. Finally, the universalism of the liberal project and the perceived urgency of economic development has eroded (though not completely erased) the contrast in late imperial statecraft between promoting "peasantization" in truly internal colonies (for example, by helping Han Chinese move into the Guangdong and Guangxi highlands, often pushing out the Miao) and discouraging such projects in true border regions such as Manchuria or Xinjiang: development is now the assumed goal for territories from Tibet to Heilongjiang. Nonetheless, the liberal project in China has remained powerfully inflected by these older traditions of political economy and political ecology, in ways that have produced distinctly Chinese variations on global predicaments.

LATE IMPERIAL WATER POLICY

By 1420 the Ming dynasty had survived a violent founding and succession struggle and put in place many of the environmentally crucial features of late imperial statecraft. The regime's primary capital was in Beijing, on the north China plain, not in the economic heartland of the lower Yangzi valley (see map 5.1). Beijing required large amounts of southern grain, to be shipped either along the coast (with the route shortened a bit by cutting a canal across the Shandong peninsula), or by the Grand Canal.[3] The sea route was cheaper and involved less commitment to centrally managed water projects. The inland route offered greater military security. Initially the Ming wished to maintain both systems, but by the mid-fifteenth century, coastal shipping of tribute grain had virtually disappeared, and the inland waterway system became an ever-greater commitment.[4]

It is tempting to place this policy shift in the context of a general Ming retreat from the sea, with the prime example being the suspension of Zheng He's voyages of exploration in the 1430s. Some historians have gone still further and seen the Ming as marking a fateful turn toward xenophobia (particularly as compared to the Mongols' cosmopolitan Yuan dynasty), anticommercial agrarian fundamentalism, or both. These characterizations seem overstated, even for the fifteenth century; and certainly sixteenth-century China saw both an extraordinary commercial boom and a great increase in contacts with foreigners. But in other ways, the Grand Canal did cement a political-economic orientation that remained crucial until at least the 1850s. It focused more on reproducing the Chinese empire, and on managing the

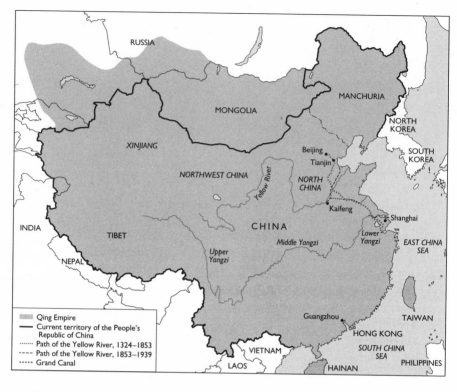

MAP 5.1.
China.

empire's vast ecological and economic differences, than on gaining control over external resources.

Though Ming statesmen were powerfully aware of threats from Central Asian nomads, their most crucial task was to contain internal threats to their power. These took two principal forms: mass movements of the discontented poor (such as the one their founder, Zhu Yuanzheng, had ridden to power), and interference with monarchic power by wealthy and culturally empowered elites (many of whom served in the government's bureaucracy).[5] The latter threat was localized in the rich and populous Yangzi delta. The former was most serious in various poorer parts of the country, above all north China, which combined a dense population with serious flood and drought problems; and northwest China, much of which was agriculturally marginal, and which occupied a transitional zone between the Central Asian khanates and the north China heartland.

In these ecologically fragile zones, Ming and especially Qing policy provided a variety of subsidies for family farming. (In some parts of the northwest, these families were descendants of farmer-soldiers, but in most places they were freeholders.) Lucrative salt-monopoly contracts were granted to merchants willing to ship grain to deficit regions of the Northwest.[6] Settlement of sparsely populated zones was encouraged through grants of land, loans, seed, and information.[7] Well digging was subsidized at various times and places.[8] Land-tax rates were low, and reclaimed land was often left off the tax rolls entirely.[9] The civilian granary system—which provided both a cushion against harvest failure and loans to smooth out seasonal supply and price fluctuations—received far more state support in poorer regions, particularly in the north.[10] In the Qing dynasty, strong efforts were also made to encourage sericulture and cotton handicrafts in these regions, both to provide farm families with an additional source of income and to help instill among the area's women the diligence and other qualities deemed necessary for proper family life.[11]

The Grand Canal and Yellow River were central to this statecraft, though in ways that were probably not fully understood at first. Moving north from the Yangzi delta, the canal had to cross the Yellow River almost at right angles on its way to Beijing. Without effective control of the Yellow River, the canal was useless. Too strong a current would block or flood the canal; dike breaks upstream would lead to too little water being fed into the canal, and perhaps water trying to enter the canal bed at the wrong places. And because the canal was the "throat of Beijing"—southern tribute grain probably accounted for more than half the capital's food supply in the mid-eighteenth century (before significant development of grain production in southern Manchuria), and still for one-third in the mid-nineteenth century[12]—allowing it to be blocked was unthinkable. Consequently, residents of the north China plain were to be protected from major floods at virtually any cost. (The exception to this policy was the last two hundred miles of the river, after it crossed the canal; this was, indeed, the least protected part of the riverbank until the twentieth century.) The bill was paid by Yangzi delta taxpayers (and those of a few other wealthy areas) through a surcharge on the grain tribute. That surcharge covered the cost of transporting the grain to Beijing; most of it went for Yellow River control and Grand Canal maintenance. By 1821, these costs had risen fivefold since 1732, and maintenance of the Grand Canal and Yellow River consumed between 10 and 20 percent of total government spending (not including a huge amount of corvée labor).[13]

Most work on the Yangzi, on the other hand, was organized and paid for by local elites, with limited oversight from local officials. In effect, the elites of the lower Yangzi received a fair amount of autonomy—which allowed them, within broad limits, to shape flood control so that it benefited their reclamation, irrigation, and transportation goals—in return for bearing the costs of keeping their poorer northern compatriots (literally) above water.

This is not to say that the system cost northerners nothing. Receiving central government largesse meant subordination to central government priorities. It was illegal for farmers to cultivate land behind the first set of barriers but within the outer walls along the Yellow River, or to withdraw water from the canal for irrigation (both of which they did regularly after 1850, when central control weakened). Canal work blocked the flow of various local streams, creating problems of waterlogged and saline soil (as Gu Yanwu had already noted in the 1640s). Supply requisitions and corvée labor were sometimes quite burdensome.[14] But overall, the area benefited from far more effective flood control than it ever could have paid for on its own, and from a north-south transport artery that it otherwise would have lacked. (The latter, among other things, facilitated imports of wood and stone, allowing areas along the canal to support more people than they could have if they had had to be self-sufficient in such land-intensive products.)

Overall, then, the effects on rural north China of provisioning Beijing this way contrast sharply with the economic and ecological pain inflicted on the hinterlands of many other early modern capitals, such as Madrid, Berlin, and Paris.[15] In the region immediately surrounding the capital, the canal also exacerbated some drainage problems, but the state more than compensated for these, lavishing funds on flood control, irrigation, and efforts to stabilize both urban and rural food prices.[16]

For the state, the system had obvious benefits—and some less-obvious benefits and costs. It fed the capital and stabilized strategic north China; it did not require elaborate naval defenses; and it fitted the conventional understanding of imperial benevolence and the virtues of rural life. (North China, a land of small freehold farms, in some ways fitted the Chinese rural ideal better than the wealthy lower Yangzi, which had more cities and higher tenancy rates.) The system also helped contain the power of lower-Yangzi elites, whom both Ming and Qing rulers found threatening. (For the same reason, quotas limited the number of civil service exam winners from the lower Yangzi.) Not only did it take away some of their wealth, which otherwise sustained lifestyles that some Ming and Qing rulers found dangerously decadent; it also focused their managerial attentions on local projects rather than central government concerns.

At the same time, the state sacrificed some of its ability to intervene in the ecology of some of its richest areas. By the end of the eighteenth century, local projects designed to reclaim and irrigate additional farmland were seriously overbuilt along various parts of the Yangzi, leading to increased flooding and other ecological problems.[17] The difficulties were quite apparent both to the government itself and to members of a few of the most exalted families of the Yangzi delta (whose interests in the continued health of the bureaucracy, the dynasty, the tax base, and overall social stability tended to outweigh the narrower interests they shared with other local landowners). But all efforts to eliminate counterproductive private dikes failed, as did efforts to reform tax collection and generate more money for government-managed water control.[18] Although the state had some limited success in curbing land clearance in the Yangzi highlands, which was carried on by much poorer people, this clearance probably contributed less to flooding than did reclamation by lowland elites, whom the state found it could not check.[19]

This system of reproductive statecraft was increasingly undermined by large-scale demographic, economic, and ecological developments, which were partly due to its successes. Beginning in the sixteenth century, the lower Yangzi and other parts of coastal China entered a long period of commercialization and economic growth (as did much of the rest of north Africa, Europe, and Asia); although the middle to late seventeenth century brought a serious contraction, growth resumed at an even faster pace in the eighteenth century. By roughly 1750, the delta had a population of roughly five hundred people per square kilometer (compared with roughly sixty-two for the Netherlands), with one of the highest standards of living in the world.[20]

Much of this prosperity came from the extraordinary productivity of well-managed rice paddies in a generally favorable setting. Some also came from very efficient resource-saving strategies: efficient stoves, stir-frying rapidly in very thin cookware, minimal use of large animals for traction, very labor-intensive fuel gathering, and so on. But it also depended on large imports of primary products: grain, raw cotton, timber, sugar, and soybeans (mostly for beancake fertilizer).[21] In return, the delta exported manufactured goods (mostly cloth); some adjacent prefectures, which were similarly import-dependent and nearly as prosperous, specialized in salt and related products.

The scale of these trades dwarfed any other eighteenth-century commerce in bulky products.[22] Being essential to the Yangzi delta's prosperity, they also allowed it to keep subsidizing other regions.

LIMITS OF GROWTH—AND OF LATE
IMPERIAL STATECRAFT

Even the Yangzi delta's remarkable trade networks could not meet expanding needs forever: markets, state, culture, and the outside world all saw to that. Export opportunities and general commercialization led to accelerated population growth (through both immigration and natural increase) in key peripheries, and population growth ultimately cut into the surplus of primary products that the region could export. Moreover, several of these peripheries began to produce their own handicrafts. North China, which used to export most of its raw cotton, began to spin and weave it locally once people figured out how to keep the thread from snapping during the arid months; the middle Yangzi and upper Yangzi began to grow more cotton (as well as tea and, later, opium) and produce their own cloth.[23]

This change was partly a market-driven process of shifting comparative advantage. As the very best rice land filled up, the most accessible forests were cut down, and a growing local population made specialization more economical, some labor was bound to switch from primary products to handicrafts, and having more people in the area who were not food producers was bound to decrease export surpluses. In a world in which most technology was embodied in fairly cheap, easy-to-copy machines, and where transport costs rose steeply with distance from the riverbank, such developments represented reasonable responses to the market, not any sort of market failure or institutional blockage to the further industrialization of the core. Indeed, I have argued at length elsewhere that it was Western Europe's peripheries in Eastern Europe and the Americas which had institutional blockages (serfdom, slavery, colonial monopolies) that inhibited such developments and so prolonged their export orientation.[24] More-open markets tended to spread protoindustrialization more evenly across the landscape—furthering the Ming-Qing reproductive vision at considerable cost to the Yangzi delta's chances for further specialization and industrial growth.

But the state did not just leave such things to the market. Tax structures, support for migration, and other policies favored growth in peripheries, often at the expense of the most advanced areas. The Qing promotion of silk and cotton handicraft by women is one example. Most Chinese families also believed that work that allowed women to produce income for the family without leaving the courtyard was preferable to work that exposed them to others (including field labor). This was another reason why, as peripheral regions became more prosperous, they did not put all available labor into maximizing output of farm products for export and continue to import cloth, even though in some regions (especially in the middle Yangzi) additional labor inputs could still have raised yields and price trends increasingly favored agriculture over handicrafts. Under the circumstances, per capita growth in advanced regions ceased, and population growth in these regions lagged far behind the average. The Yangzi delta's population was almost unchanged from 1770 to 1850, whereas China's population as a whole almost doubled.[25]

The relatively dense settlement of China's internal peripheries before the onset of modern growth, combined with an overall size that has made it difficult to rely on imports for a large share of primary products, has meant that the "first get rich, then clean up" approach to economic development and environmental protection is probably not an adequate option for China: policy has had to focus much more on preventing waste and balancing different resource demands during industrialization, without the luxury of placing large areas (except perhaps in the non-Han far west) off limits to all but very low-intensity recreational use. (It is also true, as Nicholas Menzies has pointed out, that Chinese thought has rarely placed much value on completely unused "wilderness" and sees wild lands as linked to wild people, fit perhaps for non-Han areas that should not be changed too rapidly for political reasons, but not for China proper.)[26]

In the short run, the slowing of growth in core regions did not make it any easier for them to bear the fiscal burdens that helped stabilize ecologies elsewhere in the empire, burdens that rose as population grew in less advanced regions. Serious deforestation in northwest China, for instance, increased erosion along the upper reaches of the Yellow River, which already bore a heavier silt burden per cubic meter of water than any other major river in the world (34 times heavier than the Nile's and 3.4 times worse than that of the very muddy Colorado).[27]

Meanwhile, the political underpinnings of Grand Canal and Yellow River management helped to ensure that the work would be done each year, but not very efficiently. It was understood that the canal must be kept functioning at virtually any cost (at least until the grain tribute got through), but the state lacked both the technical means and the grass-roots presence necessary to keep the Yellow River channel thoroughly dredged (still an extremely difficult task). Instead officials reinforced the walls along the river and built them higher each year as sediment raised the bed. By the early nineteenth century, the last four hundred miles of the river bed lay as much as forty feet above the land outside the walls. (Another part of the river-control strategy that was adopted—setting the walls far apart—increased the rate of sedimentation further, because it allowed the river to meander.)[28]

Thus any flood could go many miles before finding a new channel; the potential consequences increased the urgency of preventing it at any cost. Consequently, large dike-reinforcement projects were undertaken every year, along with periodic projects that involved more fundamental rebuilding; and getting the job done was much more important than scrutinizing and minimizing costs.[29] Between 1820 and 1850, annual repairs on the Yellow River and Grand Canal were consuming perhaps 12 percent of central-government spending, in addition to heavy expenses borne by local people. Many ancien régime states spent less than this on all projects combined, other than war, debt service, and maintaining the court.[30] The price of shipping a load of tribute rice to the north rose roughly 500 percent between 1700 and 1820, and the cost was borne almost entirely by Yangzi valley taxpayers.[31]

Other pressures were also growing. Despite Qing efforts to keep most of the northeast as a hunting preserve where Manchus could be Manchus, a good deal of southern Manchuria was cleared by Han farmers during the seventeenth, eighteenth, and early nineteenth centuries: after first felling the trees and exporting the logs, these settlers began exporting large amounts of soybeans to the Yangzi delta, mostly as fertilizer for the cotton fields.[32] By the early 1800s, they were also shipping large amounts of grain to Beijing, supplying perhaps as much as one-third of the capital's food supply by 1850.[33] Meanwhile, the boats that took soybeans to the Yangzi delta and cloth and iron goods to Manchuria had a lot of empty space on the northward journey (as manufactured goods occupied less space than an equal value of soybeans). This space was used to carry grain tribute when emergencies blocked the canal (as they did in 1820, 1824, and 1826).[34] Some increasingly assertive Yangzi delta elites wanted to see this transport become routine.[35] In short, more market-driven ways of feeding Beijing were emerging and gaining adherents. But abandoning the canal could have been environmentally devastating for north China, and such a switch did not *have* to be made—until, that is, foreign incursions and internal rebellions changed the nature of the Chinese state.

The Taiping Rebellion (1851–64) was the largest of four huge midcentury uprisings and probably the most destructive civil war in history. It deprived the central government of firm control over its richest region for twelve years. Rebuilding Yangzi valley society after the war was felt to require massive tax cuts for the region. These cuts successfully brought wealthy people (many of whom had fled to Shanghai during the war) back to smaller cities and towns and, to a lesser extent, villages; these incentives also encouraged returning elites to rebuild irrigation works, schools, and temples, and to resume a leadership role in society.[36] Here, in contrast to poorer regions, there was no thought of the government itself taking control of these functions: indeed, both the defeat of the rebels (which depended heavily on locally raised forces after central government armies largely failed) and the task of reconstruction considerably increased the control of local elites over Yangzi valley society.[37] Nevertheless, such tax cuts were possible only if the grain-tribute burden was significantly reduced, which in turn required abandoning the commitment to the Grand Canal–Yellow River system. Meanwhile, maintenance had lapsed during the wars; enormous floods followed, which moved the mouth of the Yellow River more than three hundred miles north, left much of the Grand Canal without a source of water, and made restoring (as opposed to simply maintaining) the old system even more expensive.

While this shift in priorities tore at reproductive statecraft from within, other forces tore at it from without. As China faced increasing pressure from foreign powers over the next several decades (pressures which had also helped unleash the Taiping Rebellion), it became clear that survival in a world of competitive nations and empires required industrial development; and heavily commercialized, primarily coastal areas seemed most suited to industrialization. Moreover, treaty ports and foreign concessions threatened Qing sovereignty over some of these very areas, and that threat was exacerbated by real (or perceived) inadequacies in public services. Westerners used problems in policing and road work as excuses to expand the areas they controlled around Shanghai; Japanese and Russian forces threatened to seize more of Manchuria if modern public-health measures were not instituted (and epidemics controlled before they threatened foreign interests), and Japan later threatened to seize areas near the mouth of the Yellow River (again, near existing concessions) if flood control was not improved.[38]

In this environment, twentieth-century Chinese nationalists began to assess all sorts of Chinese problems in relationship to China's struggles with imperialism. Thus, for instance, twentieth-century forestry officials announced that the priority areas for reforestation would be those near railroad lines (for obvious reasons) and those near the coast that were currently "wasting" foreign exchange by importing wood.[39] (One publication estimated how much of China's heavily mortgaged rail system could be bought back from foreign banks with the money "wasted" in this way; Sun Yat-sen, noting that some imported wood was used for coffins, wrote about the humiliation of being dependent on foreigners even in death.)[40] Inland areas, where shortages were taking a much higher human toll—in part precisely because residents could not import wood, in part because the regions had become overpopulated during the days of ecological subsidization—were almost totally ignored.[41]

The new statecraft changed Yellow River work in two ways. First, river-control funds in general were sharply reduced, especially after 1890; this money went directly to debt service, military modernization, and a series of "modernizing" projects on the coast (such as deepening harbors). Second, the remaining flood-control money went to different locations. More money was spent on protecting newly strategic areas near the coast and near railroad crossings; once-favored poor areas were abandoned. And the strategy worked, in a narrow sense: flooding was reduced sharply in the places that mattered most to China's battles with foreign powers. But flooding in inland areas reached its worst levels on record.[42]

For the most part, this new statecraft—and new patterns of environmental disaster—held from the late nineteenth century into the 1930s. Relatively accessible regions suffered various traumas, to be sure, but did not fare too badly in ecological terms: foreign trade often provided new sources of land-intensive products; increased government solicitude (for both sovereignty-preserving and developmentalist reasons) helped considerably; and several of the private civic organizations emerging in more urbanized areas provided technical assistance, disaster relief, and other ecologically useful services. But for many interior areas (especially in north and northwest China), increased flooding was just part of a general downward ecological spiral that brought increasingly severe droughts and erosion (in part due to ever-greater deforestation in desperately fuel-short regions), increasing salinization of the soil (because changes in the Yellow River blocked drainage of local streams), and so on.

By the 1930s at least two incipient responses to that crisis had been formulated. The first was a largely technocratic one, which we might associate with the developmentalist project, and which envisioned large, multipurpose dams, river-basin-wide planning, and large-scale industrialization with substantial central government control. The second was a populist and restorationist response, which imagined a series of largely local, labor-intensive adjustments to enable people to restore a viable life based on farming, handicrafts, and petty commerce. Though neither proposal could get far amid the violence and chaos of the 1930s and 1940s, both had important influences on the new society and ecology that emerged after the Communists came to power in 1949.

The populist response—or rather responses—emerged among north China peasants faced with the need to sustain a subsistence income in increasingly degraded environments. Ecological decline and population pressure often meant that handicraft industry and commerce became increasingly important parts of the subsistence strategies of these peasants. In Wugong, Hebei, the problem of a falling water table (which caused total arable land to decline between 1740 and 1930) was accompanied by rising taxes, banditry, and other indicators of a state that took more and gave less to hinterland regions. Here, traditional local specialties of rope making and traveling to other villages to castrate pigs became even more important parts of the local economy (at least in part because they were relatively drought-resistant). These sidelines actually provided the key to survival for the village's misnamed "agricultural" cooperative, founded under the Communist aegis during the anti-Japanese war.[43]

Similarly, in parts of eastern Henan, increased salinization of the soil after the Yellow River shift rendered much of the land largely or completely useless for agriculture. But it facilitated a boom in bootleg salt production and later in various other sideline activities that used salt: tanning, pickling, and even the making of explosives. (China had a government salt monopoly, both under the empire and the Republic, which imported heavily taxed sea salt to this area.) Although these activities made the area more prosperous for a while, they also set it on a collision course with a reinvigorated state during the Nationalist period, because the new government, having pledged salt-monopoly revenues as security for foreign loans, became increasingly insistent and brutal in its enforcement of the monopoly. It was this clash with the state—more than either village-level class struggle or the Japanese invasion—that seems to have made this area a fertile base for the Communist revolution.[44]

Neither the peasants of eastern Henan nor their compatriots elsewhere in the north China base areas were thinking of a modernizing developmentalist project, in either its capitalist or state-socialist form. Their goals, instead, seem to have been to use increasing market participation to restore enough economic stability to secure their access to traditional ideas of the good life: the ability to marry, bury parents, and celebrate the annual ritual cycle appropriately. For a time, this threw them into the arms of the Chinese Communist Party (CCP), which provided crucial support against the Nationalists and Japanese, and which moved for a time in the direction of a populist, "peasant" agenda (downplaying or abandoning for the time being numerous other elements of its program, from rapid industrialization to collective farms to women's rights).[45] But in the longer run, the CCP was committed to a developmentalist agenda that often clashed with these populist initiatives—and had much greater affinity for the technocratic approach to environmental and other crises that had appeared in an earlier form during the Nationalist period.

The technocratic approach to river control owed much to foreign models, especially from the United States, Germany, and the Soviet Union. As William Kirby has shown, once the Nationalist Party (Guomindang, or GMD) had achieved some control over large portions of China, it organized engineers (most of them foreign-trained) into groups charged with planning for rapid industrialization, with an emphasis on defense-related heavy industry.[46] These groups were largely insulated from the political process and unconcerned with obtaining popular consent (much less enthusiasm) for their projects. Their ultimate goals resembled the new kinds of developmentalism that began to emerge in the late nineteenth century. However, the peculiar circumstances of the 1930s gave their projects some important new elements.

First, they envisioned a far more state-centered kind of development than before. The government would plan, build, and run major flood-control, irrigation, and hydroelectric facilities with virtually no local input; the resulting hydropower was to be allocated to new industries based on government priorities, not market mechanisms. This statism reflected a combination of factors. One factor was a set of then-prestigious foreign models—particularly those of the Soviet Union, World War I war economies (especially Germany's), and early Fascist regimes. Even the less-statist model of development planning represented by U.S. engineers and their students featured a very large role for the state in water projects. Moreover, despite the huge amounts of hydropower ultimately generated by water projects in the U.S. West, power generation was at first largely an afterthought there: because of the need to win support from farm constituencies, those projects initially emphasized flood control and irrigation (often in defiance of economic logic), which were of secondary interest to most Guomindang planners. A statist approach was also encouraged by the urgency of national defense planning in the face of growing Japanese pressures, the general state-building strategy of the GMD, and the undeniable fact that popular preferences would not have reflected government plans: hydropower, for instance, would certainly have run a poor fourth behind flood control, irrigation, and transportation.

Even where immediate crises required that priority be given to flood control, GMD water control planning was remarkable for its nonparticipatory nature. When the northern warlord regimes (not noted for their democratic commitments) had developed plans for rebuilding the Grand Canal and adjacent waterways in western Shandong between 1914 and 1920, the planners had solicited the ideas of local elites about what the top priorities should be. In response, they developed a plan that emphasized land reclamation and would be financed in large part by sales of and taxes on reclaimed land; they also delegated to a board of local elites substantial power to adjudicate existing claims on the land. Thus in many ways this plan (which was eventually scuttled by government financial problems and international politics) borrowed from late imperial patterns of management for local water-control projects (and medium-sized projects in richer regions). When the GMD turned to flood control in this area a decade later, their plan was developed without any local participation and financed largely through the use of corvée labor under the supervision of soldiers from outside the area; engineers dispatched from a provincial office were given absolute authority to settle all local conflicts (including land claims) related to the project; non-office-holding local elites seem not to have been consulted at all; and the role of local officials (from magistrates down to village heads) was largely restricted to allocating the corvée burden assigned to each jurisdiction.[47]

The preponderant role of military planning also meant that, in contrast with late Qing developmentalism, the Nationalist period saw a return (at least on paper) to interest in planning for development of the interior—particularly for developing a heavy-industrial complex (premised on hydropower) at a safe distance from Japanese forces. A centerpiece of these plans was a huge dam on the Three Gorges section of the Yangzi River. This idea, first broached by Sun Yat-sen in 1921, now began to be seriously planned; it remained an off-and-on state project (and a symbol of Chinese modernization) for years thereafter, was given the final go-ahead in 1989, and is now operational.[48] Parallel plans were developed for large multipurpose dams on the upper reaches of the Yellow River—dams with questionable benefits for the oft-flooded lower reaches of the river, but with far more energy potential than anything that could be done in the floodplain (by the time the Yellow River reaches Kaifeng, four hundred miles from the sea, the terrain is too flat for generating hydroelectricity).[49]

Because full-fledged war with Japan began in 1937, none of the larger projects sketched by GMD engineers were begun, but the period left some legacies for post-1949 water control. Basic surveying was carried out, archives of possible plans were created, and a system of assessing those plans based on supposedly neutral (though frequently manipulated) quantitative cost-benefit analyses was instituted. Moreover, many of the actual personnel who carried out the post-1949 projects gained their early professional experience and acquired lasting habits on these projects.[50] Although water-control policy—like all other policies in the People's Republic—has been marked by frequent twists and turns, there have been important continuities as well: continuities that reflect both this dominant technocratic tradition of development planning and elements of what I have termed the populist approach to development and environmental management. In the next section, I first sketch some of these general tendencies, and then examine them in the context of water control and related environmental policies.

THE PEOPLE'S REPUBLIC: (HOW) DID
THE REVOLUTION MATTER?

With the exception of a few "model" villages, there has been very little central investment or reinvestment of urban profits in the countryside since 1949; rural areas have been expected to generate and accumulate their own capital while also transferring some surplus to the cities (just a little in some periods, a great deal in others) to build industry.[51] A number of attempts have, however, been made to redistribute urban industry across China, building up heavy industrial centers (often based on hydropower) in various inland areas of China proper, while (during the Maoist and early reform years) taxing rich coastal cities disproportionately.[52]

Rural areas have frequently been encouraged to industrialize, usually by means of labor-intensive techniques, and migration from the countryside to the cities has been limited. It was almost completely forbidden from 1960 to the early 1980s and has been gradually, but still not completely, liberalized since then. There are a number of reasons for this approach. The regime has clearly feared the costs of building infrastructure for rapidly growing cities and sought to avoid the social consequences of the vast migrant-occupied shantytowns that ring many other Third World cities; it has also (until recently) sought to protect the living standards of urban workers—who held a special place in both the symbolism and the actual power base of the regime—from too much rural competition. (Before the 1980s, rural industries were generally required to concentrate on products for local use, in part for this reason.)[53] At the same time, the idea of increasing employment opportunities in the countryside—allowing people to "leave the land but not the countryside," as one slogan put it[54]—has also appealed to much of the peasant population, who would prefer not to have to choose between, for instance, better-paying jobs and being near their kin. The combination of agricultural and non-agricultural work in a given village (and, for that matter, a given family) has also done much to cushion income fluctuations.

Meanwhile, the regime has tried (with a few notable exceptions, such as persisting in catastrophic rates of appropriation despite disappointing harvests during the Great Leap Forward)[55] to place a floor under living standards for the very poor.

This effort was most obvious in the years of the most intensive collectivism, when only very limited income differences were permitted, but it remains a feature of the countryside today, despite growing income differentials between different parts of the country. Every family who wants it is still guaranteed access to some land, and to some supplies of vital inputs at subsidized prices; some villages require local industrial enterprises to spread jobs out among village families, to limit the income differential between their best- and worst-paid workers, to reinvest locally, and to subsidize social services (or sometimes simply incomes) for those in the village who continue to farm (an occupation which generally pays less than other work).[56] Though inequality among rural residents has risen dramatically since the beginning of the reforms, some recent data suggest that it may be starting to decline again, at least in more successful regions, as income from wages becomes more widely dispersed across an increasingly industrialized countryside. Moreover, it appears that the greatest inequalities throughout China are between different communities and regions rather than between households in a given place.[57] These data, too, suggest that local policies to limit inequality still matter, even in this much less egalitarian era.

Consequently, the countryside shows evidence of a number of different, even contradictory influences. Resource shortages are obvious; so are the legacies of Soviet-style capital accumulation at the expense of the countryside (for example, by keeping the prices received by farmers for grain artificially low). The concerns of traditional statecraft—with protecting subsistence, encouraging the spread of best economic practices across the landscape, and providing a supportive economic environment for a normative kind of rural family life—may be less apparent but remain important. So does a "populist" interest in ensuring that as many rural families as possible have the means to reproduce themselves and to engage in appropriate ritual activity. (The recent boom in rural prosperity has been accompanied by much higher spending on life-cycle rituals, much to the Party's consternation.)[58]

For water policy in particular, this convergence of influences has created an awkward, but sometimes productive, dance between central government and more local actors. The centralized bureaucracies charged with multipurpose, basin-wide planning for the Yellow River and Yangzi River, which carried over from the Nationalist period and were often staffed by Nationalist holdovers, have preferred highly capital-intensive projects using the most advanced engineering possible, and have tended to emphasize power generation above all else; large-scale irrigation projects (some of which would enable whole regions to switch to thirsty industrial crops like cotton) and urban water supply have ranked next in their priorities, and flood control is well down the list. The militarization of central-government water-control efforts—in some ways ongoing since the late Qing[59]—has reached new levels on some of these projects: since 1966, many of the largest projects have actually been carried out by a special Hydropower Command established within the People's Armed Police section of the People's Liberation Army.[60] The PLA is also legally responsible for leading emergency flood control: more than a million troops were involved in fighting the 1998 Yangzi floods.[61]

At times, these central organs also seem to have favored large state-of-the-art projects for the sake of national prestige and their own professional needs, even when they knew that the benefits would be quite limited. One of the most spectacular examples is the Sanmenxia dam and reservoir on the upper Yellow River. The People's Republic inherited various plans for upper Yellow River work, of which only one, developed by Japanese authorities during World War II, called for a dam at Sanmenxia during the first phase of work. Although such a dam would provide considerable hydropower so long as it survived, it was unanimously understood that unless more humdrum measures for erosion control (from reforestation to smaller upstream dams) were completed first, a Sanmenxia dam would silt up quickly and provide little or no lasting benefit: one scholar has described the Japanese proposal for such a project "patently exploitative."[62] Yet Soviet engineers developed a plan for such a dam in the 1950s, and after the Soviet withdrawal, Chinese authorities went ahead—in part, it seems, to prove that they could do so. The resulting dam silted up rapidly—it was 45 percent blocked within four years of completion—and continues to need complex and expensive additional work to compensate.[63]

The Three Gorges Dam—which most experts think is inferior to a series of smaller dams, even for the single purpose of hydropower—is another example.[64] As a project originally envisioned by Sun Yat-sen and blessed by Mao Zedong, it has been as much a symbol of national pride as a technical solution to specific problems: it hardly seems coincidental that after being shelved for several years, it was restored to priority status after the Tiananmen incident of 1989, or that the completion of each major stage of construction was the occasion for many hours of live television coverage.[65] It remains unclear how cost-effective it will turn out to be, but as of 2008, new environmental complications continue to surface, well after most of the construction has been finished. (One more phase, which will increase the dam's electrical-generation capacity, is scheduled to be completed in 2009; but the main structures have been in place since 1993, and the river has been dammed since 1997.) Another manifestation of the nationalist urge is the Yamdrok Tso project in Tibet, also rescued from mothballs in late 1989 (after both Tiananmen and the death of the Panchen Lama, a critic of the project). It is particularly striking because Tibet still seems many years away from needing its power, and no transmission grid exists capable of sending that power elsewhere.[66]

By contrast, local communities have generally been responsible for projects that focused on flood control or on less spectacular irrigation needs, such as reducing the violent annual fluctuations in water availability that have long plagued much of north and northwest China. These projects have generally used little capital but large amounts of labor and fairly simple technology, and they have remained under local management after completion.[67] Many consist of little more than a series of small local reservoirs linked by hand-dug canals: simple as they are, these "melons on a vine" enable villages to cushion themselves against local weather shocks and pool their risks with those faced by their neighbors. Other projects have involved the sinking of large numbers of locally funded tube wells. Because local water-control authorities have felt that the needed labor (especially for maintenance) would be forthcoming only if the benefits of the project were obvious, they have tended to concentrate on projects with immediate payoffs. (Contrary to myths of continued "oriental despotism," local authorities have generally not relied on command alone to mobilize people for water-control work, even during the Maoist period.)[68] Partly for the same reason, projects that would require the continued application of labor for a long-term payoff have generally been neglected by both central and local authorities, except during episodic campaigns.[69] (Soil conservation, as we shall see, has been spottily implemented despite the understanding of numerous engineers that more glamorous projects would soon be destroyed by silt without massive, sustained, erosion-control efforts; and although the scale of Chinese tree-planting mobilizations is legendary, relatively few seedlings receive the sustained attention that would allow them to survive.)[70]

Meanwhile, approaches to other problems have oscillated between state-sponsored megaprojects and locally funded initiatives more dependent on popular support. As far back as the 1950s, for instance, central planners were toying with the idea of an enormous project to divert billions of gallons of water per year from the Yangzi basin and south China (which accounts for 76 percent of the country's river discharge) to north and northwest China (with 51 percent of the cultivable land but only 7 percent of river discharge, and some of the worst water shortages in the world.) This project, now under way, is unprecedented in scale, with some versions calling for multiple dams in the deep, narrow gorges of the upper Yangzi, far higher than any now in existence. Aside from the possible ecological consequences of such a diversion, the enormous cost of the project seems to have scared Beijing, and the plan has been repeatedly delayed and modified. In the meantime, enormous amounts of well digging (aided by the coming of electric pumps), very small local reservoirs (designed to smooth fluctuations in supply), and other rural palliatives made the project appear unnecessary by the 1970s.[71] Various conservation measures in northern cities proved remarkably successful—particularly in light of the tendency for socialist economies with price ceilings on necessities to generate shortages—allowing the rural groundwater tapped by new wells to be used locally, despite considerable urban growth.[72]

Subsequently, however, the limits of these local solutions became more apparent, encouraging renewed interest in the south-north diversion scheme. Local reservoirs and irrigation ditches created with a minimum of outside capital tend to be lined with cheap material or not lined at all, and they have high rates of seepage: thus they provide a kind of disaster insurance, but at the price of significant waste.[73] Despite some impressive water-conservation measures, local projects have been unable to keep up with the needs of rapidly growing northern cities such as Tianjin and Beijing during the 1990s. The Beijing water table, for instance, fell eighteen feet in fifteen years—and then five feet further in 1997 alone.[74] (This rate roughly matches that at which the most severely overused parts of the Ogalala Aquifer in the United States are being depleted, but north China has a lot less margin for error.)[75] Consequently, the water-diversion megaprojects, with all their costs and risks, are now squarely back on the central government's agenda. The first stage of the Yangzi diversion project is now expected to be completed in 2010, though the largest and most complex scheme is still far in the future, slated for completion in 2050.[76] The results of these arrangements have been impressive, but at considerable social and ecological cost. It is also unclear how lasting some of the gains will be.

By almost any measure, the people of China are safer from floods than ever before. Although the extremely heavy rains of 1998 (perhaps due to El Niño), combined with serious deforestation and erosion upstream, led to terrible floods along the Yangzi, taking perhaps 3,000 lives, it is worth comparing this with the death toll from comparably high water in the early days of the Republic (perhaps 100,000 dead in 1931) and the People's Republic (perhaps 30,000 dead in 1954). Similar improvements are evident in the safety of people, crops, and buildings along the Yellow River and the Huai (despite an enormous death toll when two large dams and a number of smaller ones collapsed in 1975).[77]

However, this extra margin of safety is by no means automatic or fully embodied in durable structures. Because its erosion and siltation problems have not been addressed, the Yellow River continues to run as much as ten meters above the surrounding land along much of its course, just as it did in the Qing.[78] Huge labor mobilizations are still needed to add to and reinforce dikes during the high-water periods each year. In ordinary years these mobilizations mostly involve local people, but in crises, the army is involved as well. One can imagine various circumstances in which sufficient labor might not be forthcoming. Recently, there have also been reports that a huge number of the small and medium-sized dams built through mass mobilization of unskilled labor during the Maoist years are cracking, though no known disasters have yet resulted, and this is not the first such alarm.[79] Moreover, during high-water years, it is still necessary to inundate large expanses of countryside to protect major cities and expensive modern institutions, such as airports.

Improved flood control has allowed people in certain once-vulnerable areas, such as the lower Yellow River valley, to go on the offensive for the first time and harness river water for other uses. The irrigated land area in China has roughly tripled since 1949, with most of the gains coming in the north. This increase has been essential for enabling Chinese agriculture to keep up with the enormous post-1949 population boom.[80] (The roughly 750 million people added since the 1953 census are more than double the population of any other country, other than China itself and India.) China had fewer than 10 large reservoirs (with a capacity over 100 million cubic meters) in 1949; by 1980 it had more than 300, in addition to 1,500 medium-sized ones, and building has continued since then.[81] Improved overall water control in the huge Hai-Huang-Huai plain—long the most frequently inundated part of China—has also made it possible to drain excess water from the fields there, reducing both salinity and alkalinity enough to create a long-term improvement in the area's average soil quality since 1949 (despite many other stresses).[82]

There are serious questions about how much more can be tapped from either groundwater or (especially) surface water sources, and conflicts over water are growing increasingly serious. Moreover, providing water is not the same as providing clean water, and water quality in much of China is extraordinarily poor.[83] Nevertheless, a great deal has been done to provide more reliable water supplies to a vastly expanded population; even more than with flood control, much of the credit must go to locally managed, labor-intensive projects, buttressed by such relatively small and low-tech industrial inputs as electric motors for pumps and (less commonly) concrete to line ditches. If the township and village enterprises

(TVEs)—many of which have built on local industries developed during the Cultural Revolution drive for self-reliance or on "traditional" local specialties— have been the most important, surprising, and distinctive feature of post-1978 economic growth, it can similarly be argued that small-scale, locally managed irrigation works, which have thus far survived the decline in local cadres' ability to command people's labor, are among the most impressive and unusual achievements of Chinese ecological management. Nonetheless—again as with the TVEs—doubts persist about their long-term adequacy.

HYDROPOWER AND CHINA'S FAR WEST

It is in the development of hydropower projects that Chinese water-control strategies seem most similar to those favored by technocrats the world over. This similarity is hardly surprising, because hydroelectricity projects were developed in tandem with standardized international engineering practices linked to ideas of boundless growth and the developmentalist project. (One Soviet engineer in the 1930s aptly referred to the global fraternity of engineers sharing these ideas as the "Tekhintern" and predicted that it would ultimately prove more significant than the Comintern—an insight that his friends wisely persuaded him to keep to himself.)[84] China's hydropower efforts have been enormous. More than half of the dams exceeding fifteen meters in height in the entire world are in China, almost all of them built since 1949.[85] China still has a great deal of untapped hydropower potential—the most in the world, in fact—and, unlike those of some richer countries, its government does not seem to be having many environmentalist qualms about big dams. (Because China has relatively little natural gas—by far the cleanest fossil fuel—and surprisingly little oil, coal is the major alternative to hydropower. This makes the regime's relative imperviousness to environmental critiques of dam-building somewhat more understandable.) The Three Gorges project is thus far the world's largest, with a reservoir roughly the length of Lake Superior.[86] What have these dams done, and how?

Chinese dam builders operate in a peculiar physical and social environment. Hydro installations in most of the world tend to be built in sparsely populated areas, particularly those inhabited by politically disenfranchised minorities, for several reasons. First, because dams require submerging large amounts of land, they are most likely to be built where that land is not being intensively used and where the people who do use it have relatively little power. Second, hydropower potential is greatest where the water can be made to drop a long way into a set of turbines. This tends to be easiest amid mountains or on high plateaus—often the sort of undesirable land to which politically disenfranchised peoples have been relegated or from which nomadic peoples have not yet been displaced. The power itself, of course, is usually used elsewhere, but electricity can be moved over long distances fairly cheaply. Thus, the story of hydropower—from the U.S. West to the Amazon to India's lower Himalayas to Canada's James Bay—is often that of flooding minority peoples and "unspoiled" land. (It thus constitutes, along with other energy-related land uses such as mining, one of the ways in which one of the oldest themes in world history—the struggle between agricultural and nonagricultural peoples—continues today, though we tend to think of this issue as having been largely played out by the end of the nineteenth century.)

From a purely technical point of view, one might expect this pattern to hold in China as well. Both the Yangzi and the Yellow rivers begin in the high mountains of Central Asia and complete about 90 percent of their drop toward the sea before entering China proper.[87] Tibet alone has roughly 30 percent of China's surface water (its per capita water resources exceed those of Canada) and 30 percent of the country's hydropower potential.[88] Thus much of the People's Republic's hydropower potential lies outside the areas of Han Chinese predominance and of dense agricultural settlement. Yet until recent years almost all large Chinese hydro projects have been within China proper, with several of them requiring relocation of people on an unmatched scale: the Three Gorges project has involved the relocation of at least 1.2 million people and perhaps as many as 2 million.[89]

There are various explanations for this unusual pattern of development. Some of it no doubt has to do with the often tenuous hold of Chinese regimes (including the Qing) on parts of the far west of the country. While both late imperial and twentieth-century governments have sometimes pursued a "civilizing" policy in border areas that, in its twentieth-century form, has included efforts to accelerate economic development, it has been more common (especially with minorities occupying large contiguous areas, as opposed to hill peoples already surrounded by Han Chinese) for the state to promote stability in these areas by discouraging rapid economic development that might unsettle established ways of life, while cultivating ties to favored members of the elite. To a surprising degree, such policies continued into the People's Republic, though they now seem to be largely abandoned.

Under the circumstances, even self-consciously modernizing regimes have generally given a low priority even to examining the far western regions. There was, for instance, no systematic effort even to survey the upper reaches of the Yangzi until 1976.[90] Planners of projects on both the Yellow and Yangzi rivers are still working, to a considerable extent, on the basis of plans drawn up before 1949, when political control of these regions was considerably weaker. Moreover, given the lack of supporting infrastructure (such as roads) for massive construction projects in some of these areas, it is easier to focus on relatively accessible locations.[91] But many of the same conditions obtain in such remote regions as the upper Amazon or the Indian side of the Himalayas, where hydropower development has been more aggressive than it was in China's far west during the first forty years of the People's Republic.[92] For whatever reasons, the combination of relatively cautious hydro development in sparsely populated regions with an enormous amount of building in more developed areas (much of it done in very labor-intensive, capital-saving ways, at least for smaller dams) gave China's hydro industry a somewhat unusual shape.[93] Another partial explanation is that citizens of more densely settled parts of China have fewer legal ways to block a state project that might displace them than their counterparts in many other countries do.

Overall, the combination of water-management strategies in the People's Republic has been remarkably successful in tapping existing assets and controlling immediate dangers; nevertheless, serious degradation of existing water assets and unprecedented demands on them are clearly visible. Erosion control in the Yellow River basin, for instance, has never received the attention that everyone has agreed in theory that it deserved, in part because the payoff seemed distant and short-term solutions were urgently needed. It was difficult to imagine social stability without effective flood control, at least in the provinces of Henan and Shandong. Meanwhile, though long-term ecological stability required extensive (and labor-intensive) soil-conservation measures, these take effect very slowly even under the best of circumstances. John Cotton, who studied the problem under Nationalist auspices, urged an emphasis on soil conservation, but he also suggested that the river would carry an unusually heavy silt load for at least the next fifty years regardless.[94] Because such a wait to realize the benefit of such measures was deemed unacceptable, the regime chose to press ahead on irrigation and hydropower projects (as well as flood control) in spite of the knowledge that siltation would significantly shorten the projects' lives if they were built before soil conservation was implemented. In 1964, a planner was still citing the fifty-year wait for such efforts to pay off as a reason to go ahead with irrigation projects first.[95]

Recent work by Peter Lindert on Chinese soils adds some important nuances to this picture. Lindert points out that figures on increasing silt burdens in Chinese rivers do not tell us where in the watershed the dirt comes from, and he makes a very strong circumstantial case that erosion problems on existing farms have been exaggerated.[96] It seems likely, then, that most of the increased soil that is raising river beds comes from land that has long had little or no economic use (e.g., the most arid parts of the northwest, Xinjiang, and Mongolia), where increasing erosion could be due to nonanthropogenic factors; or places where the Chinese are attempting to exploit lands they had previously not touched. This latter category might be further subdivided into places where people are trying to reclaim land for farming, but not always succeeding (as on the desert frontier in the northwest) and places where resources are seemingly being exploited on a one-time, unsustainable basis (as with recently deforested hillsides in Tibet and parts of western Sichuan).

Lindert's findings suggest a good deal about what has and has not worked in China's unusual institutional setup. Contrary to what doctrinaire marketers might have predicted, for instance, the communal ownership system for land during the Maoist era did not necessarily lead to systematic underinvestment in the long-term maintenance of the soil, perhaps because labor was also plentiful. The reform period's combination of still-incomplete property rights in land and new opportunities for private profit might also have been expected to lead farmers to "mine" their land for short-term gains, but so far that does not seem to be a serious issue, either. Nor does rural overpópulation pressing on the "commons" seem to be the problem. Indeed, labor that is still "trapped" in the countryside by restrictions on migration (or kept there by the availability of at least some nonfarm work for family members) seems to have been put to good environmental use, whatever the other problems of population growth and keeping people in the countryside might be. Rather, what seems to be lacking are systems to value and implement environmental maintenance on lands not in economic use. Mass mobilization of work units from local communities to control excessive siltation seems impossible, as such efforts would not raise the work unit's income (except in the very long term, and even then no more so than the income of free-riding units elsewhere in the watershed). Meanwhile, the state has been unwilling to undertake capital-intensive efforts in an unglamorous, low-tech endeavor that only slowly yields benefits, and the need for sustained efforts would probably make heavy reliance on corvée labor (and forcible exclusion of people from marginal lands) very difficult even if the government was otherwise prepared to contemplate it. And, as noted before, China seems to place little value on preserving wild lands for their own sake.

The heavy siltation resulting from erosion on little-used lands has had devastating effects on the Sanmenxia Dam and on many other structures along the Yellow River. Despite huge construction efforts, flood control is still heavily dependent on large annual labor mobilizations. Although the Yangzi has always been much less silt-laden and much less flood-prone, deforestation along its upper reaches (in large part due to the post-1978 construction boom) has reached a stage at which some observers are beginning to speak of the potential for it to become a second Yellow River.[97] Restrictions on logging have been imposed (causing imports to soar), but it is unclear whether these efforts will prove sufficient.

A particularly serious erosion problem may be taking shape in Tibet. Despite statements in the seventh five-year plan (in the mid-1980s) and thereafter that the far west should serve as a raw-materials source for China proper, with its own development to be funded by primary-product exports, the state has until recently moved cautiously in exploiting Tibet's vast freshwater, hydro, and mineral resources, for technical, environmental, and political reasons. (Partly because of this circumstance, state subsidies for development in Tibet continue to far exceed the value of resources extracted and the value of locally generated investment funds.)[98] The state did, however, permitted extensive logging until recently and facilitated that logging by building roads. (The proportion of Tibet's forests that are accessible has soared since 1949, and perhaps 50 percent of the forest cover of eastern Tibet was removed just between 1950 and 1987.)[99] Serious overcutting resulted, and though there have been some government-mandated restrictions and replanting efforts since the late 1990s, there has been no way to ensure the follow-up care that the seedlings need in Tibet's harsh climate (except in some areas managed by the People's Liberation Army). This deforestation is strictly a one-shot exploitation of a resource: most of the exposed land is not even suitable for farming, and much of the indigenous population prefers herding anyway. Rapid erosion has resulted, as soil no longer held by trees slides down very steep slopes.[100] The silt burden in Tibet's rivers has increased so fast that most of the small hydro stations built in Tibet have become useless within a few years of their original construction. (In a 1986 study, almost 40 percent of these stations were found to be defunct or currently unusable, indicating that a large share of the money targeted for infrastructure development in Tibet had been wasted.)[101] Given the role of Himalayan snow in the hydrology of vast areas of China, Southeast Asia and Central Asia, and the role of the Tibetan plateau in climate regulation, the long-range dangers of uncontrolled siltation of Tibetan river beds are hard to exaggerate.

Meanwhile, water shortages in much of north China are among the most severe in the world, and existing supplies are very heavily used (more than 80 percent of Yellow River water was already in use over a decade ago); the average quality of the water in use in both many urban and rural areas falls far short of even Chinese official standards, which are well below international ones.[102] Although most projections suggest that China's population will level off in the next few decades (after adding another two hundred million or so people), further improvements in standards of living all seem to require more water per person. Barring a massive increase in imports, any increase in the consumption of dietary protein and edible oils will require higher grain yields (particularly as more land is lost to roads, houses, factories, and other development); the most effective available tool for increasing yields would seem to be more irrigation.[103] Further economic development requires more energy, most of which currently comes from extremely polluting soft coal; although intensive development of oil and gas is under way, results have been limited, and greater reliance on hydropower seems all but inevitable.

But if the strains seem inevitable, how they will be managed remains an open question. That in turn raises the question of whether the distinctive parts of China's developmental and environmental management experience have any future relevance, or whether they must eventually be seen as just expensive and unproductive detours along the path of a more widely shared "liberal project" with its own environmental quandaries.

CHINA AND THE GLOBAL ENVIRONMENT AT THE MILLENNIUM: DO THE DIFFERENCES STILL MATTER?

In many ways, China's environmental problems are now those of a "typical" developing country. Here, as elsewhere, raising per capita income has become a basic measure of success (and thus of government legitimacy), despite its rather loose relationship to more direct indicators of human welfare (such as life expectancy and literacy rates). And like the other densely populated East Asian nations with success stories, China—or more accurately, the prosperous parts of China—cannot possibly provide all of the primary products that its people demand. Indeed, the most nightmarish scenarios for China's impact on the global economic future come from extrapolating to China's much larger population the per capita primary-product demand that developed in Japan, Taiwan, and Korea as those places industrialized. This is clearly an impossible scenario in the foreseeable future: even the four hundred million or so Chinese in fairly advanced areas could never import two-thirds of their cereals or virtually all of their oil and natural gas, as Japan and South Korea do[104]—but it is clear that China will make increasing claims on global supplies of various land-intensive commodities (which will, in turn, require the rest of the world to buy more Chinese industrial goods).

However, political and ecological realities are such that a relative latecomer to prosperity as big as China will have to depend heavily on internal solutions. Regarding sources of dietary protein, for instance, the West already controls most of the world's rangeland, thanks to centuries-old conquests, and thus the supply of meat; and the other East Asian countries, plus the West, have already stretched global fisheries to their limits. China has turned heavily to aquaculture, but that, too, has environmental costs. Some significant inefficiencies remain, particularly in areas like animal husbandry;[105] but those inefficiencies that result from technical problems—failing to use existing best practices—will require resources to address them, and it seems unlikely that the gains to be realized from purely organizational change—that is, by eliminating market imperfections—are likely to be enough to solve China's water shortages.

Some farmers are very wasteful users of water, and it has been suggested that raising the price of water would induce them to change their ways; but without making water-saving technologies available cheaply (many involve sophisticated sensors and other relatively expensive electronics), it seems unlikely that much would be gained by price increases alone, unless the regime is willing to see a far greater number of marginal farmers abandon the land.[106] In the current political climate, it seems unlikely that the regime would either want to add to the already huge number of people leaving the countryside (soon to reach twenty million per year), or become more dependent on farm imports.[107] Experiments with water price reform in China have thus far yielded quite modest results;[108] and there is no reason why China, of all places, should be able to force the acceptance of a non-subsidized market in water, when so few of the places that boast of their commitment to the market have done so. (Consider, for instance, the American West.) Judging by the example of Beijing, industrial water users have already realized impressive economies through nonmarket means, though these reductions came from a baseline of great inefficiency.[109] Residential use, which has been growing much more rapidly (though not on a per capita basis) might be reduced by higher prices, but most urban homes are already under some form of water rationing, and further reducing supplies that are well below global averages does not seem consistent with even modest continued improvements in health and standards of living.[110] The biggest wastage of water is in agriculture, but it is not clear that these rates are high by international standards.[111]

A decade ago, various analysts who noted an unusually high ratio of energy consumption to GNP in China predicted huge gains in efficiency with increased marketization. Instead, it turned out that GNP estimates were too low (largely because of the problems in assigning accurate values to various goods in an economy that still had many administered prices), and energy use was not nearly as wasteful as originally thought (though huge economies have nonetheless been achieved in the last twenty years).[112] The same may be true to some extent for water.

Significant gains in *economic* efficiency would result if some of the water currently used for agriculture were reallocated to meet growing urban demand. Price incentives are likely to encourage some units which control reservoirs to do just that, though a very large percentage of irrigation water is controlled by very small local units, which tend to be responsive to their local constituents, are strongly focused on maximizing agricultural yields, and may also lack the technical prerequisites to reallocate their water to cities.[113] Moreover, any transfer of water away from agriculture, without improvements in technical efficiency, would mean more food imports. That scenario brings us back to questions about how willing China (and the outside world) is to have such a huge population, aspiring to eat better, relying on imports for a growing percentage of these needs. Let us then turn to possibilities for making more water available (and losing less of it to waste), rather than reallocating it from countryside to city.

The possible palliatives can be divided into centrally directed megaprojects and smaller, more locally controlled projects. This division reveals some of the distinctive aspects of the Chinese version of modernity. In China, as elsewhere, a group of technocrats favors very large-scale engineering projects that pose enormous environmental risks (the Three Gorges Dam, Yamdrok Tso, and other huge dams for power, and the south-north water diversion scheme for irrigation and urban water needs). These technocrats wield considerable power: a remarkable percentage of China's top leaders in recent decades have been engineers. The lack of constitutional limits on central power in China makes the realization of these projects all the more likely. Not only is the ability of affected citizens (such as those scheduled for relocation) and other dissenters (such as environmentalists) to protest severely constrained, but even local and provincial governments lack a firm legal base from which to object to national appropriation of "their" resources: interbasin water transfers, for instance, require almost none of the complex negotiations and binding agreements among states (or, in China, provinces) and the national government that have been required in the United States.[114] At first glance, what R. Bin Wong has called the "fractal" nature of Chinese state and society—in which every level of government has essentially the same agenda on a different scale, rather than having different types of tasks be the purview of different levels of government, as is common in most of the world[115]—would seem to make such projects all the more likely, but additional factors push the other way.

One such factor is fiscal decentralization. Oddly enough, though Chinese regimes have rarely recognized a set of revenues that belonged in principle to local governments, even the Qing government had considerable difficulty gaining full central control over the taxes collected in its name.[116] During the last decade of the Qing and into the Republican period, both tax rates and central government revenue grew rapidly as the state adopted a series of expensive modernization projects (and incurred heavy foreign indemnities), including the expansion and professionalization of the state itself. However, during this period, the distribution of revenue among various levels of government became more, not less, bottom-heavy, in sharp contrast to most models of the state-building process (if not necessarily counter to the reality of many states).[117] Although the early People's Republic tried again to centralize fiscal control, its successes were limited, in part by its simultaneous drive for local self-sufficiency. Because the tax system enacted early in the reform period gave the central government (in theory) the exclusive right to tax slow-growing agriculture while assigning most revenues from the rapidly-growing TVEs to local government (and those from provincially owned businesses to the provinces), a further fiscal decentralization occurred; it was partly, but not fully, reversed by a new set of reforms in 1994 and 1995.[118] Consequently, the tax burden is far less unevenly distributed across space than is income: it falls disproportionately on those in the countryside, and above all on those rural areas that remain overwhelmingly agricultural.[119] China may in principle have no limits on central government supremacy over local authorities, but, as Wang Shaoguang has pointed out, as of a few years ago its central government commanded one of the lowest percentages of total revenues of any regime in the world.[120] Despite some subsequent recentralization, fiscal arrangements still place limitations on the proponents of megaprojects: it is no accident that the first top-ranking official to publicly question the Three Gorges Dam was the premier and market-oriented budget hawk Zhu Rongji.[121]

Moreover, this fiscal decentralization is not merely a sign of the incomplete triumph of central power but part and parcel of the victory of a particular developmentalist vision. The reason for giving local governments such exclusive command over revenues from local industry was, after all, to make sure that those governments would encourage such growth (this was by no means an obvious outcome in the early 1980s, with so many Cultural Revolution–era cadres still in power); and at least part of the reason for central control over agricultural taxes was to prevent local governments from taxing agriculture in ways that would drive people out of farming. (More recently, the government has taken further steps, including abolishing all taxes on farming; but this move has been only partially successful, as various semilegal and illegal nuisance fees have multiplied in jurisdictions that do not have enough local industry to support their activities.)[122] Thus, the "leave the land, but not the countryside" approach to development—with its many echoes of Qing development policies—continues to give a distinctive cast to China's environmental options as well. By 2030, China will probably be about 65 percent urban, nearly (though not completely) converging toward expectations for such an industrialized country and thus reducing this distinctiveness; but the passage of another generation before this convergence is more or less complete represents a large window in which these patterns will still matter, especially at current rates of economic and environmental change.[123]

The environmental implications are mixed. At a very basic but also speculative and almost certainly unquantifiable level, there are reasons to think that rural industrialization, as opposed to more purely urban growth, may ease environmental strain. Keeping more people in the countryside reduces the need for additional transport infrastructure (and energy for shipping), and makes it possible to get by with simpler sorts of sanitation and other public works. It has also facilitated the use of various supplementary resources that are generally not worth shipping (e.g., using crop residues and small bits of wood for fuel). It is also possible that the continued strength of kin-based identities and other elements of "traditional" culture may provide some counterweight to the endless pursuit and discarding of consumer goods as a form of self-expression, though it seems clear that the former influences are not very effective in the long run. Moreover, life expectancy in the People's Republic has reached levels close to those in the West at a much lower level of per capita income. In consequence, arguably, the whole task of maximizing income growth is somewhat less urgent, though there is no sign the government has reduced its commitment to that goal.

On the other hand, a bottom-heavy fiscal system requires that the kinds of local efforts needed to address environmental strains will need to be funded primarily from local budgets. To the extent that needed inputs are relatively low-tech and cheap—such as concrete to line irrigation ditches and reduce seepage—more prosperous localities should be able to finance them out of TVE profits, but they may not be able to underwrite the purchase of sophisticated, expensive sensors and pollution-control devices (often developed to suit the more centralized industry and agriculture of the West and Japan). Also, repairing many of the poorly built, low-tech water projects from earlier eras will be difficult in an era in which mass mobilization has become much harder and more expensive: it is likely to eat up a large portion of the funds available for environmental protection and infrastructure in many jurisdictions.[124] (It is not clear how many of the facilities built in more recent years, using more capital-intensive methods, are also in poor shape.)

Furthermore, the close connections between government and local industry that make it fiscally possible to fund local environmental amelioration can also make it politically difficult to do so. The ties between government cadres and local industry—which often involve substantial private income for the cadres and those connected to them, as well as much of local public revenue—often make regulation difficult. Many scholars have concluded that, on the whole, TVEs are more environmentally harmful than urban industries in China.[125]

Such a bottom-heavy structure also limits the government's ability to force adjustments that might be environmentally beneficial overall but are costly to local communities. Lindert has argued that whereas government and foreign reports have tended to blame the increase of flooding on the Yangzi on logging and consequent erosion in the upper Yangzi, the greater problem is that excessive reclamation of wetlands and ponds deprives a swollen river of safe outlets.[126] This choice between emphasizing upstream or downstream problems is strikingly reminiscent of the situation in the first half of the nineteenth century, before the enormous casualties of the Taiping Rebellion relieved pressure on the land in this region. Then, as we saw, officials who had delegated Yangzi valley water control to local elites were unable to stop their excessive building of private dikes and instead targeted the poorer people who were deforesting parts of the Yangzi highlands. Lindert rightly notes that much of the excess wetland reclamation in the People's Republic was the result of a misguided central government initiative—the Maoist emphasis on grain as the "key link."[127] But because the investments have long since been made, and both labor and grain markets remain highly imperfect, price signals alone are unlikely to induce local communities to let this land be submerged again. The central government may well have better luck intervening in the highlands, where much of the land does not yet belong to any local production unit—but only if it is willing to commit substantial resources.

Last, but by no means least, we should remember that many of the most environmentally fragile communities—especially in the northwest and southwest—are also among the poorest and least industrialized communities in China proper. Such communities face a double fiscal handicap: not only is local income scarce, but almost all of it is agricultural, and thus is not supposed to be taxed. Consequently the differences in per capita government revenue between rich and poor communities in China are many times larger than the differences in per capita income.[128] Much like the frontier areas in the Qing, such areas will need significant central government help even to implement environmentally necessary miniprojects, and it is not clear that this help will be forthcoming. The still more fragile ecologies and generally poorer economies of the non-Han far West (Xinjiang, Qinghai, and Tibet) continue to receive net inflows of central funds; but efforts to balance development with social and environmental stability have not produced clearly sustainable growth for the inhabitants of these regions, much less the significant relief for China proper that various leaders predicted would come from the far west's exports of primary products to east and central China.[129] The state's concern for development is increasingly overriding the fear of destabilizing various frontier peoples and ecologies, as evidenced in its dam-building and mining practices, growing infrastructural investment, increased Han immigration to Tibet, and the increasingly stringent application of intrusive birth-control policies to "national minorities" who were for a time exempt from these policies—but the political, economic and environmental consequences are still far from clear.[130]

China's environmental future is thus murky. To be sure, increased consumerism, technocratic planning, and state efforts to build monuments to its own modernizing efforts will be important, as they have been almost everywhere in the twentieth-century world, but the valorization of rural life, which has generally been out of sync with that kind of developmentalism, remains influential. Heavy reliance on local water-supply projects run by people who are not credentialed experts will also persist. A bottom-heavy fiscal structure that cramps the style of central government technocrats (and of those who would subsidize the poorest regions) and some substantial public ownership of productive assets (especially in the interior provinces) are likely to endure. The continuity that seems to be fading away fastest is the long-standing tendency to tread cautiously in minority regions, rather than to either encourage accelerated development or close off land to economic uses entirely; but even this trend could conceivably reverse if the financial and other costs of the "go West" policy mount too quickly. China will continue to face environmental challenges shaped in part by a late imperial political economy that favored the diffusion of a preferred kind of subsistence across ecologically varied regions rather than a concentration of growth in favored ones.

NOTES

1. The best summary of these aspects of Chinese liberalism—which argues powerfully against treating them as a simple "misreading" of Western liberalism—remains Benjamin Schwartz, *In Search of Wealth and Power: Yen Fu and the West* (Cambridge, MA: Harvard University Press, 1964).

2. The Han are China's dominant ethnic group, constituting more than 90 percent of the population; there is no consensus on the geographic boundaries of the group or on when it became a self-conscious grouping. They expanded gradually from northern China across the rest of the empire (or nation) and were until quite recently a small minority in Xinjiang, Tibet, and other outlying areas.

3. Hoshi Ayao, *Dai unga* (Tokyo: Kinfu shuppansha, 1971); Edward Farmer, *Early Ming Government: The Evolution of Dual Capitals* (Cambridge, MA: Harvard University Press, 1976), 153–62; and Hou Renzhi, *Xu Tianxia jun guo li bing shu: Shandong zhi bu* (Beijing: Yanjing xuebao, 1941; reprint, Washington, DC: Center for Chinese Research Materials), 21.

4. Farmer, *Early Ming Government*, 156–62, provides a quick summary.

5. G. William Skinner, "Cities and the Hierarchy of Local Systems," in *The City in Late Imperial China*, ed. G. William Skinner (Stanford, CA: Stanford University Press, 1977), 307–46.

6. Terada Takanobu, *Sansei shonin no kenkyu* (Tokyo: Toyoshi kenkyu kai, 1972), 17–80, 101–6, 120–57.

7. James Lee, "The Legacy of Immigration in Southwest China, 1250–1850," *Annales de demographie historique* 18 (1982): 284–93; Sun Xiaofen, *Qingdai qianqi de yimin zhen Sichuan* (Chengdu: Sichuan daxue chubanshe, 1997), 30–34.

8. Susan Naquin and Evelyn Rawski, *Chinese Society in the Eighteenth Century* (New Haven: Yale University Press, 1987), 24; Ming-te Pan, "Rural Credit Market and the Peasant Economy (1600–1949): The State, Elite, Peasant and Usury" (Ph.D. diss., University of California, Irvine, 1994), 116–18.

9. Wang Yeh-chien, *Land Taxation in Imperial China, 1753–1908* (Cambridge, MA: Harvard University Press, 1973), 26–31, 88, 95, 113, 128.

10. Carol Shiue, "Local Granaries and Central Government Disaster Relief: Moral Hazard and Intergovernmental Finance in Eighteenth- and Nineteenth-Century China," *Journal of Economic History* 64, no. 1 (2004): 297–98; Pierre-Étienne Will and R. Bin Wong, *Nourish the People: The State Civilian Granary System in China, 1650–1850* (Ann Arbor: University of Michigan Press, 1991), 114–15. Shiue suggests that state relief efforts were targeted at areas that had poor geographic conditions for market integration; this is not the same as targeting poor areas per se, but would still be compatible with the argument here.

11. Susan Mann, "Household Handicrafts and State Policy in Qing Times," in *To Achieve Security and Wealth: The Qing State and the Economy*, ed. Jane Kate Leonard and John Watt Leonard (Ithaca, NY: Cornell University Press, 1992), 75–96, esp. 86.

12. Such figures are necessarily approximations, especially because grain tribute was often sold or otherwise redistributed by recipients preferring fresher local grain. See, for instance, Alison Dray-Novey and Lillian Li, "Guarding Beijing's Food Security in the Qing Dynasty: State, Market, and Police," *Journal of Asian Studies* 58, no. 4 (November 1999): 1000–1004; Wu Jianyong, "Qingdai Beijing de liangshi gongying" in *Beijing lishi yu xianshi yanjiu* (Beijing: Zhonghua shuju, 1989): 167–86, esp. 172–73.

13. Hoshi Ayao, *Dai unga*, 223–27; Kenneth Pomeranz, *The Making of a Hinterland: State, Society, and Economy in Inland North China, 1853–1937* (Berkeley: University of California Press, 1993), 166–68.

14. Charles Greer, "Chinese Water Management Strategies in the Yellow River Basin of China" (Ph.D. diss., University of Washington, 1975), 35; Hu Ch'ang-t'u, "The Yellow River Administration in the Ch'ing Dynasty," *Journal of Asian Studies* 14, no. 4 (1955): 503–13; Huang He shuili weiyuanhui, shuili bu, *Huang he shuili shi shuyao* (Beijing: Shuili dianli chubanshe, 1982), 321–22.

15. David Ringrose, *Transportation and Economic Stagnation in Spain* (Durham, NC: Duke University Press, 1970), 27; Charles Tilly, "Food Supply and Public Order in Modern Europe," in *The Formation of National States in Western Europe*, ed. Charles Tilly (Princeton: Princeton University Press, 1975).

16. Lillian Li, *Fighting Famine in North China: State, Market, and Environmental Decline, 1690s–1990s* (Stanford, CA: Stanford University Press, 2007), 38–249.

17. Peter Perdue, *Exhausting the Earth: State and Peasant in Hunan, 1550–1850* (Cambridge, MA: Harvard University Press, 1987), 211–19; James Polachek, "Gentry Hegemony in Soochow," in *Conflict and Control in Late Imperial China*, ed. Frederick Wakeman and Carolyn Grant (Berkeley: University of California Press, 1975), 219–20, 226.

18. Perdue, *Exhausting the Earth*, 219–33; Polachek, "Hegemony," 226–49.

19. Anne Osborne, "The Local Politics of Land Reclamation in the Lower Yangzi Highlands," *Late Imperial China* 15, no. 1 (1994): 25–31, 37–38.

20. Colin and Richard Jones McEvedy, *Atlas of World Population History* (New York: Penguin, 1978), 62–63; Wang Yeh-chien, "Food Supply and Grain Prices in the Yangtze Delta in the Eighteenth Century," *Second Conference on Modern Chinese History* 2 (1989): 427, adjusted by omitting the three prefectures (Yangzhou, Tongzhou, and Haimen) north of the Yangzi which Wang includes in his definition of the region; Kenneth Pomeranz, *The Great Divergence: China, Europe, and the Making of the Modern World Economy* (Princeton: Princeton University Press, 2000), 37–38, 116–21, 27–38, and appendix F.

21. See Pomeranz, *Great Divergence*, 34–35, 225–39, 42–44, for more detail and sources. Interestingly, while the Jiangnan diet included a lot of fish, mostly from rivers, aquaculture, and nearby shallow ocean waters, fishing on the high seas was much less developed than in either Japan or northwestern Europe, where it became an increasingly important nutritional source and a source of vital fertilizer as well. The richest deep-water fisheries in China were off the north China and Manchurian coasts, where the maritime tradition was weaker and population pressure much less. See Hiroshi Kasahara, *Fisheries Resources of the North Pacific Ocean* (Vancouver: Institute of Fisheries, University of British Columbia, 1961), 8–9.

22. Pomeranz, *Great Divergence*, 34–35.

23. On north China, see Francesca Bray, *Technology and Gender: Fabrics of Power in Late Imperial China* (Berkeley: University of California Press, 1997), 217; Pomeranz, *Great Divergence*, 139–44. On the middle Yangzi, see Li Bozhong, *Agricultural Development in Jiangnan, 1620–1850* (New York: St. Martin's Press, 1998), 108. On the upper Yangzi, see Yamamoto Susumu, "Shindai shikawa no chi-iki keizai," *Shigaku zasshi* 100, no. 12 (1991): 7–8, 10–11, 15; Yamamoto Susumu, "Shōhin seisan kenkyū no kiseki," in Mori Masao, ed., *Min shin jidaishi no kihon mondai* (Tokyo: Kyūko shōin, 1997), 88.

24. Pomeranz, *Great Divergence*, 75–80, 215–17.

25. Ho Ping-ti, *Studies on the Population of China, 1368–1953* (Cambridge, MA: Harvard University Press, 1959), 46, 64, 281–2; Li Bozhong, "Cong 'fufu bing zuo' dao 'nan geng nu zhu,'" *Zhongguo jingji shi yanjiu* 11, no. 3 (1994): 31–37; Skinner, "Cities," 213; and to adjust, G. William Skinner, "Sichuan's Population in the Nineteenth Century: Lessons from Disaggregated Data," *Late Imperial China* 8, no. 1 (June 1987): 1–79. Compare Wang Yeh-chien, "Food Supply and Grain Prices," 427.

26. Nicholas Menzies, "Strategic Space: Exclusion and Inclusion in Wildland Policies in Late Imperial China," *Modern Asian Studies* 26, no. 4 (1992): 719–33.

27. Greer, "Chinese Water Management," 19; He Bochuan, *China on the Edge: The Crisis of Ecology and Development* (San Francisco: China Books and Periodicals, 1991), 30, gives an even higher figure.

28. Shuili bu, *Huang he shuili shi shuyao*, 288–347.

29. Hu Ch'ang-t'u, "Yellow River Administration," 505–13; Pomeranz, *Hinterland*, 167–68.

30. Pomeranz, *Hinterland*, 167.

31. Hoshi Ayao, *Dai unga*, 223–27.

32. Adachi Keiji, "Daizu kasu ryūtsū to shindai no shōgyōteki nōgyō," *Tōyōshi kenkyū* 37, no. 3 (1978): 35–63.

33. This figure was calculated based on northeastern trade in particular: see Wu Jianying, "Beijing liangshi," 173–74.

34. Hoshi Ayao, *Dai unga*, 219–30; Jane Kate Leonard, "'Controlling from Afar': Open Communications and the Tao-Kuang Emperor's Control of Grand Canal-Grain Transport Management," *Modern Asian Studies* 22, no. 4 (1988): 665–99.

35. Polachek, "Hegemony," 226–27, 52–55.

36. Polachek, "Hegemony," 223–27; Pomeranz, *Hinterland*, 273, 275; Mary Wright, *The Last Stand of Chinese Conservatism* (Stanford, CA: Stanford University Press, 1962), 163–67.

37. Philip Kuhn, *Rebellion and Its Enemies in Late Imperial China* (Cambridge, MA: Harvard University Press, 1970); Mary Rankin, *Elite Activism and Political Transformation in China: Zhejiang Province, 1865–1911* (Stanford, CA: Stanford University Press, 1986).

38. Carl F. Nathan, *Plague Prevention and Politics in Manchuria, 1910–1931* (Cambridge, MA: Harvard University Press, 1967), v, 5, 42, 74; Frederick Wakeman, *Policing Shanghai, 1927–1937* (Berkeley: University of California Press, 1995).

39. Pomeranz, *Hinterland*, 138–42. Note the parallels to the ways in which opium and prostitution were increasingly discussed not as problems of the individual customer and his family, but as a waste of national resources; Alexander DesForges, "Opium/Leisure/Shanghai: Urban Economies of Consumption," in *Opium Regimes*, ed. Timothy Brook and Bob Tadashi Wakabayashi (Berkeley: University of California Press, 2000), 178; Gail Hershatter, *Dangerous Pleasures* (Berkeley: University of California Press, 1997), 249–50.

40. Pomeranz, *Hinterland*, 140; Wu Jinzan, "Zhonghua minguo linye fazhan zhi yanjiu—minguo yuan nian zhi minguo sanshiwu nian" (Ph.D. diss., Zhongguo wenhua daxue, 1982), 71–3.

41. Pomeranz, *Hinterland*, 138–42, 46–52.

42. Pomeranz, *Hinterland*, 159–62, 201–11.

43. Edward Friedman, Paul Pickowicz, and Mark Selden, *Chinese Village, Socialist State* (New Haven: Yale University Press, 1991), 1, 9–10, 13–14, 70, 73–74.

44. See Ralph Thaxton, *Salt of the Earth* (Berkeley: University of California Press, 1997), 23–197.

45. Thaxton, *Salt of the Earth*, 198–319. See also Friedman, Pickowicz, and Selden, *Chinese Village, Socialist State*, 111–30; and Judith Stacey, *Patriarchy and Socialist Revolution* (Berkeley: University of California Press, 1983), 108–94.

46. William Kirby, "Engineering China: Birth of the Developmental State, 1928–1937," in *Becoming Chinese*, ed. Yeh Wen-hsin (Berkeley: University of California Press, 2000), 141–52. See also David Pietz, *Engineering the State: The Huai River and Reconstruction in Nationalist China, 1927–1937* (London: Routledge, 2002).

47. Pomeranz, *Hinterland*, 222–34, 53–65, gives these two stories.

48. Kirby, "Engineering China," 138, 51–52; Lyman van Slyke, *Yangtze: Nature, History, and the River* (Reading, MA: Addison-Wesley, 1988), 181–89.

49. Greer, "Chinese Water Management," 22.

50. Greer, "Chinese Water Management," 69–85; Kirby, "Engineering China," 143–53. See also Pietz, *Engineering the State,* 122, for similar findings for the Huai River engineering.

51. Nicholas Lardy, *Agriculture in China's Modern Economic Development* (Cambridge: Cambridge University Press, 1983), 98–145.

52. Nicholas Lardy, *Economic Growth and Distribution in China* (Cambridge: Cambridge University Press, 1978), 10–13, 137, 53–64; Lynn T. White, *Shanghai Shanghaied? Uneven Taxes in Reform China* (Hong Kong: Centre of Asian Studies, University of Hong Kong, 1989), 1–22.

53. Samuel P. S. Ho, "Rural Non-agricultural Development in Post-reform China: Growth, Development Patterns, and Issues," *Pacific Affairs* 68, no. 3 (1995): 360.

54. Quoted in Ho, "Rural Non-agricultural Development."

55. Yang Dali, *Calamity and Reform in China: State, Rural Society, and Institutional Change since the Great Leap Forward* (Stanford, CA: Stanford University Press, 1996), 42–67.

56. Chun and Wand Yijiang Chang, "The Nature of the Township-Village Enterprise," *Journal of Comparative Economics* 19 (1994): 440–41; Jean Oi, *Rural China Takes Off* (Berkeley: University of California Press, 1999), 95–99.

57. See Azizur Rahman Khan, "Growth and Distribution of Household Income in China between 1995 and 2002" (Department of Economics, University of California, Riverside, cited 2004; www.economics.ucr.edu/seminars/spring04/05-28-04AzizurKhan.pdf). See especially pp. 5, 8, and 12 on rural inequalities. Results in this area remain controversial for a number of reasons; for a recent assessment placing less weight on regional differences, see Dwayne Benjamin, Loren Brandt, and John Giles, "The Evolution of Income Inequality in Rural China," *Economic Development and Cultural Change* 53, no. 4 (July 2005): 769–824.

58. Among many examples, see Helen Siu, "Recycling Rituals: Politics and Popular Culture in Contemporary Rural China," in *Unofficial China,* ed. Perry Link, Richard Madsen, and Paul Pickowicz (Boulder, CO: Westview, 1989), 126–32; Yan Yunxiang, *The Flow of Gifts: Reciprocity and Social Networks in a Chinese Village* (Stanford, CA: Stanford University Press, 1996), 225–26.

59. There were hereditary groups assigned to Grand Canal work under quasi-military designations *(tun)* before 1850, but these "troops" had no weapons or institutional relationship to the armed forces. After the midcentury civil wars and the Yellow River shift, some ex-soldiers were assigned to long-term canal and Yellow River work while remaining part of armed units: this seems to have been an ad hoc measure designed to deal with flood-control emergencies and to ease the problems of demobilizing troops into a weak economy. Around 1900, many of these battalions *(ying)* were disbanded; the remaining ones were given both increased flood-control training and heavier arms.

These groups remained in place through the early Republic but were dispersed some time in the 1920s. The Nationalists, as we have seen, relied on close cooperation between soldiers and engineers for their one major water-control success in north China (the Wan Fu He project), and created strong ties between the military and engineers in general; but, so far as I know, they did not create new water-control units within the army. That innovation seems to have emerged from the "Serve the People" campaigns of the Cultural Revolution period; its effect was to make the building of centrally backed megaprojects even more autonomous from local society than if they had relied on mobilizing local labor. On pre-1850 *tun*, see Hoshi Ayao, *Dai unga*, 169–215. On post-war *ying* and their reform at the end of the nineteenth century, see Pomeranz, *Hinterland*, 193–96.

60. On the People's Hydropower Command, see Free Tibet Campaign UK, *Death of a Sacred Lake: The Yamdrok Tso Hydro-electric Power Generation Project of Tibet* (London: Free Tibet Campaign UK, 1996).

61. "Flood Control and Flood Fighting: Article 43," in *Flood Control Law of the People's Republic* (www.mwr.gov.cn/english1/laws.asp, accessed January 13, 2006); on 1998 mobilizations, see OCHA, "China: Floods OCHA-07: 21-Aug-98," in *International Natural Disaster Reports* (Center for International Disaster Information; http://iys.cidi.org/disaster/98b/0041.html, accessed January 13, 2006); and Lester R. Brown and Brian Halweil, "The Yangtze Flood: The Human Hand, Local and Global," *Worldwatch Institute* (www.worldwatch.org/press/news/1998/08/13, accessed January 13, 2006), which gives an even higher estimate of 1.6 million troops.

62. Greer, "Chinese Water Management," 77.

63. James Nickum, ed., *Water Management Organization in the People's Republic of China* (Armonk, NY: M.E. Sharpe, 1981), 10; Vaclav Smil, "Land Degradation in China: An Ancient Problem Getting Worse," in Piers Blaikie and Harold Brookfield, eds., *Land Degradation and Society* (London: Methuen, 1987), 216.

64. Patricia Adams and Gráinne Ryder, "China's Great Leap Backward," *International Journal* (October 1, 1998; www.probeinternational.org/pi/index.cfm?DSP=content&ContentID=723, accessed January 13, 2006); John Thibodeau, Philip Williams, and Dai Qing, eds., *The River Dragon Has Come: The Three Gorges Dam and the Fate of China's Yangtze River and Its People* (Armonk, NY: M.E. Sharpe, 1998), 9; Vaclav Smil, *China's Past, China's Future: Energy, Food, Environment* (London: Routledge Curzon, 2004), 199.

65. See, for example, Environmental News Network, reprinting an Associated Press story: "Three Gorges Dam Evictions Open Emotional Floodgates," *Environmental News Network* (ENN, November 6, 2002; www.enn.com/arch.html?id=342, accessed January 13, 2002), and "The Yangtze Dam: Feat or Folly?" *Washington Post*, November 9, 1997, A1.

66. Free Tibet Campaign UK, *Death of a Sacred Lake*, 7–8, 21.

67. Nickum, *Water Management*, 40.

68. Greer, "Chinese Water Management," 159, 80–84; Nickum, *Water Management*, 37–41.

69. Greer, "Chinese Water Management," 139, 50.

70. Vaclav Smil, *The Bad Earth* (Armonk, NY: M.E. Sharpe, 1984), 14; Vaclav Smil, *China's Environmental Crisis: An Inquiry into the Limits of National Development* (Armonk, NY: M.E. Sharpe, 1993), 61.

71. Greer, "Chinese Water Management," 95–100, 159–60.

72. James Nickum, "Beijing's Maturing Socialist Water Economy," in James Nickum and K. William Easter, *Metropolitan Water Use Conflicts in Asia and the Pacific* (Boulder, CO: Westview Press, 1994), 37–60.

73. Examples of such waste in individual projects abound. However, James Nickum, among others, suggests that the wastage rates for Chinese irrigation projects overall may not be higher than the international average, and that because seepage generally returns to local aquifers, overall water loss may be lower than that calculated for individual projects. See James Nickum, "Is China Living on the Water Margin?" *China Quarterly* 156 (1998): 891.

74. *China News Digest*, May 21, 1998.

75. Marc Reisner, *Cadillac Desert: The American West and Its Disappearing Water* (New York: Penguin, 1993), 438.

76. Xinhua News Agency, "North-South Water Diversion Project Heading for Early Finish" (China.org, March 5, 2003; www.china.org.cn/english/2003/Mar/57396.htm).

77. See Yi Si, "The World's Most Catastrophic Dam Failures: The August 1975 Collapses of the Banqia and Shimantan Dams," in Thibodeau, Williams, and Dai, *The River Dragon Has Come*, 25–38.

78. He Bochuan, *China on the Edge*, 30; Nickum, *Water Management*, 10.

79. "30,000 Chinese Reservoirs Facing Serious Safety Problems," *Interfax Information Services* (Interfax, June 3, 2004), forwarded by International Rivers Network, Berkeley, CA. E-mail version in author's possession.

80. James Nickum, "Is China Living on the Water Margin?" 884; Vaclav Smil, "Will There Be Enough Chinese Food?" (review of Lester Brown, *Who Will Feed China?*), *New York Review of Books*, February 1, 1996, 32–34.

81. Nickum, ed., *Water Management*, 6.

82. Peter Lindert, *Shifting Ground: The Changing Agricultural Soils of China and Indonesia* (Cambridge, MA: MIT Press, 2000), 91–97, esp. 97.

83. He Bochuan, *China on the Edge*, 177–84; Smil, *Environmental Crisis*, 45–51.

84. Loren Graham, *The Ghost of the Executed Engineer: Technology and the Fall of the Soviet Union* (Cambridge, MA: Harvard University Press, 1993), 43.

85. Joel Cohen, *How Many People Can the Earth Support?* (New York: W. W. Norton, 1995), 321.

86. Vaclav Smil, "China's Energy and Resource Uses: Continuity and Change," *China Quarterly* 156 (1998): 935–39.

87. On the Yangzi, see Tao Jingliang, "Features of a Reservoir," in *Mega-project: A Case Study of China's Three Gorges Project*, ed. Shiu-hung Luk and Joseph Witney (Armonk, NY: M.E. Sharpe, 1993), 68; Van Slyke, *Yangtze*, 15. On the Yellow River, which completes 80 percent of its drop on its upper course (at the end of which it is still in Inner Mongolia), see Shuili bu, *Huang he shuili shi shuyao*, 4–7.

88. Free Tibet Campaign UK, *Death of a Sacred Lake*, 7; Wang Xiaoqiang and Bai Nianfeng, *The Poverty of Plenty* (New York: St. Martin's Press, 1991), 20.

89. On the Three Gorges relocation, see the articles by Qi Ren, Chen Guojie, Ding Qigang, Zheng Jiaqin, Mou Mo and Cai Wenmei in Thibodeau, Williams, and Dai, *The River Dragon Has Come*. A more recent journalistic account (among many) is Jasper Becker, "Chinese Dam Looms but Villagers Stay Put," *San Francisco Chronicle* (December 1, 2002; www.sfgate.com/cgi-bin/article.cgi?file=/chronicle/archive/2002/12/01/MN172781.DTL). On the location of hydropower installations to date, see Chinese National Committee on Large Dams, *Large Dams in China* (Beijing: China Water Resources and Electric Power Press, 1987), 188.

90. Van Slyke, *Yangtze*, 16.

91. See also Bruce Stone, "China's Chang Jiang Diversion Project: An Overview of Economic and Environmental Issues," in *The Social and Environmental Effects of Large Dams*, vol. 2, *Case Studies*, ed. Edward Goldsmith and Nicholas Hildyard (Camelford, U.K.: Wadebridge Ecological Centre, 1990), 314. He notes that western routes for the proposed south-north water-transfer project have "never been surveyed as intensely as the other routes," though they would provide cleaner water and displace far fewer people.

92. See Bharat Dogra, "The Indian Experience with Large Dams," and Elizabeth Monosowski, "Brazil's Tucuruí Dam: Development at Environmental Cost," both in Goldsmith and Hildyard, *Social and Environmental Effects of Large Dams*.

93. See, for one contrast, Dogra, "Indian Experience," 201; noting the extremely large share of total Indian storage capacity that comes from a relatively few gigantic dams.

94. Cited in Greer, "Chinese Water Management," 76.

95. Greer, "Chinese Water Management," 148.

96. Lindert, *Shifting Ground*, 108–14.

97. Lindert, *Shifting Ground*, 159–60, argues that the contribution of recent defor-estation to the 1998 Yangzi floods may have been exaggerated; he notes that most of the rains fell in areas that had been largely deforested for at least a century. Official

reports, however, suggest that the recent timber boom played a large role—something that the regime would probably not be eager to admit. (See, for instance, "Yangtze Floods and the Environment," an August 1998 report of the U.S. Embassy, citing official Chinese sources, at www.usembassy-china.org.cn/sandt/fldrpt.htm, accessed January 25, 2005—particularly the section titled "Less Water but a Bigger Flood: Deforestation the Cause.") Nor would it be necessary for the heavy rains that did help create this particular flood to fall in the same place where the most recent deforestation occurred, creating some of the background problems that increase the flooding problem in general. On the recent increase in the Yangzi's silt burden, see Economic Construction Group of the Chinese People's Political Consultative Committee, "The Three Gorges Project Should Not Go Ahead in the Short Term," in Luk and Witney, *Mega-project,* 15, 113–14. For a particularly pessimistic view, see He Bochuan, *China on the Edge,* 31.

98. Wang Xiaoqiang and Bai Nianfeng, *Poverty of Plenty,* 66–74, 87–89, 139.

99. Free Tibet Campaign UK, *Tibet Facts,* nos. 7 and 8, included as appendixes in Free Tibet Campaign UK, *Death of a Sacred Lake;* S. D. Richardson, "The Forest Economy of Tibet," *Commonwealth Forestry Review* 67, no. 3 (1988): 254.

100. Free Tibet Campaign UK, *Tibet Facts,* no. 8; Richardson, "Forest Economy," 254, 262; Smil, *Environmental Crisis,* 62, 106.

101. Free Tibet Campaign UK, *Death of a Sacred Lake,* 7; Wang Xiaoqiang and Bai Nianfeng, *The Poverty of Plenty,* 89; Free Tibet Campaign UK, *Tibet Facts,* no. 7.

102. He Bochuan, *China on the Edge,* 35–40; Nickum, "Beijing's Maturing Socialist Water Economy," 37, 41; Van Slyke, *Yangtze,* 189.

103. See Lester Brown, *Who Will Feed China?* (New York: W. W. Norton, 1994), for dire projections of China's future grain deficits; Vaclav Smil, "China Shoulders the Cost of Environmental Change," *Environment* 39, no. 6 (July–August 1997): 32–34, for estimates of how China can, with further irrigation, keep these deficits manageable; and Lindert, *Shifting Ground,* for a relatively optimistic assessment of China's agricultural capacity (though he does not expect China to feed itself completely, pointing to its comparative advantage in certain kinds of manufacturing).

104. On food, see Smil, *China's Past;* for oil and natural gas figures, see U.S. Department of Energy Information Administration on South Korea (www.eia.doe. gov/emeu/cabs/skorea.html) and Japan (www.eia.doe.gov/emeu/cabs/japan.html), both accessed January 13, 2006.

105. See, for example, Smil, "China Shoulders the Cost," 34.

106. See Nickum, "Is China Living on the Water Margin?" 892; and see Gu Di, "Popularization of China's Water-Saving Irrigation Equipment," China.org (www.china.org.cn/ChinaToday/Today/ChinaToday/Ct7e/Ct7e/7e-11.htm), for one example. Much existing water-saving irrigation technology is designed for large

farms and thus not useful in much of China: see "Irrigation in China Demands More Efficient Technologies," U.S. Department of State; www.usembassy-china.org.cn/sandt/mu2irig.htm, accessed January 13, 2006.

107. Wang Feng and Andrew Mason, "Population Aging in China: Challenges, Opportunities and Institutions," in *China's Economic Transitions: Origins, Mechanisms, and Consequences,* ed. Loren Brandt and Thomas Rawski (Cambridge: Cambridge University Press, 2008), 136–66.

108. Peng Yan and Jim Stover, "Water Pricing Issues and Potential Legal Reforms in China," Professional Association for China's Environment, cited 1998; www.erm.com/ERM/Loc/erm_china.NSF, accessed January 13, 2006.

109. Elizabeth Economy, "The Case Study of China, Reforms and Resources: The Implications for State Capacity in the PRC," Occasional Paper, Project on Environmental Scarcities, State Capacity, and Civil Violence, 1997 (www.library.utoronto.ca/pcs/state/china/china1.htm, accessed July 18, 2007), 12.

110. He Bochuan, *China on the Edge,* 37–40; Nickum, "Beijing's Maturing Socialist Water Economy," 52.

111. Nickum, "Is China Living on the Water Margin?" 891.

112. Smil, "China's Energy and Resource Uses," 947; Smil, *Environmental Crisis,* 72–75, 126–28.

113. Jan Gustafson, *Water Resources Development in the People's Republic of China* (Stockholm: Royal Institute of Technology, 1984), 141, 149. A more recent and somewhat more optimistic view can be found in Nickum, "Is China Living on the Water Margin?" 895.

114. Nickum, "Beijing's Maturing Socialist Water Economy," 54.

115. R. Bin Wong, *China Transformed: Historical Change and the Limits of European Experience* (Ithaca, NY: Cornell University Press, 1997), 121–22, 25–26, 169–77.

116. Madeline Zelin, *The Magistrate's Tael* (Berkeley: University of California Press, 1984).

117. Prasenjit Duara, *Culture, Power, and the State: Rural North China, 1900–1942* (Stanford, CA: Stanford University Press, 1988), 58–85.

118. See Oi, *Rural China Takes Off,* 17–57, on fiscal decentralization under the reforms in general, and 54–56 on the attempted, but only partially successful, recentralization in 1994. For the current distribution of rural tax burdens, see Thomas Bernstein and Xiaobo Lü, *Taxation without Representation in Contemporary Rural China* (Cambridge: Cambridge University Press, 2003), 48–72, 241–44, 49–50.

119. Bernstein and Lü, *Taxation without Representation.*

120. Wang Shaoguang, "The Rise of the Regions: Fiscal Reform and the Decline of the Central State Capacity in China," in *The Waning of the Communist State,* ed. Andrew G. Walder (Berkeley: University of California Press, 1995), 103–4.

121. Jasper Becker, "Notes on China," *South China Morning Post,* May 27, 1999, forwarded by International Rivers Network. E-mail in author's possession.

122. See China Development Gateway, "2,600-Year-Old Agricultural Tax Abolished," China.org (www.china.org.cn/english/2005/dec/153739.htm, accessed July 18, 2007); Bernstein and Lü, *Taxation without Representation;* Oi, *Rural China Takes Off,* 17–57; Loraine A. West and Christine P. W. Wong, "Fiscal Decentralization and Growing Regional Disparities in Rural China: Some Evidence in the Provision of Social Services," *Oxford Review of Economic Policy* 11, no. 4 (1995), 70–84.

123. See "Urban Migration to Get a Boost," China Development Gateway (www.china.org.cn/english/215350.htm, accessed July 18, 2007).

124. Nickum, "Is China Living on the Water Margin?" 886.

125. See, for instance, Ho, "Non-agricultural Development," 375.

126. Lindert, *Shifting Ground,* 159–60.

127. Lindert, *Shifting Ground,* 160.

128. William A. Byrd and Alan Gelb, "Why Industrialize? The Incentives for Rural Community Governments," in *China's Rural Industry: Structure, Development, and Reform,* ed. William A. Byrd and Lin Qingsong (Oxford: Oxford University Press, 1990), 368; West and Wong, "Fiscal Decentralization," 79, 80.

129. Wang Xiaoqiang and Bai Nianfeng, *Poverty of Plenty,* 66–67. See also *China News Digest,* November 3, 1999, for yet another statement by a political leader (Zhu Rongji) that development of western China is an urgent priority.

130. On the more stringent application of birth-control policies to minorities (which has gone along with an increased emphasis on eugenics as well as population control, and with the promulgation of measurements by which minority peoples are shown to be "inferior"), see Frank Dikotter, *Imperfect Conceptions: Medical Knowledge, Birth Defects, and Eugenics in China* (London: Hurst and Co., 1998); Zhang Yi, "Zhongguo de 18ge baiwan ren yishang shaoshu minzu renkou suzhi fenxi," *Minzu yanjiu* 5 (1995): 19–24.

SIX · The Rhine as a World River

MARK CIOC

The Rhine is one of the world's great commercial streams, second only to the Mississippi in the tonnage of freight it carries annually. It drains eight European states along its northwesterly path from the Alps to the North Sea: Switzerland, Austria, Liechtenstein, Germany, France, Belgium, Luxembourg, and the Netherlands. Four are central to Rhine political and ecological affairs: Switzerland, home to its headwaters, the Alpenrhein and the Aare; Germany, wherein slightly over half its watershed lies; France, which controls half of the biologically rich rift valley between Basel and Strasbourg; and the Netherlands, where the Meuse and Rhine (known there as the Waal) merge into a common delta.

Among Eurasian rivers, the Rhine ranks only ninth in size. Its length is just 1,250 kilometers (775 miles), roughly one-fifth that of the Nile. Its catchment area is so small—185,000 square kilometers (71,400 square miles)—that it would take thirty Rhine basins to equal the Amazon basin. Its average delta discharge is 2,200 cubic meters per second (2,875 cubic yards per second), less than half that of the Danube, its closest neighbor. Like most alpine rivers, the Rhine flows steeply and quickly in its upper reaches, becomes slower and (if left to its own devices) braided in its middle stretches, and then grows sluggish as it reaches its delta. It picks up tributary waters along the way, averaging a discharge of 1,100 cubic meters per second at Basel and 2,200 at Emmerich. Its year-round flow is more consistent than that of most rivers, largely because of a naturally balanced discharge regime: its alpine tributaries (those upstream, or south, of Basel) shed their waters during the warm summer months when the snow meltoff is highest, whereas its nonalpine tributaries (those downstream, or north, of Basel) peak during the rainy winter months. Seasonal variations thus offset each other, creating a stable year-round flow favorable to navigation.[1]

The most striking feature of the Rhine today is its centrality to Europe's industrial and urban life. Rotterdam's Europoort, on the Rhine mouth, is the main destination for Mideast oil tankers and the world's largest ocean harbor.[2] Duisburg-Ruhrort, situated at the center of the coal-rich Ruhr region, possesses the world's largest inland harbor. The Lippe, Emscher, Ruhr, Mosel, Lahn, Nahe, Main, Neckar, Ill, and Aare are all commercially important tributaries. German canals connect the Rhine to the Baltic, while French canals connect it to the Atlantic and Mediterranean. Since 1992 the Rhine has also been linked to the Black Sea via the Main-Danube canal.

More than fifty million people live in the Rhine watershed, making it one of the most densely settled river basins in the world. Some of Europe's largest iron, steel, automobile, aluminum, textile, potash, and paper firms are located on the Rhine. So are some of the world's largest chemical and pharmaceutical firms—including Bayer, BASF, Sanofi Aventis, Novartis, and Roche. The Rhine also stands at the center of western Europe's energy grid, generating hydroelectricity, transporting coal, and providing cooling water for nuclear reactors. Take away the Rhine, in other words, and industrial production in the western half of Europe would come to a halt for lack of infrastructure.

The Rhine is used simultaneously for transportation, industrial production, urban sanitation, and energy production. Largely for that reason, the Rhine is also one of the most biologically degraded streams in the world. Few streams have experienced as much habitat destruction and loss of biodiversity as the Rhine over the past two hundred years. Most visible to the eye is the sheer drop in the amount of living space available to the river's nonhuman organisms. The Rhine's main channel has been shortened by more than one hundred kilometers, which represents about an 8 percent drop in bank and channel habitat for aquatic and semi-aquatic species. Hundreds of kilometers of secondary channels and braids have also been removed, representing a further loss of channel and bank space and also the near-complete destruction of the microhabitats (backwaters, deep pools, and riffs) so essential to fish for feeding, spawning, and nursing. In addition, more than three thousand islands have been removed from the channel, each scooped-out island representing a loss of habitat for a variety of species. Finally, more than 80 percent of the river's original floodplain—the forests, meadows, and wetlands on the channel's edge, on which most river organisms depend for their survival—has been usurped for farms, cities, and industries.

The Rhine channel now flows more swiftly and with less variation than it did in the past, making it a more hostile environment for most fish. Hydro dams and locks have created longitudinal obstacles for migratory fish, making it impossible for them to migrate from headwaters to ocean as their life cycles dictate. Reinforced banks, meanwhile, block the lateral movement of fish from main channel to backwaters, where fish normally feed and breed. Water pollution too has wreaked havoc on riverine organisms, creating an environment that allows only those species resistant to salts, heat, and chemicals to survive. Despite cleanup efforts over the past thirty years, the river's chloride load (salt content) is still so high that the upper stretches of the river have taken on some of the brackish characteristics usually associated only with estuaries and deltas. Thermal pollution has reduced seasonal variations in water temperature to such an extent that the Rhine almost never freezes over in winter as it once did; and chemical pollution has led to accumulation of heavy metals and persistent organic compounds in the river's silt and sediment. As a result, the river can no longer support many of its native species and has come to depend on the influx of newcomers adapted to saltier, warmer, and eutrophic (deoxygenated) river water.

This essay examines how the Rhine emerged as one of the world's greatest commercial waterways and how it simultaneously became one of the world's most biologically degraded rivers. The two processes were intertwined: the Rhine's destruction as a biological habitat is a direct consequence of political, economic, and hydraulic ideologies and practices rooted deep in Europe's past. More specifically, the manner in which the Rhine was engineered to serve the needs of industrial Europe during the nineteenth century brought with it negative ecological consequences that are still with us today. Some were foreseen and accepted as inevitable consequences of progress; most were not foreseen but were accepted as faits accomplis nonetheless.

Three changes have had a particularly noticeable impact on Rhine ecology: channel straightening, which was done for purposes of water regulation and navigation; floodplain destruction, a consequence of land reclamation (flood-control) policies; and water pollution, the price of using the river as an industrial and urban sewer. All three have imposed a uniformity of habitat on the Rhine that has in turn undermined the river's ability to support biological diversity. The Rhine thus illustrates in microcosm the environmental problems besetting many regions that have undergone European-style commercial and industrial development over the past two centuries.

CONSTRUCTING A WORLD RIVER

The Rhine's rise to prominence as one of the world's great commercial rivers began in 1815, when the Vienna Congress decided to establish the Central Commission for Rhine Navigation and place the river under an "international regime." Now headquartered in Strasbourg, the Rhine Navigation Commission is the oldest continuous interstate institution in Europe and therefore marks the first step toward the Common Market and European Union. But the manner in which the river was constructed between 1815 and 1975 was more a reflection of Europe's past than its future. The modern Rhine (like modern Europe itself) is the product of ideologies and practices inherited from the Italian Renaissance, the Enlightenment, the French Revolution, and nineteenth-century liberalism.

Virtually all European rivers are products of Renaissance-era engineering practices. River manipulation is an age-old art that first came to Europe during the Roman Empire and was later kept alive through Dutch, Spanish, and Italian (Venetian) contacts with the Muslim world. The era of European dominance in this field began with the publication of Benedetto Castelli's *Della misura dell'acque correnti* (1628) and Domenico Guglielmini's *Della natura de' fiumi* (1719). Castelli developed the mathematical formula for determining the amount of water flowing in any given river at a given time (by measuring width, depth, and velocity). Guglielmini, meanwhile, provided engineers with a practical and easily accessible guide for channeling water from its source to its mouth as quickly and efficiently as possible to reduce flooding and maximize land reclamation for agriculture. The Renaissance engineers themselves were not particularly skilled river manipulators— they inadvertently caused many disasters from their imperfect understanding of floodplain geomorphology, and their activities struck fear into the hearts of seventeenth-century Europeans—but they nonetheless created the scientific basis for the practice of widening and shortening rivers.[3]

Renaissance-era Italian practices spread to Switzerland, the Netherlands, the German states, and France, where they became an integral part of the curricula of military engineering schools in the eighteenth century. These schools championed the notion that river engineering was central to the state-building process, demonstrating that it was possible for an "enlightened despot" to reclaim land for agricultural development, manage water resources, and improve commerce at the same time. "Engineers were ready to be at once the doctors and surgeons for water," wrote André Guillerme about the graduates of these schools. "At the request of political authorities, they sponged, curetted, and cauterized the open wound that the surface water network had become. And they were more successful, especially because, to unreliable practices inherited from the Renaissance were now added the more reliable methods of hydraulics, Enlightenment science par excellence, pursued in all engineering schools."[4]

One can see these Renaissance-Enlightenment principles at work in the blueprints of Johann Gottfried Tulla (1770–1828), the Baden engineer who oversaw the first Rhine rectification project in 1817. Tulla is still famous among hydraulic engineers for the maxim that guided his work: "No stream or river, the Rhine included, needs more than one bed; as a rule, multiple branches are redundant."[5] This straight-and-fast approach came directly from his reading of the Italian engineers. As a Paris-trained student of hydraulics, Tulla was also schooled in the Enlightenment tradition. "In agrarian regions," he wrote in his Rhine blueprint, "brooks, streams, and rivers should, as a rule, be canalized, and their flow harnessed to the needs of people who live along their banks."[6] And he shared fully in the optimistic spirit of his era. "Everything along this stream will improve once we undertake the rectification work," he claimed in his Rhine blueprint. "The attitude and productivity of the riverbank inhabitants will improve in proportion to the amount of protection their houses, possessions, and harvests receive. The climate along the Rhine will become more pleasant and the air cleaner, and there will be less fog, because the water table will be lowered by nearly one-third and swamps will disappear."[7]

Common to all European engineering textbooks was the notion that rivers were in need of being "domesticated," "tamed," or "harnessed." Some of this antagonistic mentality originated from the danger of flooding, which periodically made life hazardous for those who dwelled on European river banks; but much of it stemmed from the fact that rivers posed serious limitations to the movement of troops during wartime, which meant that engineers were an indispensable part of every European army. Most hydraulic engineers, Tulla included, started out as members of the military profession and only later became civil engineers, by which time the metaphors of war were deeply lodged in their heads. In 1812, the year Napoleon invaded Russia, Tulla was referring to his Rhine blueprint as a "general operational plan" for a "defense against a [Rhine] attack." And in 1825, a German official praised the Tulla Project as "a war strategy against the Rhine's waters."[8] Equally prevalent among engineers was the notion that free-flowing rivers were by nature defective and therefore in need of "rectification" and "amelioration." Blueprints for canal construction commingled with blueprints for river rectification, and with the blueprints went the mentality of improvement. Almost all

European engineers shared the belief that an "ideal" river was actually a canal—straight, predictable, designed for navigation, and not prone to flooding. That mentality goes a long way to explaining why most European rivers today look more like canals than natural-flowing streams— "straight as a dead snake," in Aldo Leopold's memorable phrase.[9]

If river rectification had its intellectual roots in the Italian Renaissance and European Enlightenment, the idea of an international river originated in the ideology of the French Revolution. When French troops seized control of the Rhine in 1792, they permanently transformed the political structure that had prevailed there for centuries. The Hapsburgs, who lost the Austrian Netherlands (Belgium) to France in 1795, never returned to the Rhine as a riparian power. Similarly, the Lilliputian German principalities of the ancien régime Rhine gave way to new middle-sized Napoleonic creations: Baden, Württemberg, Hesse, Nassau, Berg, Westphalia, and Rhineland. France's overarching influence waned with Napoleon's defeat in 1815, but the Vienna Congress's delegates decided against restoring the Rhine principalities of yesteryear and instead accepted the Napoleonic states as legitimate. To have done otherwise would have meant the restoration of ninety-seven independent German political entities between Alsace and the Netherlands—not the kind of political situation that would have permitted river rectification work on a grand scale.

On economic issues, too, the French Revolution's legacy was immense, especially as regards the establishment of liberal trade policies. The Vienna diplomats used the Convention de l'Octroi, which had been signed between Napoleonic France and its German satellite states in 1804, as a guide in formulating their own unified commercial codes. Similarly, the Magistrat du Rhin, a Napoleonic agency created in 1808 to handle commercial and engineering matters on the Rhine, served as a model for the Rhine Navigation Commission (Tulla, for instance, formulated his Rhine blueprint while serving as Baden's liaison officer to the Magistrat). By agreeing to an international Rhine, the Vienna diplomats were tacitly accepting yet another French revolutionary goal: "The restrictions and obstacles formerly placed on Rhine sailing and trading directly conflict with natural law, to which all Frenchmen are sworn to uphold," stated the French Executive Council decree of November 16, 1792. "The flow of rivers is a common asset, not given to transfer or sale, of all states whose waters feed them."[10] The Vienna delegates were more prosaic—"Navigation on the Rhine, from the point where it becomes navigable to the sea *[jusqu'à la mer]* and vice versa, shall be free, in that it cannot be prohibited to any one"—but the end result was identical.[11]

Moving from liberal economic theory to liberal economic practice was a messy matter, on the Rhine as elsewhere in nineteenth-century Europe. The Dutch, determined to protect their monopoly on colonial tea, salt, and spice imports, interpreted the phrase "*jusqu'à la mer*" to mean "up to the sea" and not "into the sea," thus exempting their seaports from the Vienna agreement. They also arbitrarily decided that the name *Rhine* referred only to the Neder-Rijn (the Rhine's secondary branch) and not the Waal (its main branch), where most trading took place.[12] In the face of this intransigence, other riparian states and cities (notably Cologne) refused to give up their own trade privileges until the Dutch returned to the negotiating table. It took sixteen years to resolve most of these conflicts (by the Mainz Acts of 1831) and another thirty-seven years to resolve the rest (by the Mannheim Acts of 1868). No doubt it would have taken longer, but increased competition from the railroads after 1848 finally turned the Rhine riparian states into unabashed free traders.[13]

Nationalism, in the form of Franco-German rivalry over Alsace and Lorraine, also worked against the cooperative spirit embodied in the idea of an international regime. The root problem was that five of the seven original members of the Rhine Navigation Commission—Prussia (Rhineland and Westphalia), Hesse, Nassau, Baden, Bavaria (Palatinate), France (Alsace and Lorraine), and the Netherlands—were German states. Bismarck's wars of unification exacerbated this imbalance. First, Prussia annexed Nassau after the Austro-Prussian war of 1866. Then Baden, Hesse, and Bavaria joined the new German empire in 1871, as did Alsace and Lorraine, which France lost as a result of the Franco-Prussian war. From 1871 to 1918, only the presence of the Netherlands on the commission kept the navigable stretch of the Rhine from becoming "Germany's river but not Germany's border," as Ernst Moritz Arndt proclaimed in 1813. When France returned to the Rhine at the end of World War I, it reclaimed Alsace and Lorraine, moved the commission to Strasbourg, and expanded its membership to include Switzerland, Belgium, Italy, and Great Britain, all for the purpose of diluting German influence (articles 354–62 of the Versailles Treaty). Nazi Germany and Fascist Italy quit the commission in the mid-1930s, and it all but disappeared during World War II. It was not until 1950, when the Federal Republic of Germany joined the commission, that the Rhine became a fully functioning international river in spirit as well as in fact.[14]

With rare exceptions, however, these politico-military disputes had surprisingly little effect on the pace and scope of the various Rhine engineering projects. The Rhine navigation commissioners and their bevy of engineers kept the spirit of cooperation alive because they all spoke the common language of mathematics and shared the goal of maximizing the river's potential as a navigational waterway. Personnel, blueprints, and ideas crossed borders with ease. The Vienna Congress placed the Rhine's future not so much in the hands of the various riparian governments as in the hands of hydraulic engineers. The Rhine Navigation Commission's influence from above in the setting of goals, and the Rhine engineers' influence from below over implementation, kept the riparian governments in check even in an age of militant nationalism.

Yet this arrangement also had a major drawback. Missing from the equation were any organizations or personnel interested in safeguarding the Rhine as a biological habitat. All of those in control of the Rhine thought in terms of global trade; none concerned themselves with such local issues as the fishing industry or the timber trade. In this sense, the Vienna Congress inadvertently created an ecological vacuum that gave rise to a "tragedy of the commons": all of the riparian states were interested in developing the Rhine, but none in preserving it; all fretted about the gradual decline in water quality, yet none had any particular incentive to do anything about it. Not until 1950 did the European governments create the Rhine Protection Commission as a counterweight to the Rhine Navigation Commission, by which time most of the ecological damage had already been done.

THE ECOLOGY OF RHINE ENGINEERING

Rivers can be envisaged in a variety of ways: as a line in the landscape, as the trunk of a watershed, or as the artery of a biological habitat. The first image suggests that a river is fundamentally just a sluiceway for channeling water and sediment downstream (in keeping with the Latin root for river, *ripa*, meaning *bank*). The second image highlights the inseparability of a bank and channel from a watershed—the headwaters, floodplains, valleys, mountains, tributaries, islands, underground flow, delta, and everything else that makes up a drainage system. The third image is the fullest, as it suggests that rivers—as carriers of water—lie at the conflux of the physicochemical and biological worlds, providing space for fish, snails, birds, trees, and people. Rhine engineers, schooled as they were in the Renaissance-Enlightenment tradition of river engineering, viewed rivers in the narrowest sense: as a sluiceway. They therefore thought in mechanical rather than organic terms as they constructed the river.

Because the Rhine's geomorphology and ecology are too diverse to treat as a single ecosystem, scientists have traditionally divided the river into two parts, each with several subdivisions. The Alpine part includes the Alpenrhein tributary system, the Aare tributary system, and the high Rhine. Trout and grayling are the indicator fish species (species that delineate a bioregion), with alder and willow as the most common trees. Most of the engineering projects on these stretches have focused on hydroelectric development and flood control. The non-Alpine part includes the upper Rhine, middle Rhine, lower Rhine, and delta Rhine, all of which are open to sea traffic. These stretches belong to the barbel, bream, and (at the delta) flounder bioregions, with oak and elm as the dominant trees. A quick overview of the major engineering projects on the non-Alpine stretches suffices to show the negative impact that navigational improvements have had on the river's flora and fauna. For simplicity, these projects can be grouped together under national rubrics: the delta Rhine is associated with the Netherlands, the lower and middle Rhine with Germany, and the upper Rhine with Germany and France.

Work on the delta Rhine (from Pannerdens near the Dutch-German border to the Hook of Holland) was handled almost exclusively by the Netherlands. From an engineer's perspective, the delta Rhine's drainage pattern had two natural defects: the channels were too shallow and lacking in gradient to carry sediment and ice floes efficiently to the North Sea, and the river's many delta mouths were too narrow to keep all the water flowing in channels during peak discharge periods. The most immediate problem was the partial confluence of the Waal and the Meuse at Heerewaarden and again at Loevestein. When the Waal ran high, as it often did in summer, the Meuse tended to overflow its banks regularly. Nearly as problematic was the narrow channel between Rotterdam and the North Sea, which restricted drainage and limited ship size on the Waal.[15]

The Netherlands' Department of Public Works and Water Management over-saw all phases of the rectification work. The first undertaking, the Merwede Project (1850–1916), concentrated on a section of the commingled Waal-Meuse waters between Gorinchem and Dordrecht. Workers began by constructing a new riverbed—the Nieuwe Merwede—for the middle portion of the Merwede river, which in its natural state was more a series of interflowing creeks than a river. The new bed provided the Waal and Meuse with a deeper and wider conduit to the sea, and it worked well for flood control as well as navigation. Next on the agenda was the stretch downstream from the Nieuwe Merwede, known as the Boven Merwede. Its bed was so wide (six hundred meters) from the combined Waal and Meuse flow that during low-water periods it easily became obstructed by sandbars. To rectify this problem, the Dutch dug a new mouth system for the Meuse—known as the Bergse Maas—which greatly reduced the amount of commingling between the

Waal and Meuse and opened up traffic to the sea via the Hollandsch Diep. Once Meuse waters no longer encumbered the Boven Merwede, engineers were able to reduce its width to make it navigable year-round.[16]

During the same period, Dutch engineers began the Nieuwe Waterweg Project (1860–72) to canalize the thirty-five-kilometer stretch of the Waal between Rotterdam and the North Sea. Following a plan developed by Pieter Caland, engineers cut a trench through the Hook of Holland, dammed the old river channel, and then let the river forge a new mouth through the force of its own current. Dredgers then deepened this new navigational channel, creating the preconditions for Rotterdam's phenomenal rise to become the world's largest harbor. More Rhine-related projects followed. From 1875 to 1906, the Waal and the Bovenrijn (the short stretch of the Lower Rhine between the German border and Pannderdens canal) were reengineered to maintain a minimum depth of three meters. These alterations made it possible for large ships to travel quickly and easily between the highly industrialized Ruhr region and Rotterdam. At the same time, the Nederrijn (the secondary Rhine bifurcation below Pannerdensch) was reengineered to maintain an alternate shipping route at a minimum depth of two meters. Then, from 1920 to 1932, engineers dammed the Zuiderzee, transforming the Ijsselmeer into an estuary (also a Rhine mouth). The widening and canalization of the Meuse (1918–42) and the Nederrijn (1954–69) followed. In the 1930s the Amsterdam-Rijn canal (1931–38) was built, providing Rhine ships with yet another route to the North Sea.[17]

Work on the lower and middle Rhine (from Bingen to Pannderdens) was handled mostly by the Prussian government. It commenced with the establishment of the Rhine River Engineering Administration in Koblenz under the directorship of Eduard Adolph Nobiling in 1851. The basic engineering challenge on the lower Rhine was to maximize navigational efficiency by maintaining a uniform flow at a predictable velocity. Minimum depths of two meters were established for the Bingen-to-St. Goar stretch, two-and-a-half meters for the St. Goar-to-Cologne stretch, and three meters for the Cologne-to-Pannderdens stretch. To achieve these depths, the river had to be artificially narrowed to a width of 90 meters from Bingen to Oberwesel, 120 meters from Oberwesel to St. Goar, and 150 meters from St. Goar to the Dutch border. The Lower Rhine had a number of meanders and braids, so Nobiling and his staff began with a series of cuts designed to shorten and steepen the stream. The distance between Bonn and Pannderdens was reduced by twenty-three kilometers. Islands were removed or connected to their adjacent banks. Sandbars and other navigational hindrances were dredged, embankments fortified, and harbors added. Nobiling's most original contribution was the design of a new type of wing dam—a concave structure about a meter wide and six meters long that extends into the river from the shore—to direct the flow toward the middle of the stream so as to maintain a minimum shipping depth during low-water periods.[18]

Work on the upper Rhine (from Basel to Bingen) was undertaken in three different phases, twice by the Germans and then once again by the French. The first, the Tulla Project (1817–76), focused mostly on flood control. It provided the upper Rhine with an artificial bed of uniform width: 200 meters between Basel and Strasbourg, and 230–250 meters from Strasbourg to Mannheim. The river's length was reduced by a total of 82 kilometers: 31 kilometers were removed from Basel to the mouth of the Lauter river (14 percent of the original 218.5 kilometers), and 51 kilometers from the Lauter mouth downstream to Mannheim (37.1 percent of the original 135.1 kilometers). More than two thousand islands were removed in the process. The Tulla Project, however, had one fatal drawback: it greatly aggravated channel erosion, so much so that this stretch of the river became less navigable than in the past. Another round of engineering work—the Honsell-Rehbock Project (1906–36)—addressed this problem by reworking the upper Rhine so that it conformed to the standards of the just-completed Prussian and Netherlands projects. Here the goal was to create a riverbed two meters deep and eighty-eight meters wide that would permit all-year navigation from Mannheim to Basel. Dikes, dams, and wing dams were needed, as were reinforced riverbanks and harbors. Special attention had to be paid to the problem of maintaining the water level, because (unlike the lower Rhine) the upper Rhine was supplied mostly by Alpine runoff and was therefore prone to seasonal droughts. By the 1920s, the Honsell-Rehbock Project had made it possible for large ships to travel beyond Mannheim (the endpoint of Rhine shipping during most of the nineteenth century) to the new ports of Karlsruhe and Kehl/Strasbourg.[19]

Overcoming the navigation restrictions farther upstream, along the Alsace-Baden border (from Strasbourg to Basel), was far more problematic. One obstacle was the Istein rapids, an inadvertent byproduct of Tulla's engineering. Circumventing them necessitated an elaborate lock system. A related problem was the water table in Baden. Any rectification work that entailed extensive canalization of the riverbed would inevitably lower the water table and potentially endanger Baden's agricultural productivity. The German government was in no hurry to open up Basel to sea traffic, especially if it might lower the water table in Baden, so work on this stretch did not begin until after World War I, when France returned to the Rhine and initiated work on the Grand Canal d'Alsace (1921–59). The idea, as envisaged by René Koechlin, the Alsatian engineer in charge of the project, was to divert most of the water from its original bed and direct it instead through a series of hydroelectric dams running parallel to the left bank. Aside from producing hydropower, the Grand Canal established a year-round transportation link connecting Basel, Mulhouse, Colmar, and Strasbourg. The first hydro dam, at Kembs, was completed in 1932. The next three—at Ottmarsheim (1952), Fessenheim (1956), and Vogelgrün (1959)—had to await the end of World War II. Yet another four hydro dams were subsequently built at Marckolsheim (1967), Rhinau (1963), Gerstheim (1967), and Strasbourg (1970), this time to protect Baden's water table. Two more locks—one at Gambsheim with a hydro dam and one at Iffezheim without one—were added in 1974 and 1978, respectively, to control erosion.[20]

From a Renaissance-Enlightenment engineering perspective, the Dutch, German, and French projects turned the Rhine into something approaching an ideal river: a cement-lined canal that flows steadily and predictably most of the time. From an ecological viewpoint, however, the Rhine's new bed and bank deprived it of most of the features on which its biodiversity depended. The chief purpose of river straightening is to funnel water from land to ocean as quickly as possible. In practical terms, this means turning the river into an efficient drainage system by removing its braids, oxbows, islands, rivulets, backwaters, deep spots, shallow pools, and marshlands—in other words, by removing the sites that provide most riverine organisms with a niche. Aquatic organisms, especially fish, depend on a diversified, not a uniform, channel. Well adapted to the natural rhythms of a river, they can withstand floods, droughts, and innumerable other changes, but not a geometric assault from river engineers. As late as 1900, biologists could still distinguish four bioregions on the navigable stretch of the Rhine from Basel to Rotterdam, distinguished by the dominant fish species: the grayling-barbel region (the upper half of the upper Rhine), the barbel region (lower half of the upper Rhine and most of the middle Rhine), the bream region (most of the lower and delta Rhine from Bonn to Dordrecht), and the sea bream–flounder region (near the delta mouth). Nonstop river engineering, however, transformed the entire navigable Rhine into a single biocommunity.[21]

Migratory fish—chief among them salmon, shad, and sturgeon, once the mainstays of the Rhine fishing industry—were hardest hit. But all fish were affected to one extent or another because they all depend on longitudinal, lateral, and vertical pathways for feeding and spawning. The Rhine's longitudinal pathways disappeared with the construction of dams and locks on the upper Rhine, which blocked the migration route between the Alps and the North Sea. The salmon industry, for instance, suffered a major blow when the Kembs hydroelectric plant was completed in 1932, because it cut the salmon off from their Alpine spawning habitat. Though less immediately lethal to nonmigratory fish, the hydro dams and locks have nonetheless limited their ability to disperse and colonize, which in turn has reduced the number of fish that the river now supports. The river's lateral pathways (also known as river-edge habitats) disappeared with the construction of artificial banks and the simultaneous removal of braids and back channels. These changes destroyed the low-velocity areas fish need to feed, spawn, and nurse. Vertical river pathways (also known as river-groundwater interactions) are particularly important to salmon, trout, and other fish that spawn on gravel depressions, where surface water and groundwater mix and where fine sediment is at a minimum. These pathways disappeared as a consequence of gravel extraction, a concomitant of almost all river rectification work.[22]

Two hundred years ago the Rhine supported forty-seven fish species. Today, only thirty-eight of those species are still found in the river, and many of them have become either rare or wholly dependent on artificial propagation for survival. Migratory salmon and shad were once plentiful in the river, as were to a lesser extent the lampern, sea lamprey, North Sea houting, sea trout, and sturgeon. All of them are now gone or rare, the victims of river engineering. Most numerous today in the river, by far, are three fish from the Cyprinidae (carp) family: the roach (36.1 percent), bleak (25.6 percent), and common bream (11.8 percent). Tolerant of polluted and degraded streams, they now account for 73.5 percent of all fish swimming between Basel and the delta. The next six most common species today are the eel (6.8 percent), dace (6.8 percent), perch (4.3 percent), chub (2.3 percent), white bream (1.6 percent), and gudgeon (1.4 percent), which collectively account for another 23.2 percent of the river's fish. The remaining extant species—including grayling, smelt, pike, mud minnow, ide, barbel, bitterling, minnow, rapfen, souffie, loach, burbot, stickleback, bullhead, and flounder—now collectively account for a mere 3.3 percent of the fish population. Thus a mere nine species account for well over 95 percent of all fish in the Rhine between Basel and Rotterdam.[23]

Although fish have been most directly affected by river engineering, river mammals, aquatic birds, and amphibians have also been displaced. Beaver and otter populations have all but disappeared, their place largely taken by the nonnative muskrat, a species well adapted to cement banks. Nearly all birds that nest on riverbank vegetation and feed on freshwater species are endangered to one extent or another on the Rhine, including herons, songbirds, terns, ducks, geese, falcons, and rails. Three amphibian species—the tree frog, dice snake, and adder—have become endangered, in each case because the rectification work has deprived them of their natural living space. Moreover, even the most adaptable species find themselves marginalized by the new river for the simple reason that four-fifths of the river's former floodplain no longer exists, having been usurped for urban, industrial, and agricultural development.[24]

THE ECONOMICS OF WATER POLLUTION

It is well known that the Mercator projection—the famous two-dimensional world map designed in 1569 by Gerhard Krämer—exaggerates Europe's size and geographic centrality while peripheralizing and diminishing the rest of the world. As a map of the Rhine, however, it is ideal: it places Duisburg (Krämer's home) and Rotterdam at center stage, the span between them being, then as now, the most navigable and lucrative stretch of the river. In Krämer's day, timber, fish, and wine were mainstays of Rhine commerce. Since the nineteenth century, coal and chemicals have dominated.

Coal mining has had the single greatest impact on the Rhine's natural hydrology, affecting not only the pace and scope of river engineering and canal construction but also giving rise to the first great spurt of urban sprawl on its banks and the first signs of severe water pollution in its catchment area. Especially hard hit by coal-related water pollution were the lower Rhine and one of its tributaries, the Emscher, which flow through the Prussian-controlled provinces of Rhineland and Westphalia (the Ruhr region), home to Europe's largest bituminous reserves. Coal extraction caused ground depressions around the mines, pockmarking the landscape and creating stagnant pools that helped breed water-borne diseases. Coal cleaning and coke processing allowed phenol and other contaminants to enter the Emscher and Lower Rhine.

Because the Emscher, a short river (109 kilometers) with a small watershed (850 square kilometers), snakes right through the middle of the Westphalian coalfields, it was an irresistible target for the dumping of industrial effluents. It earned a reputation as an open-air sewer (or *cloaca maxima*, as it was later dubbed) in the early days of coal mining; and the dirtier it got, the more entrenched its status became. By the early twentieth century, the Emscher was receiving discharges from 150 coal mines, 100 related factories, and 1.5 million urban residents each year. By 1910 only about half of its annual water budget came from natural runoff; the remainder, nearly 100 million cubic meters, came from industrial (89 percent) and urban (11 percent) discharges. The coal industry alone accounted for most of the contaminated water. Westphalia's bituminous mines tended to be extraordinarily deep, and water pumps were therefore needed to keep the tunnels from flooding. On average, 1,700 liters of mine water were pumped out of the mine for every ton of coal extracted, much of it laden with chlorides. The mine water was used to wash the coal and then was dumped (along with the chlorides and coal dust) untreated into the Emscher. The coking process produced an additional waste product—phenol—which lent the Emscher valley its distinctive stench.[25]

The Emscher was poorly suited to its designated role as a sewer. Its gradient was slight, its water level varied greatly from winter to summer, and its pathway meandered all over its valley. Its waters therefore easily stagnated, making it a good host for typhoid, cholera, and malaria. Discharges from industry doubled its flow without accelerating its velocity, creating even more problems with stagnation than before. Chlorides, coal dust, and phenol overwhelmed the stream's self-cleaning capacity, killing vegetation and fish and clogging the streambed. In some places the salt content was so high that it damaged the nearby agricultural fields. Sent to investigate a typhoid epidemic that killed three hundred people in Gelsenkirchen in 1901, Rudolph Emmerich filed this report on water conditions on the Emscher: "Here we find a black, thick, swampy, rotten and fermenting manure, which hardly moves: during summer, gas bubbles burst, poisoning the surrounding area. . . . The fermentation and putrefaction of these enormous quantities of disgustingly dirty and muddy waste water are intensified to the highest degree by the hot water from innumerable steam engines; as a consequence, the waste water often reaches breeding temperature. The waste water to be found in Gelsenkirchen is the most disgusting in the world."[26]

In 1904 the Prussian government responded to the river's deterioration by creating the Emscher Cooperative, a quasi-governmental, quasi-private association that included all the corporate entities using the Emscher and its feeder streams for waste disposal, as well as the urban communities that once relied on the river for drinking water. In principle, the goal of the Emscher Cooperative was to coordinate water policy between water suppliers and water users throughout the Emscher's catchment area. In practice, the polluting industries held the purse strings, and they kept the cooperative focused on the narrower task of waste disposal on the cheap. Protection of the Emscher as an ecological habitat was nowhere on the agenda.

The cooperative gave top priority to reengineering the Emscher to make it a more efficient version of the open-air sewer it had already become. Its length was shortened by twenty kilometers, which gave it a steeper gradient and therefore a faster flow. Its bank and bed (and that of its entire tributary system, some three hundred kilometers in length) were lined with cement to prevent seepage and to counteract the land depressions induced by underground mining. In polder areas, the cooperative installed special pumps and drainage systems so that stagnant water could be routinely returned to the Emscher or one of its feeder streams.[27] Predictably, the cooperative found that the least expensive disposal method was to channel the pollutants as swiftly as possible down the Emscher and into the Rhine. "The Rhine is capable of absorbing far more pollution than it now receives from the Emscher without any danger," the cooperative's water experts claimed in 1912 as a justification for this shortsighted practice.[28]

The notion of sacrificing a Rhine tributary to industrial production, and of using the Rhine as the sink for wastewater disposal, was subsequently adopted by the chemical industry when it muscled its way onto the Rhine in the 1860s. "Sacrificed stretches," wrote Curt Weigelt, the chief spokesperson for the German chemical industry, in 1901, "are spans of the river where pollution should be permitted either because the situation is such that industries can find no other possibility for getting rid of their wastewater without endangering profits and jobs, or because local conditions simply do not allow the cleansing of the water to its original state."[29] The chemical industry, however, differed from the coal industry both in its geographic reach and in its production capabilities. Unlike the coal industry, the chemical industry did not have to remain clustered atop the Westphalian bituminous reserves on the Lower Rhine and Emscher. It could spread to any stretch of the river from Switzerland to the Netherlands where coal, hydroelectricity, or petroleum could reach, and thus it could multiply almost indefinitely the number of river stretches that could be sacrificed. Moreover, the huge variety of its products—acids, bases, dyes, fertilizers, explosives, pharmaceuticals, film, and petrochemicals, to name but a few of the early ones—made the number and toxicity of chemical waste products almost limitless.

The Rhine basin was an ideal site for chemical manufacturing because it offered a steady stream of fresh water (for production, heating, cooling, and dumping) and a superb network of navigation links. Sulfur, pyrite, salt, chalk, phosphorus, and other essential raw materials were either locally accessible or easily imported on Rhine barges. Westphalia's coal provided a cheap fuel source and a superabundance of coal tar, the chief ingredient in dye production. Acid,

soda, and dye factories also found it profitable to settle close to their best cus-
tomers, the well-established textile mills on the Wupper, Ruhr, and Rhine.
Superphosphate production relied on a ready supply of sulfuric acid as well as
phosphate deposits in the Rhineland province and on the Lahn tributary. Potash
from Alsace and phosphatic slag from Lorraine also made the Rhine central to
that sector of the fertilizer industry. Cellulose plants also found the timber, caus-
tic soda, and water they needed for their pulp and paper operations ready at hand
on the Rhine.[30]

German and Swiss chemical firms led the way. The three most successful
German firms—BASF (Badische Anilin und Soda Fabrik), Bayer, and Hoechst—
were all founded in the 1860s with the advent of the artificial dye industry. They
settled on all stretches of the "German" Rhine (the lower, middle, and upper
Rhine) as well as on the Neckar, Main, and Wupper tributaries. Switzerland's most
successful firms—Ciba, Geigy, Sandoz, and Hoffmann–La Roche—all clustered
on the Upper Rhine near Basel, the endpoint of Rhine navigation. They too started
out as dye firms and then moved into pharmaceuticals and other specialty products.
The chemical industry in Alsace (also on the Upper Rhine) got its start when the
region came under German control in 1871. The Germans focused on potash-
fertilizer production through the exploitation of the local silvinite mines; the
French later branched out into other chemical sectors as well. The Dutch-based
industry, centered on the delta Rhine in and around Rotterdam, came to the forefront mostly after 1945, when the European chemical industry started using olefin
(derived from petroleum) instead of coal tar as its basic feedstock.[31]

Dye manufacturing had the first and most direct impact on water quality in the
Rhine basin, and it set the tone for later wastewater disposal methods. The early
aniline dyes required huge quantities of arsenic acid for production. Some of the
waste arsenic could be reprocessed and reused, but much of it found its way into
the Rhine and the North Sea. In the early years, dye firms were utterly indiscriminate in their dumping practices: some let their waste seep into the groundwater,
others dumped it into the North Sea, and still others poured it into the Rhine.[32]
Arsenic-related deaths were so prevalent between 1860 and 1872 that a public panic
ensued, forcing the riparian states to take the highly unusual step of signing an
international convention prohibiting arsenic dumping in the North Sea and into
local water supplies. All that did, however, was to reinforce the practice of dumping waste arsenic into the Rhine and its tributaries. Most other dye chemicals also
escaped regulation even if their toxicity was well known, the assumption being that
the Rhine would render everything harmless by dilution. Hydrogen sulfide, sulfitic

acid, arsine, aniline vapors, sulfuric acid, phenol, xylene, toluene, nitrotoluene, benzene, and nitrobenzene—all part of the dyeing process—were dangerous to one degree or another. When absorbed by the human body in small doses over time, these chemicals could damage the liver, kidneys, and bone marrow, a fact that dye workers came to learn firsthand.[33] The dyes penetrated not just into the skin and nostrils of workers but also into surrounding rivers and streams. By 1902, the BASF plant in Ludwigshafen had six pipes that led to the Rhine, emitting enough red dye that a distinct trail was visible all the way to Worms, many kilometers downstream; and by 1905, Bayer had ninety-five pipes dumping wastewater into the Wupper. Yet so widespread was the belief in the Rhine's self-cleansing capacity that Carl Duisberg, head of the Bayer Chemical Company, asserted in 1912 that "one could pour Germany's entire annual production of sulfuric acid into the Rhine at Cologne and not find a trace of it downstream at Mülheim" without fear of contradiction.[34]

The toleration of large-scale local pollution in Westphalia in the establishment of the modern coal and coking industries was short-sighted enough; but the continued toleration of river dumping once the chemical industry spread up and down the Rhine was a prescription for environmental disaster. By the 1960s, when the Rhine Protection Commission first began to undertake measures designed to restore the river's health, water quality between Basel and Rotterdam had already deteriorated so severely as a consequence of industrial and urban pollutants that for all intents and purposes the entire river had already been transmogrified into one long sacrificed stretch, much like the Emscher before it.[35] A study undertaken by a consortium of Rhine waterworks in the 1970s demonstrated that fully half of the pollutants came from the chemical industry, and most of those pollutants could be traced back to just six major sources: cellulose factories in Strasbourg and Mannheim, the Alsatian potash industry, the Bayer chemical plant at Leverkusen, and the urban centers of Basel and Strasbourg.[36]

Rhine water pollution can be divided into three basic categories: thermal pollution, which originates when water used for cooling conventional and nuclear power plants is returned to the river; chloride pollution, caused by excess salt discharges from potash production and agricultural runoff; and chemical pollution, caused especially by the bioaccumulation of heavy metals (zinc, copper, chromium, lead, cadmium, mercury, and arsenic) and persistent organic compounds such as organophosphates. Thermal pollution, not toxic per se, has raised the average yearly water temperature of the Rhine to such a degree that it has greatly affected both the number and composition of river species. The most pronounced effects are immediately below the nuclear plants, but the impact can be observed on all stretches of the river. Chlorides are common salts that enter the river through a variety of agricultural and industrial activities. They have no effect on humans and cause no harm once they have reached the sea, but in excessive quantities they make it impossible for freshwater species to survive. In 1970, for instance, the Rhine Protection Commission determined that the river's chloride load had reached an unprecedented 365 kilograms per second at the Dutch-German border, about three times the natural load. Most of the human-induced salt load came from the Alsatian potash mines, the rest from a variety of coal and chemical plants. Collectively, that amounted to 2.5 million metric tons of excess chlorides entering the Rhine each year.[37]

The third category—chemical pollutants—have proved to be the most pernicious because they are toxic to human and nonhuman organisms inside and outside the streambed. The level of copper in the Netherlands' floodplain, for instance, stood at 160 parts per million in 1974, more than six times the level considered safe for arable soils. Mercury and cadmium levels in the soil were twenty-five times higher than levels considered safe. Zinc levels were eleven times higher, lead levels seven times higher, arsenic levels five times higher, and chromium levels four times higher than acceptable limits. Research also indicated that the Rhine was carrying fifteen metric tons of nonbiodegradable organic substances every day, chiefly chlorinated hydrocarbons from pesticides and industrial processes. These substances were particularly worrisome because they pass through sewage-treatment plants without being removed from the water.[38]

The combined impact of thermal, salt, and chemical pollutants has profoundly transformed the number and composition of the river's invertebrate macrofauna—including bryozoa, mollusks, insects, crustaceans, leeches, flatworms, and sponges—which are generally considered to be the best indicators of water quality. As late as 1900, there were 165 known species living on the Rhine. By 1971, that number had dropped to just 27. The biggest drop came in insect populations, chief among them the mayfly, stonefly, and caddis fly, all crucial to the river's food chain. Their taxa numbers, which stood at 111 in 1900, fell to just three in 1971. Taxa richness rose again as water quality improved, but as recently as 1980 there were still only forty-six taxa found on the Rhine, less than half the original number.[39] Meanwhile, water pollution has opened up new opportunities for a few species. The most notable newcomer is the zebra mussel, a coin-sized black-and-white striped mollusk from the Caspian Sea. Highly tolerant of salt, and a voracious consumer of phytoplankton, it has come to dominate the Rhine's benthic (bottom-dwelling) community by sheer force of numbers between Basel and Rotterdam. Other newcomers—the freshwater crayfish, shrimp, beach flea, river snail, and bladder snail, among them—are all physiologically, morphologically, and behaviorally adapted to industrial pollutants, dissolved salts, and other harsh river conditions.[40]

Water pollution has thus proved to be as powerful a force as hydraulic engineering in imposing a biological homogeneity on the Rhine: it has reduced or eliminated all organisms that cannot tolerate the contaminants and favored only the few that can.

THE LIMITS OF RESTORATION

Karl Wittfogel's analysis of the relationship between irrigation politics and social power in ancient Egypt, China, and India is well known. Growing populations and persistent water shortages, he argued, gave rise to the world's first "hydraulic societies" based on large-scale dams, canals, and irrigation projects—highly stratified agro-urban civilizations ruled from above by emperors and kings and from below by bureaucrats and construction engineers.[41] His central thesis—that these supposedly early versions of "oriental despotism" explain modern-day Asian politics— has been repeatedly challenged. His notion of "hydraulic societies," however, has some merit when applied to modern-day Rhine affairs: something akin to an "occidental despotism" emerged on the Rhine during Wittfogel's lifetime and near his birthplace in Germany.

The Rhine Navigation Commission formed the upper stratum of this despotic regime, keeping all Rhine-related projects focused on one goal alone: the maximization of the river's potential as a navigational artery, regardless of its impact of that effort on the river as a biological habitat. Blueprints for bridges, canals, bank reinforcement, harbors, and everything else related to the development of the river as a shipping lane passed through the commission's offices. But all matters having to do with fishing and other related activities were forwarded to the various national fisheries commissions and governments, as if there were no connection between river engineering and fish stocks. Dutch supremacy over the delta, Prussian supremacy over Westphalia, and France's (eventual) supremacy over Alsace imposed a middle tier of water despotism on the navigable Rhine between Basel and Rotterdam. Here the sole purpose was maximization of the river's commercial and economic development, with little or no attention paid to protecting the river's banks and floodplain as a riparian habitat.

The German government went a step further, turning over the management of the Emscher and later other Rhine tributaries to water cooperatives. This move allowed the polluting industries to exercise a local despotism, arrogating for themselves the right to turn the tributaries into an industrial faucet or sewage gutters as they saw fit. It was the cooperatives, not local residents, who determined how the water would be used; it was industries, not farmers, who got the lion's share of water resources; and it was the engineers, not the local fishermen, who ultimately triumphed. The cooperatives favored minimal cleansing at minimal cost, and invariably that meant using the feeder streams as conduits to transport wastewater and other debris from industrial sites to the Rhine as efficiently as possible. The underlying (and ultimately incorrect) assumption was that the Rhine's volume and velocity were so great that no amount of coal dust, phenol, chlorides, metallic tailings, arsenic, or other pollutants could possibly turn the river into a larger version of the Emscher.

This multilayered navigational-industrial regime imposed yet another despotism on the Rhine: the tyranny of the irrevocable past. Today, not even the most old-fashioned river engineer would hack and chop at a river the way earlier generations sliced up the Rhine. Engineers have belatedly come to realize the importance of preserving a river's microhabitats as they reconstruct it. The old rules of river engineering, based on the notion of a single straight, wide, swift channel, have been discredited. Even canals today are built with biological principles in mind. The new Rhine-Main-Danube canal, for all its artificiality, snakes through the Altmühl valley more like a river than a canal. Instead of cutting a straight line through the hills, engineers followed the contours of the valley landscape, added artificial backwaters and river-edge habitats to facilitate lateral movement of aquatic species, and inserted artificial tributaries to replicate the dynamics of a natural stream. As a result, the canal looks in many respects more like a natural river than do the three rivers that it connects. Building from scratch, however, is infinitely easier than undoing what has already been done. Renaissance and Enlightenment-era engineering is permanently embedded in the Rhine today in the form of concrete banks, hydro dams, locks, and similar structures. To remove them would be to endanger the network of cities, towns, villages, roads, and factories that have taken over the former floodplain and become fixtures of the riverscape. Some agricultural fields can be (and are being) renaturalized, but in practical terms it is simply not possible to restore the Rhine to anything even remotely approximating what it looked like two hundred years ago.

A quick glance at current restoration projects reveals just how limited are their purpose and scope. The most highly publicized project, known as Salmon 2000, had as its foremost goal the reestablishment of the Rhine salmon population by the year 2000 (later extended when it did not achieve its goals in time). Suitable gravel beds, however, can be found today only on a handful of the Rhine's small tributaries and subtributaries—the Sieg, Bröl, Lahn, Saynbach, Bruche, Ill, and Lauter—for the most part streams that were too small to have caught the attention of industrial developers. Even the most optimistic estimates suggest that the Rhine will never support more than around twenty thousand salmon per year, a tiny fraction of its former population.[42] Another habitat restoration project—the Stork Plan—focused on the reconstruction of a few patches of former alluvial forestland and islands in the Dutch delta, especially at Millinger Waard, Sint Andries, Blauwe Kamer, and Duurse Waarden on the Waal. But the Netherlands' government soberly realized it would be impossible to engage in more extensive undertakings without upsetting various delta drainage schemes or removing valuable land from agricultural and urban use.[43] Similarly, the Action Plan on Flood Defence, which began in 1998, has been focusing on restoring as much of the upper Rhine's former floodplain as feasible. But it was clear from the outset that only a tiny fraction of the river's former floodplain could be renaturalized: there is simply too much built environment there today.[44]

Ultimately, the most important legacy of Rhine engineering has been environmental damage. The river was modified and transformed on the basis of an international free-trade agreement made in 1815 by all of the major European states. It made economic sense to take the river out of the hands of local princes and to place the river under an international regime. Under the aegis of the Rhine Navigation Commission, trade on the river increased with every year, rising from 10 million metric tons in 1825 to a staggering 288 million by 1978.[45] The commission's phenomenal success, moreover, helped establish a model for economic cooperation that moved Europe slowly but inexorably in the direction of the Common Market and European Union; but placing the Rhine in the hands of Eurocrats was a Faustian bargain that ought to give some discomfiture to today's free traders. By almost every ecological metric—from fish counts to water quality—the Rhine deteriorated significantly as a biological habitat even as it vastly improved as an economic waterway. By placing no environmental restrictions on economic growth at the outset, and by failing to reassess the purpose and goals of the Vienna regime as environmental problems first came to light, the European governments bequeathed to future generations a level of environmental damage that for the most part cannot be undone.

NOTES

This article summarizes and expands on the arguments I developed in *The Rhine: An Eco-biography, 1815–2000* (Seattle: University of Washington Press, 2002).

1. Statistics from the International Commission for the Hydrology of the Rhine Basin (CHR), *Der Rhein unter der Einwirkung des Menschen*, 13. If the Meuse basin is included, the Rhine's catchment area is 225,000 square kilometers.

2. Egbert Wever, "The Port of Rotterdam: 'Gateway to Europe,'" in *The Rhine Valley: Urban, Harbour and Industrial Development and Environmental Problems; A Regional Guide Dedicated to the 28th International Geographical Congress, The Hague, 1996*, ed. Heinz Heineberg, Norbert de Lange, and Alois Mayr (Leipzig: Institut für Länderkunde, 1996), 13. Rotterdam overtook the Port of New York as the world's largest port in 1962.

3. Cesare S. Maffioli, *Out of Galileo: The Science of Waters, 1628–1718* (Rotterdam: Erasmus, 1994), 268; and Norman Smith, *Man and Water: A History of Hydro-technology* (London: Charles Scribner's Sons, 1975), 43–45.

4. André E. Guillerme, *The Age of Water: The Urban Environment in the North of France, A.D. 300–1800* (College Station: Texas A & M University Press, 1983), 176. See also 196–209.

5. Johann Gottfried Tulla, "Bericht an das Großherzogliche Ministerium der auswärtigen Angelegenheiten über die Grundsätze, nach welchen die Rheinbauarbeiten künftig zu führen sein möchten, vom 1.3.1812," cited in Max Honsell, *Die Korrektion des Oberrheins von der Schweizer Grenze unterhalb Basel bis zur Grossherzogthum Hessischen Grenze unterhalb Mannheim* (Karlsruhe, 1885), 5.

6. Johann Gottfried Tulla, *Denkschrift: Die Rektifikation des Rheines* (Karlsruhe, 1822), cited in Heinz Musall, *Die Entwicklung der Kulturlandschaft der Rheinniederung zwischen Karlsruhe und Speyer vom Ende des 16. bis zum Ende des 19. Jahrhunderts* (Heidelberg: Geographisches Institut der Universität Heidelberg, 1969), 197.

7. Cited by H. Wittmann in "Tulla, Honsell, Rehbock," *Bautechnik-Archiv* 4 (1949): 12.

8. All three citations from Traude Löbert, *Die Oberrheinkorrektion in Baden: Zur Umweltgeschichte des 19. Jahrhunderts* (Karlsruhe: Institut für Wasserbau und Kulturtechnik, 1997), 98–99.

9. Aldo Leopold, "Wilderness," in *The River of the Mother of God and Other Essays*, ed. Susan L. Flader and J. Baird Callicott (Madison: University of Wisconsin Press, 1991), 227.

10. Pierre Ayçoberry and Marc Ferro, *Une histoire du Rhin* (Paris: Éditions Ramsay, 1981), 370–71.

11. On the negotiations, see the *procès verbaux* of the Vienna Congress's Commission on the Free Navigation of Rivers, in *Rheinurkunden: Sammlung zwischenstaatlicher*

Vereinbarungen, landesrechtlicher Ausführungsverordnungen und sonstiger wichtiger Urkunden über die Rheinschiffahrt seit 1803, part 1 (Munich: Duncker & Humblot, 1918), 55–162. The citation, from article 5 of the Paris Peace Treaty (1814), is on p. 36.

12. For the Dutch position, see H. P. H. Nusteling, *De Rijnvaart in het tijdperk van stoom en steenkool (1831–1914)* (Amsterdam: Holland Universiteits Pers, 1974), 5–9. The phrase *jusqu'à son embouchure* comes from the Vienna Final Acts (1815), article 109; see *Rheinurkunden,* part 1, 42–43.

13. The text of the Mainz and Mannheim acts appears in *Rheinurkunden,* part 1, 213–283, and part 2, 80–106. For a detailed analysis of the diplomacy from 1815 to 1866, see J. P. Chamberlain, "The Regime of the International Rivers: Danube and Rhine" (Ph.D. diss., Columbia University, 1923).

14. The Rhine Commission's history can be found in Ursula von Köppen, "Die Geschichte der Kommission und die Rechtsordnung der Rheinschiffahrt," in *150 Jahre Zentral-Kommission für die Rheinschiffahrt* (Duisburg-Ruhrort: Binnenschiffahrts-Verlag, 1965), 21–28; and Kurt Lenzner, "Die internationale Rechtsordnung des Rheines," in *Der Rhein: Ausbau, Verkehr, Verwaltung,* ed. Wasser- und Schiffahrtsdirektion Duisburg (Duisburg: Rhein Verlagsgesellschaft m.b.H., 1951), 389–99.

15. G. P. van de Ven, ed., *Man-Made Lowlands: History of Water Management and Land Reclamation in the Netherlands* (Utrecht: Matrijs, 1993), 227–28.

16. Ven, *Man-Made lowlands,* 232–33.

17. Ven, *Man-Made Lowlands,* 233–34; Ben Wiebenga, "Pieter Calands Plan," *Beiträge zur Rheinkunde* 24 (1972): 19–24; Johan van Veen, *Dredge, Drain, Reclaim: The Art of a Nation* (The Hague: Martinus Nijhoff, 1962), 80–105.

18. Gerhard Mantz, "Zur Erinnerung an Leben und Werk des Geheimen Regierungsrathes und Strombaudirektors Eduard Adolph Nobiling," *Beiträge zur Rheinkunde* 34 (1982): 22–38.

19. Wasser- und Schiffahrtsdirektion Duisburg, *Der Rhein: Ausbau, Verkehr, Verwaltung* (Duisburg: Rhein Verlagsgesellschaft m.b.H., 1951), 115–25.

20. J. Dieterlen, "Kembs: Premier échelon du Grand Canal d'Alsace," *La navigation du Rhin* 10 (November 1932): 405–66; and CHR, *Der Rhein unter der Einwirkung des Menschen,* 80–92. For a good summary of Baden's water-table concerns, see Badischer Landwirtschaftlicher Hauptverband, *Steppe am Oberrhein? Der franzözische Rheinseitenkanal* (Freiburg: Badischer Landwirtschafts-Verlag, 1954).

21. Thomas Tittizer and Falk Krebs, eds., *Ökosystemforschung: Der Rhein und seine Auen; Eine Bilanz* (Berlin: Springer, 1996), 272, 286.

22. Ian G. Cowx and Robin L. Welcomme, eds., *Rehabilitation of Rivers for Fish: A Study Undertaken by the European Inland Fisheries Advisory Commission of FAO* (Oxford: Fishing News Books, 1998), 11–18.

23. Anton Lelek and Günter Buhse, *Fische des Rheins: Früher und heute* (Berlin: Springer, 1992), 37–38.

24. Tittizer and Krebs, *Ökosystemforschung*, 195–199, 218–21.

25. Ulrike Klein, "Die Gewässerverschmutzung durch den Steinkohlenbergbau im Emschergebiet," in Hans-Jürgen Teuteberg, ed., *Westfalens Wirtschaft am Beginn des "Maschinenzeitalters"* (Dortmund: Gesellschaft für Westfälische Wirtschaftsgeschichte, 1988), 341–44; and Thomas Rommelspacher, "Das natürliche Recht auf Wasserverschmutzung," in *Besiegte Natur: Geschichte der Umwelt im 19. und 20. Jahrhundert* (Munich: C. H. Beck, 1987), 57–61.

26. Cited by Franz-Josef Brüggemeier, "The Ruhr Basin, 1850–1980: A Case of Large-Scale Environmental Pollution," in *The Silent Countdown: Essays in Environmental History*, ed. P. Brimblecombe and C. Pfister (Berlin: Springer-Verlag, 1990), 212.

27. D. A. Ramshorn, *Die Emschergenossenschaft* (Essen: Emschergenossenschaft, 1957), 5–35. See also August Heinrichsbauer, *Industrielle Siedlung im Ruhrgebiet in Vergangenheit, Gegenwart und Zukunft* (Essen: Glückauf, 1936), 10–13.

28. Untitled report in Nordrhein-Westfälisches Hauptstaatsarchiv Düsseldorf, Regierung Düsseldorf, No. 55904, 1912.

29. Curt Weigelt, "Die Industrie und die preussische Ministerialverfügung von 20. Februar 1901," *Die chemische Industrie* 24 (October 15, 1901): 555.

30. Ralf Henneking, *Chemische Industrie und Umwelt* (Stuttgart: Franz Steiner Verlag, 1994), 35–37; and Frauke Schönert-Röhlk, "Die räumliche Verteilung der chemischen Industrie im 19. Jahrhundert," in *Gewerbe- und Industrielandschaften vom Spätmittelalter bis ins 20. Jahrhundert*, ed. Hans Pohl (Stuttgart: Steiner, 1986), 417–55.

31. On the European chemical industry, see Fred Aftalion, *A History of the International Chemical Industry* (Philadelphia: University of Pennsylvania Press, 1991), esp. 103–13.

32. Karl Otto Henseling and Anselm Salinger, "'Eine Welt voll märchenhaften Reizes . . . ,' Teerfarben: Keimzelle der modernen Chemieindustrie," in *Das blaue Wunder: Zur Geschichte der synthetischen Farben*, ed. Arne Andersen and Gerd Spelsberg (Cologne: Volksblatt, 1990), 89–90.

33. Gerd Spelsberg, "'Im Fieber des Farbenrausches': Eine Siegesgeschichte," in Andersen and Spelsberg, *Das blaue Wunder*, 4–25.

34. "Wasserwirtschaftlicher Verband: Hauptversammlung, Berlin, 24.2.1912," *Zeitschrift für angewandte Chemie* 25 (April 26, 1912): 835–36.

35. Der Rat von Sachverständigen für Umweltfragen, *Umweltprobleme des Rheins 3: Sondergutachten März 1976* (Stuttgart: Kohlhammer, 1976), esp. 47–65.

36. *Rhein-Zeitung*, June 7, 1977.

37. T. H. Elkins and P. K. Marstrand, "Pollution of the Rhine and Its Tributaries," in *Regional Management of the Rhine: Papers of a Chatham House Study Group*, ed. Royal

Institute of International Affairs (London: Chatham House, 1975); and L. J. Huizenga, "Suitable Measures against the Pollution of the Rhine by Chloride Discharge from the Alsatian Potash Mines," *Pure and Applied Chemistry* 29 (1972): 345–53. The Rhine Protection Commission's figures were based on a German chloride study.

38. Statistics in P. P. Jansen et al., *Principles of River Engineering: The Non-tidal Alluvial River* (London: Pitman, 1979), 26–28.

39. Ann Schulte-Wülwer-Leidig, "Ecological Master Plan for the Rhine Catchment," in *The Ecological Basis for River Management*, ed. David M. Harper and Alastair J. D. Ferguson (Chichester: John Wiley & Sons, 1995), 511; and Tittizer and Krebs, *Ökosystemforschung*, 194–95, 247, 256.

40. Ragnar Kinzelbach, ed., *Die Tierwelt des Rheins einst und jetzt* (Mainz: Naturhistorisches Museum Mainz, 1985), 37; and Tittizer and Krebs, *Ökosystemforschung*, 247, 251–53.

41. Karl Wittfogel, *Oriental Despotism: A Comparative Study of Total Power* (New Haven: Yale University Press, 1957).

42. International Commission for the Protection of the Rhine, *Ist der Rhein wieder ein Fluss für Lachse? "Lachs 2000"* (Koblenz: ICPR, 1999).

43. For a comprehensive overview of the Stork Plan, see Dick de Bruin et al., *Ooievaar: De toekomst van het rivierengebied* (Arnhem: Stichting Gelderse Milieufederatie, 1987), 9–20.

44. International Commission for the Protection of the Rhine, *Action Plan on Flood Defence* (Koblenz: ICPR, 1998).

45. 1825 figures from Christian Eckert, *Rheinschiffahrt im XIX. Jahrhundert* (Leipzig: Verlag von Duncker & Humblot, 1900), 154. Figures for 1978 from Commission Centrale pour la Navigation du Rhin, *Rapport annuel de la Commission Centrale pour la Navigation du Rhin* (Strasbourg: Commission Centrale pour la Navigation du Rhin, 1985), 53.

SEVEN · Continuity and Transformation

Colonial Rice Frontiers and Their Environmental Impact on the Great River Deltas of Mainland Southeast Asia

MICHAEL ADAS

For Americans at least, the term *frontier* conjurers up images of the Great Plains or the West, of ranchers and sod-house farmers, cavalrymen, and Native American resistance to the inexorable advance of Euroamerican settlement. But the United States frontier was only one example of a larger type of settler expansion into areas from Australia and Argentina to Russia and Canada that have been aptly termed "neo-Europes" because of the invasions of European domesticated and feral animals, plants, and diseases that accompanied the influx of human invaders into these temperate zones.[1] And European settler frontiers that were established overseas represented only one variant of several patterns of frontier expansion over much of the globe through most of the early modern and modern periods. Frontier expansion in the neo-Europes was predated by movements of peoples in Eurasia, Africa, and the Americas that were often far greater in their duration and numbers, the amount of land brought under cultivation, and the environmental transformations they set in motion or accelerated. Therefore, in thinking about the ecological impact of the unprecedented spread of human, animal, and plant populations in recent centuries, we need to take into account frontiers in Africa, Latin America, Eurasia, and Oceania that differed in important ways from those opened by European settlers.

In the nineteenth and early twentieth centuries, some of the most dramatic examples of these alternative modes of frontier expansion—both in terms of the size of the social and ecological transformations involved and their impact on the global system—occurred across the vast deltaic plains formed by each of the three great river systems of mainland Southeast Asia. Long before humans moved into the region, rivers carried rich alluvial soil from the mountainous interior of southern China and mainland Southeast Asia south toward the sea: the Irrawaddy river, which defines present-day Burma (Myanmar); the Chao Phraya, which is the main *menam* or river system of Thailand; and the Mekong, which dominates Nam Bo, or the southern third of Vietnam. Over thousands of millennia, their flow formed extensive, relatively flat, and well-watered deltas that have proved superb locations for the cultivation of wet rice, which is the staple food of much of the population of mainland and island Southeast Asia as well as that of neighboring east and south India, Bangladesh, and south and central China. As late as the first decades of the nineteenth century, each of these great deltas was sparsely populated, frequently flooded, and covered with mangrove swamps and monsoon rain forests. During the century that followed, massive peasant migrations, European colonial imperatives, market linkages, and the prodigious expansion of cultivated acreage transformed the deltas into some of the key frontier regions not only of mainland Southeast Asia, but of the world. Collectively, they became one of the great surplus-food exporting regions of the global capitalist system.[2]

Nineteenth- and early twentieth-century promoters of European imperialist expansion tended to attribute these developments, which they considered wholly positive, almost exclusively to enlightened European rule, or, in the case of Siam (today's Thailand), to political pressures and economic incentives applied by competing European powers, especially Great Britain and France. In this account of the opening of the three delta frontiers (which has striking parallels to settler histories of the wheat and herding frontiers of the American West, Australia, and Argentina), these fertile areas were wild and undeveloped before the coming of European colonial conquest and territorial expansion.[3] In each of the three delta areas, European colonizers abolished the export embargoes that indigenous rulers had imposed to control food prices or to ensure that surpluses were available for times when flood or drought threatened famine. The Europeans also abrogated sumptuary laws (restrictions on the type of consumer goods that could be purchased by merchants, peasants, or other commoners) that the monarchs of Siam, Burma, and Vietnam enforced to maintain the material and symbolic status markers that clearly separated the tiny elites of their kingdoms from the subject population. Encouraged by European colonial officials, European merchants and entrepreneurs also established trading and processing centers and transportation and communications networks to link peasant production in each of the deltas to the global market. Under European auspices, the monetary systems and weights and measures of these areas were reformed and standardized; and legal codes, based on European precedents, were imposed that upheld the sanctity of contracts, private property, and the other pillars of market capitalism. Taken together, advocates of European colonial expansion argued, these reforms and innovations gave rise to infrastructures and political and social contexts in which agricultural expansion could thrive and peasant and immigrant labor would flock to settle in the dynamic frontier regions of mainland Southeast Asia.

Those who celebrated the rice-frontier variant of the triumphal, civilizing-mission ideology of the European colonizers viewed all of these developments as wholly progressive and conducive to the "improvement" (to use the term frequently employed at the time) of the colonized peoples and the lands they occupied. But in recent decades, and even occasionally in the last years of the imperialist interlude, the role of colonialism as an agent of development of the great rice frontiers has been strongly contested by a growing corpus of historical research and writing.[4] These revisionist accounts reveal, for example, that in at least the Irrawaddy and Mekong deltas, there was considerable settlement and development in the precolonial era.[5] The monarchs and administrators of indigenous dynasties, whose power base was centered to the north of each of these deltas (the Dry Zone in upper Burma and Trung Bo or Annam in central Vietnam; see map 7.1), sporadically promoted peasant migration and the expansion of wet-rice cultivation in areas they sought to annex to their kingdoms. These patterns of migration and settlement were linked to the southward movement of the Burmese and Vietnamese that had begun many centuries earlier. And they threatened indigenous peoples—in lower Burma, the Mons, and in the Mekong area, the Khmers—who had long inhabited these regions. In Thailand, by contrast, the severe seasonal flooding of most of the central plain north of Bangkok formed by the Chao Phraya River had historically made it all but impossible for sedentary cultivators and long-term settlements to be established in the region.[6] As a consequence, the centers of Siamese civilization had long been located in regions to the north of the delta, though the city of Thonburi (Bangkok) on the lower Chao Phraya had been established following the destruction of the Ayudhya in 1767.

Although wet-rice cultivation had been established in limited areas of each of the mainland deltas (with lower Burma the most extensively developed and Siam the least) before European influence or control was established in the second half of the nineteenth century, the boom time of these rice frontiers came during the last decades of the nineteenth century and the first decades of the twentieth. The deltas' sagas of

MAP 7.1.
Southeast Asian rice deltas.

agrarian development and market growth have been narrated numerous times—
though often from highly contested perspectives. Colonial and royal officials
attempted to introduce alternative crops, but by the early twentieth century each
delta had been transformed into a classic monoculture economy, based overwhelmingly on the cultivation, processing, and marketing of rice. In a matter of
decades, the three regions together had become by far the largest rice-exporting
area in the world.

In Burma, where the boom began first, after the British took control of the
Irrawaddy delta in the early 1850s, the area under rice cultivation increased from an

estimated 700,000 to 800,000 acres in the 1850s to more than 8,400,000 by the early 1930s. In the same period, rice exports rose from 162,000 tons to nearly 3,000,000.[7] The official date for the opening of central Siam to market production in rice is 1855. In that year the British plenipotentiary, Sir John Bowring, pressured the court of the Siamese monarch, Rama IV, to end a royal monopoly on the export of rice that had been shipped to Malacca in Malaya for centuries.[8] But the real rice boom along the Chao Phraya began in the late 1870s, in conjunction with a major extension of canal and dike construction by concessionary companies under contract to the royal government.[9] Between 1905 (when the first reasonably reliable statistics were compiled) and 1934, the area planted in rice in the Chao Phraya delta area increased from about 6.5 million *rai* (1.18 million hectares) to more than 16.5 million *rai* (3 million hectares). In the same period, rice exports, which contemporary observers noted came almost entirely from the central plain, increased from just over 11 million *picul*s (roughly 660,000 metric tons) to well over 25 million *picul*s (approximately 1.5 million metric tons). Less reliable records suggest that during the early decades of the expansion of rice production on the central plains, between the late 1870s and early 1900s, rice exports grew from 3.5 million *picul*s to the 11 million recorded in 1904.[10]

In the Mekong delta region, which was incorporated piecemeal into France's growing empire in Indochina beginning in the 1860s, the rapid expansion of rice production was delayed by the need to build irrigation canals and dikes to control flooding and drain salt water from the neighboring Sea of Siam and the South China Sea. The French need to cover the costs of colonization by bringing the area into market production led to extensive government and private investment in canal dredging and drainage. At the same time, peasant migrants moving into the region undertook dike construction on the lands they cultivated, or they were compelled by government officials to work on larger irrigation projects throughout the delta. Between 1880 and 1937, the area under rice cultivation in Cochinchina, where most of the expansion of paddy production was concentrated, increased from 522,000 hectares to 2,200,000. Rice exports from Saigon, the provincial capital and the main port city for the Mekong region, rose in the same period from 284,000 to 1,548,000 imperial tons.[11]

The advance of the rice frontier in each of the great delta regions of mainland Southeast Asia attracted a steadily accelerating influx of migrants from neighboring regions and overseas. The migration of hundreds of thousands of peasants from the densely populated regions of the Dry Zone in Burma and the Red River delta or Bac Bo and coastal plain (Trung Bo) of Vietnam was essential to the advance of rice cultivation in the Irrawaddy and Mekong deltas. Though the flow of Thai peasants was somewhat smaller, by the 1930s substantial migration from largely subsistence areas surrounding the central plain along the Chao Phraya had made possible the dramatic increase in export rice production that had by the early 1900s enmeshed south-central Siam, like the southern portions of Burma and Vietnam, in the world economy. These massive movements of population served to alleviate severe population pressure in the areas of origin, which had been seriously depleted by centuries, and in some cases millennia, of cultivation. Key areas of heavy peasant emigration to the rice frontiers—especially the Dry Zone in Burma, northeast Siam, and central Vietnam—were also famine-prone: the monsoon rainfall was often precarious at best or arrived too late at worst. Thus, the development of the great delta-region rice frontiers not only provided areas for settlement by the peoples from other regions within the British and French colonies and the pressured but independent Siamese kingdom; they also generated prodigious surpluses of a staple food that could be shipped to other districts threatened by famine or simply in need of additional sustenance for their relatively dense populations.

Much of the rice exported found its way to other heavily populated areas elsewhere in Asia, including India, Java, and south China. In addition, Indian and Chinese immigration helped to swell the flow of migrant labor, capital, and entrepreneurial and technical skills into each of the rapidly expanding frontier regions. Indian peasants from throughout Britain's South Asian empire, but especially the densely packed east and southeast coasts, not only settled land as smallholders in lower Burma but also took up positions, in the tens of thousands, as tenant producers and rural and urban laborers. And though the Chao Phraya and Mekong deltas were brought under cultivation mainly by Thai and Vietnamese peasants and laborers, Chinese millers, merchants, moneylenders, and landowners also played vital roles. Chinese migrants, including thousands of laborers, were also present in lower Burma. But from the mid-nineteenth century, Indians predominated as merchants and moneylenders through much of the Irrawaddy delta. In many areas they vied with Burmese rice merchants and British and Burmese mill owners for control of credit supply and processing facilities, as well as the internal and export trade that undergirded the colonial economy. Thus the rice deltas provided surplus food for substantial populations overseas and migration outlets from areas where overcrowding and unemployment were chronic sources of widespread poverty and malnutrition.[12]

The question of which social and ethnic groups gained the most from the conversion of the sparsely settled deltas of mainland Southeast Asia into major granaries of the world system vexed colonial officials and social scientists for most of the past century.[13] In broad terms, small landowner-producers were the key to agrarian expansion in lower Burma and central Siam. In the Irrawaddy districts, the majority reaped substantial material rewards in the early decades of the opening of the rice frontier, and they enjoyed a high living standard relative to peasants in neighboring regions of Asia; but the laissez-faire policies that the British colonizers stubbornly pursued, despite clear signs of increasing cultivator indebtedness and land alienation, fed growing social and ethnic tensions that centered on the growth of large landed estates and the consequent impoverishment of a substantial portion of the laboring, tenant, and small-landholder social strata, both Burmese and Indian. By the 1920s, worsening economic conditions fed an epidemic of banditry and other modes of peasant "avoidance resistance." With the onset of the Great Depression in the 1930s, serious riots spread from Rangoon (Yangon) to other major towns in the delta, and a major nativist rebellion—directed against the British colonizers, Indian and indigenous landlords, merchants, and moneylenders—spread through the delta and into upper Burma.[14]

In Siam, where market production increased at a slower pace, peasant cultivators who opened most of the new areas brought under cultivation often became indebted to or the tenant-clients of large landowners, mainly Thai nobles and Chinese entrepreneurs. Although social tensions and sporadic outbreaks of violence punctuated the steady advance of the Chao Phraya rice frontier, patron-client reciprocity, Buddhist buffers, and a lesser dependence of the Siamese economy on global market conditions made for lower levels of protest and perhaps fewer indirect reprisals such as flight, arson, and banditry.[15]

In the Mekong delta, huge land concessions granted by the colonial regime to French *colons*, Vietnamese notables, and Chinese investors ensured that large estates would dominate rice production for export. The estates were worked, usually on very unfavorable terms, by Vietnamese peasant tenants, or under oppressive conditions by migrant laborers, again mainly Vietnamese. Despite great disparities in land control and consequently in living standards, the Mekong delta was not ravaged by rebellions comparable to those that broke out in the north-central provinces of Nghe-An and Ha-Tinh in the early years of the Great Depression. But throughout the French period, the countryside proved fertile ground for sectarian and millenarian movements and, by the 1930s, Communist cadre recruitment and localized uprisings.[16]

The insistence of European officials, and subsequently many historians, that the expansion of the rice frontiers in the great river deltas of mainland Southeast Asia was overwhelmingly a process stimulated by European colonial initiatives, or (in Thailand) diplomatic and mercantile pressures, meant that the resulting environmental transformations should also be seen as a legacy of Western colonization and capitalist market expansion. But few of those who observed and described these developments gave serious attention to their ecological dimensions. In fact, like the mythic sagas of the settling of the American West, contemporary accounts of the expansion of the delta rice frontiers celebrated the vast acreage brought under cultivation, the unparalleled increases in rice exports, and the improved living conditions the booming mainland economies provided for hundreds of thousands of peasant immigrants and populations overseas whose staple food supply was made more secure by the deltas' surpluses. Colonial rhetoric resoundingly valorized economic development and summarily dismissed the precolonial deltas as gloomy, unhealthy, and unproductive "wastelands." The impact of the advancing rice frontiers on the indigenous plant and animal life of the deltas was subsumed under stirring descriptions of the clearing of tropical forests to extend rice cultivation and the retreat of bands of "primitive" hunting and gathering peoples and wild "beasts" in the face of the forces of improvement and progress.

Despite the lack of detailed or systematic contemporary studies of the ecological impact of the expanding rice frontiers in any of the three delta regions, the overall contours of a prodigious process of environmental transformation can be pieced together from accounts and government documents focused on other issues. The great influx of sedentary peasant cultivators and their domestic animals, and the subsequent conversion of much of the area of each of the deltas to rice monocultures, led to widespread (but unquantifiable because of the absence of detailed records) displacement of indigenous species of wildlife, from large cats and wild elephants to reptiles and birds. Indigenous plant life was cut down or burned off to make way for rice. Much of the area cleared had been covered by tall, densely growing and sharp-edged grass (*kaing* in Burmese, *cognon* in Thai) that had long rendered overland travel extremely difficult. But extensive stands of tropical rain forest in lower Burma and in the Mekong delta had all but disappeared by the early years of the twentieth century. Particularly in the southernmost districts on the Irrawaddy delta plain, these mixed forests were dominated by tall *kanazo* trees that reached heights of more than 45 meters in freshwater areas. Precolonial cartographic evidence and travelers' accounts indicate that as many as three million hectares of the great *kanazo* forests had been cut down by the end of the British colonial period in 1941.[17]

In both the Irrawaddy and Mekong regions, extensive stands of mangrove played a critical role in the advance of the deltas into the sea and protected them from storms and tidal surges. In the western districts of the area, dominated by the province the French called Cochinchina, were nearly two million hectares of mangrove forests that had been little disturbed by humans until the mid-nineteenth century. In the decades on either side of the turn of the century, the more accessible of these forests were cut down so that rice could be sown amid the rotting stumps. In the Irrawaddy region, and apparently the Chao Phraya basin as well, the mangrove forests were largely confined to thin strips of land along, and frequently flooded by, the rivers. The seasonal inundation and the brackish water made mangrove areas less attractive to prospective cultivators than freshwater areas further north. As a consequence, mangrove stands often survived despite the extensive settlement surrounding them. In Cochinchina, where mangrove forests were more pervasive, the French invested heavily in drainage operations and dike building that were designed to either desalinate deforested areas or protect them from flooding so that they could be brought into rice production. The clearing of mangrove forests took a heavy toll on the fish and shellfish that thrived in the zones where the forests ran into the rivers and creeks that meandered through each of the great deltas.[18]

The steady influx of settlers that sustained the moving rice frontiers in each of the delta regions was also a source of considerable environmental change and very often of degradation. Villages sprang up amid the rice paddies, and major cities such as Rangoon, Bangkok, and Saigon emerged as political and financial centers. Waterways were fouled by significant increases in human waste, and in the larger towns and urban centers, rice mills and other processing industries proved to be major sources of both air and water pollution. Because these were not aspects of colonial development that the European authorities deemed worth monitoring, we have no way to gauge the extent of the pollutants discharged or their short- and long-term effects. But periodic epidemics of diseases such as malaria, typhus, and cholera, which were often associated with land clearing, hydraulic projects, and polluted rivers and drinking water, took a heavy toll on those who migrated to the deltas.[19]

Because economic development and social change in each of Southeast Asia's great river deltas was centered on the production of river-nourished wet rice, the environmental damage of the transformations of the colonial era was less pronounced than in many other frontier areas, including the American West and the rain-forest regions of Brazil or island Southeast Asia. The more limited amount of environmental disruption involved in the extension of wet rice cultivation is clearly demonstrated in Lucien Hanks's analysis of the different forms of human adaptation in the Chao Phraya basin, which were mirrored in both the Irrawaddy and Mekong regions. He chronicles several phases in the transformation of the Chao

Phraya delta from a sparsely inhabited expanse of fertile land, flooded much of the year, into one of the granaries of the world economy. Hanks identifies several adaptations, which he plots on a continuum from what he terms a "niche" pattern at one extreme to a "holding" response at the other.[20]

In the early settlement of central Siam, the niche pattern was predominant. Small bands of shifting cultivators sowed their paddy seeds broadcast rather than laboriously transplanting paddy shoots from seedbeds. Making no attempt to construct even rudimentary dikes or irrigation canals, they planted and harvested their rice staple with little disturbance to the existing topography, flora and fauna, or seasonal patterns of flooding and drought in the areas they passed through. Centuries before the colonial era, sedentary cultivators were established in many areas in lower Burma, and both Khmer and Vietnamese peasants cultivated rice in enclaves scattered about the Mekong delta. Rice was often broadcast sown by villagers whose settlements dated back generations, but who attempted only very limited diking and drainage projects. Depending on the degree of labor and time invested in these alterations to the existing environment, these sedentary cultivators could be plotted along the middle range of Hank's imaginary continuum between niche and holding patterns.[21]

As in lower Burma and French Cochinchina, the massive influx of settlers into the Chao Phraya delta starting in the last decades of the nineteenth century led to the growing predominance of holding-pattern adaptations associated with wet-rice cultivation, and the increasing marginalization of groups practicing different modes of cultivation at the niche end of the continuum. In newly settled areas, where land was plentiful in the early stages of frontier expansion, cultivators often sowed their rice broadcast in areas where flooding was less severe and extensive diking thus unnecessary. But as rice cultivation spread and the peasant populations in each of the deltas rose dramatically, transplanting, which represented the extreme mode of the holding pattern in wet-rice agriculture, came to dominate social and economic development on the rice frontiers of mainland Southeast Asia. In each area, but more in the deltas to the east than in the Irrawaddy region, extensive irrigation projects proved essential. In fact, capital-intensive schemes, underwritten by foreign investors—British and Indian in Burma, European and Chinese in Siam, and French and Chinese in Cochinchina—were necessary for rice production. The system of cultivation came overwhelmingly to depend on a pattern of sedentary cropping that began with seedlings sprouted in nurseries; these were then transported to and transplanted in flooded fields and finally matured and harvested after the river water had been drained off.

The building and maintenance of huge networks of dikes and field bunds were critical to the emerging rice-export industries. In addition, in many parts of Siam and French Cochinchina, massive and expensive engineering projects were required to flush salt residues from the soil to render it suitable for rice cultivation. Transport and irrigation canals were dug, which often redirected or connected existing natural waterways. These projects resulted in significant reconfigurations of the riverine and topographical features. They also generated pollutants, which apparently no contemporary noticed, much less attempted to quantify; and they significantly altered the natural cycles that brought rain, river water, and vital soil nutrients to the increasingly heavily cultivated and populated lands of the rice frontiers.[22]

As extensive as these environmental transformations proved to be, and as unsettling to previous ecological adaptations by humans, plants, and feral animals, in many ways the expansion of wet-rice agriculture was the optimal form of large-scale economic development then available. Beginning with the presupposition that human populations have historically transformed the natural environments they inhabit and would inevitably continue to do so, colonial officials and agricultural experts assumed (if they thought about it at all) that wet-rice expansion was the most "natural" and beneficial, and the least ecologically unsettling, way for these changes to occur. Wet-rice agriculture remains by far one of the most productive modes of generating a staple food. Rice is also one of the most nutritious of all of the staple foods cultivated by humans for millennia.[23] The rice economies of the deltas not only supported rapidly growing immigrant and indigenous populations in each area, but they also generated impressive and rising surpluses, which fed millions in more densely populated and less productive areas in Asia and beyond. Export provided a major stimulus for the growth of regional market linkages, and, particularly in lower Burma and central Siam, led to the emergence of substantial markets for imported consumer goods, from kerosene lanterns to bicycles and capital equipment for processing rice and extending railway and steamboat transport systems.

The spread of wet-rice agriculture, though clearly toward the holding end of Hank's continuum of human modes of adaptation, was far less disruptive of existing ecological systems than many other processes of agricultural expansion and frontier settlement. A growing number of studies demonstrate that ecological transformations and (almost invariably) the degree of degradation inflicted on pre-existing environments have been much more extensive in frontier areas where different crops and agricultural systems provided the impetus for the expansion of settlement, extraction, and production. Striking contrasts can be readily demonstrated, for example, between rice frontiers and wheat-farming frontiers in the prairie lands of Canada and the United States, the spread of market-oriented crops like peanuts and cotton in the African Sahel, and the clearing of heavily forested areas in Brazil and South Asia.[24] Wet-rice cultivation in the deltas of mainland Southeast Asia involved significant adaptation to the existing environment rather than the extreme displacement of existing ecosystems that predominated in these other frontier regions.

The water supply for rice cultivation was supplied naturally by monsoon rains and the great rivers that had over eons also deposited the fertile soil that made possible the deltas' seaward advance. Seasonal flooding also carried vital soil nutrients to large areas adjoining the rivers. Canals and dikes extended and directed the range of the water flow or controlled the extent of flooding, but they did not, at least initially, disrupt the natural cycles that made each of the deltas superb regions for rice cultivation. The water cover that was essential to the early growth of the rice crops also protected the soil from leaching and ultimately laterization (hardening) by the tropical sun and heat.

Although rice production on the large estates that came to dominate the rice economy in some areas of the Mekong delta became increasingly mechanized, cultivators in lower Burma and central Siam worked the paddies with simple plows, hoes, sickles, and other implements that had been used for millennia.[25] In all three areas, rice production continued to rely on the nutrients deposited naturally by the rivers and draft animals rather than on chemical fertilizers. But because the prodigious extension of dike and bund construction steadily constricted the flooding of the soil over heavily cropped areas, fertility declined on all but the newly settled and cropped lands. Except to some extent in the estate areas of French Cochinchina, local techniques and local knowledge, rather than the scientific findings of government-sponsored experiment stations, laboratories, and model farms, overwhelmingly informed rice-cultivation practices. Thus, on the moving rice frontiers of the mainland deltas, as in most wet-rice-growing regions, the spread of the holding pattern combined human control over and reconfiguration of the environment with a high degree of preservation of natural inputs and the maintenance of seasonal cycles. Humans were clearly reshaping the delta environments over vast areas, but they were fashioning lush gardens, which, as Michael Pollan has perceptively observed, may well represent the best possible balance between necessary human interventions in the natural world and concern and care for the sustenance of the larger ecological systems on which we, like all creatures, depend.[26]

Nevertheless, research carried out since 1945 has revealed a number of serious ecological repercussions of wet-rice agriculture as practiced in these areas. Some of these were short-term and quite apparent to perceptive contemporary observers; these have been generally downplayed or justified as inevitable side effects of necessary social and economic development. But perhaps the most serious ecological consequence of the expansion of the rice frontiers of the mainland deltas of Southeast Asia, as well as those in other areas of the world, was utterly unknown, even to the handful of forestry officers and agricultural experts who were most attuned to the environmental consequences of the massive transformations that occurred.

Among the readily apparent consequences of expanded rice cultivation was the depletion of feral animal species and forests in the river basins. This deprived peasant farmers and urban communities of easy and cheap access to forest products—from handicraft and building materials to food supplements and firewood—that were once vital sources of their livelihood. The destruction of mangrove forests and swamplands also undercut the fishing and shellfish industries that had provided critical dietary supplements in the precolonial era. As policy makers in all three areas were also acutely aware, the decline in the diversity of sources for subsistence, and in some cases for market production, compounded the potential socioeconomic and environmental costs of dependence on a single market crop, rice. The extensive building of dikes and bunds for the seasonal regulation of the water supply that was essential for successful rice cultivation also led over time to the depletion of the delta soils by blocking the deposition of fresh soil and critical nutrients carried by river floodwaters. It also led in many areas to the silting up of river tributaries and critical navigation canals.

Although there was a general trend to reduce the variety of rice strains planted, both indigenous and introduced rice varieties remained far more diverse than has been the case in the past couple of decades throughout much of Southeast Asia and neighboring regions, where the plant homogenization associated with the Green Revolution has dominated production.[27] But the rice monoculture overall has been a major contributor to the socioeconomic and political crises that have recurred in all these delta regions from the late 1920s onward. As overseas market outlets shrank and the global terms of trade turned increasingly against primary-product producing areas, which included virtually all colonial economies worldwide, large numbers of peasant cultivators faced landlessness and impoverishment and, at times in Vietnam, starvation.[28] Depression and then world war let to drastic reductions in sources of credit, the decimation of the mercantile and processing sectors of the rice economies, and the flight of immigrant laborers, managers, and traders.[29]

Since 1945, the policies of Burma's military juntas have dramatically reduced the Irrawaddy region's participation in the world market. Revolution and two colonial wars reduced South Vietnam, and much of the Mekong region, to rice-importing areas by the mid-1960s. And though Thailand has remained active as a rice exporter and escaped the devastation of war, the importance of the rice production of the Chao Phraya delta in the global economy steadily diminished until the early 1980s, when there was a marked upturn.[30]

However significant from a regional perspective, these ecological repercussions and socioeconomic setbacks are dwarfed by a more fundamental global environmental concern that was identified only a decade or so ago. Despite the relatively high degree to which wet rice accommodates the ecosystems into which it is introduced, the paddies in which it is grown turn out to be major producers of methane gas, which is one of the main sources of global warming. The "stew" of oxygen-deficient muck, rotting plants, stagnant water, and organic and mineral nutrients that is so conducive to the cultivation of rice also nurtures prodigious quantities of methane-manufacturing bacteria. And maturing rice plants turn out to be superb, strawlike conduits for the transmission of the methane into the atmosphere. When it escapes in this manner, rather than being burned off, it traps many times more radiant heat than better-known greenhouse gases, such as carbon dioxide, and thus contributes even more than they to planetary warming.[31]

Thus the massive extension of rice cultivation presents a profound but little-recognized dilemma for all humankind. Because so much of the earth's human population is dependent on wet-rice production for its staple food supply, alternative crops cannot be developed in the foreseeable future. But even the stabilization of paddy production at current levels and with existing technologies will continue to funnel well over a hundred million tons of unburned methane gas into the atmosphere annually. Because the greenhouse effects of these emissions could have devastating effects on the global environment, it becomes imperative for us to modify rice-growing techniques extensively and rapidly enough to reduce, and perhaps eventually to eliminate, the massive emission of methane. But unlike the pervasive global alarm regarding carbon dioxide emissions and the consequent determination to bring them under control, the recognition of the polluting side-effects of wet-rice cultivation, and consequently the will to address the problem, has been slow to develop. Given the magnitude of the annual greenhouse emissions produced by rice paddies, the considerable time lag involved in even recognizing—much less acting upon—the dangers posed, gives cause for serious concern. Because measures to reduce high-profile pollutants, such as carbon dioxide or chlorofluorocarbons, have often been stalled by denial, indifference, and outright resistance, one wonders how much longer it will take to win acceptance for expensive modifications to wet-rice cultivation practices and technologies that presently support a substantial portion of the world's human population.

NOTES

1. Alfred W. Crosby, *Ecological Imperialism: The Biological Expansion of Europe, 900–1900* (New York: Cambridge University Press, 1986).

2. Norman Owen, "The Rice Industry of Mainland Southeast Asia, 1850–1914," *Journal of the Siam Society* 59, no. 1 (1971): 75–143.

3. Michael Adas, "Imperialist Rhetoric and Modern Historiography: The Case of Lower Burma before and after Conquest," *Journal of Southeast Asian Studies* 3, no. 2 (1972): 175–92.

4. John Furnivall, *An Introduction to the Political Economy of Burma* (Rangoon: Burmese Advertising Press, 1931); Charles Robequain, *L'évolution économique de l'Indochine française*, Centre d'Études de Politique Étrangère (Paris: Hartmann, 1939).

5. Pierre Brocheux, *The Mekong Delta: Ecology, Economy, and Revolution, 1860–1960* (Madison, WI: Center for Southeast Asian Studies, 1995); Michael Adas, *The Burma Delta: Economic Development and Social Change on an Asian Rice Frontier, 1852–1941* (Madison: University of Wisconsin Press, 1974).

6. Yoshikazu Takaya, "Land Form and Rice Growing," and "Land Reclamation in the Chao Phraya Delta," in *Thailand: A Rice-Growing Society*, ed. Yoneo Ishii (Honolulu: University of Hawaii Press, 1978).

7. Cheng Siok-Hwa, *The Rice Industry of Burma, 1852–1940* (Kuala Lumpur: Oxford University Press, 1968); and Adas, *Burma Delta*.

8. Yoneo Ishii, "History and Rice-Growing," in Ishii, *Thailand*.

9. S. Tanabe, "Historical Geography of the Canal System in the Chao Phraya Delta," *Journal of the Siam Society* 65, no. 1 (1977): 23–72; and Takaya, "Land Reclamation."

10. James Ingram, *Economic Change in Thailand Since 1850* (Stanford, CA: Stanford University Press, 1955).

11. Brocheux, *Mekong Delta;* Robequain, *L'évolution économique.*

12. Adas, *Burma Delta;* Cheng, *Rice Industry of Burma;* Tanabe, "Historical Geography"; Ingram, *Economic Change;* G. William Skinner, *Chinese Society in Thailand: An Analytical History* (Ithaca, NY: Cornell University Press, 1957); Brocheux, *Mekong Delta;* Yves Henry, *Économie agricole de l'Indochine* (Hanoi: Gouvernenment Général de l'Indochine, 1932); Francesca Bray, *The Rice Economies: Technology and Development in Asian Societies* (Oxford: Basil Blackwell, 1986).

13. Willem van Schendel, *Three Deltas: Accumulation and Poverty in Rural Burma, Bengal and South India* (New Delhi: Sage Publications, 1991).

14. Adas, *Burma Delta;* Michael Adas, *Prophets of Rebellion: Millenarian Protest Movements against the European Colonial Order* (Chapel Hill: University of North Carolina Press, 1979) and "Bandits, Monks and Pretender Kings: Patterns of Peasant Resistance and Protest in Colonial Burma, 1826–1941," in *Power and Protest in the Countryside,* ed. Robert P. Weller and Scott E. Guggenheim (Durham, NC: Duke University Press, 1982); Van Schendel, *Three Deltas;* and Cheng, *Rice Industry of Burma.*

15. Skinner, *Chinese Society in Thailand;* Ian Brown, "Rural Distress in Southeast Asia during the World Depression of the Early 1930s," *Journal of Asian Studies* 45, no. 5 (1986): 995–1025; David Feeny, *The Political Economy of Productivity: Thai Agricultural Development, 1880–1975* (Vancouver: University of British Columbia Press, 1982).

16. Brocheux, *Mekong Delta;* Cao Duong Pham, *Vietnamese Peasants under French Domination* (New York: University Press of America, 1985); Robert Sansom, *The Economics of Insurgency in the Mekong Delta of Vietnam* (Cambridge, MA: MIT Press, 1970); Hy Van Loung, "Agrarian Unrest from an Anthropological Perspective," *Comparative Politics* 17, no. 2 (1985): 153–174; William Duiker, "The Red Soviets of Nghe-Tinh: An Early Communist Rebellion in Vietnam," *Journal of Southeast Asian Studies* 4, no. 2 (1973): 186–99; and Hue-Tam Ho Tai, *Millenarianism and Peasant Politics in Vietnam* (Cambridge, MA: Harvard University Press, 1983).

17. Michael Adas, "Colonization, Commercial Agriculture and the Destruction of the Deltaic Rain Forests of British Burma in the Late Nineteenth Century," in *The World Economy and Forest Depletion in the Nineteenth Century,* ed. J. F. Richards and R. Tucker (Durham, NC: Duke University Press, 1983).

18. André Henry, *Étude sur les forêts de la Cochinchine* (Saigon: n.p., 1891); Brocheux, *Mekong Delta.*

19. Ken de Bevoise, *Agents of the Apocalypse: Epidemic Disease in the Colonial Philippines* (Princeton: Princeton University Press, 1995).

20. Lucien Hanks, *Rice and Man: Agricultural Ecology in Southeast Asia* (Chicago: Aldine, 1972).

21. Adas, "Imperialist Rhetoric"; Brocheux, *Mekong Delta.*

22. Tanabe, "Canal System of the Chao Phraya"; Feeny, *Thai Agricultural Development;* Brocheux, *Mekong Delta.*

23. Bray, *Rice Economies.*

24. On North America, see Helen Wheatley, "Power Farming: A Comparative History of Cotton Culture in the United States and Australia" (PhD diss., Johns Hopkins University, 2001); Ernest L. Schusky, *Culture and Agriculture: An Ecological Introduction to Traditional and Modern Farming Systems* (New York: Bergin & Garvey, 1989). On Africa, see Richard Frank and Barbara Chasin, *Seeds of Famine: Ecological Destruction*

and the Development Dilemma in the West African Sahel (Montclair, NJ: Allanheld & Osmun, 1980); and Michael Watts, *Silent Violence: Food, Famine and Peasantry in Northern Nigeria* (Berkeley: University of California Press, 1983). On Asia and Brazil, see Madhav Gadgil and Ramachandra Guha, *This Fissured Land: An Ecological History of India* (Berkeley: University of California Press, 1993); and Susanna Hecht and Alexander Cockburn, *The Fate of the Forest* (New York: Harper, 1990).

25. Brocheux, *Mekong Delta;* Feeny, *Thai Agricultural Development;* Adas, *Burma Delta.*

26. Michael Pollan, *Second Nature: A Gardener's Education* (New York: Dell, 1991).

27. Michael J. G. Parnwell and Raymond L. Bryant, *Environmental Change in South-East Asia: People, Politics and Sustainable Development* (London: Routledge, 1996); P. L. Pingali, M. Hossain, and R. V. Gerpacio, *Asian Rice Bowls: The Returning Crisis?* (Wallingford, U.K.: CAB International, 1997).

28. Brown, "Rural Distress during the World Depression"; Charles P. Kindleberger, *The World in Depression, 1929–1939* (Berkeley: University of California Press, 1973).

29. Feeny, *Thai Agricultural Development;* Brocheux, *Mekong Delta;* Adas, *Burma Delta.*

30. Randolph Barker, Robert W. Herdt, and Beth Rose, *The Rice Economy of Asia* (Washington, DC: Resources for the Future, 1985).

31. H. U. Neu, L. H. Ziska, R. B. Matthews, and Q. Dai, "Reducing Global Warming: The Role of Rice," *Geojournal* 35, no. 3 (1995): 351–62; Pingali et al., *Asian Rice Bowls;* Bill McKibben, *The End of Nature* (New York: Doubleday, 1999).

PART THREE · LANDSCAPES, CONQUESTS, COMMUNITIES, AND THE POLITICS OF KNOWLEDGE

EIGHT

· Beyond the Colonial Paradigm

African History and Environmental History
in Large-Scale Perspective

WILLIAM BEINART

Human beings are, before anything else, biological entities. Their interactions with other species and with the natural environment, and their appropriation of the natural resources without which life is impossible, must be central elements in human history. Significant sorties have been made into this terrain in a variety of historical writing, and perhaps more in other disciplines. Some earlier Western intellectual traditions evinced a strong environmental determinism to explain different forms of society, racial characteristics, and social division. This tendency has now largely been jettisoned by historians. A simultaneous concern, however, evident at least since the Enlightenment, has been analysis of human effects on the natural world. This strand, fueled by an anxious environmentalism and by the reaction to concrete modernism, has been dominant in recent environmental history, especially in writing about the consequences of European imperialism.

Alfred Crosby placed the earth-shattering environmental consequences of European expansion over the last five hundred years at the heart of world history. Eurasian diseases and immunities, together with the technology gap and ruthless conquest, facilitated the devastating depopulation of the Americas and their repopulation by invaders—human, animal, and plant.[1] The taming of nature and indigenous peoples emerges as the central motif for Crosby and those influenced by him.[2] Such approaches offer striking insights into both rapid environmental change and global race relations, because they help to explain how particular demographic balances were established in various parts of the colonized world.

The new environmental history has provided a useful stimulus to Africanists because it shares many of their well-established moral concerns and perspectives. In the roughly fifty years since African countries began to shake off colonial control, major advances have been made in revealing the African past, and a vast volume of literature has been produced that will remain an enduring legacy. The subdiscipline of African history has initially been informed by a set of assumptions that might broadly be conceived as corrective. Research has dwelled on the achievements of precolonial states and societies, on the exploitation and colonial conquest of Africa, and on the repressive nature of colonial rule and racial segregation. In fulfillment of the stirring 1960s call by Terence Ranger, historians demonstrated African agency, African initiative, and the salience and legitimacy of African resistance.[3] This broad approach survived the disillusionment with African nationalism in the 1970s and has been extended into the subsequent attention to peasants, workers, women, and popular politics and religion.

Environmental issues, long of interest to historians and social scientists working on Africa, slipped easily into the anticolonial framework and also in important respects extended it. These issues have provided additional scope for interdisciplinary interaction with geographers and archaeologists as well as natural and medical scientists, whose fields contain deep wells of accumulated research. Environmental concerns have necessitated moving away from well-thumbed administrative files to explore new archival sources. They have opened the way to consideration of fascinating nonhuman agents in history, such as fire and water, animals, insects, and plant invaders. They have raised further questions for oral fieldwork on themes strongly familiar to the majority of Africans who, until recently, lived in rural settings. Both African people and the settlers and colonists who came to the continent debated environmental issues intensely; nature and landscape have also been evoked in many different modes of cultural expression. An environmental approach facilitates the mining of rich but still-neglected seams of intellectual and cultural history, from African fables and ecoreligions to the colonial fascination with botany and wildlife.

This chapter, focused on areas of Africa that came under British control, is divided into two sections. I illustrate briefly six interlinked lines of analysis in recent African environmental history; all bear considerable import for understanding the relationship between colonizer and colonized, white and black. Such approaches are beginning to assume the status of a new paradigm and have successfully inverted colonial stereotypes that celebrated Western knowledge and bemoaned Africans as environmentally profligate. I then raise questions about this new paradigm and offer some alternative propositions that might move the debate beyond inversions of colonial narratives.

First, the environmental consequences of colonial incursions have been explored, including appropriation by companies and settlers of natural resources such as wildlife, forests, minerals, and land. This process was at the heart of European expansion from its very inception: a core myth of the foundation of Madeira, one of the first islands colonized outside Europe, was a seven-year fire by which this densely wooded landscape was cleared for settlement.[4] Spanish conquistadors claimed tracts of the Americas not only by reading proclamations and by warfare, but also by symbolically striking trees or lopping branches with their swords.[5]

Some Africanist writing shared what John MacKenzie calls the apocalyptic vision of global environmental history, based on the profoundly disruptive colonial encounters in the Americas and Australia.[6] Helge Kjekshus's *Ecology Control and Economic Development in East Africa* (1977) is a somber account of early colonial rule in Tanzania, sketching the impact of war and diseases such as smallpox and chiggers. Critically, he argued that colonialism spread the endemic tsetse fly and trypanosomiasis, causing sleeping sickness in humans and effectively excluding cattle from large areas.[7] Ecological catastrophe was reflected in a period of demographic halt or decline, perhaps comparable to the period of the slave trade in parts of West Africa.[8] In *The Empire of Nature*, MacKenzie himself vividly illustrates the predatory character of settler and imperial hunting in southern Africa, which catastrophically reduced wildlife and was responsible for the extinction of a couple of species.[9] Environmental decay is discussed in many studies of partial displacement, or compression of African societies into smaller areas of land, as a result of settler colonialism from South Africa to Kenya.

Second, it has been recognized that colonial states in Africa became concerned about environmental regulation, including forest protection, wildlife preservation, soil erosion, and water conservation. They also attempted to eradicate, through environmental management, human and animal diseases, such as malaria, trypanosomiasis, and tick-borne maladies, whose complex ecological etiology was becoming apparent. But colonial environmental management has been characterized as highly intrusive.[10] Approaches to forestry, it has been argued, were drawn from the scientific and commercial models of Europe and India that excluded rural people.[11] Similarly, purity in conceptions of wilderness resulted in the depopulation of national parks.[12] "Fortress conservation," excluding African people from reserves (while allowing access to tourists and scientists), came to characterize wildlife management before and after independence.[13]

Conservationist interventions, linked with other imperatives of agricultural development and social control, also fed into wholesale attempts to change African patterns of land use. Such interventions, whether attempts to sedentarize transhumant pastoralists, or villagize societies with scattered settlement, have been seen in themselves as a major cause of rural degradation, both social and environmental.[14] Colonial development and conservation projects, rooted in a scientific and modernizing logic, have been subjected to particularly critical scrutiny because they outlived the colonial era and remained central in the development strategies of independent African states and international agencies.

Third, the inadequacy of colonial and Western science has frequently been stressed, an argument strengthened by the failure of many major schemes even after independence. Although political resistance and bureaucratic incapacity played a part in the mishaps of planning, nevertheless lack of research, misunderstanding, scientific hubris, and technical weakness have all been demonstrated by researchers. Interventions designed to control trypanosomiasis by the slaughter of game or removal of people in the early decades of this century may instead have facilitated its spread. Kate Showers argues that faulty colonial contour-bank construction in lowland Lesotho, one of the most eroded landscapes on the continent, resulted in stormwater welling up, breaking through, and forming new gullies.[15]

A striking example, which rapidly achieved paradigmatic status in the literature, is Fairhead and Leach's West African research in *Misreading the African Landscape*. They illustrate how, over many years in Guinea, French colonial officials and subsequent experts interpreted the patches of forest to be found in the savannah zone as evidence of deforestation, and framed their interventions with this assumption in mind. By contrast, Fairhead and Leach found that "elders and others living behind the forest walls provide quite different readings of their landscape and its making. At their most contrasting, they bluntly reverse policy orthodoxy, representing their landscape as half-filled and filling with forest, not half-emptied and emptying of it. Forest islands, some villagers suggested, are not relics of destruction, but were formed by themselves or their ancestors in the savanna."[16] In this analysis, settlement brought forests. Scientific understanding and interventions were flawed by their lack of social understanding, or their subservience to colonial political and cultural agendas.

Fourth, as a corollary, the validity and salience of local knowledge about the environment, and means of living in it, have become an increasingly rich area of research as well as a powerful ideological factor in the debate over the right to manage resources. It is a point made with equal force in respect of Australian aboriginal people or Native Americans, although the argument has potentially greater policy import in Africa and Asia, where so many indigenous peoples were comprehensively disposessed.

Perhaps it is not coincidental that some of the most trenchant statements have come from West African contexts, in that this region was least affected by settler colonialism and maintained particularly innovative forms of agricultural production. In his influential book *Indigenous Agricultural Revolution*, Paul Richards explored the capacity of West African smallholders to make "the best of natural conditions, ... capitalizing on local diversity."[17] "This ecological knowledge" he argued, was "one of the most significant of rural Africa's resources" and was by no means simply a "hangover from the past." He focused on food-crop strategies, especially low-technology, wetland rice cultivation in Sierra Leone, where "people's science" was at work in the deployment of locally evolved seed varieties to cater for small variations in natural conditions.[18] Any outside aid, he argued, should work flexibly with local knowledge and techniques. His research feeds into concerns articulated by Calestous Juma in *The Gene Hunters* about the intellectual property rights of local people everywhere over both wild and cultivated species in the face of a new international "scramble for seeds."[19]

Local knowledge has also been addressed in debates about the thorny question of the environmental vulnerability of common-property regimes. Most Africanists have rejected simple renditions of the "tragedy of the commons," in which individuals maximize exploitation of a free common resource at the cost of the resource itself.[20] Counterarguments have noted that private landholding has been no guarantee against environmental degradation: freeholders have frequently mined the land and moved on.[21] Moreover, people have gained access to commons as members of communities, with traditions of socially circumscribed usage; local authorities, customs, and religious ideas often reinforced constraints on exploitation.

In a key article on overgrazing controversies, Homewood and Rodgers argued further that common management systems show limited evidence of serious degradation. They questioned calculations of fixed carrying capacities for East African pastures and suggested that overgrazing is frequently invoked but not botanically demonstrated. Referring to Baringo District in Kenya, they maintained that "the history of the area is more suggestive of a series of oscillations in stock numbers and vegetation conditions precipitated by . . . climatic fluctuations governing this semiarid area, rather than a long-term trend of anthropogenic environmental destruction."[22] An avalanche of studies in range ecology has developed such findings.[23] In sum, they suggest that the economic and social benefits, especially for poor people, of access to common grazing for animals, vital for multiple uses such as draft, milk, meat, and exchange, are not generally outweighed by the environmental costs.[24]

South Asian and Latin American literature about the "environmentalism of the poor" provides a parallel.[25] Poor people, especially in rural areas, who are immediately dependent on natural resources have an overwhelming interest in retaining them in usable form as well as maintaining equitable access. Appreciation of local knowledge has been accompanied by sensitivity to gender relations and recognition of the role of African women, as the continent's main cultivators, on the front line of managing nature.

Fifth, scholars have systematically illustrated the centrality of conflicts over natural resources and environmental issues in rural anticolonial movements and rebellions. Following the Second World War, developmental strategies overlaid trusteeship as a guiding philosophy of empire in what has been called the second colonial occupation in Africa. State intervention helped both to trigger protest and to drive peasants into the arms of nationalists. My own research in African history began nearly twenty-five years ago with an attempt to investigate the Pondoland revolt in South Africa in 1960—perhaps the country's most serious rural rebellion of the twentieth century. It was too difficult to research at the time, but with new material and fresh perspectives gathered in the last few years, I have become more aware of its environmental origins.[26] Rural people were disturbed about the government's conservation-driven rehabilitation program; anger seethed over denial of access to reserved forests; and conflict also simmered over a succession dispute, prompted many years before by the state's dismissing a chief for failing to cooperate in locust eradication. Chieftaincy was a lightning rod for such conflicts both because of the intermediary role of traditional authorities and their responsibility for many aspects of environmental management.

Last, the fortunes of African societies have long been enmeshed in global economic and social forces and have thus been increasingly susceptible to environmental calamity. Elias Mandala's investigations of rural economy and ecological management in the lower Tchiri Valley in Malawi demonstrate how global and regional processes shaped its people's options in responding to floods in the 1930s.[27] Drawing on Amartya Sen's idea of entitlements to food, rather than drought, as the major factor behind famine, Megan Vaughan and others have explained the centrality of markets and economic and gender differentiation in mapping susceptibility to hunger.[28] The far-reaching environmental and social repercussions of African civil conflicts bred in the Cold War have also been investigated. Warring parties shot elephants for their ivory in Angola and Mozambique; millions of involuntary refugees placed intense pressure on resources in receiving areas. Debt and structural adjustment have prompted the stripping of natural resources for export and compounded environmental losses.

In summarizing and juxtaposing a range of arguments, I have inevitably simplified individual studies and connections between them. This increasingly wide-ranging literature is now a valuable resource in a number of disciplines. It captures not only the recent mood of Africanist scholarship but also certain striking features of both the colonial relationship and postcolonial states. Academic research is by no means the only vehicle for such ideas. Nevertheless, inverting colonial ideas about environmental degradation has been part of a far-reaching critique of asymmetrical power relations, both within particular countries and between the global North and South. Fundamental assumptions about knowledge, consumption, and rights to resources, as well as about inequality, have been challenged. At least at the level of development rhetoric, if not always in its practice, sensitivity to local knowledge and participatory planning, rather than root-and-branch intervention, are widely advocated. Development strategies designed to be both pro-peasant and gender-sensitive, such as dispersed agroforestry or social forestry rather than afforestation in plantations, have reflected these new directions.

These analytical and policy gains must not be lost. However, these lines of analysis are now sufficiently robust to withstand examination and extension. Arguments rooted in an anticolonial and sometimes populist discourse can present us with too neat an inversion and analytical closure, which is not always appropriate in a postcolonial world and might obscure important lines of research. We need to find routes forward without losing sight of issues of equity or the imperative to combat racial assumptions in respect of resource use and management.

Other branches of African studies, where the recent political travails of the continent have helped to provoke uneasiness, offer guidance. Historians of the slave trade and slavery, long a touchstone for developments in African history, have evolved a more complex sense of responsibility and morality. Their view recognizes the slave trade not only as a European-controlled system of exploitation but also as a trade with African participation and with many complex outcomes.[29] The rise of great West African empires, notably Asante, Dahomey, and Oyo, was intimately linked with slave capture, trade, militarization, and intensified forms of internal slavery. Similarly, although analysts of contemporary African governance differ in their explanations, some are forging a historically informed vision integrating the legacy of colonialism with a critique of African political practice and

African modes of authority.[30] This literature opens up questions of responsibility and agency that we need to address in environmental history.

One route forward may be to consider a longer time span and a comparative approach. The environmental history of the Americas has provided one model by which to explore the African case. But, as Crosby notes, the two continents' experiences differ fundamentally. Unlike most indigenous peoples in the Americas and Australasia, Africans weathered the storm of colonialism, demographically speaking. Certainly, important new human diseases were introduced during the early colonial period, as well as the epizootic rinderpest in the 1890s, which devastated cattle herds. But Africans in many regions had the immunities, and the demographic and political weight, to withstand disease and displacement. (The Khoisan peoples of southern Africa were an exception in this respect.) In the longer term, the demographic explosion of the twentieth century (and earlier in some places) is far more notable than any temporary halt. African populations increased eightfold, perhaps more in some countries, during the twentieth century. Moreover, it is now commonplace to argue that direct colonial control was a relatively brief episode in much of Africa, lasting less than a century in most places and little more than sixty years in some. This observation applies even in parts of southern Africa, where settlers gained the strongest foothold; and European agrarian settlement has been decisively driven back in most of the subcontinent during the past few decades. Environmentally and demographically, colonialism was less cataclysmic than in North and South America, the Caribbean, Australia, and New Zealand.

This is not to suggest that African societies were unconnected to the extraordinary global interchange of species and techniques that accompanied imperial expansion over the past half-millennium. Some crops, including species of palm, sorghum, millet, yams, rice, teff, and coffee were domesticated in Africa, or, like bananas, came very early from farther east. But Africans absorbed many new species through the European maritime empires because plants domesticated elsewhere offered enhanced food security, productivity, variety, labor savings, or cash-crop opportunities—notably, but by no means only, American crops and fruits such as maize, cassava, tomatoes, beans, chilies, potatoes, tobacco, cocoa, prickly pear, and avocados. A strand in the literature sees the introduction of maize, the most important of these crops, in some areas as a colonial imposition. But as James McCann shows, maize came early to Africa: it was widely reported in the seventeenth century, well before any direct colonization, and traveled along African routes. The crop was, for example, "part of the historical conjuncture that resulted in Asante's historical prosperity and hegemonic growth."[31] The Asante kingdom became perhaps the most populous and powerful in West Africa during the eighteenth and nineteenth centuries. The spread of such plants was a testament to agricultural innovation rather than to colonial imposition. In turn, new species fundamentally altered the range and balance of edible plants in the continent, helping to shape demography, farming systems, and environmental impact over the long term. This impact was not predictable. Although a valuable food source, maize also probably helped to spread malaria and exhausted the soils in areas where it was cultivated intensively and continuously.

We need also to understand that Africans, and especially Bantu-speaking black Africans, were migrants and colonizers in the continent. In his overview, *Africans,* John Iliffe places environmental control consequent on such migration at center stage: "Africans have been and are the frontiersmen who have colonized an especially hostile region of the world on behalf of the entire human race. That has been their chief contribution to history. It is why they deserve admiration, support, and careful study."[32] Some may be uneasy about according environmental control quite so central a role in the contributions of Africans to world history, and clearly women as well as men were at the cutting edge of these frontiers. Nevertheless, there is evidence that precolonial land settlement and subsequent demographic and economic growth could involve exhaustion of resources as well as beneficial use.

The spread of Bantu-speaking people from West Africa through much of the rest of sub-Saharan Africa, about two to three thousand years ago, together with the techniques, livestock, and crops which they were developing, necessarily involved unsustainable demographic expansion in local areas.[33] Interpretations of the decline of Great Zimbabwe in the fifteenth century have invoked the exhaustion of soils, firewood, and pastures. "Without fundamental changes in technology and agricultural system," Graham Connah concludes, "it was fated to destroy itself."[34] Robert Harms compares the Nunu of the Congo Basin to the New England settlers at much the same time, concerned primarily with taming the land and maximizing their take of fish.[35] Sutton discusses sophisticated East African irrigation and terracing systems capable of supporting dense settlement, which broke down by the early nineteenth century, probably because of declining yields under intensive exploitation.[36] The Bemba practice of *citimene,* or ashbed cultivation, involving the lopping and burning of trees, helped transform this part of Zambia, even if it was relatively containable in times of land plenty.[37] The Bemba symbol of masculinity was the ax.

All human survival disturbs nature, itself a dynamic set of forces, and this is a condition of development. Clearly, the impact of hunter-gatherers is of a different order from that of industrial society, but, as now seems to be accepted, the earliest aboriginal settlers in the Americas and Australia, even without iron tools or livestock, contributed to the extermination of animal species. Critically, historians must allow for changes within societies at particular phases of their encounters with nature. Trade, markets, and technological change, both international and local, have given specific natural resources value as commodities. The ivory trade is a case in point, and it is worth stressing that for any agrarian African society elephants were among the most dangerous animals, trampling and eating crops. Commercialization of palm oil in nineteenth-century coastal West Africa led to removal of some forest cover and the establishment of new plantations. Fairhead and Leach's illustration of African capacities to afforest land around their settlements does not prove that deforestation is a myth. Their work is a valuable corrective to overarching narratives of degradation, and we must be cautious about generalizations. But the dominant trend over the twentieth century in many African countries is more likely to have been deforestation, and satellite imagery for the last couple of decades suggests this trend is accelerating in some areas.

Everywhere, new techniques of hunting by firearms, fishing with nets, and cultivating with plows could alter relationships between people and nature. In her discussion of soil erosion in Lesotho, Showers focuses on colonial interventions and responsibility, but the Sotho themselves transformed their agrarian, military, and transport systems in the nineteenth century. They adopted horses and sheep, as well as ox-drawn wagons and sledges; they intensified plow cultivation of the lowlands with new crops of wheat and maize; and they colonized mountain zones.[38]

This argument does not preclude periods of relative stability in particular locales, nor do I suggest that all environmental transformation is best conceived as degradation. Moreover, it certainly allows for a dynamic view of local knowledge; and we still have a great deal to learn about the accommodations reached between people and nature, the way these were interpreted in different societies, and the way they were policed. Environmental regulation could be expressed in part through customary and religious practices, and, as David Maxwell and Terence Ranger have argued, the eco-religious elements in Zimbabwean territorial cults did not disappear in the twentieth century.[39] They may in fact have been reinforced as an explanation of agro-ecological stress and as a popular critique of state intervention.

The same logic might apply to management of common property resources. Although Africanists are correctly wary of simplified models depicting a tragedy of the commons, we should not, conversely, assume that common-property regimes are environmentally beneficial. When control and accountability do break down, degradation can occur under the pressure of social change, urbanization, markets, war, and drought.[40] Examples can be found from the West African Sahel to the Eastern Cape in South Africa. Where land boundaries are tightening, continued transhumance can be a recipe for conflict. In some peri-urban contexts with very rapid population growth, uncertainty over land rights has exacerbated difficulties in providing urban services and developing urban environmental controls. Mary Tiffen, Michael Mortimore, and Francis Gichuki demonstrate in their book *More People, Less Erosion* that peasants greened their land in Machakos district, Kenya, over a period of fifty years from an environmental low point in the 1930s, despite increases in population. In many respects, the study echoes others in praise of local knowledge. But they also suggest that a key factor in the transition from "badlands to farmlands" was the landholders' ability to secure effectively private rights over, and to invest in, both arable and grazing land.[41] In other cases, such as in the Eastern Cape, common property together with lack of resources have inhibited investment, improvement, and effective land management. We have to allow for variable outcomes.

More-complex readings of the history of science and knowledge, an exciting area of academic enterprise, may also be valuable. First, scientific developments, research agendas, and institutions, even when government-funded, were rooted in far broader intellectual networks than could be shaped by any particular state; the relative autonomy of scientific investigation, debates within disciplines, and battles between scientists and officials are all evident. Second, the dichotomy between Western science and local knowledge also requires modification. Although some encounters were characterized by mutual incomprehension, systems of knowledge have often been porous and plural over a long period. On the one hand, for example, Steven Feierman argues that African medical ideas were open to many new influences.[42] On the other, even at the height of colonial control, there was a significant sprinkling of sensitive scientists, not least in ecological, agricultural, and medical fields, as well as innumerable anthropologists whose record of local knowledge and techniques is now a baseline for research.[43] Transmission of ideas and practices was clearly mediated by relationships of power, but that imbalance did not in itself halt the process.

Third, scientific work, past and present, shapes our very capacity to think about environmental change, about the history of relevant disciplines that must be part of environmental history, and about ecological interactions that are far beyond the powers of historians and social scientists to research. Richards, often cited as a key advocate of African knowledge, also insists that social scientists listen to natural scientists. He has celebrated John Ford's analysis of the history of trypanosomiasis in Africa precisely because it required the understanding of a natural scientist to unravel complex issues of habitat, vectors, and immunities. He distances himself from those social scientists who wish "to mine the natural sciences" very largely "for material that might lend itself to cultural critique" and to examine only "the marginal cases, where the bioscientific problem was framed in an unprofitable way," as in the "excesses of colonial agricultural planning."[44]

Failures in planning have perhaps been better rehearsed by historians than the rapidity with which scientists in Africa grappled with, and sometimes understood, complex diseases, ecologies, and natural phenomena. Historians must remain critical and identify instances where the intersection of scientific practice and state power has disadvantaged poor people or women, but they must also remain humble in recognition of the limits of our discipline. Local knowledge also has its limitations, sometimes tragically, in respect of diseases such as AIDS. All knowledge exists to be tested, rejected, and built upon. Where local communities have limited capacity for many types of environmental and disease management, it may be wise to bring sensitive science and the state back in.[45] Not all experts are outsiders, and such debates are increasingly generated within African countries.

Science and the state remain potentially powerful allies for poor people. Elizabeth Colson's study of the consequences of building the Kariba Dam on the Zambezi River helped initiate valuable anthropological research into the social and environment costs of big dams.[46] In South Africa and Zimbabwe, the unequal distribution of reservoir water to commercial farms and white suburbs was a fundamental aspect of discrimination and apartheid. But not all big dams are bad dams. Leaving aside the vexed question of irrigation, African countries are urbanizing rapidly and irrevocably. Social justice, urban health, and environmental improvement demand clean water. Dams, diversion of water, flooding of dam catchments in rural areas, and water processing may all be a necessary consequence. The environmentalism of the poor in the urban areas increasingly focuses on the demand for such services at an affordable rate; in South Africa, at least, the same needs are evident in dense rural settlements.[47]

Moreover, ecological outcomes, whether in zones managed by local communities or by national states, are unpredictable, as both history and the natural sciences tell us. So may folklore. I suggested at the outset that one of the most exciting areas opened up by an environmental focus lies in cultural history—well explored in the British historiography of landscape and literature, attitudes, and art, but less so in African studies.[48] Fables were one sphere of African culture that explored encounters with the natural world. Such stories are sometimes good to think with.

Many fables illustrated perceived animal characteristics and abounded with metaphors and observations drawn from nature, but they also offered a mirror on human society. They could be moral tales, explanatory myths, or more open-ended narratives. They clearly changed through time and, like other local knowledge, incorporated new influences. In Khoisan and African stories of South Africa, for example, the jackal and hare were usually tricksters. Khoisan jackal fables collected in the mid-nineteenth century wove wagons, farmers, and sheep into their narratives.[49] Settlers not only brought with them parallel folklore but also recorded and reworked indigenous fables that had meaning for them. The imbrication of these traditions, reflecting also social and agrarian change, is a fascinating topic in itself.

Destruction of species and even conservationist interventions have often produced unexpected consequences. The partial eradication of jackals in early twentieth-century South Africa, supported by conservationists who wished to stop the daily driving and kraaling (corralling) of livestock, contributed to a rapid rise in the number of sheep and thus to South Africa's equivalent of the Dust Bowl in the early 1930s.[50] Unpredictability can also work in the opposite direction. In the late nineteenth century, the future for wildlife in much of southern Africa seemed bleak. Some wild animals were, however, protected in enclaves, and the system of parks and reserves was gradually extended throughout the region. From the 1950s, these efforts were supplemented by game farming on private land, partly as a source of meat and trophies and partly as an alternative to pastoral farming, from which returns were declining. Initiatives such as the Campfire Program in Zimbabwe have attempted to extend this trend into communal areas. In the vast area that encompasses South Africa, Botswana, Zimbabwe, and Namibia, wildlife numbers have increased in the past couple of decades to their highest level since 1900. The state, by reserving land; capitalist farmers, by switching land use rapidly; and science, in the shape of veterinary medicine and zoology, have all contributed to this outcome. Biodiversity has benefited, but the recovery of wildlife has not yet produced a more equitable division of rural resources.

Although the bulk of academic writing sees wildlife conservation as a product of the colonial state, serving white and Western interests, new studies are beginning to reveal African agency in this sphere. The origins of the Moremi National Park in Botswana, now at the heart of the valuable Okavango delta reserve, can be traced to the enthusiasm of African advisers to the local BaTawana chieftaincy in the 1950s and 1960s. They worked with white adventurers and sometimes in the face of opposition from the colonial Bechuanaland protectorate.[51] The history of African ideas and practices regarding animals, which in many parts of the continent shaped the rhythms of everyday life, has been less well researched. From a rich base of anthropological material it is patent that certain species, at least, were sometimes protected. Similar exciting but neglected fields are the history of landscape and the built environment—not least because relatively few structures were made by specialists. As in the case of environmental history as a whole, their study demands a multifaceted, totalizing approach that draws on analysis of production, technology, environmental change, and style.

I have sought to test contrasting narratives written about African environmental history. Time scales, disciplines, and ideological vantage points all inform the interpretations offered. Although I emphasize human capacities to shape the environment, other themes, notably vulnerability and the all-pervasive environmental constraints on human activity, deserve attention. But I do not believe that these views need always be mutually exclusive, and indeed a number of the texts discussed demonstrate that they are not. Mahmood Mamdani, who sees the primary divide in African studies as between communitarians and modernists, argues not only for an awareness of the roots of these positions but also for a synthesis.[52] Achieving it may not be easy. A profound ambivalence can be detected in recent Africanist writing, by scholars both in Africa and outside, which, while emphasizing the asymmetry of global relations and the history of racist assumptions, struggles to free historiography and social studies from narratives of dependency, victimhood, and romanticism. We must continue to explore not only African creativity and resistance but also other forms of African agency, not least the shared human capacity to wield power for ill as well as good, over nature as well as people.

NOTES

1. Alfred W. Crosby, *The Columbian Exchange: Biological and Cultural Consequences of 1492* (Westport, CT: Greenwood Press, 1972) and *Ecological Imperialism: The Biological Expansion of Europe, 900–1900* (Cambridge: Cambridge University Press, 1986); William Cronon, *Changes in the Land: Indians, Colonists, and the Ecology of New England* (New York: Hill and Wang, 1983).

2. William Beinart and Peter Coates, *Environment and History: The Taming of Nature in the USA and South Africa* (London: Routledge, 1995).

3. T. O. Ranger, *The Recovery of African Initiative in Tanzanian History* (Dar es Salaam: University College, 1969) and *Rhodes, Oxford, and the Study of Race Relations* (Oxford: Clarendon Press, 1989); John McCracken, "Terry Ranger: A Personal Appreciation," *Journal of Southern African Studies* 23 (1997): 175–85.

4. Crosby, *Ecological Imperialism*, 76.

5. Stephen Greenblatt, *Marvelous Possessions: The Wonder of the New World* (Chicago: University of Chicago Press, 1991), 56.

6. John MacKenzie, "Empire and the Ecological Apocalypse: The Historiography of the Imperial Environment," in *Ecology and Empire: Environmental History of Settler Societies*, ed. Tom Griffiths and Libby Robin (Edinburgh: Keele University Press, 1997), 215–28.

7. Helge Kjekshus, *Ecology Control and Economic Development in East African History* (London: Heinemann, 1977); Leroy Vail, "Ecology and History: The Example of Eastern Zambia," *Journal of Southern African Studies* 3 (1977): 129–55.

8. Kjekshus, *Ecology Control*, 25. He notes that this must be a speculative conclusion. For a discussion, see Juhani Koponen, *People and Production in Late Precolonial Tanzania: History and Structures* (Helsinki: Finnish Society for Development Studies, 1988), 362 ff.

9. John MacKenzie, *The Empire of Nature: Hunting, Conservation and British Imperialism* (Manchester: Manchester University Press, 1988).

10. William Beinart, "Soil Erosion, Conservationism and Ideas about Development," *Journal of Southern African Studies* 11 (1984): 52–83; David Anderson and Richard Grove, eds., *Conservation in Africa: People, Policies and Practice* (Cambridge: Cambridge University Press, 1987).

11. Ravi Rajan, "Imperial Environmentalism or Environmental Imperialism? European Forestry, Colonial Foresters and the Agendas of Forest Management in British India, 1800–1900," in *Nature and the Orient: The Environmental History of South and Southeast Asia*, ed. Richard H. Grove, Vinita Damodaran, and Satpal Sangwan (Delhi: Oxford University Press, 1998): 324–71.

12. Jane Carruthers, *The Kruger National Park: A Social and Political History* (Pietermaritzburg: Natal University Press, 1995); Terence Ranger, "Whose Heritage? The Case of the Matobo National Park," *Journal of Southern African Studies* 15 (1989): 217–249, and *Voices from the Rocks: Nature, Culture and History in the Matopos Hills of Zimbabwe* (Oxford: James Currey, 1999).

13. Dan Brockington, *Fortress Conservation: The Preservation of the Mkomazi Game Reserve, Tanzania* (Oxford: James Currey, 2002).

14. Anderson and Grove, *Conservation in Africa;* F. Wilson and M. Ramphele, *Uprooting Poverty: The South African Challenge* (Cape Town: David Philip, 1989); Pat McAllister, "Resistance to 'Betterment' in the Transkei: A Case Study from Willowvale District," *Journal of Southern African Studies* 15 (1989): 346–68; Nancy Jacobs, *Environment, Power, and Injustice: A South African History* (Cambridge: Cambridge University Press, 2003).

15. Kate B. Showers, "Soil Erosion in the Kingdom of Lesotho: Origins and Colonial Response," *Journal of Southern African Studies* 15, no. 2 (1989): 263–86, and *Imperial Gullies: Soil Erosion and Conservation in Lesotho* (Athens: Ohio University Press, 2005).

16. James Fairhead and Melissa Leach, *Misreading the African Landscape: Society and Ecology in a Forest-Savannah Mosaic* (Cambridge: Cambridge University Press, 1996), 2–3, and *Reframing Deforestation: Global Analysis and Local Realities: Studies in West Africa* (London: Routledge, 1998); Melissa Leach and Robin Mearns, eds., *The Lie of the Land: Challenging Received Wisdom on the African Environment* (Oxford: James Currey, 1996).

17. Paul Richards, *Indigenous Agricultural Revolution: Ecology and Food Production in West Africa* (London: Unwin, 1985), 41; Paul Richards, "Ecological Change and the Politics of African Land Use," *African Studies Review* 26 (1983): 1–72.

18. Richards, *Indigenous Agricultural Revolution*, 142.

19. Calestous Juma, *The Gene Hunters: Biotechnology and the Scramble for Seeds* (London: Zed Books, 1989); Amos Kiriro and Calestous Juma, eds., *Gaining Ground: Institutional Innovations in Land-Use Management in Kenya* (Nairobi: Acts Press, 1989).

20. Graham Hardin, "The Tragedy of the Commons," *Science* 162 (December 1968): 1243–48.

21. Gavin Williams, "Introduction: Farmers, Herders and the State," *Rural Africana* 25–26 (1986): 1–23.

22. Katherine Homewood and W. A. Rodgers, "Pastoralism, Conservation and the Overgrazing Controversy," in Anderson and Grove, *Conservation in Africa*, 123.

23. Roy Behnke, Ian Scoones, and Carol Kerven, *Range Ecology at Disequilibrium* (London: Overseas Development Institute, 1993); Ian Scoones, ed., *Living with Uncertainty: New Directions in Pastoral Development in Africa* (London: Intermediate Technology Publications, 1995).

24. Ben Cousins, "Livestock Production and Common Property Struggles in South Africa's Agrarian Reform," *Journal of Peasant Studies* 23, nos. 2–3 (1996), special issue on "The Agrarian Question in South Africa," ed. Henry Bernstein, 166–208.

25. Ramachandra Guha and Joan Martínez-Alier, *Varieties of Environmentalism: Essays North and South* (London: Earthscan, 1997).

26. William Beinart, "Environmental Origins of the Pondoland Revolt," in *South Africa's Environmental History: Cases and Comparisons,* ed. Stephen Dovers, Ruth Edgecombe and Bill Guest (Cape Town: David Philip, 2002), 76–89.

27. Elias C. Mandala, *Work and Control in a Peasant Economy: A History of the Lower Tchiri Valley in Malawi, 1859–1960* (Madison: University of Wisconsin Press, 1990).

28. Megan Vaughan, *The Story of an African Famine: Gender and Famine in Twentieth-Century Malawi* (Cambridge: Cambridge University Press, 1987); Alex de Waal, *Famine That Kills: Darfur, Sudan, 1984–5* (Oxford: Clarendon Press, 1989) and *Famine Crimes: Politics and the Disaster Relief Industry in Africa* (Oxford: James Currey, 1997).

29. Paul E. Lovejoy, *Transformations in Slavery: A History of Slavery in Africa* (Cambridge: Cambridge University Press, 1983); Patrick Manning, *Slavery and African Life: Occidental, Oriental and African Slave Trades* (Cambridge: Cambridge University Press, 1990).

30.   Jean-François Bayart, *The State in Africa: The Politics of the Belly* (London: Longman, 1993); Jean-François Bayart, Stephen Ellis, and Beatrice Hibou, *The Criminalization of the State in Africa* (Oxford: James Currey, 1999); Patrick Chabal, *Power in Africa: An Essay in Political Interpretation* (Basingstoke: Macmillan, 1994); P. Chabal and Jean-Pascal Daloz, *Africa Works: Disorder as Political Instrument* (Oxford: James Currey, 1999); Mahmood Mamdani, *Citizen and Subject: Contemporary Africa and the Legacy of Late Colonialism* (London: James Currey, 1996); George B. N. Ayittey, *Africa Betrayed* (New York: St. Martin's Press, 1992).

31.   James McCann, *Maize and Grace: Africa's Encounter with a New World Crop, 1500–2000* (Cambridge, MA: Harvard University Press, 2005), 43.

32.   John Iliffe, *Africans: The History of a Continent* (Cambridge: Cambridge University Press, 1995), 1.

33.   Jan Vansina, in *Paths in the Rainforests: Toward a History of Political Tradition in Equatorial Africa* (London: James Currey, 1990), does not see exhaustion of resources as a necessary part of the process.

34.   Graham Connah, *African Civilizations: Precolonial Cities and States in Tropical Africa: An Archaeological Perspective* (Cambridge: Cambridge University Press, 1987), 209.

35.   See Robert Harms, *Games against Nature: An Eco-cultural History of the Nunu of Equatorial Africa* (Cambridge: Cambridge University Press, 1987), 245—although he probably pushes the analogy too far.

36.   J. E. G. Sutton, "Irrigation and Soil-Conservation in African Agricultural History," *Journal of African History* 25, no. 1 (1984): 25–42.

37.   Audrey Richards, *Land, Labour and Diet in Northern Rhodesia: An Economic Study of the Bemba Tribe* (London: International Africa Institute, 1939); Henrietta Moore and Megan Vaughan, *Cutting Down Trees: Gender, Nutrition, and Agricultural Change in the Northern Province of Zambia, 1890–1990* (London: James Currey, 1994).

38.   Showers, *Imperial Gullies*.

39.   David Maxwell, *Christians and Chiefs in Zimbabwe: A Social History of the Hwesa People, c. 1870s–1990s* (Edinburgh: Edinburgh University Press, 1999), 53 ff.; Terence Ranger, *Voices from the Rocks: Nature, Culture, and History from the Matopos Hills of Zimbabwe* (Bloomington: University of Indiana Press, 1999).

40.   Cousins, "Livestock Production and Common Property Struggles," 171; he notes especially Trond Vedeld, "Local Institution-Building and Resource Management in the West African Sahel," Pastoral Development Network, Overseas Development Institute, Network Paper 33c (1992), and Trond Vedeld, *Village Politics: Heterogeneity, Leadership, and Collective Action among the Fulani of Mali* (Ås: Agricultural University of Norway, 1997).

41.   Mary Tiffen, Michael Mortimore, and Francis Gichuki, *More People, Less Erosion: Environmental Recovery in Kenya* (Chichester: John Wiley, 1994), 5.

42. Steven Feierman, "Struggles for Control: The Social Roots of Health and Healing in Modern Africa," *African Studies Review* 28 (1985): 73–147; Steven Feierman and John M. Janzen, eds., *The Social Basis of Health and Healing in Africa* (Berkeley: University of California Press, 1992).

43. Helen Tilley, "African Environments and Environmental Sciences," in *Social History and African Environments,* ed. William Beinart and JoAnn McGregor (Oxford: James Currey, 2003), 109–30.

44. M. Priscilla Stone and Paul Richards, "The Integration of the Social and Natural Sciences: The View from the Program on African Studies," unpublished paper.

45. Ben Fine and Colin Stoneman, "Introduction: State and Development," *Journal of Southern African Studies* 22, no. 1 (1996): 5–26, quoting Peter B. Evans, et al., *Bringing the State Back In* (Cambridge: Cambridge University Press, 1985).

46. Elizabeth Colson, *The Social Consequences of Resettlement* (Manchester: Manchester University Press, 1971).

47. David A. McDonald, ed., *Environmental Justice in South Africa* (Athens: Ohio University Press, 2002); David A. McDonald and Greg Ruiters, eds., *The Age of Commodity: Water Privatization in Southern Africa* (Sterling, VA: Earthscan, 2006).

48. Keith Thomas, *Man and the Natural World: Changing Attitudes in England, 1500–1800* (London: Penguin, 1984); Simon Schama, *Landscape and Memory* (London: Fontana, 1996). But see Ute Luig and Achim von Oppen, eds., "The Making of African Landscapes," special issue of *Paideuma: Mitteilungen zur Kulturkunde* 43 (1997).

49. W.H.I. Bleek, *Reynard the Fox in Africa; Or Hottentot Fables and Tales* (London: Trüber and Co., 1864).

50. William Beinart, *The Rise of Conservation in South Africa: Settlers, Livestock, and the Environment, 1770–1950* (Oxford: Oxford University Press, 2003).

51. Maitseo Bolaane, "Chiefs, Hunters and Adventurers; The Foundation of the Okavango/Moremi National Park, Botswana," *Journal of Historical Geography* 31 (2005): 241–59.

52. Mamdani, *Citizen and Subject.*

NINE · Environmental Histories of India

Of States, Landscapes, and Ecologies

MAHESH RANGARAJAN

THE SETTING

Environmental change in colonial India was once largely outside the purview of historical scholarship but is now a flourishing subject. The sheer size of the population of the country, now accounting for one in six people on the planet, and its centrality to European projects of global domination since the late eighteenth century make it inevitable that imperial impact and its aftermath should form a major trope of the global environmental history narrative. There are also enduring legacies of state building and diverse social formations in the subcontinent.

India's role in the wider world is also connected to its geographic heterogeneity. The vast Indus-Ganges-Brahmaputra plains in the north constitute the largest lowland floodplains in Asia other than those of the Yellow and Yangzi rivers in China. To the west of the geologically young and tectonically active Himalayas lie the highlands of central-west Asia; to the east are the associated hill ranges of Burma. The Indian peninsula has smaller floodplains and a whole range of hills, plateaus, and mountain ranges—none as high as those to the north, and most composed of older rock formations.

It is easy to forget that humans share this living space with more than ten thousand varieties of flowering plants and five hundred species of mammals, a reflection less of India's size (the nation today is one-third the size of the continental United States and one-seventh the size of Russia) than of its topographical diversity. A 3,000-kilometer-long coastline and numerous small water bodies, some seasonal in nature, add to this heterogeneity. The complex and contesting claims over nature and living spaces within have a deep bearing on the world at large, given the number of humans and the diversity of species involved. But what matters to a historian are the ways in which these dilemmas and clashes can be set against the backdrop of complex historical legacies.

Recent high-quality scholarship drawing on sources from the precolonial period has helped to place recent events in a longer-term context, though it also leads us to question some claims made in earlier works. Increasing attention is also being given to regional and local histories, vital in recording the past of a large, populous, and diverse subcontinent. India's engagement with the wider world, in particular as an integral part of the *Pax Britannnica*, has deeply influenced the choice and nature of issues under debate.[1]

A question often discussed is to what extent the colonial and imperial period altered the ways in which people related not only to each other but also to their geophysical and biological environment. Connected to this question is that of the extent to which imperial legacies reshaped the environment of India after independence in 1947. For if the unmaking of an older order underpinned the new polity of the company state and then, after 1858, of the Crown, the developmental choices of the modern state have also drawn from debates and dilemmas of the colonial era.[2] Less than two decades after the first ecologically informed study of a peasant movement, a welter of fresh monographs has appeared.[3] From an initial focus on forestry policies and irrigation, the agenda is broadening to include topics ranging from fisheries to urban air pollution, and attitudes are shifting from an emphasis on fauna to histories of science and knowledge systems.[4] Yet the main unifying theme in these studies remains the nature and significance of the colonial experience.[5] The only book presenting an overview of the processes of change is an ambitious attempt to span centuries and subregions to map the changing patterns of prudence and profligacy in resource use.[6] Recent collections have tended to explore the larger agro-ecological context and to pay more attention to the complex experience of crafting large polities in a subcontinent with more than eight hundred agro-climatic zones. The heterogeneity was well expressed in a Hindavi (old Hindi) proverb observing that the water, as well as the language, changed with every ten *kos* traveled.[7]

Lenin once wrote that Marx's thought had three components: German philosophy, French socialism, and British political economy. Analogously, British imperial land management in the subcontinent had three dimensions: government forestry, perennial canal networks, and new ways of regulating or controlling large fauna.[8]

These distinct but interconnected projects were also specific to South Asia. Thus, state forestry was more central to the British experience in India than in southern or eastern Africa, where stock control and watershed management were much more prominent.[9] The canal networks in northern and southern India were among the most ambitious ventures of their time and influenced the creation of modern irrigation systems in the United States.[10] Conversely, the preservation of wildlife never acquired, at least in colonial times, the significance that it had in the United States or in southern Africa. It was seen as an adjunct to sport hunting and forestry practice: perhaps the canopy forest was less conducive to game viewing, whereas the wildlife of the open plains was devastated long before the onset of aesthetic elite sensibilities.[11] This triad of government forestry, canal irrigation, and carnivore control has left a deep and abiding mark on the ecological landscape of the sub-continent.[12] Despite enormous variations in revenue arrangements and agro-ecologies in different regions, these issues were critical components of colonial, and in many ways of postcolonial, policy.

Public concern about the adverse aspects of this legacy has contributed to fresh research. The new wave of work does have roots in older traditions, especially those of fieldwork in anthropology and agrarian studies, but a major driving force has come from outside the discipline.[13] In common with popular history and gender history, ecologically informed social history has links with social movements.[14] The focus on the fight for the forest in the past mirrors present-day concerns about the contest between commercial forestry and the livelihood and rights of the rural poor. Similarly, the interest in exploring alternative techniques of irrigation reflects anxieties about the adverse social and ecological impact of large dams.[15] The interest in "traditional" technologies and in discovering alternatives to state control and capitalist market economies is evident in much of the research. Colonialism, unsurprisingly, is often seen as a crucial divide.

The pioneers of Indian environmental history tended to set up an opposition between the equilibrium of people and nature before colonialism, and the disharmony that arose as a result of British intrusion. Previous rulers had rarely intervened in woods and pastures; when they did, it was mainly to assert monopolies over valuable animals, like elephants. Gadgil and Guha have also argued that the use of natural resources was regulated mainly by caste and custom.[16] Such an approach focuses on the consequences of imperial policy for rural producers and also reverses any notion of a long period of decline before the coming of *Pax Britannica*. Despite its merits, this paradigm does not take adequate account of the relations between precolonial regimes and the hinterland: it assumes a stasis or a "long equilibrium" in the precolonial period. Although the idea of a colonial ecological watershed remains valid, it needs to be examined and critiqued.

IMPERIAL IMPACTS

Increase the forests that are near your
frontier fortresses and destroy all that are in
the middle of your territory. Then alone you
will not have trouble from robbers.

> *Amuktamalyada*, sixteenth-century Telugu
> manual of statecraft

The environmental implications of the changes on the agrarian frontier in the early modern era demand more attention than they normally receive. British policies and actions differed from those of their predecessors, but understanding this disjuncture requires a more attentive assessment of the environmental impact of precolonial society. States dependent on land-based revenues had long tried to extend their reach into forest and hill areas. In turn, some polities emerged from such locales.

Successive rulers tried to extend their domain of settled, cultivated arable land to increase revenue and strengthen their kingdoms. These efforts had significant consequences for the floral complex as well as for more mobile forms of life. The establishment of human settlements in the passes of Dohad and Rajpipla by 1761 cut off the elephants in the Gujarat forests from those in central India. The crucial aspect of such changes is not merely the extension of town and farm at the expense of wildlife habitat.[17] After all, despite such changes, the overall scene was arguably one of harmony. But such a view would overlook the significance of such changes. The fragmentation of the habitat of large mammals—so marked in the nineteenth and twentieth centuries—had antecedents, albeit less pronounced, in the Mughal and post-Mughal eras.[18]

In the seventeenth century, the Mughal Empire bore down heavily on the nomadic tribes in the hilly and the deltaic regions of Sind. A combination of military might, religious proselytization, and revenue remissions were employed to try and induce settlement among the nomadic peoples.[19] The clearing of fresh lands for cultivation was also given a fillip by religious institutions like the *math* (seminary) of Bodh Gaya, established in 1590.[20] The expansion of rice cultivation into the vast delta of the Ganges and Brahmaputra was facilitated by land grants to Muslim holy men. Islam gained new adherents even as it was remade to conform to peasant life in a land where, unlike any other place in the Indian subcontinent, tigers regularly preyed on humans.[21] The influx of caste Hindu colonists into the middle Indian highlands and valleys was a staggered process, encouraged by landholders and rulers eager to reap more revenue. The tug of war between the agrarian heartlands and the drier or forested hinterland was not specific to colonial rulers; earlier, however, there was more of a continuum of forest and savannah, or, alternatively, of scrub jungle and cultivated arable land. At its apogee, the Mughal Empire extended over half of central Asia. By the late sixteenth century, urban centers in central India such as Sanchi, known for its Buddhist stupa (shrine), and Khajuraho had receded from prominence in politics and history. Large surrounding tracts were overgrown with jungle to such an extent that neither center finds mention in Abu al-Fazl's *Ain i Akbari*, compiled in 1596. Its last great ruler, Aurangzeb (d. 1707), issued an edict asking local chiefs to maintain forest tracks for hunting by members of the imperial household.[22]

Even though states did not normally promote direct management of uncultivated lands as in imperial China or regulate forest use as in Japan, disincentives and incentives did retard or speed up the process of agrarian extension.[23] In 1761, the Peshwa—recognizing the rights of Ramachander Bascottah—commended the latter for his work in the Nimar region on repelling attacks by Bhil tribal peoples: "Jungles having overgrown the once cultivated fields, I therefore ordered you to restore these *mahals* to cultivation and inhabitants."[24] The classical associations of settled agrarian lands with family and caste and the wastes with the home of the warrior and war band were striking. This opposition was not an isolated case: settling the land entailed cutting back the jungle, guarding against wild-animal attack, and repelling raids by mobile peoples.[25] Nor was this approach peculiar to Indian rulers: a study of environmental change in late imperial south China refers to a triad of "bandits, snakes, and robbers" that had to make way for cultivated arable land.[26] In India, the priorities may have been different, given the need to protect cattle from large predators that found them easy, slow-moving prey in comparison to wild herbivores.

Such relations were not solely antagonistic. A lively exchange of animals bred or captured beyond the cultivated arable land mediated ties between settlers and other peoples. Despite the interest in extending cultivation and the reach of pioneer peasants, rulers still relied on other producers in a variety of ways. The Banjaras, with their trains of pack bullocks, provided vital support to the Mughal army in campaigns by transporting grain and supplies. They also provided credit and linked remote areas with the market. The best calves were sold to sedentary peasants, who benefited from such exchanges. The size of these *tandas* or caravans deserves mention: in the seventeenth century they included as many as two hundred thousand bullocks. Even in the 1840s, a caravan of forty thousand on the north Indian plains elicited little comment.[27] The elephant, too, served as a link between states and residents of hillside and forested lands. The capture of wild elephants had been vital for more than two millennia: the animals were used as siege engines and for transport. Supplies were especially critical for the Turk and Mughal rulers in north India. Elephants could be bred in captivity, but it was easier to trap and train them. Unlike their African cousins, female Asian elephants rarely have tusks: in any case, it was the African species whose tusks were preferred by ivory carvers across the ages. Asian elephants were more valuable alive than dead. Under the Mughals, their possession inspired the composition of court poetry. Individual elephants were highly prized possessions, Akbar's own elephant Gajraj being a case in point. A special elephant tax was levied, though it was waived in the northern Deccan because of the poverty of the peasantry.[28] In Akbar's time (1556–1605), captive elephants in the Muhgal dominions numbered perhaps seventeen thousand.[29] Elephant use in warfare largely ended in China before 1700 C.E., but the animals continued to be used in India until well into the twentieth century.[30]

Just as fauna and flora were in flux, so too were human settlements. There is little evidence of self-reliant village communities. On the contrary, trade and the exchange of high-value commodities could strengthen and not just weaken land-extensive forms of production. For example, even trade contact with the Portuguese following the voyages of Vasco da Gama did not rupture swidden cultivation in the western Indian highlands: rather, it enabled swidden cultivators to expand their production of spices. The limited reach of the Portuguese into the hinterland and the high value of commodities like pepper helped stabilize long-fallow cultivation in parts of Kanara on the southwest coast.[31] Post-Mughal polities—whether Maratha or Rajput—did not make as sharp a break as British rule did. This is not to argue for the concept of self-reliant autarkic village economies—against which there is now overwhelming evidence from different regions—but the fluidity of the division between farm and forest was more than matched by a wealth of resources and opportunities for peoples on the fringe of lowland agriculture. The kings of the forest in central and western India often gained from their deep knowledge of local conditions. Both the Portuguese and the Mughal leaders acceded to the demands of the Kolis in the northern Konkan and the hills of Baglan as the latter avoided set-piece battles in the plains. Koli power in the hills ensured that their terms were often met by rulers. When larger polities were in crisis, the forest chiefs could turn the tables. The hills and forest were the birthplace of many a dynastic royal household. This kind of fluidity, though not limitless, was significant enough to raise doubts about close long-term parity between endogamy and ecological function.[32] Caste did not rigidly define the ecological role played by groups of humans.

The very structure of the polity sustained dispersed forms of production. There was no functional harmony in the process, and conflicts did occur. The dispersal of habitations over a wider geographical area had major ecological consequences. Land was more abundant than labor, and the extent of pasture and jungle made it easy to procure good fodder. The density of human population in India increased from an estimated five people per square kilometer around 200 C.E. to thirty-five by 1650. With more than three-fourths of the land area not under permanent cultivation at the start of the seventeenth century, this low population density made for a very different scenario from the present day.[33] Recent works have focused increasingly on the association of the cultivated arable land to the expanses that lay beyond or at the edge of it, or were frequently in transition. This relationship has been demonstrated for the Mughal period, but the proposition would also hold true in large parts of the subcontinent until well into the modern era. This abundance of arable land distinguishes India from China. Until well into the last two decades of the nineteenth century, labor, not land, was the limiting factor in the expansion and maintenance of cultivation.[34] But the terms began to shift against itinerant, nomadic, and land-extensive forms of settlement even before demographic expansion accelerated in the 1920s.

The British differed from Indian rulers, tribal leaders, and landholders in their notion of political power. Kings and rent receivers had looser, more flexible political arrangements and revenue systems, especially in hilly and dry regions. Irruptions and raids redressed at least in part the flow of wealth from the hills to the plains.[35] Under the British, these raids were curbed with an iron fist. The British put an end to such cycles of expansion and decay and began creating a cordon sanitaire for the lowlands. This move tipped the scales in favor of a village-centered peasant economy and new commercialization of forest lands.[36] This process of "pacification" and enforcing sedentary settlement initially derived from concerns for law and order and a desire to make it easier to collect land revenue. In the Rajmahal hills, early attempts to recruit the hill peoples, or Paharias, into colonial military service failed. A three-hundred-mile-long masonry wall was built around the hill range, symbolizing the British cordon sanitaire. The tract beyond the wall was settled with Santhals, who were seen as more amenable to settled cultivation.[37]

Such areas had been key elements in the precolonial polity, but in a loose and fluid way. Now, with the termination of tribal raids, the inner frontier was closed.[38]

This change was only the prelude to more intrusive policies in mountains and forested regions. In the aftermath of the 1857–58 rebellion (or mutiny), there was widespread disarming of the countryside, which put an end to the age-old tradition of an armed peasantry. The old order was conducive to more dispersed patterns of production and settlement: slash-and-burn farming, stock keeping, hunting, nomadic trade, and trapping. There was an intimate connection between the more disaggregated forms of political power and the heterogeneity of human ecology. Now, attempts to impose or promote sedentary settlement and agrarian production, as distinct from a nomadic and itinerant way of life, were sustained with far more vigor. The Bhils of Khandesh and the Bhattis of the Delhi region became targets for sedentary settlement in the 1820s, and these initiatives were considerably expanded elsewhere later in the century.[39] The British were not dependent on tribal or pastoral peoples for services. They dispensed with the Banjara transporters and set up their own commissariat.[40] In southern India, the Koravas had earlier earned a living and sustained trade through a mix of occupations: salt trading; magic and sorcery; casual labor; and breeding and raising cattle.[41]

Change did not move at the same pace everywhere, but it runs like a thread through narratives of different regions. Inclusive and accommodative modes of power were elbowed out as the new polity took shape. The privileging of certain modes of resource use, especially of sedentary cultivation, was accompanied by another significant departure from past practice. It also set the stage for regulation of the uncultivated wastes that had earlier only lightly felt the ingress of polities. In place of tribute or the tapping of skills of those who used the wastelands, the British actually began to intervene in the production process itself. A pleader who appeared before a committee of the Poona Sarvajanik Sabha in 1872 aptly summed up the colonial disjuncture. Vitallput of Colaba near Bombay lamented that "under previous rulers only rice-producing lands were assessed before: barren lands used for subsidiary purposes were not assessed . . . and the cultivator was permitted to collect decayed vegetable matter from the jungles and hillsides which he is not allowed to do now."[42]

The annexation or the regulation of uncultivated lands was both an index and a consequence of the break with the past. The portrait of the transition sketched here is only tentative, but it might help take the debate beyond the polarity of "harmony" and "disequilibrium." Adivasis (or tribal peoples) and Banjaras had not been outside the power structures in the precolonial era. Despite major changes, they retained varying degrees of autonomy within such state systems. The change in the nature of the polity now pushed such groups to the margins of power.

The process began long before the enactment of the forest legislation in the 1860s and 1870s.[43] In fact, the drive to transform the forests into managed landscapes has to be seen against the backdrop of previous interventions. The British Empire in South Asia was part of a global network: not only did it expose resources to new pressures, but it could also draw on sources of power outside the region. It was thus more insulated from pressures within the subcontinent than previous regimes. Little of the hill, pasture, or jungle was left untouched by the transition to a more intrusive political order and a harsher fiscal regime. The creation of a new kind of polity under the Raj was a precursor of the wide-ranging interventions that followed the enactment of the Forest Act of 1878.[44]

By 1900, well over one-fifth of the land area of British India had been taken over as government forest. In the short run, this solved the crisis of timber supply for the railways that were extending over much of the subcontinent; it also marked a huge shift in property relations. Such extension of executive authority was possible only because of decades of a more intrusive state. The Forest Department, founded in 1864, was important beyond the immediate context of the imperial experience in South Asia. The founder of the Forestry Service in the United States, Gifford Pinchot, never concealed his deep admiration for Dietrich Brandis, the first inspector general of forests in India, and said his counterparts and predecessors in India had "accomplished on the other side of the world what I might hope to have a hand in doing in America."[45] Fractious fights over forest and pasture meant that there was more to the issue than mere scientific and administrative achievement. The department may well have been, in the words of Michael Williams, a "jewel in the Imperial Crown, a model for the rest of the world, and a highly efficient and profitable enterprise. But it proved to be one of the festering sores in the body of the Indian subcontinent that has still not healed."[46]

CONTESTED NATURE

In 1997 the social historian Shail Mayaram stated with regard to Alwar, a princely state in Rajasthan (western India), that "the Secretary of the Agrarian Grievances Committee complained vociferously of the ban on *shikar* [hunting] for pigs and deer ruined the crops. When the maharaja [king] was told this he exploded and said 'This is all that I have to show to the English. If this is finished, what will I have? The Commission Report was buried.'"[47]

Environmental histories of the colonial period are in large part about the fates and fortunes, the strategies and struggles, and the changing practices and consciousness of underprivileged or marginal groups. More often than not, these are groups living on the fringes of the cultivated arable land. Alternatively, they might be cultivators, but in areas where rainfall is low, the reliance on rainfall high, and the cycle of crop production historically tied to the use of uncultivated land. The narratives follow a familiar line in which the Adivasis—peasants, keepers and breeders of livestock, fisher folk, and artisans—are marginalized by a combination of colonial policies and the growth of capitalism. These processes facilitated the rise of market- and state-oriented patterns of production, which were and are more ecologically disharmonious than the systems they supplanted. The retreat of the jungle, itinerant peoples, and swidden cultivators is central to stories of environmental transition in South Asia.[48] The twin themes of the decline of older patterns of land use and the degradation of ecosystems are interwoven in the narratives; even so, blending such complex and multifaceted processes into wider histories of social change is a challenging task.

Despite the history of attempts at homogenizing social and ecological diversities, South Asia retained a level of heterogeneity that is perhaps without parallel. Many "traditional" resource users proved resilient enough to adapt, innovate, survive, and in rare cases, even flourish through the colonial era and into the present day. By contrast, in America, the arrival of new settlers and the pathogens, plants, and animals that accompanied them overwhelmed indigenous peoples and organisms. This story of ecopolitical conquest, the theme of Alfred Crosby's concept of ecological imperialism, would, in any case, hardly hold true for southern Asia. Not only did invasion by exotic animals remain a nonstarter, but even the environmental changes had more to do with social processes than purely biological ones. This situation makes it all the more necessary to trace the career of political conflicts, for they had much to do with changes in the land.

Insurgencies and rebellions were exceptional, but their infrequency does not connote passivity among the population. Contests over nature and how to treat with it often grew out of radically differing views of who would decide how to use the land. Ajay Pratap's work on the Rajmahal hills examines the interaction of the British with the Paharias, a tribe that practiced a form of shifting cultivation known as *khallu*. The more numerous Santhals, who staged a major rebellion in 1855, were better acquainted with settled cultivation. Pratap focuses on the impact of land regulation and state forestry on the Paharias and their attempts to limit such intrusion. For the Paharias, the curbs on slash-and-burn agriculture precipitated a major crisis.[49] Similarly, the Baigas, a small tribe in the central provinces, found their system of swidden cultivation coming under intense pressure from the 1860s onward.

The more numerous Gond, who played a central role in the forest movement in the 1930s, were more amenable to the limitations on mobility. Their greater familiarity with the plow made colonial forest regulations less painful.[50]

Both the Santhals and the Gonds found relations with the British forest and revenue departments marked by tensions. But even other smaller tribal peoples who played a less spectacular role in rebellions did influence the course of events. The use of Forest Department records and oral sources has helped shed light on resistance as well as cooperation in everyday life. This vital point about the diversities of the subaltern experience should help qualify a bleak and generalized view of disempowerment and decline. Neither process was a uniform one.

In fact, even the losers in these conflicts can be said to have had an influence, in at least two distinct ways. First, they were often central to the cognition of colonial officials. In addition to addressing concerns about generating revenue and appropriating resources such as labor and forest wealth, these officials were concerned with putting an end to lawless and environmentally harmful mobility. The design and implementation of this highly interventionist project, or series of initiatives, can yield rich insights into colonial rule. Was failure due more to imperial designs inappropriate for particular ecologies, or to the absence of land rights and adequate capital to enable sedentary settlement?[51] This question provides the starting point for many a recent history, with obvious resonance for the problems of displacement and rehabilitation in the present day. Either way, even rural land users like Paharias and Santhals, Banjaras and Baigas, Koravas and Gonds, who were marginal in terms of power and entitlement, were central at critical junctures in history.

Second, the expansion of the powers of the company Raj or the market was not a complex process. This part of the tale may lack the epic element inherent in histories of rebellions but is nonetheless crucial. There is no disputing the overall direction of changes. The forest and the people who lived within it were more intensively managed as a resource in a wider system of production. Increased fiscal pressure and the drain of wealth away from the hills were indeed marked features of the Raj.[52] Yet accommodation was often unavoidable in day-to-day interactions, especially given the need to procure labor for road works and bridge building, pollarding and logging, laying fire lines, and cutting down weeds.

The kind of tug-of-war in daily life differed from one place to another. It was part of a continuing process of the redefinition of both state and society. It was not a conflict of state versus civil society (which in any case are not entities that can easily be isolated from one another) but a multifaceted contest within each of these realms.[53] This emerges clearly in the constitution of the *van panchayats* (literally, forest committees) in the western Himalayas, which marked a deeper level of engagement by the government and also strengthened certain dominant local players. The government attempted via this institution to cede a degree of community control and reinforce state authority.[54] Nomadic cattle breeders won a measure of support, as the heifers they bred were seen as critical as draft cattle. Draft power in settled agriculture was being adversely affected by poor pasturage and curbs on mobility of the itinerant husbandmen.[55] As long as labor remained scarce, hill peoples retained some leverage. The annexation of a patch of land by foresters or a new land revenue settlement did not extinguish their lifestyle. Their responses—varied and complex as they were—did leave a mark on policies. This outcome is clearest with forest-management techniques, which in the early twentieth century often eased up on strict exclusion simply because it was not workable.[56]

None of these qualifications can disguise the reality of the severe impact of colonial policy in the decisive decades of the nineteenth century. Although the timing and nature of the impact varied widely across India, clear patterns emerge. In the hill ranges of western India, small dam systems that had been kept in good repair often fell apart. Unlike previous rulers, the British did not advance zero-interest loans to assist in their maintenance. To make matters worse, the new land-revenue system reduced the availability of cash and surplus labor, making upkeep very difficult.[57] Across much of the subcontinent, a range of strategies aimed at killing off animals labeled as vermin deeply affected target species. Species that were typical of the open country in north and central India—such as the lion and the cheetah—were confined to tiny, shrinking pockets of a once-huge home range.[58] The expansion of the irrigation networks often complemented and paralleled this process of extirpation. In the Indus basin, which contained two-thirds of the irrigated acreage of early twentieth-century India, double-cropped wheat fields were tilled by peasant settlers of the Punjab, whose sons and brothers made up a disproportionate number of the British Indian Army. But these new cultivators had replaced an older landscape. Camel breeders and shepherds made way for wheat fields. Many of these changes were part of a larger process of economic growth, but the specific ways in which they came about distributed costs unevenly, both on peoples and on different landscapes.[59]

NEW HORIZONS

Colonial land management had widely divergent effects on different regions. For instance, the adverse consequences of modern canal irrigation in the southern peninsula were never quite as marked as in north India. Whereas in the Ganges basin, British engineers mainly had to design and construct new canals, their counterparts in the Madras presidency repaired and revived old works. Southern rivers such as the Kaveri, the Godavari, the Krishna, and the Tungabhadra were seasonal, unlike north India's river systems, which were fed by year-round snow melt. The switch from well to canal irrigation in the north led to increased salinity because drainage was inadequate. In the south, the very different topography and the incorporation of the old systems into the new ones limited such adverse consequences. The relationship between different technologies of resource use was, therefore, not always an adversarial one.[60]

The contrast between different regions is also clear in the role of trees in the alluvial plains of Uttar Pradesh and Punjab as compared with hilly regions. In the former areas, peasants relied mainly on dung for fuel, and the absence of tenant rights severely limited the growing of trees. Farmers did grow trees, but the social and ecological milieu in which they did so has to be located and identified carefully. These caveats are all the more necessary because the emphasis on the interdependence of rural society may convey the impression of harmony and stasis, with colonial intervention being the sole agent of decline.[61]

Vandana Shiva's work, for example, undoubtedly opens up the role of modern science and knowledge systems for critical analysis. In common with the work of others who are skeptical about the Enlightenment project and knowledge systems originating in the Western world, her critiques pave the way for a serious consideration of alternative traditions. Shiva's critics have largely focused on the issue of gender, arguing that the role of women in environmental change is often far more complex than Shiva admits. Briefly put, these other scholars have stressed the importance of the changing social context and the consciousness of women and men, in place of an essentialist notion of women being at peace with nature.[62] Missing from the debate is discussion of the problems posed by this approach in assessing the colonial experience. The point, which neither Shiva nor her critics make, is a simple but vital one. In the bid to give legitimacy to "traditional" resource use, the colonial experience is being seen in a simplistic way. In this paradigm, colonial or modern knowledge is seen as being inherently anti-nature and anti-people. The corollary to this view is that the systems they displaced are viewed uncritically as benign to nature and to people. Aside from specific objections to such a view of society or ecology prior to colonialism, this argument has serious limitations.[63]

For one, scientific knowledge is not a monolithic, as Shiva herself has admitted. It includes many diverse traditions. Yet the awareness of this diversity is not integrated into a broader perspective on the legacy and pitfalls of science. As Donald Worster has demonstrated in the specific case of ecology, the "imperial" view of nature was often in contention with the "Arcadian" one.[64] Whereas the former emphasized the conquest and domination of the natural world, the latter focused on the discovery of harmony and the unifying processes in nature. This division is crucial, and Worster argues that today's ecologically conscious ideologues have their roots in the latter tradition. Second, by imposing a timeless teleology on the West (at least after Francis Bacon and René Descartes), the East/West dichotomy ignores changes within the Western world. The term *Orientalism* has often been used to describe the ascription of essentialist qualities to colonized lands and peoples. In this case, the reverse process is at work. An "Occidentalist" view of the West is clearly in the making. Whatever its political affinities or moral claims, it can hardly help us comprehend the roots of present-day ecological dilemmas in East or West.

No student of South Asia's environmental record can possibly ignore the fissures and cracks within the colonial state. Richard Grove's most significant contribution, after all, lies in showing how surgeons and botanists working for the East India Company state sounded alarm bells about the ecologically deleterious impact of unrestrained laissez-faire as early as the 1830s. In this respect they were actually at the cutting edge of scientific knowledge.[65] Grove's study points to the key role of internal critics and dissenters within the state apparatus. He implies that colonial officials were not simply transplanting ideas and technologies from core to periphery. The ecological character of tropical colonies, with sharp climatic fluctuations and soils vulnerable to erosion, made environmental damage caused by unbridled free enterprise much more rapidly evident than in Europe. Officials of the company state also had more leeway to regulate private property than their counterparts in England. So the in-house critics did not simply impose "Western scientific practices" on South Asia. On the contrary, many critical concepts in conservation evolved in the island colonies in the Indian Ocean and on the subcontinent. Their ideas evolved in a complex setting where the roughly eight hundred botanists and surgeons were an early technical and scientific elite trying to attract state support for specific policies. There have been valid criticisms of the extent to which such ideas actually played a role in changing officials' minds. They could often be "a small voice in the wilderness" confronting the "stinginess of the East India Company in terms of long term investment." But the primary aim of men like Alexander Gibson in western India was surely to ensure a supply of revenues and logs from lands of what he labeled "tangle and noxious jungle."[66] A second observation relates to the broader British view by the 1820s and 1830s of India not as a land with a fragile ecology, but a dangerous one. Diseases of which little was known still claimed the lives of more British soldiers than combat operations did. The idea of a land of pestilence and danger could be much more powerful an influence than notions that the soils and waters were imperiled by unwise land use.[67] Yet neither desiccation nor the notion of a land where death came in myriad forms fits a simple conquest-of-ecology model.

Moreover, the logic and dynamics of state-society relations were far from static. Often, institutions evolved and changed in unexpected ways. Significant shifts in sensibility at key moments had long-term consequences. In 1900, for example, Lord Curzon, a figure rightly reviled by nationalists for his racially ordered views of empire, refused to go on a lion shoot in the Gir hills in western India. Instead, he strongly supported curbs on hunts put in place by the rulers of the principality of Junagadh. This was a small but critical step in saving the last population of lions in Asia from extinction, a population that remains intact to this day. Earlier that year, he undertook initiatives to help protect architectural monuments, not only to catalogue and study them but also to protect them from the ravages of modernization and the march of time. Short-term interests in trade or hunts had initially played havoc with the natural as well as architectural and monumental heritage; over time, these gave way to more consolidated attempts at statist regulation. The government's response was to assert control over selected sites either directly (through such agencies as the Forest Department or the Archaeological Survey of India) or through intermediaries (such as the princes of Junagadh and adjacent states). The introduction of expertise, whether of German foresters and botanists or of Oxbridge historians, gave teeth to such intentions.

The long-term consequences of statist control were mixed. It is vital to see such historically contingent developments as marks of the evolution of a more complex system. To ignore such institutional developments does not do justice to the complexity of the colonial encounter with peoples and its landscapes in colonial India.[68] Such impulses did not spring forward in full maturity; they had deeper roots in locally significant aesthetic concerns and ideologies. But such specific initiatives achieved larger ends when they caught the imperial eye.[69]

Even externally driven ideas or processes had complex effects that varied with local conditions and legacies. Knowledge networks often worked in unexpected ways. The South Asian experience has now been relocated in the wider framework of the ideas and networks of expertise in the British Empire in the twentieth century. Empire forestry conferences distilled and made available for a wider audience the decades-long experience of Indian foresters, whose work was drawn on in several other colonized countries as well as in the United States.[70] The wheel was set to turn with the emergence of the United States itself as a powerful player in the tropical world, not only in the flow of commodities and resources but also as a fount of ideas and influences. In the Western Himalayas, British perceptions of pastoral grazing and its impact on Himalayan ecology and agriculture were influenced by views of the Dust Bowl in the American Midwest in the 1930s. Concerns were raised about the threat to the plains of floods and soil erosion from overgrazing on the hill slopes and in water catchments. Itinerant pastoralists like the Gaddis and Gujjars were targeted by foresters and other bureaucrats.[71] The same justifications had been supplied for the pressures exerted on swidden cultivators across swathes of middle India in the late nineteenth century, but the evocation of the American experience was a distinctive and new feature.

Engagement between Indians on environmental issues was also sophisticated and complex, defying any convenient categories. India's intelligentsia has a long history of engagement with the wider world. Many lower-caste leaders, notably Bhimrao Ambedkar (1891–1956), saw modern technologies as a positive force for change and were strongly critical of figures like Mohandas Gandhi (1869–1948), who valorized rural community life as a refuge from the ills of modernity. Ambedkar even served on the Viceroy's Executive Council in the mid-1940s, helping to oversee the induction of American experts for the Damodar Valley Authority (DVA), a multipurpose hydro scheme in eastern India. Such large engineering projects were seen as offering waged work in modern industry to those born into a menial caste. Here Ambedkar was on solid ground, for it was work in textile mills and the railways and even earlier service in the nineteenth-century presidency armies that had provided many "Untouchables" in the nineteenth century with an alternative and more dignified livelihood.[72] Support for such projects also came from modernizers like Jawaharlal Nehru. For both Ambedkar and Nehru, the fact that the DVA was consciously modeled on the TVA (Tennessee Valley Authority, in the United States) was a matter of pride. Given the salience of large dams in independent India, these ideological impulses merit attention.[73]

Even as lower-caste reformers and left-leaning nationalists saw the passage of the old ways of life as worthy of celebration, sections of the middle class were romanticizing the forest. Prathama Banerjee has remarked on the tendency of a section of the intelligentsia to discover traits of nobility and rootedness in the history of tribal peoples, particularly in Bengal. A conflation of anthropology and poetics, prose and verse went into the creating of a mythical people beyond the pale of city and village life, from whom there was much to learn.[74] Bibhutibhushan

Bandopadhyay, the manager of a land estate in eastern India in the late 1920s, bemoaned the fact that his main contribution to posterity was the clearance of forest to make way for cultivation. His diary notes were the first step to the crafting of a memoir that makes poignant reading. But his *Aranyak of the Forest* not only eulogized the trees and fauna of the disappearing forest; it also saw forest clearing as the final step in an age-old conflict against forest peoples that dated back to the Aryan conquest. Bandopadhyay is now better known for his work *Pather Panchali*, immortalized in Satyajit Ray's film of the same name, but the lament in his *Aranyak* rings true: "I felt sad wondering how long I would be able to keep untouched the forest around Saraswati kundi. The *hansalata* (snake root), the wild *shefali* (night jasmine)—would they all disappear? In their stead, innumerable stalks of maize would rear their heads; rows of tiled huts stand cheek by jowl, strong cots before them, and muddy yards where the cattle chewed their fodder."[75] This was a landscape being mourned even as large chunks of it were being destroyed.

Complex ways of seeing the colonial encounter can enrich views on ecological as well as sociological transitions. Far from being perfected in the metropole and exported to the periphery, colonial ecological control actually evolved through close interaction with local peoples and ecologies. The asymmetry of power was always inescapable: a hundred years ago, fewer than three hundred thousand whites ruled over three hundred million Indians. But the interaction was a changing and fluid one: the view of India as a well of limitless resources gave way to selective appropriation for imperial ends that was seen, more often than not, as "conservancy." Inevitably, the responses of the intelligentsia were far from uniform: the disparate views of the forest, city, and the village were only tiny instances of larger, more bitter, and more heated debates on how to blend aspirations for self-rule with a life of dignity for all. The problem with an East/West dichotomy is not that it sheds no light on colonial rule or its impact, for there were profound differences between the Raj and its predecessors; but these differences grew out of specific victories and calamities, of historically evolving processes, not out of a morality play that opposed East and West, science and local knowledge, the modern and the traditional. The multiple strands of opinion gave Indian debate a richness it retains to this day.

CONCLUSION

Histories of environmental change have much to offer a student of South Asian history and society. They lead back to larger issues of how and when human relations change in immutable and irreversible ways, with deep, even irreversible consequences for the nonhuman environment. The Raj was a new kind of power: its mode of organizing and asserting authority put an end to the fluidity and mobility of power structures across the subcontinent. India did not have a millennia-long record of statecraft to match China's, but certainly hierarchies of landscapes as well as of people long preceded colonial rule. Despite more than half the land's being tillable, only in the twentieth century did the plow reshape the countryside, denuding large swathes of their tree cover. The monsoon forest was less a primeval thicket than a mosaic of landscapes in transition. The great change came in two phases: first with the policing, disarming, and sedentarization of itinerant peoples, and then with the sequestering of forest and the expansion of canal irrigation. These were not simple shifts, and the continuing struggles over livelihoods and environments are testimony to the persistence and emergence of alternative currents.[76]

To the British, the long-term structural features of the environment—such as the alternation of monsoon rainfall and long, dry spells—were as complex as the bewildering array of fauna that had to be conquered and subdued. The early phase of all-out aggrandizement gave way over time to more localized and specific attempts at systematic extraction of revenue. Yet the imperative of political control—never easy to achieve in such a vast land—imposed its own restraints. Many insights have sprung from a growing realization that just as the fear of rebellion often restrained exclusion or resource appropriation, so too the ecologies of forest, delta, and hillside were complex and unpredictable enough to confound foresters, hydraulic engineers, and civil officials. Unlike the settler societies of the Americas or Australia (or, to a lesser degree, South Africa), India never became conducive to white settlement, except in a few hill-station enclaves. But its mixed bag of diverse livelihoods—one that combines elements of a flourishing industrial and postindustrial sector with dry grain farming, long-distance transhumance, and a growing middle class and far larger underclass—took shape in the colonial era. Such divisions deeply color its environmental legacies. The resulting tapestry, of many hues and colors, is not easily amenable to the imposition of homogeneity, whether imperial or nationalist.

NOTES

This is a substantially reworked and rewritten version of a paper originally published in *Environment and History* 2, no. 2 (1996). The editor, Richard Grove, deserves a special word for his encouragement and advice.

I have incurred many intellectual debts over the years. The Nehru Memorial Museum and Library and the Mario Einaudi Center for International Studies at

Cornell University have provided a sanctuary and base. The Department of History at Jadavpur University in Kolkata, with which I was affiliated, has been unfailing in its support. I also thank the Department of History, University of Delhi, where I am now based.

I am grateful to Sara Ahmed, C. A. Bayly, Neeladri Bhattacharya, Richard Drayton, Ramachandra Guha, Sumit Guha, Najaf Haider, Ron Herring, the late Ravinder Kumar, M. D. Madhusudan, Dilip Menon, Tapan Raychaudhuri, Anindya Sinha, Kalyanakrishnan Sivaramakrishnan, Nandini Sundar, Megan Vaughan, and Joanne P. Wagehorne for their insights.

I am also indebted to all participants in the workshops on imperialism, ecology, and politics and to my students at Cornell University and in Bangalore for asking stimulating questions. I thank Lotte Hughes and William Beinart for sharing sections of their *Environmental History of the British Empire* (Oxford: Oxford University Press, 2008) before publication.

1. For recent reviews, see Rohan D'Souza, "Nature, Conservation and the Writing of Environmental History," *Conservation and Society* 1, no. 2 (2003): 317–32; Kalyanakrishnan Sivaramakrishnan, "Nationalism and the Writing of Environmental History," *Seminar* 522 (2003): 25–30. A more detailed bibliography may be found in Mahesh Rangarajan, "Colonialism, Ecology and Environment, Departures and Beginnings," in *India and the British Empire*, ed. Nandini Gooptu and Douglas Peers (Oxford: Oxford University Press, in press).

2. The East India Company ruled large parts of India from 1757 until 1858, after which it was under the direct rule of the British Crown until 1947.

3. The pioneering monograph was Ramachandra Guha, *The Unquiet Woods: Ecological Change and Peasant Resistance in the Western Himalaya* (Delhi: Oxford University Press, 1989; 2nd ed., 2000).

4. Two collections are David Arnold and Ramachandra Guha, eds., *Nature, Culture and Imperialism: Essays on the Environmental History of South Asia* (Delhi: Oxford University Press, 1995), and Richard H. Grove, Vinita Damodaran, and Satpal Sangwan, eds., *Nature and the Orient: Essays in the Environmental History of South and Southeast Asia* (Delhi: Oxford University Press, 1998). On fauna, see J. M. Mackenzie, *The Empire of Nature: Hunting, Conservation and British Imperialism* (Manchester: Manchester University Press, 1988); and Mahesh Rangarajan, *India's Wildlife History: An Introduction* (Delhi: Permanent Black, 2001). On irrigation, see Rohan D. Souza, *Drowned and Dammed: Colonial Capitalism and Flood Control in Eastern India* (Delhi: Oxford University Press, 2006). The history of science is examined in S. Ravi Rajan, "Imperial Environmentalism: The Agendas and Ideologies of Natural Resource Management in British Colonial Forestry, 1800–1950" (PhD diss., Oxford University, 1994, now revised and published as *Modernizing Nature: Forestry and Imperial Eco-development, 1800–1950* (Delhi: Orient

Longman, 2007). Also see Richard Drayton, *Nature's Government: Science, Imperial Britain, and the "Improvement" of the World* (New Haven: Yale University Press, 2003).

5. An early pioneer in this respect was David Hardiman: see "Power in the Forests: The Dangs, 1820–1940," in Arnold and Guha, *Nature*, 89–147. For regional histories, see Marlene Buchy, *Teak and Arecanut: Colonial State, Forests and People in the Western Ghats, 1800–1947* (Pondicherry: French Institute, 1996). Mahesh Rangarajan, *Fencing the Forest: Conservation and Ecological Change in India's Central Provinces, 1860–1914* (Delhi: Oxford University Press, 1996); Ajay Skaria, *Hybrid Histories: Forests, Frontiers and Wildness* (Delhi: Oxford University Press, 1998); Haripriya Rangan, *Of Myths and Movements: Writing Chipko into Himalayan History* (Delhi: Oxford University Press, 2001).

6. Madhav Gadgil and Ramachandra Guha, *This Fissured Land: An Ecological History of India* (Delhi: Oxford University Press, 1992).

7. A *kos* is about three kilometers. The original proverb is "Har das kos paani badle aur har bees boli," cited in *Social Nature: Resources, Representations and Rule in India*, ed. Arun Agrawal and Kalyanakrishnan Sivaramakrishnan (Delhi: Oxford University Press, 2000). See also Gunnel Cederlof and Kalyanakrishnan Sivaramakrishnan, *Ecological Nationalisms* (Delhi: Permanent Black, 2006).

8. On the imperial impact on fauna, see Raman Sukumar, *The Living Elephants: Evolutionary Ecology, Behaviour and Conservation* (Delhi: Oxford University Press, 2003), especially chapter 2. On vermin extermination, see Mahesh Rangarajan, "The Raj and the Natural World: The War against 'Dangerous Beasts' in Colonial India," in *Wildlife in Asia: Cultural Perspectives*, ed. John Knight (London: Routledge Curzon Press, 2004), 207–32.

9. For insights on Africa, see the classic work by David Anderson and Richard H. Grove, *Conservation in Africa: People, Problems and Practice* (Cambridge: Cambridge University Press, 1988); and William Beinart, *The Rise of Conservation in South Africa: Settlers, Livestock and the Environment, 1770–1950* (Oxford: Oxford University Press, 2003). There are two joint collections of papers on South and Southeast Asian ecological history: Grove, Damodaran, and Sangwan, *Nature and the Orient;* and Paul Greenough and Anna Lowenhaupt Tsing, eds., *Southern Projects in Nature* (Delhi: Orient Longman, 2005).

10. There is now a global history of environmental ideas and ideologies that does not place Europe or the United States at the center. See Ramachandra Guha, *Environmentalism: A Global History* (Delhi: Oxford University Press, 2000). On irrigation in the United States, see Donald Worster, *Rivers of Empire: Water, Aridity and the Growth of the American West* (New York: Pantheon Books, 1985).

11. For an interesting comparative view, see Paul Sutter, "What Can U.S. Environmental Historians Learn from Non-U.S. Environmental Historiography?" *Environmental History* 8, no. 1 (2003): 109–35.

12. Most of the sources in this paper are on colonial India, which includes modern India, Pakistan, Bangladesh, and Burma (Myanmar), but see Nihal Karunaratna, *Forest Conservation in Sri Lanka from British Colonial Times, 1818–1912* (Colombo: Trumpet Publishers, 1987); Krishna Ghimire, *Forest or Farm? The Politics of Poverty and Hunger in Nepal* (Delhi: Oxford University Press, 1992); and Indu Agnihotri, "Ecology, Land Use and Colonization: The Canal Colonies of Punjab," *Indian Economic and Social History Review* 33 (1996): 37–58.

13. Ramachandra Guha, "Writing Environmental History in India," *Studies in History* 9 (1993): 9–129. Ramachandra Guha, ed., *Social Ecology* (Delhi: Oxford University Press, 1994) includes several key papers on historical and contemporary debates.

14. A major stimulus was the publication of the successive State of India's Environment Reports since 1982. The first was Anil Agarwal and Ravi Chopra, eds., *State of India's Environment: A Citizen's Report* (Delhi: Centre for Science and Environment, 1982).

15. On forests, see a perceptive popular publication, People's Union for Democratic Rights, *Undeclared Civil War: A Critique of the Forest Policy* (Delhi, 1982). For references on the history of irrigation, see Rohan D'Souza, "Damming the Mahanadi River," *Indian Economic and Social History Review* 40, no. 1 (2003): 81–105.

16. Gadgil and Guha, *This Fissured Land*, 106–8. The argument on caste is outlined on 91–109. The most thoughtful and serious alternative view is that of Sumit Guha, *Environment and Ethnicity in India, 1200–1991* (Cambridge: Cambridge University Press, 1999).

17. Irfan Habib, "The Geographical Background," in *The Cambridge Economic History of India*, vol. 1, ed. Irfan Habib and Tapan Rayachaudhuri (Delhi: Cambridge University Press, 1984), 2; Jean Deloche, *Transport and Communications in India prior to Steam Locomotion*, vol. 1, *Land Transport* (Delhi: Oxford University Press, 1993), 5–10, 52 n. 21, 118.

18. John F. Richards, *The Unending Frontier: An Environmental History of the Early Modern World* (Berkeley: University of California Press, 2004).

19. Sunita Zaidi, "The Mughal State and Tribes in Seventeenth-Century Sind," *Indian Economic and Social History Review* 27 (1989): 343–62. On Punjab, see Chetan Singh, *Region and Empire: Panjab in the Seventeenth Century* (Delhi: Oxford University Press, 1991), 263–70.

20. Gyan Prakash, *Bonded Histories: Genealogies of Labour Servitude in Colonial India* (Cambridge: Cambridge University Press, 1990), 70.

21. Richard M. Eaton, *The Islamic Frontier in Bengal, 1204–1760* (Delhi: Oxford University Press, 1994), 228, 239. The expansion was a long-term trend, as Eaton's title suggests, and the Mughals only accelerated the process.

22. Deloche, *Transport*, 1:118.

23. Nicholas Menzies, "Exclusion and Inclusion in Wild Land Policies in Late Imperial China," *Modern Asian Studies* 26 (1992): 119–35; Conrad Totman, *Green Archipelago: Forestry in Preindustrial Japan* (Berkeley: University of California Press, 1989); Michael Williams, "Ecology, Imperialism and Deforestation," in *Ecology and Empire: Environmental History of Settler Societies,* ed. Tom Griffiths and Libby Robbin (Seattle: University of Washington Press, 1997), 169–84.

24. John Malcolm, *Report on the Province of Malwa and Adjacent Districts* (Calcutta, 1822), 408. A *mahal* is a revenue circle.

25. J.C. Heesterman, *The Inner Conflicts of Tradition: Essays in Indian Rituals, Kingship and Society* (Chicago: University of Chicago Press, 1985), 170–71.

26. Robert B. Marks, *Tigers, Rice, Silk and Silt: Environment and Economy in Late Imperial South China* (Cambridge: Cambridge University Press, 1998), 324–26. Still, there is little evidence in India for state-sponsored campaigns to wipe out large wild animals.

27. Irfan Habib, "Merchant Communities in Pre-colonial India," in *The Rise of Merchant Empires: Long Distance Trade in the Early Modern World,* ed. James Tracy (Cambridge: Cambridge University Press, 1990), 371–99.

28. Anne Marie Schimmel, *The Empire of the Great Mughals: History, Art and Culture* (Delhi: Oxford University Press, 2005), 215–18.

29. Sukumar, *The Living Elephants,* 75–76.

30. Mark Elvin, *The Retreat of the Elephants: An Environmental History of China* (New Haven: Yale University Press, 2004), 9–19. By contrast, more than three thousand elephants were used by armies under Mountbatten's command in Southeast Asia in the 1940s. The longer-term strategic role of elephants in warfare has been studied in two pioneering works: Simon Digby, *War-Horse and Elephant in the Delhi Sultanate; A Problem of Military Supplies* (Karachi: Oxford University Press, 1974), and Thomas R. Trautmann, "Elephants and the Mauryas," in *India, History and Thought: Essays in Honour of A.L. Basham,* ed. S.N. Mukherjea (Calcutta: Firma L. Mukhopadhyay, 1982), 254–81.

31. Kathleen Morrison, "Environmental History, the Spice Trade and the State in South India," in Cederlof and Sivaramakrishnan, *Ecological Nationalisms,* 43–64.

32. S. Guha, *Environment and Ethnicity,* 43.

33. Sumit Guha, *Health and Population in South Asia* (Delhi: Permanent Black, 2001), 58–60.

34. Habib, *Cambridge Economic History,* 1:6.

35. Seema Alavi, *Sepoys and the Company: Tradition and Transition in Northern India, 1770–1870* (Delhi: Oxford University Press, 1995), 155–93, esp. 192–93.

36. This point about peasantization was first made by C.A. Bayly in *The New Cambridge History of India,* vol. 2, *Indian Society and the Making of the British Empire,* part 1 (Cambridge: Cambridge University Press, 1988), 138–45. It remains a case of

intuitive insight into a long-term process based on limited documentary evidence but amply borne out in later researches on regional polities.

37. Alavi, *Sepoys*, 192–93.

38. Ajay Skaria, "A Forest Polity in Western India: The Dangs, 1800s–1920s," (PhD diss., University of Cambridge, 1992), 84. Skaria's book, *Hybrid Histories*, while deeply insightful on larger issues of historical method, needs to be read in conjunction with the unpublished thesis.

39. Bayly, *Indian Society*, 141; Alavi, *Sepoys*, 187–88.

40. Robert Varady, "North Indian Banjaras: Their Evolution as Transporters," *South Asia* 2 (1979): 1–18; Neeladri Bhattacharya, "Pastoralists in the Colonial World," in Arnold and Guha, *Nature*, 49–85.

41. Meena Radhakrishna, *Dishonoured by History: Criminal Tribes and British Policy* (Delhi: Orient Longman, 2000).

42. *Report of the Subcommittee on the Poona Sarvajanik Sabha Appointed to Collect Information to Be Laid before the East India Finance Company on Matters Relating to India* (Poona, 1872), 59, 67.

43. The distinctions between differing kinds of forest legacies are made in Mahesh Rangarajan, "Imperial Agendas and India's Forests: The Early History of Indian Forests, 1800–1878," *Indian Economic and Social History Review* 21 (1994): 147–67.

44. This point is forcefully made by Amrita Tulika, "Bhils of Western India, 1800–1900" (PhD diss., Delhi University, 2004).

45. R. Guha, *Environmentalism*, 35.

46. Michael Williams, *Deforesting the Earth: From Prehistory to Global Crisis* (Chicago: University of Chicago Press, 2004), 168.

47. Shail Mayaram, *Resisting Regimes: Myth, Memory and the Shaping of a Muslim Identity* (Delhi: Oxford University Press, 1997), 81. The same region in eastern Rajasthan is the subject of a lucid and moving study based on oral evidence: Ann Grodzins Gold and Bhoju Ram Gujjar, *In the Time of Trees and Sorrows: Nature, Power and Memory in Rajasthan* (Delhi: Oxford University Press, 2003).

48. Bayly, *Indian Society*, 138–42, 161.

49. Ramachandra Guha and Madhav Gadgil, "Forestry and Social Conflict in British India: A Study of the Ecological Bases of Peasant Protest," *Past and Present* 123 (1989): 141–77.

50. Ajay Pratap, *The Hoe and the Axe: An Ethnohistory of Shifting Cultivation in Eastern India* (New Delhi: Oxford University Press, 1999).

51. The forest movements are analyzed by David Baker, "A Serious Time: Forest Satyagraha in Madhya Pradesh, 1930," *Indian Economic and Social History Review* 21 (1984): 71–90. For the story of the Baigas, see Rangarajan, *Fencing the Forest*, 95–137.

52. Indra Munshi Saldanha, "The Political Ecology of Traditional Farming Practices in Thane District, Maharashtra (India)," *Journal of Peasant Studies* 17, no. 3 (1990): 433–43.

53. Nandini Sundar, Roger Jeffrey, and Neil Thin, *Branching Out: Joint Forest Management in India* (Delhi: Oxford University Press, 2001).

54. Arun Agrawal, "State Formation in Community Spaces? Decentralization of Control over Forests in the Kumaon Himalayas," *Journal of Asian Studies* 60 (2001): 9–40.

55. Shanti George, "Nomadic Cattle Breeders and Dairy Policy in India," *Nomadic Peoples* 19 (1985): 1–20; on forestry practice, see Kalyanakrishnan Sivaramakrishnan, "Transition Zones: Changing Landscapes and Local Authority in Southwest Bengal, 1880s–1920s," *Indian Economic and Social History Review* 36, no. 1 (1999): 1–34.

56. Raymond Bryant examines a similar process in a very different region in "Shifting the Cultivator: The Politics of Teak Regeneration in Colonial Burma," *Modern Asian Studies* 27 (1994): 225–50.

57. David Hardiman, "Small Dam Systems of the Sahyadaris," in Arnold and Guha, *Nature.*

58. See Rangarajan, "The Raj and the Natural World," for details.

59. Indu Agnihotri, "Ecology, Land Use and Colonization: The Canal Colonies of Punjab," *Indian Economic and Social History Review* 33 (1996): 37–58.

60. Elizabeth Whitcombe, "Irrigation," in *The Cambridge Economic History of India,* vol. 2, *C.1757–c.1970,* ed. Dharma Kumar (Delhi: Cambridge University Press, 1984): 677–736. Whitcombe's classic work remains *Agrarian Conditions in Northern India: The United Provinces under British Rule,* vol. 1, *1860–1900* (Berkeley: University of California Press, 1972).

61. This point is forcefully brought out in a fine paper by Vinay Gidwani, "Labored Landscapes: Agro-ecological Change in Central Gujarat, India," in *Agrarian Environments: Resources, Representations, and Rule in India,* ed. Arun Agrawal and Kalyanakrishnan Sivaramakrishnan (Durham, NC: Duke University Press, 2000), 216–50. Revenue settlements through the nineteenth century enabled the Kanbis to stabilize agriculture even as the settlements disempowered the Kolis.

62. Vandana Shiva, *Staying Alive: Women, Ecology and Survival in India* (New Delhi: Kali for Women, 1988). For the disturbing ways in which such views of a seamless past get appropriated by sectarian groups, see Uma Chakravarti, *Gendering Caste through a Feminist Lens* (Calcutta: Stree, 2003). See also Bina Agrawal, *A Field of One's Own: Gender and Land Rights in South Asia* (Cambridge: Cambridge University Press, 1994); Sarah Jewitt, *Environment, Knowledge and Gender: Local Development in India's Jharkhand* (Hampshire: Ashgate, 2002). Symbols of ecological renewal and resistance can also be appropriated by sectarian groups, as with those of the Hindu revivalists: see Mukul Sharma, "Saffronizing Green," *Seminar* 515 (2002): 26–30.

63. For instance, the tank irrigation systems of southern Tamil Nadu date back centuries but have been maintained only by appropriating the labor of the menial "Untouchable" groups, who were landless. See David Moss, *Rule of Water: Statecraft, Ecology and Collective Action in South India* (Delhi: Oxford University Press, 2003).

64. Donald Worster, *Nature's Economy: A History of Ecological Ideas,* 2nd ed. (Cambridge: Cambridge University Press, 1994).

65. Richard H. Grove, *Green Imperialism: Colonial Expansion, Tropical Island Edens and the Origins of Environmentalism, 1600–1800* (Cambridge: Cambridge University Press, 1995); Richard H. Grove, *Ecology, Climate and Empire: Colonialism and Global Environmental History* (Cambridge: Cambridge University Press, 1997).

66. Henry J. Noltie, *The Dapuri Drawings: Alexander Gibson and the Bombay Botanical Gardens* (Bombay: Mapin, 2002), 35–36.

67. David Arnold, *Tropics and the Travelling Gaze: India, Landscape and Science, 1800–1856* (Delhi: Permanent Black, 2006), 71–73. Between 1815 and 1840, more than one hundred thousand British soldiers died in India from disease (238 n. 5).

68. On lions, see Divyabhanusinh, *The Story of Asia's Lions* (Bombay: MARG, 2005), 127, 142. On monuments, see Nayanjot Lahiri, *Finding Forgotten Cities: How the Indus Civilization Was Discovered* (Delhi: Permanent Black, 2005), 42. I am grateful to both authors for continued insights they have shared over the years. Curzon's note on monuments was written in February 1900; his intervention with the lions came in October.

69. For instance, planters in the Nilgiris had begun conserving *shola* forests by the mid-nineteenth century (having played a key role in their obliteration over larger hill tracts); see Deborah Sutton, "What a Splendid Wood: Sholas, Forest Plantations and Colonial Conservancy in the Nilgiris, 1837–1880," paper presented at the Conference on the Environmental History of Asia, New Delhi: Jawaharlal Nehru University, December 2002. Similarly, the Junagadh nabobs had begun to fret about protecting lions as early as 1879, when there was still a bounty on the animals in British India; see Divyabhanusinh, "Junagadh State and Its Lions: Conservation in Princely India, 1879–1947," *Conservation and Society* 4 (2006): 522–40.

70. See S. Ravi Rajan, "Foresters and the Politics of Agro-ecology: The Case of Shifting Cultivation and Soil Erosion, 1920–50," *Studies in History* 14 (1998): 217–36.

71. Vasant Kabir Saberwal, *Pastoral Politics: Shepherds, Bureaucrats and Conservation in the Western Himalaya* (Delhi: Oxford University Press, 1998).

72. Gail Omvedt, *Ambedkar: Toward an Enlightened India* (Delhi: Viking Penguin, 2004), 111–12.

73. Daniel Klingensmith, "Building India's Modern Temples: Indians and Americans in the Damodar Valley Corporation, 1945–60," in *Regional Modernities,* ed. Kalyanakrishnan Sivaramakrishnan and Arun Agrawal (Delhi: Oxford University Press, 2003), 122–40. Yet at the same time very different Indo-American relationships

were being forged—not to build dams but to study bird ecology and taxonomy. See Michael Lewis, *Inventing Global Ecology: Tracking the Biodiversity Ideal in India, 1945–97* (Delhi: Orient Longman, 2003), 51–69. There is less on India in the magisterial work of Richard Tucker, but it does set events against a larger background. See *Insatiable Appetite: America's Impact on the Tropical World* (Ann Arbor: University of Michigan Press, 2002).

74. Prathama Banerjee, "The Work of Imagination: Temporality and Nationhood in Colonial Bengal," in *Subaltern Sudies,* vol. 12, *Muslims, Dalits and the Fabrications of History,* ed. Shail Mayaram, M. S. S. Pandian, and Ajay Skaria (Delhi: Permanent Black, 2006), 280–322, esp. 308–14. Romantic views could be assimilated into conservative projects by rising middle-class nationalism, as is shown by Archana Prasad, *Against Ecological Romanticism: Verrier Elwin and the Making of an Anti-modern Tribal Identity* (Delhi: Three Essays Collective, 2003).

75. Bibhutibhushan Bandhopadhyay, *Aranyak of the Forest* (1938), translated from Bengali by Rimli Bhattacharya (Kolkata: Seagull Books, 2002), 225–26.

76. Amita Baviskar, "Nature Red in Tooth and Claw: Looking for Class in Struggles over Nature," in *Social Movements in India: Poverty, Power and Politics,* ed. Raka Ray and Mary Fainsod Katzenstein (Delhi: Oxford University Press, 2006), 161–78. For another view, see Vasant Kabir Saberwal and Mahesh Rangarajan, eds., *Battles over Nature: Science and the Politics of Conservation* (Delhi: Permanent Black, 2003).

TEN · Latin American
Environmental History
A Shifting Old/New Field

LISE SEDREZ

In 1902 the Brazilian author Euclides da Cunha published a riveting work about a regional rebellion against the newly established republic and its subsequent suppression by the federal government.[1] A masterpiece on identity, race, and nation building, it contained, to the despair of the following generations of high school students, a long and detailed chapter on the dry land of the Brazilian northeast and on the unforgiving nature that had shaped the *caboclo* and his history. Da Cunha was not a historian; he was a military engineer. In the following years, his book was heavily criticized for its "geographical determinism" and for the racial overtones about the *caboclo*. Yet *Rebellion in the Backlands* is still revered as a foundational text of Latin American historiography.

Even before da Cunha, writing on nature and history in Latin America went back a long way—although nature was usually depicted in a more generous light. In the early nineteenth century, Edenic narratives abounded, as the new Latin American nations sought to distinguish themselves from the European powers by boasting of the hidden potential for wealth in their newly independent territories. A century later, nation, nature, and race still obsessed Latin American intellectuals like da Cunha, who dreamed of rooting this elusive Latin American identity in the land.[2] But it was only in the 1980s that the development of environmental history encouraged Latin Americanists to discover new, challenging approaches to traditional questions. Environmental history relieved historians of the ghost of geographic determinism. The new discipline invited scholars to understand nature in its shifting, dialectic interaction with human societies: nature, after all, was neither the powerful ruler of the destiny of countries nor the static, malleable source of commodities. Instead, environmental history proposed to understand nature as a complex, shifting network of human and nonhuman communities, of biotic and nonbiotic elements.

In recent years, Latin American environmental history has shown a remarkable vitality, which is a consequence of its particular genesis within Latin American historiography. Although nature has long been part of the national and regional historical narratives, it was not necessarily historians who addressed these questions (as da Cunha's example illustrates). When Latin American historians in the late 1980s eventually began to define a niche for environmental history, they had to engage in a three-way dialogue. First, they drew from a large literature on nature and history written not only by historians but also by economists, anthropologists, geographers, and others. Second, they derived much of the theoretical framework for the new discipline from their dialogue with environmental historians of North America, where the field had developed earlier. But the field also draws from Latin American research agendas and interdisciplinary practices. It has matured in recent years, combining the influence of these three bodies of literature into a promising and evolving discipline. In this article, I analyze briefly the current state of the field, its origins, perspectives, and main lines of research.

WRITING ENVIRONMENTAL HISTORY IN LATIN AMERICA

With few exceptions, Latin American historians have been slow to embrace environmental history as compared to their North American colleagues. In part, this is because other disciplines within Latin American studies have occupied the niche for academic research on the relations between nature and society over time. Historical geographers, anthropologists, and demographers have produced a vibrant body of knowledge on the theme since World War II, effectively blurring disciplinary boundaries. Certainly, the interdisciplinarity of environmental history is not exclusive to Latin American scholarship. Don Garden has pointed to the lack of historians in the rise of environmental history in Australia.[3] Nevertheless, the weight of historical geography was felt particularly strongly in Latin America. As Carl Sauer, a Latin Americanist, revolutionized the field of geography, his work influenced many young geographers who followed him in discussing time, place, and societies on the continent.[4] The strong tradition of historical geography in

Latin America invites scholars to avoid parochial definitions of environmental history and embrace interdisciplinary collaboration.

Thus, when Alfred Crosby's *Ecological Imperialism* and Warren Dean's *Brazil and the Struggle for Rubber* were published in the 1980s, they represented more than groundbreaking books for Latin American historiography; they granted historians the confidence that they had something unique to add to the ecological debate and showed that environmental history in Latin America was not simply historical geography by another name.[5] Both Dean and Crosby had already made impressive contributions to Latin American history earlier in their careers; Crosby's *Columbian Exchange* was widely reviewed in professional journals at the time of its publication, and Dean's *Rio Claro* was acclaimed as a classic study on coffee plantations in Brazil.[6] *Ecological Imperialism* put plants, animals, and disease at the forefront not only of the conquest of America but also in the reproduction of European landscapes in the New World. Dean's work on the failure of the rubber industry in the Brazilian Amazon also offered an intriguing narrative in which nature played a key role in the development of capitalism and national projects. Eventually, Dean's *With Broadax and Firebrand*, a posthumous publication and a masterpiece in its own right, brought the discipline from the fringes of Latin American studies closer to the mainstream.[7]

Crosby and Dean are correctly identified as two of the founders of environmental history in the United States, but their work also marked a new moment in the literature produced not only *about* Latin America, but also *in* Latin America. Other scholars, such as Donald Worster, William Cronon, Joan Martínez-Alier, and Richard Grove, secured a faithful Latin American audience, either as they translated their works into Portuguese and Spanish or as Latin American scholars completed their training in the United States or Europe.[8] Beyond questions of the origins of the discipline, however, one must ask what consequences these international influences had on the development of environmental history in Latin America. Did it matter whether Latin American environmental history was produced in Latin America or elsewhere? If the sources were sound, the field stimulating, the ideas creative, and the analysis rigorous, should we not just welcome the work instead of asking about its nationality?

For the historian Guillermo Castro Herrera, at least, if the field was to flourish in Latin America, nationality did matter. According to Castro Herrera, "In the absence of a significant internal cultural demand for a historical approach to the environmental problems of the region, environmental history has been developed by making use of the opportunities created 'from the outside.'" He argues that this "outside" framing of the discipline undermined its ability to generate a theoretical systematization and methodological development. Moreover, it posed risks of "an even greater delay in the construction of a vision of our own; the indiscriminate importation of problems and alternatives constructed from the visions of the others; a permanent fragmentation of the field of study, in space as well as in time, and the loss of true, useful contact between this field and others of doubtless importance—in themselves and for the environment—in which Latin America has already achieved results of great value, such as political, social, economic and cultural history."[9]

Although Castro Herrera may have overstated some of the risks, he is correct about the need for an autonomous tradition of environmental history to free the discipline from being confined to textbook sidebars. A discipline structured from outside was likely to face resistance in Latin American intellectual circles, never becoming more than the token afterthought for environmental concerns. Without the acceptance of Latin American historians, environmental history risked isolation, as Castro Herrera warned, and it would fail to connect to the larger questions that have dominated Latin American historiography, such as the formation of the states and the region's connections with global systems. But to develop environmental history in Latin America, it was also necessary to convince scholars of the relevance of the new discipline. As Stefania Gallini argues, Latin American scholars cultivate a strong sense of social commitment and responsibility: advocacy and scholarship often go hand in hand. Thus a larger question that looms in the background is, "Why is writing environmental history socially and politically important?"[10] Among so many other Latin American crises and problems—including political repression, economic instability, rapid urbanization, and violence—what is the relevance of the environment?

Again, answers to this question come not only from historians but also from scientists, economists, and other scholars who incorporate sometimes tentative but always critical historical perspectives in their investigations of current environmental issues. Pointing out how much historical narratives inform scholarly work on environmental issues in Latin America, Enrique Leff, a leading Mexican economist from the Universidad Nacional Autónoma de México who has coordinated the Red de Formación Ambiental for the United Nations since 1986, called for Latin American historians to create an epistemological framework to support this interdisciplinary analysis.[11] This perspective, curiously, places the emphasis not on the contribution from other disciplines to Latin American environmental history, but on the potential support that environmental historians may offer for other environment-related areas of investigation in Latin America.

NATURE AND HISTORY
IN LATIN AMERICA

If theoretically the field of environmental history is a late bloomer within Latin American historiography, nature and society are nevertheless intertwined in the formation of the concept of Latin America, even in the most traditional historical narratives. Moreover, representations of nature are by no means absent in the historiography. Particularly in the twentieth century, linking historical work to struggles for social justice was important to Latin American historians, and few social conflicts have been more defining for Latin American history than the disputes over access to land, land distribution, and land conversion.

In both the Portuguese and the Spanish Americas, land grants and royal monopolies of valuable resources determined the occupation of the territory, creating a powerful landed elite. State functions in the colonies were closely connected to the protection of these monopolies and to ensuring the success of these land grants in ways that would benefit the colonial project. Although the strategies of colonization varied widely throughout Latin America, they all included radical transformations of the landscape—through large-scale mining or sugarcane plantations, for instance—and continuous control over labor that carried on these transformations—through African slavery or *encomiendas* and *mitas* (forced-labor obligations).

In the national period, particularly the nineteenth century, land use in Latin America answered to the new needs of the Industrial Revolution. The integration of Latin America's natural resources into a world system increased, as did the representation of Latin America as a region with an "agrarian calling" *(vocación agraria)*. The export-led growth model dominated the region, and the new independent nations mostly specialized in one or two primary products for export. The tight connection between international trade and nation formation in Latin America left the region vulnerable to cycles of boom and bust, not only because of fluctuations of the market but also because of the overexploitation and exhaustion of the commodified resources. By the early twentieth century, in several countries of Latin America, whaling had declined; mining cities had disappeared; coffee growers had moved to greener lands, leaving exhausted plantations behind them and increasing the pressure on forests; plant diseases had decimated export-crop plantations; huge domestic and international migration had followed the new export products, with rural workers and new urban populations escaping from famine and forever altering the demographic map of Latin America; and rubber and guano millionaires found themselves impoverished, remembering the good—if brief—old days.

The close links between nature, land, labor, nation formation, and world trade, as well as their influence on Latin American society over time, did not of course escape the attention of Latin American historians. On the contrary, during the 1960s and 1980s, much of the Marxist historiography in Latin America discussed the dependence of the region on international trade and produced ground-breaking studies on the export-commodity economies and the world they created.

However, although nature has clearly been present in more "traditional" narratives of Latin American historiography, these narratives lacked a broader understanding of environmental processes in history, not only as reflections of human agency but also as unique, dynamic phenomena. Thus, although I argue for a less parochial concept of environmental history that acknowledges the contributions of many different disciplines, I also argue that environmental history in Latin America can and should go beyond these contributions to develop its own theoretical framework, one that draws from more traditional Latin American historiography, from sister disciplines such as historical geography, and from North American environmental history.

ORGANIZING THE FIELD

In the past few years, historians from many Latin American countries have joined forces to prevent the fragmentation and isolation of environmental history feared by Castro Herrera and to expand the answer to the "relevance question": why environmental history matters in Latin America. The movement began with independent local initiatives in Panama, Cuba, Brazil, Mexico, Colombia, and Chile in the 1990s. There were few connections between these initiatives, although they all engaged in dialogue with North American environmental historians. At this point, websites and discussion lists, such as the one managed by the American Society for Environmental History, played an important role in fostering debate among Latin American scholars.[12]

Since then, these first tentative contacts have developed into a productive and ongoing exchange that has resulted in conferences and engaging new literature. In August 2001, Germán Palácio organized the first conference on the environmental history of Latin America in Bogotá, Colombia, with participation of scholars from Peru, Brazil, the United States, and Mexico, as well as Colombia.[13] In July 2003, a larger symposium took place in Santiago, Chile, and a second meeting was held in Havana, Cuba, in October 2004.[14] Building on these efforts, in April 2006, the third Symposium on Latin American Environmental History in Carmona, Spain, saw the founding of the Sociedad Latinoamericana y Caribeña de Historia Ambiental, based in Panama City. The assembly of more than sixty members elected Guillermo Castro Herrera as the president of the new organization, and a fourth meeting was planned for May 2008, in Belo Horizonte, Brazil.

These meetings offered more than a chance for historians to exchange ideas; they also provided opportunities to reflect on the limits and the potential of the discipline and to develop new theoretical considerations.[15] In this context, Alberto Guillermo Florez-Malagon wrote an excellent study on the relationship of environmental history to other social sciences.[16] Stefania Gallini and Silvia Meléndez investigated the sources and methodologies of Latin American environmental history.[17] Germán Palácio wrote on the influence of foundational works of North American environmental historians in the creation of a Latin American research agenda on ecology and society.[18] Instead of isolated, tentative essays, these were works that actually built on each other, forming the basis of a promising critical literature.

In recent years the annual meetings of the American Society for Environmental History have also hosted an increasing number of panels and presentations focused on the region, usually with the presence of Latin American scholars. Thus, the development of an internal debate on environmental history in Latin America did not prevent the continuation of a dialogue with North American and European scholars, but it provided the discipline with new questions, new research agendas, and practices of its own. For instance, as mentioned previously, one of the strengths of Latin American environmental history is its ability to claim partnership with more traditional disciplines while retaining its own innovative approach. This interdisciplinary experience is one possible contribution by Latin American historiography to the development of environmental history in general.

NEW DEVELOPMENTS

With this mixture of continuity, domestic and international dialogue, and theoretical reflections, the early twentieth-first century is an exciting time for the environmental history of Latin America. It is also a time when historians are challenged to embrace more sophisticated research, building on earlier works but still tackling the main questions: why environmental history matters for Latin American scholars and how environmental history can contribute to the understanding of Latin America.

A first recent shift in the historiography is the criticism of the prevalence of declensionist narratives. From Eduardo Galeano's *Open Veins of Latin America* to work by Nicolò Gligo and Dean's *With Broadax and Firebrand*, studies on environment and society in Latin America have emphasized the degradation of nature and the destruction of traditional ways of life.[19] In part, this emphasis reflects attempts to find a place for the environment among so many other urgent and critical research topics, among them democracy, justice, and socioeconomic inequality. On the other hand, despite William Cronon's warnings on the risks of too many declensionist narratives, sometimes the stories told are tragic and declensionist because the sources point to histories that *are* tragic and declensionist.[20] By the end of the twentieth century, the Atlantic rain forest, the subject of Dean's last work, was reduced to less than 10 percent of its fifteenth-century area, by the best estimates; there are not many ways to place these data in an optimistic light. Environmental history in Latin America includes many works that highlight the degradation of nature, mismanagement, habitat loss, community displacements, and violence; this is because there is not one environmental crisis in contemporary Latin America, but many, which include all of these elements. And, after all, these are the stories that energize and mobilize historians.[21]

At the same time, narratives drawing from interdisciplinary dialogues have increased the possibilities for more success stories and fewer declensionist narratives. Many of these stories focus on recent case studies and have the laudable goal of promoting models. But the concept of crisis remains strong. Thus, although declensionist narratives often result from the awareness of the huge challenges that Latin American communities face today, such as access to water, sewage treatment, loss of biodiversity, deforestation, erosion, and pollution, success narratives often result from the eagerness of historians to contribute to the resolution of these crises. From this perspective, both success stories and declensionist stories share a similar inclination—and similar risks.

Without dismissing the urgency of these narratives of crisis, new studies have questioned their effectiveness in helping us understand the environmental history of Latin America. Echoing some of Cronon's remarks, Stefania Gallini argues that the hegemony of a "negative teleology" in Latin American environmental history risks reducing complex histories to linear narratives while reinforcing the dichotomy of nature and culture. In addition, these narratives use present crises as keys to understanding the past, obscuring alternative voices and the changed patterns of relations between society and nature. New research must overcome this model while maintaining the dialogue with contemporary environmental debate. As Gallini writes, environmental history demands that Latin American scholars "abandon the economics-oriented unilinearity of history."[22] Although it is a timely warning, moving beyond declensionist narratives requires a fine balance between avoiding this negative teleology and understanding the historical processes that have shaped the current relations between nature and society—which is not by any means a dilemma unique to Latin America.

A second potential shift is related to units of analysis. Environmental historians initially adopted national narratives, which proved useful for exploratory studies or for studies on the national political institutions.[23] Like declensionist narratives, national environmental histories also argued for the relevance of the new discipline; they complemented and challenged traditional national narratives, introducing nature and the transformation of nature into the understanding of national projects. As the literature grows, however, historians are increasingly being challenged to cross national boundaries and embrace new units of analysis to compose a version of Latin American environmental history that is more than the sum of several national narratives. By proposing alternative units of analysis, environmental historians may address some of the larger questions that permeate Latin American studies— such as whether it makes sense to speak of Latin America at all. What do Belize and Uruguay or Guatemala have in common, or even Brazil and Chile? The concept of Latin America is no less problematic and intriguing than the many national projects. Research that focuses on bioregions, instead of national borders, reveals that diversity within a single country is no less startling than between two countries. Analyses of transboundary bioregions may yield new understandings of the similarities or dissimilarities in the way Latin American countries have constituted themselves. For instance, research in the Amazon region, which includes nine countries, has produced remarkable works that focus on both regional and national perspectives, as David Cleary has shown.[24] Analysis of bioregions allows studies on a small or large scale, and as diverse as Elinor Melville's *Plague of Sheep*, about the Mezquital Valley during the Spanish conquest, and Dean's *Brazil and the Struggle for Rubber*, on the twentieth-century Amazon.[25] Here again, the interdisciplinary tradition of Latin American environmental history offers a clear advantage. One of the best transnational studies that focused on bioregions was written not by a historian but by a brave anthropologist. Using national boundaries to his advantage, William Durham described how different communities shared similar cultures, competed for natural resources, and, because of this sharing and competition, brought their countries to the verge of war over transnational resources.[26]

Stuart McCook proposes a different framework for understanding how environmental history is structured in Latin America in his essay on the environmental history of Spanish America. Instead of opposing scholars of nations and bioregions,

McCook argues that the field is split into three different groups, which he calls truffle-hunters, parachutists, and topographers. The first group, truffle-hunters, has contributed to the creation of "superb empirical work on Latin American environmental history." These scholars accumulate case studies, searching in the archives for the most revealing and well-documented stories on how societies and nature have interacted in Latin America.[27] Parachutists, on the other hand, are those who seek a bird's-eye perspective of the discipline, privileging large narratives and laboring over useful periodizations. The problem is that truffle-hunters and parachutists sometimes fail to communicate, and the gap between them hampers the advancement of future studies. To close this gap, it is necessary for more participation from the third group, the topographers, who combine the synthesis produced by the parachutists and "the detailed soundings made by the truffle-hunters into a rich, informative map of the intellectual landscape. The topographer can help refine the parachutist's concepts and categories" by means of rigorous empirical work.[28] For McCook, the unit of analysis is less important than the overall perspective and the historian's ability to combine large periodizations with well-documented case studies. Thus, "topographical" works include not only Dean's *With Broadax and Firebrand* (which studies the Atlantic forest bioregion), but also Brailovsky and Foguelman's *Memória verde* (which is limited to Argentina's national boundaries).[29]

Like the perspectives and units of analysis, the lines of research for Latin Americanists in environmental history have multiplied in the last few years. Here I classify the field into four major research topics. Each of these topics has sub-themes, which, like bioregions, often cross their conceptual boundaries. Although I discuss mostly recent research, it is important to keep track of the classic works that established the parameters for each of these topics and of the related disciplines that contribute to environmental history.

The first of these research topics is what I call "encounters." In classic environmental history, the "encounter" refers to the meeting of the Old and New Worlds. Crosby's definition of the Columbian exchange set the parameters for future studies of this encounter between biotic communities, with their humans, parasites, and other biota, which had been separated for millennia.[30] In her equally classic *Plague of Sheep*, Melville further developed the theme of the encounter by underlining not only the astonishment and inexperience of the New and Old World inhabitants but also the power of inequality and the radical cultural and ecological transformations caused by the encounter.[31] However, the topic goes beyond that initial shock. Encounters usually imply conflicts between human communities that compete for land and nature, often resulting in the expansion of one society over another. This expansion, together with the dehumanization of the conquered space, characterizes much of the frontier narrative, heavily inspired by North American historiography. In the Latin American version, frontier histories usually mean deforestation, which was one of the earliest subjects of its environmental historiography. This emphasis on frontiers and forests was due probably to a sense of urgency about the state of the Latin American forests in the 1980s (when the discipline was first developing) and also to the fascination that the Amazon forest holds for the global imaginary. Besides, the frontier in the Amazon is still active, and some of the contemporary issues recall classic historical dilemmas in frontier narratives.[32]

Frontier narratives imply also the dispute over the environment between settler communities and traditional or indigenous groups. Conflicts between Indians and settlers were well documented in both the colonial and the modern era, and historical anthropology has contributed to the understanding of the mechanisms of negotiation of meaning and manipulation in these conflicts.[33] Ironically, some of these anthropological studies are inspired by U.S. environmental history, such as in the article by Conklin and Graham on Amazon Indians and ecopolitics. Conklin and Graham argue that indigenous groups appropriate environmental discourses to restate their claim to ancestral land whenever it is expedient, much as North American Indians played European powers against each other to protect their interests, as described by Richard White.[34] Underlining the issues of power, alterity, nature, and culture, the rubric of "encounters" also covers studies of the conflicts between dominant societies and other traditional but nonindigenous groups, such as *quilombolas* (runaway slaves), fishing communities, and rubber tappers. Nonindigenous traditional communities have been relatively unexplored in environmental history, though social scientists and anthropologists have developed a solid literature.[35] Claudia Leal, in her studies on the black communities in the Colombian forests, addresses some of these issues and offers interesting insights on issues of race, class, and the environment in Latin America, another largely unexplored theme.[36]

The second large topic is intellectual environmental history. Scholars have repeatedly stressed how ideas of nature changed over time, from observations of the Jesuit priests to the naturalists' travel diaries to the manifestos of the environmental movement. Scientists, humanists, and activists have contributed to the development of different concepts of nature. Inspired by Antonio Gerbi's 1930s work on the impact of the New World's biota on the intellectual circles of Europe, this intellectual history of Latin America's environment is also a history of encounters.[37]

Ideas in Latin America have always been part of a dialogue with Europe or the United States, in a continuous quest by intellectuals to find their own standing. At the same time, ideas of nature are not shaped in purely abstract terms but are connected to transformations in society and in the landscape. José Pádua's excellent study on conservationist thought in Brazil over five centuries illustrates this connection between the dialogue with European ideas and the changes in the Brazilian environment, as physiocratic concepts of efficient natural-resource management clashed against the realties of slavery and a slash-and-burn culture.[38]

Historians of science have also contributed to the field by focusing on the explorations of naturalists such as Carl von Martius, Alexander von Humboldt, and Charles Darwin in Latin America and their impact on modern science.[39] The interface of nature and science, moreover, has produced excellent works that reach beyond a Latin American research agenda. For instance, Jorge Cañizarres-Esguerra's *How to Write the History of the World* argues that the creation of a Creole science, based on a peculiar understanding of nature and natural sciences in the colonial period, challenged the basis of European scientific hegemony.[40] Likewise, McCook's *States of Nature* offers an innovative view of the state as it binds together national projects, sponsored science, and a view of nature as commodity against the backdrop of a nature that is not as tamed as scientists and statesmen would wish.[41]

In the history of environmental ideas, the history of the environmental movement and conservationism in Latin America has been one of the most productive niches for environmental historians, producing a rich collaboration with social scientists. It has also been disappointing and uneven. Sometimes a simplistic overview of the movement prevails, yielding stories that are as unilinear as any declensionist narrative. A cartoon structure of such books would show a preexisting Eden, the fall from grace (through European conquest or industrialization, depending on how far back the author wants to go), a disastrous present, and finally hope for redemption through the environmental movement. Some good texts, however, have sought to break this pattern by incorporating a multidimensional narrative. Some, for instance, stress the conflicts that environmentalism has generated not only with governments but also with other contemporary social movements in national and international contexts.[42] A larger, continental story of environmentalism, comparing different national perspectives, still awaits an author.

The third large topic is economic environmental history. Nature is associated with commodities and the management of natural resources, such as hydropower energy, timber, and fisheries, instead of with rivers, forests, and aquatic fauna. This topic has greater resonance in traditional Latin American historiography. In his foundational text in Brazilian historiography, for instance, Celso Furtado proposed a periodization based on export cycles of natural commodities (brazilwood, sugarcane, gold, and coffee) and their effect on the organization of the Brazilian society.[43] Environmental history makes a valuable contribution to traditional economic history of natural resources by underlining the complexity of nature's role in history and challenging the mere commodity perspective. For instance, some economic historians stress the importance of land-use institutions and property rights in assessing the history of agricultural production and forestry in Latin America; but although land-use institutions may be the same within one country, the same rules may have very different consequences in different landscapes and types of production. For example, forests in Paraná or Chile, fairly homogeneous and with fertile soil, have a different carrying capacity (and consequently, generated a different agrarian society) from the forests of the Amazon, with poor soils and a very heterogeneous forest.[44] Without the perspective of environmental history, economic analyses may fail to grasp these differences.[45]

The debate on property rights from traditional economic history offers some very interesting questions for environmental history, as Shawn Miller argues.[46] In Latin America, as Miller points out, rights over land did not imply rights over everything that was above or under that land. In the colonial era, timber was a valuable royal monopoly. This situation encouraged deforestation because neither the landowner nor the crown stood to gain from sound management of timber. Miller's argument on conflicting property rights could also apply to other royal monopolies, such as whales, salt, and minerals. Except for mining and guano, there are still few studies on these monopolies and their impact on the environment, but some exploratory articles are encouraging.[47] Unfortunately, modern mining has received even less attention than mining in the colonial era, and we know very little about the residues of mercury and other toxic metals in mining areas, the environmental impact of mining technology, or conflicts over water use in the mining regions.

Economic historians have contributed extensively to the field, as in the recent edited volume by Steven Topik, Carlos Marichal, and Zephyr Frank, *From Silver to Cocaine;* but their focus has been mostly on the terms of trade rather than on the environmental processes.[48] In contrast, more attuned to classic environmental history, John Soluri's work on the banana economy in Central America analyzes the social and cultural practices that resulted both from the international capitalist system and the characteristics of banana production.[49]

The fourth and last topic in this scheme is "landscapes and places." Its themes, as in the previous cases, connect with all the other topics, but here the emphasis is on landscape transformation and the places it creates.[50] Just recently, environmental historians have begun to explore urbanization and industrialization in Latin America.[51] It is not too soon. Urban environmental history has been sorely neglected, although 80 percent of the population in Latin America lives in urban areas and the region has four of the world's largest cities (São Paulo, Rio de Janeiro, Mexico City, and Buenos Aires). Fortunately, historical geographers have done a better job than environmental historians in this area.[52] New research on landscapes has explored the connections between cities, hinterland, and rural communities, partially influenced by William Cronon's *Nature's Metropolis*.[53] This fourth topic is a promising new territory rather than a well-established research agenda, and the potential for future studies is large. Beyond the issue of urbanization, there has been little historical research on large state-sponsored projects such as dams and highways that assesses their impact on the environment and human communities over time. Pollution appears as an important motivator for the organization of environmental movements, but most studies fail to analyze how communities negotiate their livelihood in polluted ecosystems and how pollution represents not only degraded nature, but also a new landscape.

Environmental history of Latin America has come a long way since its first exploratory attempts to establish itself as a legitimate field within Latin American scholarship. Some of its limitations are structural to Latin American studies. For instance, a restricted and risk-averse publishing market, as compared to that of Europe and the United States, is a clear hindrance to the expansion of new disciplines and the exchange of ideas within the region. Yet the field cannot grow healthily if it depends too heavily on works produced outside the region, failing to win over mainstream Latin American historians. Nevertheless, a small but eager group of historians has recently invested much enthusiasm in developing the field, exploring alternative ways to foster productive scholarship.

This schematic structure I present here is merely indicative and not at all conclusive. It shows, however, intriguing gaps in this new literature that have yet to be addressed. For instance, although there are several studies on the impact of capitalistic production on the Latin American environment, few studies have analyzed consumption in the region. Research on class, gender, and race, which is fairly advanced in other areas of Latin American studies, has merited little attention from environmental historians. Another potential avenue for research is intercontinental collaboration. Although environmental historians maintained a dialogue with U.S. (and on a smaller scale with European) environmental historians, there has been little exchange with African or Asian scholars. The framework of environmental history could provide, as in the Columbian exchange, the opening for a more fruitful interaction between these three young historiography communities.

In 2003, Paul Sutter published an article suggesting what U.S. environmental historians could learn from non-U.S. environmental historians.[54] Expanding on his essay, we might ask not only what Latin American history could learn from U.S. environmental historians—as this is an ongoing dialogue—but also what environmental history in Latin America could contribute to the development of environmental history in general. I have argued here that Latin American historians have not simply reflected questions proposed by their North American counterparts but instead have drawn from multiple influences. Among the very specific characteristics resulting from these influences are multidisciplinarity and a broader definition of environmental history. They also include the persistence of traditional questions from Latin American historiography, such as social justice, power and inequality disputes, and the global position of the region (which is marked by its own inequalities). For good or bad, these characteristics have defined many of the questions proposed by scholars studying Latin American environmental history, and they may well present a valuable contribution to the field in general.

After all, if environmental historians may be, as McCook asserts, parachutists, truffle-hunters, and topographers, why not bridge builders?

NOTES

1. Euclides da Cunha, *Os sertões (Campanha de canudos)* (Rio de Janeiro: Livraria Francisco Alves, P. de Azevedo & cia, 1911).

2. For a discussion on precursors of the environmental history of Latin America, see Lise Fernanda Sedrez, "Historia ambiental de América latina: Orígenes, principales interrogantes y lagunas," in *Repensando la naturaleza: Encuentros y desencuentros disciplinarios en torno a lo ambiental*, ed. Germán Palácio Márquez and Astrid Ulloa (Bogotá: Universidad Nacional de Colombia–Sede Leticia, Instituto Amazónico de Investigaciones Imani, 2002); and Guillermo Castro Herrera, "The Environmental Crisis and the Tasks of History in Latin America," *Environment and History* 3 (1997): 1–18.

3. Don Garden, "Where Are the Historians? Australian Environmental History," American Society for Environmental History, www.h-net.org/~environ/historiography/australia.htm, cited June 18, 2003.

4. Carl Ortwin Sauer, *The Early Spanish Main* (Berkeley: University of California Press, 1966); and Carl Ortwin Sauer and Martin S. Kenzer, *Carl O. Sauer: A Tribute* (Corvallis: Oregon State University Press, 1987).

5. Alfred W. Crosby, *Ecological Imperialism: The Biological Expansion of Europe, 900–1900* (Cambridge: Cambridge University Press, 1986); Warren Dean, *Brazil and the Struggle for Rubber: A Study in Environmental History* (Cambridge: Cambridge University Press, 1987).

6. Alfred W. Crosby, *The Columbian Exchange: Biological and Cultural Consequences of 1492* (Westport, CT: Greenwood Press, 1973); Warren Dean, *Rio Claro: A Brazilian Plantation System, 1820–1920* (Stanford, CA: Stanford University Press, 1976).

7. Warren Dean, *With Broadax and Firebrand: The Destruction of the Brazilian Atlantic Forest* (Berkeley: University of California Press, 1997).

8. Among these authors, particularly influential were Donald Worster, ed., *The Ends of the Earth: Perspectives on Modern Environmental History* (Cambridge: Cambridge University Press, 1988); William Cronon, *Changes in the Land: Indians, Colonists, and the Ecology of New England* (New York: Hill & Wang, 1983); Richard H. Grove, *Green Imperialism: Colonial Expansion, Tropical Island Edens, and the Origins of Environmentalism, 1600–1860* (Cambridge: Cambridge University Press, 1995); and Joan Martínez-Alier and Manuel González de Molina Navarro, *Historia y ecología* (Madrid: Marcial Pons, 1993).

9. Guillermo Castro Herrera, *Environmental History (Made) in Latin America*, American Society for Environmental History; www.h-net.org/~environ/historiography/latinam.htm, cited June 18, 2003.

10. Stefania Gallini, "Invitación a la historia ambiental," *Cuadernos digitales: Publicación electronica en historia, archivistica y estudios sociales* 6, no. 18 (2002), http://historia.fcs.ucr.ac.cr/cuadernos/c18-his.html.

11. Enrique Leff, "Vetas y vertentes de la historia ambiental latinoamericana: Una nota metodológica y epistemológica," *Varia historia* 1 (2005): 17–31. Leff's call is not uniquely for historians: he claims that many traditional disciplines must incorporate environmental concerns, from physics to psychology, from geography to engineering, to face the challenges of the modern world. See Enrique Leff and José María Montes, *Los problemas del conocimiento y la perspectiva ambiental del desarrollo* (Mexico City: Siglo Veintiuno Editores, 1986).

12. Encouraged by the late John Wirth, I contributed to these efforts toward the creation of a scholarly bibliographic website on Latin American environmental history. See Lise Sedrez, *Online Bibliography on Environmental History of Latin America*, California State University at Long Beach, www.csulb.edu/laeh, cited June 10, 2007.

13. The proceedings were published in Palácio Márquez and Ulloa, *Repensando la naturaleza*.

14. A previous symposium was held in Quito, Ecuador, in 1997, but with little follow-up. See Mauricio Folchi Donoso, Reinaldo Funes Monzote, and Fernando Ramírez Morales, *Simposio de historia ambiental americana* (História ecológica de Chile;

270 · LISE SEDREZ

www.historiaecologica.cl/simposio.htm, cited October 28, 2003); and Armando Fernández et al., *Il simposio de historia ambiental americana: "Hacía una historia ambiental de América latina y el Caribe"* (Fundación Antonio Núñez Jiménez de la Naturaleza y el Hombre; www.fanj.cult.cu/noticias/II%20simposio%20Historia%20Ambiental.htm, cited February 2, 2003).

15. See, for instance, Guido P. Galafassi, *Ambiente, sociedad y naturaleza entre la teoria social y la historia: Diálogo* (Buenos Aires: Universidad Nacional de Quilmes, 2002); and Graciela Zuppa, David Velazquez Torres, and Gilmar Arruda, *Natureza na América latina: Entre apropriações e representações* (Londrina, Brazil: Eduel, 2001).

16. Alberto Guillermo Florez-Malagon, *Ambiente y desarrollo: El campo de la historia ambiental; Perspectivas para su desarrollo en Colombia* (Bogotá: Pontifica Universidad Javerian, 2000).

17. Gallini, "Invitación a la historia ambiental"; Silvia Meléndez, "La historia ambiental: Aportes interdisciplinarios y balance crítico desde América latina," *Cuadernos digitales: Publicación electronica en historia, archivistica y estudios sociales* 7, no. 19 (2002), http://historia.fcs.ucr.ac.cr/cuadernos/c19his.rtf.

18. Germán Palácio Márquez, ed., *Naturaleza en disputa: Ensayos de historia ambiental de Colombia, 1850–1995* (Bogotá: Universidad Nacional de Colombia, 2001).

19. Eduardo H. Galeano, *Open Veins of Latin America: Five Centuries of the Pillage of a Continent,* trans. Cedric Belfrage (New York: Monthly Review Press, 1973); Nicolò Gligo, "Notas sobre la historia ecológica de América latina," in *Estilos de desarrollo y medio ambiente en América latina,* ed. Nicolò Gligo and Osvaldo Sunkel (Mexico: Fondo de Cultura Económica, 1980); and Dean, *With Broadax and Firebrand.*

20. William Cronon, "Telling Stories about Ecology," in *Major Problems in American Environmental History: Documents and Essays,* ed. Carolyn Merchant (Lexington, MA: D. C. Heath, 1993), 325.

21. For a brief overview of the many environmental crises of Latin America, see J. Timmons Roberts and Nikki Demetria Thanos, *Trouble in Paradise: Globalization and Environmental Crises in Latin America* (New York: Routledge, 2003).

22. Gallini, "Invitación a la historia ambiental." The expression *negative teleology* was coined by Piero Bevilacqua, as quoted by Gallini. See Piero Bevilacqua, *Tra natura e storia: Ambiente, economie, risorse in Italia, saggi; Natura e artefatto* (Roma: Donzelli, 1996).

23. Joel Simon, *Endangered Mexico: An Environment on the Edge* (San Francisco: Sierra Club Books, 1997); Lane Simonian, *Defending the Land of the Jaguar: A History of Conservation in Mexico* (Austin: University of Texas Press, 1995); Antonio Elio Brailovsky and Dina Foguelman, *Memória verde: Historia ecológica de Argentina* (Buenos Aires: Sudamerica, 1994); Fernando Ramírez Morales, "Apuntes para una historia ecológica de Chile," *Cuadernos de historia* 11 (1991): 149–96; Sterling Evans, *The Green Republic: A Conservation History of Costa Rica* (Austin: University of Texas Press, 1999).

24. David Cleary, "Towards an Environmental History of the Amazon: From Prehistory to the Nineteenth Century," *Latin American Research Review* 36, no. 2 (2001): 65–96.

25. Elinor Gordon Ker Melville, *A Plague of Sheep: Environmental Consequences of the Conquest of Mexico* (Cambridge: Cambridge University Press, 1994); and Dean, *Brazil and the Struggle for Rubber.*

26. William Durham, *Scarcity and Survival in Central America: Ecological Origins of the Soccer War* (Stanford, CA: Stanford University Press, 1979).

27. Stuart George McCook, "On Parachutists, Truffle-Hunters, and Topographers: Writing the Environmental History of Tropical Spanish America," paper presented at meeting of the American Society for Environmental History, Denver, CO, 2002. McCook points to a collection of essays by Bernardo Garcia-Martinez and Alba González Jácome as one of the best examples of modern truffle hunting in Latin American environmental history: *Estudios sobre historia y ambiente en la América latina* (Mexico City: Instituto Panamericana de Geografía e Historia, 1999). The parachutists would be Guillermo Castro Herrera, with his *Los trabajos de ajuste y combate: Naturaleza y sociedad en la historia de America latina* (Havana: Casa de las Americas, 1994), and Pedro Cunill, with *Las transformaciones del espacio geohistórico latinoamericano, 1930–1990* (Mexico City: Colegio de México, Fondo de Cultura Económica, 1995).

28. McCook, "On Parachutists, Truffle-Hunters, and Topographers," 4.

29. Dean, *With Broadax and Firebrand;* Brailovsky and Foguelman, *Memória verde.*

30. Crosby, *Columbian Exchange* and *Ecological Imperialism.*

31. Melville, *Plague of Sheep.*

32. On deforestation and frontiers, see Dean, *With Broadax and Firebrand,* as well as Warwick Bray, "A donde han ido los bosques? El hombre y el medio ambiente en la Colombia prehispanica," *Boletín del Museo del Oro (Bogotá, Colombia)* 30 (1991): 43–65; Domingo Cozzo, "Las pérdidas del primitivo paisaje de bosques, montes y arbustiformes de la Argentina con especial referencia a sus territorios aridos y húmedos," *Miscelanea* 90 (1992); Susan E. Place, *Tropical Rainforests: Latin American Nature and Society in Transition* (Wilmington, DE: Scholarly Resources, 1993); Donna J. Guy and Thomas E. Sheridan, *Contested Ground: Comparative Frontiers on the Northern and Southern Edges of the Spanish Empire* (Tucson: University of Arizona Press, 1998).

33. Very interesting historical perspectives for indigenous claims of nature are presented in Luis Fernando Calero, *Chiefdoms under Siege: Spain's Rule and Native Adaptation in the Southern Colombian Andes, 1535–1700* (Albuquerque: University of New Mexico Press, 1997); Nancy M. Farris, *Maya Society under Colonial Rule: The Collective Enterprise of Survival* (Princeton: Princeton University Press, 1984); Myrna Santiago, *The Ecology of Oil: Environment, Labor, and the Mexican Revolution, 1900–1938* (New York: Cambridge University Press, 2006), and William Balée,

"Indigenous History and Amazonian Biodiversity," in *Changing Tropical Forests: Historical Perspectives on Today's Challenges in Central and South America*, ed. Harold K. Steen and Richard P. Tucker (Durham, NC: Forest History Society, 1992).

34. On the myth of the environmental "noble savage," see Barbara Conklin and Laura Graham, "The Shifting Middle Ground: Amazon Indians and Eco-politics," *American Anthropologist*, no. 97 (1995): 695–710; and Richard White, *The Middle Ground: Indians, Empires, and Republics in the Great Lakes Region, 1650–1815* (Cambridge: Cambridge University Press, 1991).

35. Margaret E. Keck, "Parks, People and Power: The Shifting Terrain of Environmentalism," *NACLA Report on the Americas* 285 (1995): 36–42; and Margaret E. Keck, "Social Equity and Environmental Politics in Brazil: Lessons from the Rubber Tappers of Acre," *Comparative Politics* 27, no. 4 (1995): 409–24.

36. Claudia Leal, *Unos bosques sembrados de aserríos: Historia de la extracción maderera en el Pacífico colombiano* (Medellín, Colombia: Universidad de Antioquia, 2003).

37. Antonello Gerbi, *The Dispute of the New World* (Pittsburgh, PA: University of Pittsburgh Press, 1973), and Anthony Pagden, *European Encounters with the New World from Renaissance to Romanticism* (New Haven: Yale University Press, 1993).

38. José Augusto Pádua, *Um sopro de destruição: Pensamento político e crítica ambiental no Brasil escravista, 1786–1888* (Rio de Janeiro: Jorge Zahar Editor, 2002).

39. Joseph Ewan, "Through the Jungle of Amazon: Travel Narratives of Naturalists," *Archives of Natural History* 19 (1992): 185–207; Regina Horta Duarte, "Viagens e viajantes," special issue, *Revista brasileira de história* 22, no. 44 (2002). *História, ciência e saúde: Manguinhos*, one of most important history of science journals in Latin America, published a special edition on science and naturalists in Latin America in 2001. See *História, ciência e saúde: Manguinhos* 8, supplemento (Rio de Janeiro, 2001, www.scielo.br/scielo.php?script = sci_issuetoc&pid = 0104–59702001000 5&lng = en&nrm = isso).

40. Jorge Cañizares-Esguerra, *How to Write the History of the New World: Histories, Epistemologies, and Identities in the Eighteenth-Century Atlantic World* (Stanford, CA: Stanford University Press, 2001).

41. Stuart George McCook, *States of Nature: Science, Agriculture, and Environment in the Spanish Caribbean, 1760–1940* (Austin: University of Texas Press, 2002).

42. Keck, "Social Equity and Environmental Politics"; José Augusto Drummond, "A visão conservacionista (1920 a 1970)," in *O ambientalismo no Brasil: Passado, presente e futuro*, ed. Enrique Svirsky and João Paulo R. Capobianco (São Paulo: Instituto Socioambiente, 1997), 19–28; Eduardo J. Viola, "The Ecologist Movement in Brazil (1974–1986): From Environmentalism to Ecopolitics," *International Journal of Urban and Regional Research* 12 (1988): 211–28; M. Price, "Ecopolitics and Environmental Non-governmental Organizations in Latin America," *Geographical Review* 84 (1994):

42–58. Juan de Onis, *The Green Cathedral: Sustainable Development of Amazonia* (New York: Oxford University Press, 1992); Helen Collinson, *Green Guerrillas: Environmental Conflicts and Initiatives in Latin America and the Caribbean* (London: Latin American Bureau, 1996); Evans, *Green Republic*.

43. Celso Furtado, *Formação econômica do Brasil* (Berkeley: University of California Press, 1963).

44. See, for instance, Lee J. Alston, Gary D. Libecap, and Bernardo Mueller, *Titles, Conflict, and Land Use: The Development of Property Rights and Land Reform on the Brazilian Amazon Frontier* (Ann Arbor: University of Michigan Press, 1999).

45. From an environmental economic perspective, see Hugo Gunckel, "Utilización de la araucaria chilena en el siglo XVIII," *Noticiaro mensual (Museo Nacional de Historia Natural)* 25 (1980): 3–7; Claudio Donoso and Antonio Lara, "Utilización de los bosques nativos en Chile: Pasado presente y futuro," in *Ecología de los bosques nativos de Chile,* ed. Juan J. Arnesto, Carolin Villagran, and Mary Kalin Arroyo (Santiago: Editorial Universitaria, 1995), 363–87.

46. Shawn W. Miller, *Fruitless Trees: Portuguese Conservation and Brazil's Colonial Timber* (Stanford, CA: Stanford University Press, 2000).

47. Elizabeth Dore, "La interpretación socio-ecológica de la historia minera de América latina," *Ecología politica* 7 (1994): 49–68; A. J. R. Russell-Wood, "Technology and Society: The Impact of Gold Mining on the Institution of Slavery in Portuguese America," *Journal of Economic History* 37 (1977): 59–83; Paul Eliot Gootenberg, *Between Silver and Guano: Commercial Policy and the State in Postindependence Peru* (Princeton: Princeton University Press, 1989).

48. Steven Topik, Carlos Marichal, and Zephyr L. Frank, *From Silver to Cocaine: Latin American Commodity Chains and the Building of the World Economy, 1500–2000* (Durham, NC: Duke University Press, 2006).

49. John Soluri, "Altered Landscapes and Transformed Livelihoods: Banana Companies, Panama Disease, and Rural Communities on the North Coast of Honduras, 1880–1950," in *Interactions between Agroecosystems and Rural Communities,* ed. Cornelia Butler-Flora (Boca Raton, FL: CRC Press, 2000). Soluri expanded this theme in his award-wining book *Banana Cultures: Agriculture, Consumption, and Environmental Change in Honduras and the United States* (Austin: University of Texas Press, 2005), xiii, 321.

50. See, for instance, Andrew Sluyter, "From Archive to Map to Pastoral Landscape: A Spatial Perspective on the Livestock Ecology of Sixteenth-Century New Spain," *Environmental History* 3 (1998): 508–28.

51. Larissa V. Brown, "Urban Growth, Economic Expansion, and Deforestation in Late Colonial Rio de Janeiro," in *Changing Tropical Forests: Historical Perspectives on Today's Challenges in Central and South America,* ed. Harold K. Steen and Richard

P. Tucker (Durham, NC: Forest History Society, 1992); Exequiel Ezcurra, *De las chinampas a la megalopolis: El medio ambiente en la cuenca de México* (Mexico City: Fondo de Cultura Económica, 1991).

52. See, for instance, the connections drawn between city and hinterland by the historical geographer Christian Brannstrom in "Rethinking the 'Atlantic Forest' of Brazil: New Evidence for Land Cover and Land Value in Western São Paulo, 1900–1930," *Journal of Historical Geography* (2002): 420–39; or studies on Rio de Janeiro by Maurício de Almeida Abreu, *Natureza e sociedade no Rio de Janeiro* (Rio de Janeiro: Prefeitura da Cidade do Rio de Janeiro, 1992).

53. See Richard W. Slatta, *Gauchos and the Vanishing Frontier* (Lincoln: University of Nebraska Press, 1983); John O. Browder and Brian J. Godfrey, *Rainforest Cities: Urbanization, Development, and Globalization of the Brazilian Amazon* (New York: Columbia University Press, 1997); and William Cronon, *Nature's Metropolis: Chicago and the Great West* (New York: W. W. Norton, 1991).

54. Paul Sutter, "Reflections: What Can U.S. Environmental Historians Learn from Non-U.S. Environmental Historiography?" *Environmental History* 8, no. 1 (2003): 1–33.

ELEVEN · # The Predatory Tribute-Taking State

A Framework for Understanding Russian Environmental History

DOUGLAS R. WEINER

Without embracing yet another rigid determinism, it may be proposed that certain forms of political economy leave their own footprints on the physical landscape and bequeath identifiable environmental legacies. At least one scholar has even attempted an ecological "archaeology of colonialism."[1] One problem that the environmental historian seeks to explain is how particular socioeconomic and political orders, through the values, outlook, sense of meaning, and behaviors that flow from their structuring of common sense and everyday life—their internal logics—create particular ranges of choices for decision makers and public actors which then encumber environmental consequences. (Of course, different systems with different logics may also generate similar legacies.) Such logics provide both a comfort zone and a formidable barrier to imaginable alternatives. Not infrequently, existing systems become very durable, reproducing fundamental patterns over long periods because they have succeeded in making the case—often aided by repression or the threat of violence—that their view of "the way things are" is the most realistic one around.

This essay seeks to begin to explain how the natural (and social) landscape of post-Soviet Eurasia arrived at its current, parlous condition. The core of the argument is simple. At least since the Mongol-Tatar invasion of the thirteenth century, and particularly with the rise and expansion of the Muscovite state, and later, the Russian Empire and the USSR, a succession of militarized, predatory tribute-taking regimes have dominated the Eurasian land mass. Whatever they called themselves, the attitudes of these regimes toward the human and nonhuman (natural) resources of Russia have been similar. Unbounded by the rule of law (although constrained somewhat by custom), these regimes saw the population and the land over which they ruled as a trove of resources to be mined for the rulers' purposes. At times, those purposes have sounded noble: defense of the one true faith; the ingathering of the dispersed Russian ethnos; the creation of a just, classless society; or the engineering of a transition to a "liberal, democratic, free-market society." Nevertheless, high-minded purposes have not overshadowed the rulers' cold understandings of the prerequisites of maintaining power (although subjectively, many of Russia's rulers probably believed that they were serving noble ends); and in pursuit of these purposes, Russia's rulers have spared neither people nor land.

The cumulative environmental legacy of Russia's regimes is edifying, but hardly heartening. One does not have to subscribe to a special environmental e-mail list such as REDfiles (Russian Environmental Digest) to appreciate the scale of environmental problems in the former Soviet Union. Images of long-standing problems (e.g., European deforestation, the Aral Sea crisis, nuclear and industrial contamination from Murmansk to Sakhalin, and deteriorating levels of public health, with unprecedented modern peacetime demographic decline in Russia) produce a composite impression of a region poisoned by a civilization gone badly awry.[2] Tracing the genealogy of this landscape of risk is important not only for the people of that region but for everyone on the planet. Just as we have all been engulfed by the environmental effects of capitalist "globalization," equally, we all find ourselves downwind or downstream of Chernobyl, Kyshtym, the Novaya Zemlya and Semipalatinsk nuclear test sites, the nuclear dumping in the Arctic and Pacific oceans, and the eroded south Siberian and Kazak steppes.

The situation appears not always to have been so gloomy. On the eve of the first millennium, the Slavs seem to have been a "free" people of the forests. They practiced slash-and-burn agriculture *(liada, podseka)* but also returned to once-cultivated, and subsequently abandoned, fields after suitable intervals to allow the recovery of soil fertility (a practice known as long-fallow agriculture, or *perelog*).[3] Fields could usually be cultivated for four to five years in succession before losing their fertility.[4] They also domesticated livestock, which they pastured in forest clearings. Described by the sixth-century Byzantine commentator Procopius as "living communally, without leaders" and by the Byzantine emperor Maurice as "freedom-loving, bold, and disinclined either to slavery or to submission," the Slavs made their redoubts in the almost impassable forests and swamps along the Dnepr and Dvina basins.[5]

However much importance one ascribes to the Viking invaders from Gotland in the consolidation of the first Eastern Slav state—Kievan Rus'—and the loose federation to which it gave rise, the evidence from the Russian Primary Chronicle (Tale of bygone years) testifies to the significant role of private property, the law, and (limited) civic participation in the governance of those societies, among them the commercial republics of Novgorod and Pskov. (The more recently settled northeastern principalities of Vladimir-Suzdal and later Moscow constituted important exceptions.) Those societies were nevertheless certainly capable of exhausting their resources. As the wealth of Novgorod, in particular, was based on the export of forest products, especially pelts, that republic's energetic commercial spirit was unkind to fur bearers; the beaver was hunted out of European Russia and survived precariously on the eastern slopes of the Urals.[6] Nevertheless, the forest cover remained generally intact over Rus', yielding to a park-like mixed forest-steppe landscape only at the southern margins of Slavic settlement. Revealingly, at the time of Iaroslav the Wise (1019–54), forests blanketed 40 percent of the current territory of Ukraine (or twenty-eight million hectares), compared with 14.2 percent today.[7]

The pagan Slavs exempted areas of the forest from use, designating them either as sacred groves or as unclean places. This tradition continued even after the introduction of Christianity in 988, although these areas were now consecrated, following processions into the forest with church banners and icons. Such areas allowed the regeneration of renewable biotic resources of the forest, especially game.[8] Large oaks served as landmarks for travelers and to divide territory: felling such trees occasioned a stiff monetary fine, according to Iaroslav the Wise's law code *Russkaia pravda,* whose writ embraced Kievan Rus'.[9]

After Eurasia was absorbed into the Mongol Empire (the domain of the Golden Horde), the Russian lands evolved in a different direction. During their struggles to liberate themselves from Mongol-Tatar suzerainty (and to subjugate their rival princes), the grand princes of Moscow aggrandized their highly centralized, militarized, authoritarian polity. The commercial republics of Novgorod and Pskov were crushed and ravaged by the early sixteenth century; the grand prince, from the time of Ivan IV ("the Terrible"), was now tsar or caesar (and the successor to the *khan*). All property was subsumed into the tsar's household; the Muscovite state constituted his giant patrimonial demesne. That state had also evolved into a permanent state of belligerence. In his quest to regather the "Russian (Orthodox) lands" lost to the (Roman Catholic) Polish-Lithuanian Commonwealth and to crush neighboring (Lutheran) Livonia and the (Islamic) successor states to the Horde, Ivan IV pursued holy wars on all fronts. To support his vastly expanded military, the tsar granted estates, complete with enserfed peasants, to newly ennobled gentry on condition of service. The obliteration of Russian cities as independent commercial and political centers, a joint legacy of the Mongols and the Muscovite princes, made self-sufficient, serf-powered estates all the more necessary.[10] Society was a hierarchy of power. Gentry were "slaves" *(kholopy)* to the tsar, and enserfed peasants were bondsmen to the gentry. The autarkic, tribute-based Russian economy was coming into being.

The first environmental consequences of the Muscovite militarized service state were not long in coming. Incessant war brought in its train famine and horrific epidemics from the 1550s through the 1570s, with the consequent abandonment of plowland, exacerbated by the mass flight of peasants to the "wild fields" of the forest-steppe and steppe to escape Ivan IV's draconian policies. This flight, in turn, led to a sharp increase in the exploitation of those peasants who remained in, or were returned to, the ambit of the state's control. Increased land-based natural and money rents led peasants to intensify production by eliminating fallow, leading to a rapid loss of soil fertility and to equally devastating famine, political anarchy, and even foreign occupation during the Time of Troubles (1599–1613).[11] However, as Richard Hellie notes, the Muscovite regime did not see any alternative to the hyper-exploitation of its peasantry: "At times of economic dislocation the only means of satisfying the needs of the army, the backbone of which was the middle service class cavalry, seemed to be to limit the movement of the primary producers capable of rendering this support. This understanding was based on an unwillingness to reduce the army to a size the country could afford. Any reduction was impossible, for it would have forced the admission that Russia was indefensible or that its military aspirations were too grandiose."[12]

Russia's rulers understood that their system could function only if they closed all escape routes to their captive labor force; and that tactic in turn propelled further territorial expansion of the state. Yet expansion threatened dilution of the tsarist administration over the increasingly vast imperial territory; in consequence, the peasants and other taxable groups had to be squeezed even more, ad infinitum.

With the defeat of the Kazan and Astrakhan khanates in the 1550s, the Muscovite state expanded southward and eastward while simultaneously prosecuting an on-again, off-again war with the Polish-Lithuanian Commonwealth and Livonia (and later Sweden) in the north and west. In an attempt to secure the southern boundaries against the Crimean Khanate and its patron, the Ottoman Empire, intricate systems of defensive lines (the *zasechnaia cherta*) were constructed from the mid-1500s at the southern edge of the forest and across the forest-steppe: its culminating phase was known as the Belgorod defense line, begun in 1637. Among the most grandiose military projects in history, it included the construction of administrative garrison towns and many hundreds of miles of trenches, palisades, towers, and abatis. These were breached by the Crimean Tatars only once, in 1571, when Moscow was sacked.[13]

As late as the early seventeenth century, an unbroken ocean of grass still stretched from the Danube to Mongolia. Although the various nomadic pastoralist groups that occupied these grasslands were also skilled hunters, neither the steppe vegetation nor the fauna appear to have been noticeably affected by their presence; but we should approach with caution the conclusion that, until the appearance of the Russians, the steppe was "pristine" and untransformed. Indeed, that is the subject of an unresolved debate among ecologists and biogeographers, some of whom assert that without intensive grazing, the fescue-feathergrass assemblage, at least in the northern part of the steppe, would have yielded to a more hydrophilic meadow-type vegetation.[14] Perhaps the major effect that the nomads had on the steppe was burning, especially during wars. Most of the burning of the steppe, though, was done by Russians as a defensive measure, to deprive the nomads' horses of pasture.

By the mid-seventeenth century, the various Cossack federations (Don, Zaporozh'e, Kuban, Iaik) had been deputized by the tsarist state to protect its borders against the nomads. As they penetrated farther south and east into the steppe, they were followed by agriculturalists. Behind this advance the defensive lines, no longer needed by the end of the eighteenth century, remained undeveloped, becoming anomalous dense islands of forest amid agricultural and park-like landscapes. (The Tula abatis was preserved as the Tul'skie Zaseki Zapovednik, or "inviolable" nature reserve, from 1935 to 1951, when it was eliminated by the Stalin regime; the Kaluzhskie Zaseki reserve was established in 1992.) As such they represent one of the few "green" contributions of the Muscovite, tsarist, and Communist periods.

As the rich Black Earth region of the former western steppes in Ukraine and southern Russia became available for cropping, Slavic migrants (future Russians and Ukrainians), organized as serf labor on gentry estates, converted the steppe into a grain basket. Forest islands, especially along steppe rivers and streams, were felled for firewood, construction materials, and shipbuilding, which boomed under the patronage of Peter I ("the Great"). Whatever forest-conservation measures were promulgated by Peter, notably the ban on logging along rivers and in designated forest preserves (1722), were taken solely to ensure sufficient materials for his warships.

By the middle of the eighteenth century, these trends had already had profound effects not only on the vegetation but also on the fauna. Gone were the herds of European bison *(Bison bonasus L.)* and tarpan, or wild horse (the last one died in 1877). The last *tur*, an ancestral form of the domesticated cow, was killed in 1644, and the saiga antelope *(Saiga tatarica)*, once found as far west as Moldavia, was driven back east beyond the Don River. The steppe was cleared of beaver *(Castor fiber)* and moose *(Alces alces)* as well. The once-extensive ranges of the greater and lesser bustard (*Otis tarda L.* and *Otis tetrax L.*), common and Demoiselle cranes (*Grus grus L.* and *Anthropoides virgo L.*), and other species of steppe avifauna now contracted to isolated spots. By 1880 the Wild Field, as Slavs called the European part of the steppe, was no more.[15] The proportion of cultivated land had increased in the region from 26 percent in 1719 to 66 percent in 1881.[16] This proportion represented just about 100 percent of the *cultivable* land.

The revolution from above of Peter I and his successors also had serious effects on forests throughout European Russia. His wars, first with the Ottomans and then with the Swedes, led to a great expansion of serf-powered iron works, which in turn required vast amounts of charcoal. The world's biggest smelter of iron in the eighteenth century, the Russian iron industry as late as the 1880s was consuming almost twenty million cubic meters of timber annually, when the rest of Europe had converted to coke.[17] Potash, paper, salt production, tar, pitch, turpentine, distilling, domestic heating and home construction, railroads, telegraph poles, coal mine pit-props, and, by the late nineteenth century, a growing timber export trade took an enormous cumulative toll on the forest cover.

The tribute-taking mode of the central government was imitated by all those who held power at the lower levels of authority. Michael Confino's old but classic study of the landed gentry argues that they had the aspirations and attributes of "grand proprietors" but the "mentality of petty exploiters."[18] Permeated by a spirit of mistrust of their peasants (which was reciprocated), the gentry—infused with the logic of tribute—subscribed to a peculiar calculus of value. They confused sales price with profit owing to their failure to account for the cost of peasant labor, which they treated as a free good. Serfdom consigned Russian agriculture to low yields combined with soil exhaustion, as nobles had neither the money to buy the best technologies nor the willingness to entrust complicated machinery to the serfs.[19]

Exploring the logic of gentry estate management, Confino identifies three core impulses: the desire for more income, the unwillingness to make timely investments and the lack of patience to wait for investments to bear yields, and, finally, their desire to preserve serfdom intact.[20] Because improvements could not be permitted to affect the social relations and labor customs of the estate, the gentry retained the persistent hope that the acclimatization of new cultivars would produce quick wealth through an agronomic miracle. Ivan Bolotov even recommended growing cotton in Russia "regardless of region."[21] Although not wantonly cruel for the most part, nobles structured their production and consumption in a way that left little in reserve for bad times. The famine of 1833–34, for example, led to mass deaths of both livestock and peasants. The nobles had to purchase replacement animals, making the estate's margin of viability even more threadbare.[22]

Unable to make their estates financially viable after the loss of their bonded labor following emancipation, many members of the gentry sold off their forests to timber merchants. According to the calculations of M. A. Tsvetkov, forest cover declined in European Russia from 52.7 percent, or 213,416,000 hectares, in 1696 to 35.16 percent, or 172,378,000 hectares, in 1914; some provinces, such as Tver', were almost totally deforested, declining from 75.8 percent forest cover to 22.6 percent over that period.[23] At every level, tribute takers, be they the bureaucratic monarchy in St. Petersburg, gentry on their estates, or chartered merchants, became dependent on expansion to new areas, on rent-seeking, or on confiscation—even of their own resources—as opposed to becoming more productive, developing new products, and penetrating new markets.

In an important and perceptive study, Jane Costlow notes that some sensitive Russian artists and writers—Nikolai Nekrasov, Il'ya Repin, Leo Tolstoy, Anton Chekhov, Ivan Shishkin, and others—understood the interconnection between deforestation and what she calls "larger structures of violence and individual tales of shirked responsibility" that characterized the larger society.[24] Repin's *Procession of the Cross in an Oak Wood*, Costlow observes, shows in clear emotional terms that "the *narod* [people, masses] and the trees are both victims of violence, and inhabit a desiccated, near-apocalyptic landscape."[25]

Although some historians of the Russian Empire have suggested that a new pattern finally began to emerge after the revolution of 1905, when Tsar Nicholas II was forced to accept limitations on his powers and the creation of an enfeebled legislature (the Duma), the state continued to use its enormous repressive power to maintain the near-servile conditions of labor in the empire's military-industrial complex. An enormous quantity of the accumulated wealth generated by the biological potential of the Russian land and embodied in the tsarist military-industrial complex was squandered in World War I; even more was consumed in the resultant social explosion and civil war that engulfed the country.[26]

By perpetuating the tribute-taking state with its short-term objectives, the tsarist empire made itself less secure, not more. Promising, by contrast, a "planned," "rational," and scientific governance, the new Soviet leaders ironically ended up perpetuating the same imperial tribute-taking system, with some interesting, but ultimately unavailing, modifications.

Perhaps the most important of the novelties introduced by the Bolsheviks was the pretense of planning. Actually, the promise of a "planned economy" first beckoned during World War I, when Russian politicians and academics eagerly began to imitate the efficient and even more dirigiste German war economy.[27] To a certain extent, the new Soviet rulers initially did promote a longer view of development, as manifested in the support for Vladimir Ivanovich Vernadskii's Radium Institute and for a comprehensive geological assay of the country through the Academy of Sciences' Commission on Natural Productive Forces (KEPS, later SOPS).[28] More surprisingly, the new Bolshevik regime extended its support to the young nature-protection movement. Where prerevolutionary advocates of this cause had also spoken of a "moral duty" to nature or enthused over the aesthetic qualities of sites that they sought to protect, after 1917, in order to appeal to the materialist and economic sensibilities of the new rulers, advocates highlighted the benefits to science and to rational economic planning that nature protection could proffer.[29]

Also, because nature protection was not usually regarded by the Soviets (or by later Communist regimes) as particularly politically charged (even though we might think that it should have been so viewed), a certain amount of unpoliced social space also opened up for mobilization in this area. Led by eminent field biologists, the Soviet nature-protection movement for many decades was the arena for a fascinating sociological drama. During the 1920s these scientists managed to win the confidence of cultural officials such as Anatolii Vasil'evich Lunacharskii, people's commissar for education of the Russian Soviet Federated Socialist Republic, and were able to gain the creation of the world's first national environmental-impact body, the Interagency State Committee for Nature Protection (1925–31), which had a right to assess and hold up economic projects that were found to cause unacceptable ecological harm. Lunacharskii also assisted in the emergence of the world's first network of protected territories exclusively dedicated to ecological and scientific study *(zapovedniki)*, which were projected to serve as baselines *(etalony)* of "healthy, integral ecological communities" against which changes in surrounding, human-affected areas could be compared. On the basis of these comparisons, it was hoped, scientists could recommend the most appropriate forms of land use for each major bioregion.[30]

By 1933 there were seventy republic- and local-level reserves across the Soviet Union with a total area of six million hectares (about fifteen million acres). Additionally, in 1924 an All-Russian Society for the Protection of Nature (VOOP) was founded, which from 1928 published the bimonthly journal *Okhrana prirody* (Protection of nature). Extensive foreign contacts were forged; Daniil Nikolaevich Kashkarov, a leading ecologist, even made a coast-to-coast tour of the U.S. national parks in 1929.[31]

In 1931, however, after Stalin's ascendancy, the Interagency Committee was abolished. Articles published in *Okhrana prirody* that implied that collectivization was unnecessary—claiming that biological control of pests through habitat protection and restoration could be just as effective in augmenting the harvest—were savaged as "land mines placed under socialist construction."[32] Recent scholarship has found strong evidence that scientist-activists began to link their own freedom with that of nature. After all, Gulag projects such as the Baltic–White Sea Canal (Belomorstroi) graphically demonstrated that violence and bondage for nature and for humans went hand in hand.[33] Courageously, nature-protection activists advanced arguments against giant hydropower projects, collectivization, and the "transformation of nature" even at the height of the first five-year plan (1928–32).

Tellingly, many of these great projects had their antecedents in the tsarist period. Collectivization, after all, was nothing more than the total reenserfment of the peasantry under a tribute regime so brutal that it generated a man-made famine in Ukraine and the North Caucasus in which between five and eight million people died (the worst modern tsarist-era famine in 1891–92 "only" killed half a million).[34] It is no surprise that most of the blueprints for Stalin's canals were developed under Peter I.[35] Because of uncooperative topography and late industrialization, railways became more cost-effective ways of shipping goods in the nineteenth century, and few canals were built before the 1930s. For Stalin, however, purely economic criteria or even engineering rationality often were not the bases for undertaking large-scale projects.

This mentality is reflected in Paul Josephson's textbook *Totalitarian Science and Technology*, which highlights a pervasive feature of Soviet technology: gigantomania. Projects seemed "to take on a life of their own, so important [were] they for cultural and political ends as opposed to the ends of engineering rationality."[36] And Loren Graham shows the path not taken in his poignant study of the suppression of a humanistic approach to engineering in the USSR in the late 1920s. That is when the first showcase of the five-year plan, the Dnepr hydroelectric station, was begun. Had the Soviets based their decision on economic rationality alone, they would have abandoned the megalithic single dam in favor of several smaller plants, including coal-fired ones, as many of their engineers were suggesting. However, "the final decision to go ahead with the giant dam was based not on technical and social analysis but on ideological and political pressure. Stalin and the top leaders of the Communist Party wanted the largest power plant ever built in order to impress the world and the Soviet population with their success and that of the coming Communist social order."[37]

Even more graphic illustrations of Stalin's display technologies were the railroad from Salekhard to Vorkuta, built at great human cost by laborers of the Gulag, which sank into the permafrost, and the notorious Baltic–White Sea Canal or Belomorstroi, which proved unnavigable by the warships and large freighters it was supposed to accommodate.

In a way, the economic rationality of the projects, conventionally understood, was almost beside the point. Their real raison d'être lay elsewhere. If the Soviet leaders ever had a clear vision of a Communist utopia, at its core presumably was the figuration of late nineteenth- and early twentieth-century British, German, and American industry, with rivers of steel flowing and smokestacks belching.[38]

Many in the Bolshevik Party were left unimpressed by "attractive pictures of stateless Communism" because it was a vision that seemed to belong to the far-distant future. Iakov Gol'tsman, representing what Thomas Remington has called the party's "technocratic left" wing, wholeheartedly supported Lenin's policies of extreme centralization against the challenge of "workers' control": "Impatient with theories of statelessness, committed to modernization, [Gol'tsman's] attitude typified a current of working-class sentiment which created a base of support for Soviet dictatorship among those proletarian activists whom the revolution had thrust into prominence." Because of this group's conviction that socialism was unthinkable without industrialization, they argued that some kind of primitive capital accumulation for investment and reinvestment was required. As we know, this view became dominant under Stalin, and Remington argues that "the extraction of surplus labor became the *goal* of socialism, because, according to one author, 'the development of the communist revolution is the development of the productive forces.'"[39]

Lenin's electrification plan exemplified the use of technology for the transformation of nature and people. According to Jonathan Coopersmith, electricity, it was thought, "would eradicate the cultural and economic chasm between town and country, a major target of Russia's Marxist modernizers." In Lenin's own words, "electrification . . . will make it possible to . . . overcome, even in the most remote corners of the land, backwardness, ignorance, poverty, disease, and barbarism." H. G. Wells quipped in 1920 that Lenin "has succumbed at last to a Utopia, the Utopia of the electricians."[40]

But this utopia of the electricians could not be built without investment capital, which the mixed economy of the 1920s (New Economic Policy) was not generating quickly enough for the impatient rulers. Taking a page from Ivan IV's playbook (Stalin later "edited" Sergei Eisenstein's cinematic portraiture of Ivan to make it more sympathetic), Stalin used brute force not simply to collectivize the peasants but also to extract from them the needed "surplus" investment capital in the form of grain, and millions perished in the resulting famine. To add to the irony, the Bolshevik regime had entirely appropriated the tsarist-era style of cost accounting that treated human labor as well as natural resources as free goods, despite paying lip service to Marx's theory of labor value.

At what juncture Soviet leaders ceased to believe in the Communist future is still an open question and a very complex one. Lenin's last essays reveal a distinct agnosticism about the quick success of the Soviet project. By the late 1930s, it was clear that the Soviet economy had failed to meet elementary demands for food and shelter. Nevertheless, the existing strategies of centralized planning, monumental projects, and hyper-industrialization were retained; the regime, it appears, perceived that these features were indispensable for building legitimacy, constructing new Soviet citizens, and justifying the self-perpetuation of the enormous administrative and managerial bureaucracy on which the regime's real power rested.[41]

Peter Rutland reaches a similar conclusion, namely, that "planning" served to mask "unwelcome contradictions" at the heart of the Soviet order. "Planning offers itself as a way of asserting man's control of the economic environment, and manages to disguise the fact that it is essentially uncontrollable. It provides a rudimentary work ethic—or, in Marxist terms, it justifies the extraction of surplus labor—by telling the workers that they are laboring not merely for the wages they receive, but also for the greater good of society, in particular for the future. It functions as a device of political legitimation, i.e., it provides a further answer to the perennial question of 'why should I obey my rulers?'"[42] In this context we could comfortably substitute "the conquest of nature" for "planning."

It is possible that "planning" and "the conquest of nature" were not originally devices for the self-perpetuation of the Bolshevik elite and their new system. "Bolshevik theories of social organization," notes Thomas Remington, "although inchoate at the time of October, always presupposed that commodity exchange would be replaced by an administrative authority guided by intelligent reason. The new state would dedicate itself to developing the great natural resources of Russia that the *ancien régime,* in its folly and incompetence, had failed to exploit."[43] No one bothered to consider how "rational" economic decisions were conjured or precipitated; no one thought about the possibility of a plurality of "rationalities." That "rationality" was a social construct—always relative to some specific referent—remained unexamined before the seizure of power.

The revolution's promise of a new world even led many to devise projects "to overcome the limits of physical nature." Inventors and crackpots hatched plans to create perpetual-motion machines, to melt the glaciers of the Pamir Mountains, to warm up the Arctic, to divert the course of entire rivers, and change the climate of Eurasia. Gravity, entropy, and even death would be overcome: at least one prominent Bolshevik, the engineer Leonid Krasin, an otherwise rather reasonable political figure, "publicly stated his belief that science would one day achieve the resurrection of the dead."[44]

Conquering nature, for early Soviet ideologues, itself meant conquering death—certainly through the collective participation in the building of a utopia, whose embodiment would be monuments of metal and concrete that would survive the ages, but sometimes also in a literal sense.[45] Although "personal immortality" did not currently exist, wrote the Soviet literary spokesman Maxim Gorky, we will yield to "people who will create a new, marvelous, bright life and, perhaps, through the miraculous force of fused wills, shall defeat death."[46] For the regime, free floating without a clear blueprint for the future, without the disciplines of global and domestic markets, and unable to supply the needs of the population, a basis for legitimacy had to be found in the cultivation of "new Soviet people" and the deployment of compelling myths that would inspire loyalty, or at least the patience to accept the long wait for Communism.

Irrespective of whether the Soviet leadership actually believed that immortality could be achieved, the production of new forms of selfhood was intimately bound up with the desire to expurgate all "spontaneous," unpredictable and ungovernable traits of the old humans. Personal self-aggrandizement and individualism, although lushly practiced by the leaders as well as the people, were publicly declared impermissible "bourgeois" qualities to be rooted out. Aleksei Gastev, perhaps the most extreme theorist of the new person, promoted an Institute of Labor whose curriculum included studies of social engineering, Frederick Taylor's methods, and psycho-technology. His model for the new humans was the machine.[47] Gastev celebrated the "Americanization" of the individual, by which he meant the transformation of the ordinary individual into a completely efficient machine. Anticipating an "amazing anonymity" among future proletarians, he hailed the "steadily expanding tendencies toward standardization" in society.[48]

We remember Gorky, however, and not Gastev, as the one who linked all these transformations—nature, society, and the individual—into a single, idealistic-sounding program of action while simultaneously crafting an immense mystification to benefit the Stalinist regime. In a series of newspaper essays during the late 1920s and early 1930s, Gorky returned to an old theme: the final triumph of rationality and consciousness over spontaneity. With the advent of socialism, he averred, chaos would be banished forever from the world. Swamps, predators, drought, snakes, deserts and other "unproductive" lands, "sleepy forests," Arctic ice, hurricanes, and earthquakes would all be eliminated.[49] The propagandist of a view that humanity was a collective "god," Gorky propounded that "Man is the bearer of energy that organizes the world, creating 'second nature'—culture; man is an organ of nature, created by her as if for the attainment of self-knowledge and transformation."[50] "Imagine," he wrote,

> that in the interests of the development of our industry it is necessary for us Russians to dig a . . . canal in order to link the Baltic Sea with the Black Sea. . . . And so instead of sending millions to be slaughtered, we send a portion of them to this work which is vital to the country. . . . I am confident that those killed during three years of war would have been able in this time to drain the . . . swamps in our country, to irrigate the Hungry Steppe and other deserts, to connect the rivers of the Trans-Urals with the Kama, to lay a road through the Caucasus Mountain ridge and to accomplish still other great feats of labor.[51]

Espousing what he called "geo-optimism," Gorky decried nature worship. "There is something 'primitive and atavistic' in the sight of humans bowing before nature's beauty."[52]

As Stalin's violent collectivization and the first five-year plan were set in motion, Gorky's calls for the transformation of nature became more strident. "We live in a world of wonders created . . . by that consummate revolutionary and wonder-worker: reason," he exulted in "Drought Shall Be Annihilated," an article that appeared in a major daily. Humans were "omnipotent," and "there hardly exists anything impossible for the rational will of millions of people directed toward a single goal."[53] Declaring "a war to the death" against nature, Gorky in another article fumed that "the blind drive of nature to produce on earth every kind of useless or even harmful trash—must be stopped and eradicated."[54] "First nature" and "everything elemental (spontaneous)" would be effaced and transformed into rationally planned "second nature." Reflecting a profoundly monocultural vision in all respects, Gorky celebrated the disappearance of the "mottled impoverishment" of rural Russia: "The light-bluish strips of oats and, alongside them, a black parcel of upturned earth, then a golden strip of rye, and a greenish one of wheat, and, in general, a multicolored sadness of general fragmentation. . . . In our day huge expanses of land are colored more powerfully, in only one color."[55] This transformation of nature could reinscribe plastic and impressionable human nature, lectured Gorky. "Upbringing, my friends," he proclaimed, "is omnipotent!"[56]

Gorky inaugurated the new literary agenda with the "collectively written" apologia for the Baltic–White Sea Canal, whose motto—"In transforming nature, man transforms himself"—he personally coined.[57] An early major project of the Gulag, the canal functioned more as an icon of modernity than as a practical military or economic facility. Praising the secret police operatives of the GPU (Glavnoe Politicheskoe Upravlenie, or Main Political Administration) as "engineers of human souls," Gorky saw them as agents who were purging the hundreds of thousands of prisoner-laborers of their "elemental" backward qualities and peasant individualism and transforming them into productive "new Soviet people."[58] "These grandiose projects," he wrote, "directing the physical energy of the mass to a struggle with nature, . . . permit people to come into contact with their essential mission in life—the mastery of the forces of nature so as to put an end to their rabidity."[59]

In this drama of transformation, nature was cast as the enemy. However, nature had met its match. Pictured as an omnipotent and omniscient planner of whole continents, Stalin makes a cameo appearance in Gorky's *Belomor*. "Stalin holds a pencil. Before him lies a map of the region. Deserted shores. Remote villages. Virgin soil, covered with boulders. Primeval forests. Too much forest, as a matter of fact; it covers the best soil. And swamps. The swamps are always crawling about, making life dull and slovenly. Tillage must be increased. The swamps must be drained. . . . The Karelian Republic wants to enter the stage of classless society as a republic of factories and mills. And the Karelian Republic *will* enter classless society by changing its own nature."[60]

Whether Gorky, or Stalin, authentically believed by 1933 that such pharaonic projects could really produce the people of the future we cannot know. However, the projects did promote other strategic goals of the regime. Together with the real or imagined military enemies of the USSR, nature could always be cast in the role of enemy. This view provided the justification for mobilizing the population periodically for enormous campaigns such as the Great Stalin Plan for the Transformation of Nature, Nikita Khrushchev's Virgin Lands campaign, his construction of the Bratsk Dam in Siberia, Leonid Brezhnev's plan to reroute Siberian rivers southward, and his construction of the ill-fated Baikal-Amur railroad. Writing about the civil war period (1918–21), Remington noted that "each round of mobilization sought to unlock some hidden store of energy but produced an even greater countereffect in the form of bribery, black markets, hoarding, speculation, deception, and small-scale enterprise. Thus mobilization reduced the aggregate quantity of usable resources."[61] The same could be said of all the subsequent campaigns.

By contrast with their more nakedly pragmatic analogues in the United States, Soviet acclimatization and predator control were part of a vast "plan" to reinvent nature, turning it into the obedient servant of human society. In 1929 the academician Nikolai Kashchenko wrote: "The final goal of acclimatization, understood in the broad sense, is a profound rearrangement of the entire living world—not only that portion which is now under the domination of humanity but also that portion that has still remained wild. Generally speaking, all wild species will disappear with time; some will be exterminated, others will be domesticated. All living nature will live, thrive, and die at none other than the will of humans and according to their designs. These are the grandiose perspectives that open up before us."[62]

The writer and engineer Mikail Ilin wrote a best-selling book about the "struggle against nature." Ilin celebrated Soviets as "Conqueror[s] of their Own Country" and predicted that "within a few years all the maps of the USSR will have to be revised. In one place there will be a new river . . . in another a new lake. . . . Man will transform deserts, change water flows, and even create new species of plants and animals. . . . Man must fight the river," he admonished, "as the animal-tamer fights wild beasts."[63] That these words were not simply the utterances of academic cranks and writers is demonstrated by the vast state-sponsored campaigns for the acclimatization of exotics (including the mink, muskrat, nutria, and raccoon dog) and for predator elimination, both of which extended even into the supposedly inviolable nature reserves.[64] An order to exterminate all foxes in Ukraine was issued as late as 1958.[65] It is not difficult to hear in this, and in Trofim Denisovich Lysenko's myriad schemes, an echo of the old gentry dream that an agronomic miracle would save the decrepit estate without requiring structural changes in power relations or labor practices.[66]

Wildfire control policy represented another such campaign. The absolutist Soviet state mounted an absolute war against natural fire. By 1972, Stephen Pyne informs us, controlled burning by peasants was outlawed by the Brezhnev regime, and the state's fire brigades patrolled the skies, constituting the "largest wildland firefighting system in the world." Fires continued to burn, however, and were compounded by the furtive nature of controlled burning after 1972 as well as by the choking lack of information, including essential meteorological information. The sole reliance on fire suppression set the stage for the monumental 1987 fire in the Transbaikal region, which has been estimated to have burned over about 12 million hectares (although official reports put the area at 92,000 hectares at first and 290,000 hectares later). As Pyne insightfully concludes: "Aerial fire suppression was, in the final analysis, a political institution, an expression of the state's geopolitical will. It responded to the political ecology of a totalitarian regime."[67]

In the nineteenth century, Russian elites, unable to imagine a structurally different order, also placed their hopes for prosperity and modernity on the development of southern Siberia, along the Amur River.[68] Ultimately, they hoped that a new orientation, toward the Pacific, would transform Russia into a second United States. However, as Mark Bassin has shown, these hopes were not founded on credible geographical knowledge of Russia's Far East. This kind of wishful thinking in Russia was not limited to the nineteenth century. In fact, it reached its apogee under the Soviets—witness Stalin's infamous Arctic railroad and the more recent Baikal-Amur railroad. Although our geographies are socially constructed, not all imagined geographies are equal: there *is* still a material world out there against which we more than occasionally bump our heads. To the great cost of the Soviet human population as well as to flora and fauna, Stalin often acted and spoke as if the constraints of material reality did not matter; his was the ultimate "geography of the mind."

So strong was the regime's insistence that it was all-knowing and all-powerful that it was even prepared to defy the consensus of international science in a range of disciplines. Acting in the name of the regime, Lysenko and Isai Izrailovich Prezent's first major denunciatory campaign was launched against ecology as a science. As it happened, the leading ecologist of the day, Vladimir Vladimirovich Stanchinskii, scientific director of the Askania-Nova *zapovednik,* had advanced scientific arguments from both ecology and genetics against the acclimatization of exotic fauna. After a visit to Askania-Nova by Lysenko and Prezent in the late summer of 1933, Stanchinskii and his team were arrested as "counterrevolutionaries."[69] Not surprisingly, Lysenko and Prezent then turned to the suppression of genetics, a campaign that was crowned with success in 1948 after Stalin personally intervened. This disregard for expert counsel, particularly when such counsel implied higher costs for the regime's pet projects in order to protect humans or other "nonproduction values," was a red thread that ran through Soviet economic practices from the 1930s to perestroika.

The hostility to any limitation on the Party and state's freedom to transform and "reinvent" nature is reflected in a remark made by the chairman of a 1930s Party purge commission to Mikhail Petrovich Potemkin, a Communist and former president of the All-Russian Society for the Protection of Nature, during Potemkin's interrogation: "How can you," demanded the purge commission chair, "a member of the Party, have become involved in a cause like conservation?"[70]

Interesting parallels exist between the histories of Soviet nature protection and those of pollution control and public health during the 1920s and 1930s, although the two communities of discourse remained almost completely separate. A scientist-led field, with 1,600 public health physicians (in 1928) and environmental chemists at its core, actively pursued novel technical means of treating industrial wastes while insisting that the regime proceed with caution in its drive to industrialize. About forty research institutes were concerned with problems of air, water, and soil quality by the mid-1930s, and there was even an All-Union Conference for the Preservation of Clean Air in Kharkov in 1935. Wastewater recycling was proposed in 1934.[71]

Again, however, the repressive thirties had their dampening effect on this field. When one expert wrote in 1930 that "a new substance may be broadly introduced only after it has been determined by appropriate scientific and technical research institutes that it is harmless," the director of the All-Union Institute for Labor Hygiene and Organization rebutted: "If we took Professor Koiranskii's proposal seriously, then this would be tantamount to placing a 'veto'—in the name of science—over the industrial introduction of a whole array of new substances and new chemical production processes."[72]

The later 1930s saw mass repressions of scientists, physicians, and public figures in this area, beginning with the former chief public health inspector of the USSR and minister of public health, Grigorii Naumovich Kaminskii, whose battle to protect workers and other citizens from hazardous industrial pollution ended with his arrest in 1937 and subsequent execution. By July 1939, Vice-Premier Andrei Ianuar'evich Vyshinskii responded to entreaties for a law setting pollution standards with the rejoinder that "we have the Stalin Constitution. That is sufficient to ensure that our public hygiene and public health are the best in the world."[73]

Just as protection from pollution was textual or iconic and not real, so were some campaigns to transform nature. With the announcement of the Great Stalin Plan for the Transformation of Nature in October 1948, provinces in the steppe region were given targets of acreage for shelterbelt plantings. Vladimir Boreiko describes how the Ukrainian SSR, seeking to fulfill its plan for the Belgorod-Don shelterbelt, spent a good deal of money on an artistically designed billboard featuring the slogans of Stalin and other party leaders on the campaign. Bitterly he concludes: "It all fits. If you are producing for people, you strive for quality. If you are producing for fools, you produce something for show."[74] Because the Soviet system was not able to produce for consumers, it had to produce for show and produce a public which could consume the virtual reality.

The industrial and hydraulic models for these icons of "successful" modernity were appropriated from abroad. Because of the absence of an organic, self-propelling economic dynamism within the Soviet economy, innovations had to be borrowed continually from outside.[75] Peter Rutland writes: "Much of this 'learning from America' was largely rhetorical, but one can nevertheless see that in certain respects Soviet planners have adjusted their priorities through observation of the changing world market—the introduction of chemicals, plastics, and fertilizers, for example. But the dominant tendency in priority setting has been inertia . . . the priorities laid down in the early 1930s."[76] Although such practices assured the reproduction of the *apparat* (bureaucracy) and therefore reflected the *political* rationality of the Soviet system, they ultimately cannibalized the economy and exhausted resources, with industry essentially only able to produce enough to keep itself going.

Sham communalism resulted in a repressed and intensified egoism and survivalist mentality based on kinship, small groups of friends, and clientelism, which set the stage for today's Mafia.[77] In actuality a perpetuation of tsarist serfdom, the Soviet tribute-taking system deepened a general lack of empathy, an inability to assume responsibility, and a dangerous environment for workers and the general public. Inspired by the work of Ulrich Beck, the sociologist Oleg Yanitsky characterizes Russia as the ultimate "risk society" which had sustained "genetic damage" during the long period of totalitarianism.[78] "Over the course of eighty years," Yanitsky writes, "[the USSR] was used as a testing ground for the most divergent model schemes of modernization." By the fall of the Communist regime, an area occupying 2.5 million square kilometers of the territory of the Russian Federation, or 15 percent, was considered to represent "an acute ecological situation."[79] In this area lived 20 percent of the nation's population, sixty million, and sixty-eight cities were deemed "dangerous" by Goskompriroda (the USSR State Committee for Environmental Education). In sixteen of these cities, the concentration of air pollutants was more than fifty times the norm.[80] Safe drinking water was a particularly low priority, with only 30 percent of wastes satisfactorily treated and with such major cities as Baku, Riga, and Dnepropetrovsk lacking sewage systems.[81] In Russia alone, one million tons of lethal chemicals are stored in dubious conditions of security at more than 3,500 sites. Contaminated nuclear sites, aside from the region affected by Chernobyl, include Kyshtym in the Urals, the site of a 1957 disaster;[82] Krasnoyarsk; Tomsk Oblast; and the eastern coast of Novaya Zemlya, to name only the most seriously polluted areas.

Agriculture is another prime case of the workings of the tribute economy. Again in Russia in 1989, 60 million hectares of agricultural land were eroded, 42 million hectares had elevated acidity, and another 36 million hectares were saline. The lack of economic criteria of utility or efficiency promoted an "extensive" mode of development (for example, to increase agricultural production, you cultivate more land rather than intensify production on currently cultivated land) and a disregard for such inputs as resources, labor, and appropriate techniques. Attempting to explain the discounting of resource costs and environmental externalities in Soviet-type economies, Marshall Goldman and others argued that Marxian economic dogmas such as the labor theory of value acted as constraints on economic actors.[83] Indirectly responding to this view, Joan DeBardeleben's influential study *The Environment and Marxism-Leninism* demonstrated that Marxist-Leninist dogma could (and was beginning to) accommodate the costing of resources and externalities as well as other environmental values.[84] Regrettably, the dogma's relative flexibility made little difference in the world of practices or outcomes. That is because, in the end, outcomes are governed by political economy and actual power relations— an old Marxian saw that still cuts some wood. In the last analysis, Marxism was just a fig leaf covering an insidiously plunderous iteration of Russia's traditional tribute-taking mode of economic organization.

Closely researched multifactoral case studies of actual environmental policy making and practices (as opposed to often-meaningless decrees and regulations) have provided illuminating analyses of the political economy of the Soviet Union. Amid the growing literature in this area, two studies by Thane Gustafson capture the complexities of Soviet decision making. His first book, on water policies, amplified the point made a decade earlier by H. Gordon Skilling: that Soviet officials' visions of how to pursue economic development, among other things, diverged significantly according to the specific economic sectors for which they bore responsibility—and, we might add, from which they skimmed their tribute.[85] Because natural resources, even renewable ones such as water, are ultimately finite, and certain uses of rivers, such as water storage for hydropower, work at cross-purposes with other uses—such as shipping, fishing, and irrigation—policy conflicts emerged. These conflicts reflected the physical impossibility of simultaneously maximizing all uses and cast a long shadow on the regime's dream of transcending the "kingdom of necessity" through the directed transformation of nature. They also revealed the cost-benefit logic of the regime as it was inexorably forced to trade off some goals against others.

More often than not, those trade-offs were for short-term advantage, with heavy disregard for serious long-term costs. A classic example of this was the autarkic decision to turn Central Asia into a supplier of the Soviet Union's cotton. The goal of cotton self-sufficiency for the USSR was first proposed by Lenin in 1918. However, it was under Stalin that the regime undertook to "bridle" the Amu Darya and Syr Darya rivers for this purpose, in the words of the Uzbek Party secretary Usman Yusupov. Later, under Khrushchev, the regime extended the irrigation to Turkmenistan, building the unlined Karakum Canal (whose seepage rate was 50 percent). It was a classic case of imperialist land use: by the 1970s Central Asia could no longer feed itself, owing to the substitution of cotton for food crops accompanied by rapid population increase. Now, owing to the salinization of soils as a result of overwatering and poor drainage, much of the best agricultural land has been poisoned.[86]

If that were not bad enough, the unconstrained withdrawal of water from the two rivers has resulted in a regional environmental catastrophe on a par with Chernobyl: the disappearance of the Aral Sea. Barely fifty years ago, the Aral was the fourth largest lake in the world, covering an area of 66,000 square kilometers with a volume of 1,061.6 cubic kilometers and a salinity level of 10 parts per 1,000. Now, the Aral Sea is almost gone. For almost a decade, it has consisted of two shrinking ponds: in 1998 its total area was 28,687 square kilometers and its volume 181 cubic kilometers. Owing to the unprecedented evaporation, salinity in the lake has increased more than fourfold, to 45 parts per 1,000. Fishing, once the major industry of the region, has disappeared from the southern Uzbek basin. Large, rusting trawlers lie stranded, listing on the dry seabed, looking like a scene out of a science-fiction movie. It is difficult to imagine that forty-odd years ago the annual catch exceeded forty thousand metric tons.

The entire regional landscape underwent disastrous transformation. A toxic, manmade lake, Sarykamysh, with an area of three thousand square kilometers, was formed by the discharge of drainage water from the cotton fields. The *tugai* floodplain, a species-rich habitat of tall reeds, tamarisks, poplars, willows, and oleasters, was desiccated. Of 170 indigenous species of mammals, a mere 38 still inhabit the region, perhaps themselves doomed to go the way of the extinct Amu Darya tiger.

Epidemiologically, too, the desiccation of the Aral Sea has been a catastrophe. From the exposed seabed, tens of millions of tons of sands laden with salts, pesticides, fertilizers, and other chemicals—precipitates from irrigation wastewater discharged over decades—are carried annually to fields and towns. Dust storms, perhaps the result of regional climate change caused by the lake's disappearance, afflict the region as well. Worst hit has been the Autonomous Republic of Karakalpakstan (in Uzbekistan), bordering the former sea. A recent statistic noted that 111 children per 1,000 die before their first birthday.[87] As clean water has disappeared, viral hepatitis and typhoid fever have become widespread, as have anemia, cancers, and tuberculosis.

Finally, the desiccation of the sea poses another, global danger. During the Cold War the Soviet army tested and stored biological weapons on Vozrozhdenie Island, once located in the middle of the lake and now only three kilometers from the shore. Among the organisms were Ebola virus, plague, anthrax, smallpox, Marburg fever, and a host of other lethal diseases. No one gave a thought to the possibility that one day there might be no lake to isolate the facility. One accidental release could trigger a worldwide pandemic.

When the Party bosses of Central Asia, who had profited for decades from the cotton monoculture, realized that the Aral Sea was disappearing, they sought to counteract the damage by proposing a transfer of water from northward-flowing Siberian rivers such as the Irtysh and Ob' to their region. It was a typical reaction: solve your immediate problem by creating another one whose solution can be deferred. First considered by the Aral-Caspian Expedition of the USSR Academy of Sciences in April 1950, the proposed Sibaral Canal, dubbed "the project of the century," would have stretched for 2,200 kilometers across the Turgai trough, delivering water to the Aral. Because it considered the entire country its patrimony and therefore its testing ground, the Communist Party leadership endorsed the project, along with a similar project to divert north-flowing European rivers and waters south, to irrigate Ukraine, Kalmykia, and the North Caucasus, and to stem a further drop in the level of the Caspian Sea. Each unforeseen and undesirable consequence of the tribute-takers' "planning" was addressed by displacing the problem onto some other region, sector, or generational cohort.

When the unprecedented water diversions were proposed and then endorsed by the Brezhnev regime as another "project of the century," scientists warned of possible global-scale consequences. Such an abrupt cutoff of warmer river water to the Arctic Ocean could alter the entire heat balance of the planet, some cautioned; others drew attention to the vast amount of agricultural land in southern Siberia that would be flooded in connection with the damming of the Ob' and Irtysh rivers. Only an increasingly desperate public outcry convinced the new Soviet leaders—Mikhail Sergeevich Gorbachev and Nikolai Ivanovich Ryzhkov—to cancel the project. That decision, taken on August 20, 1986, was Gorbachev's first major signal to the educated public that there was really some kind of change in the offing. Because the Central Asian republics have been unable to shift their agricultural economies away from cotton and rice to more traditional orchard crops, the Aral Sea is now certain to disappear completely within the next two decades. At no point did the Soviet leaders or their comprador vice gerents in Central Asia look back—or forward. The crucial question is, When did a picture of the costs, or trade-offs, of development come into view? For it was then that a transparent debate should have been held. But then, transparency has never been a strong point of the militarized tribute-taking state.

In *Crisis amid Plenty*, Thane Gustafson showed how this complicated weighing of risks and trade-offs played out in energy policy. The Soviet leadership's pursuit of growth to maintain the system and shore up its legitimacy turned out to require dangerous short-term reorientations in investment. Because of existing inefficiencies, embodied in shoddy, obsolete technologies and wasteful practices, extracting or producing the energy needed to run the Soviet and CMEA (Council for Mutual Economic Assistance, or Comecon) economies required ever more exorbitant investments in the energy sector, squeezing production of consumer goods and severely limiting other investment options.

At the end of World War II the regime was presented with a windfall: the discovery of the world's second largest oil field at Samotlor in western Siberia. However, its short-term perspective led the regime to pump the field with water to extract the oil faster. By the mid-1980s, when production was at its peak, a barrel of West Siberian crude cost more to get out of the ground than it could be sold for on the world market. Nevertheless, the regime's desperation for hard-currency earnings—to purchase the food for its people that its devastated collective-farm sector could not produce—caused it to expand drilling maximally. Rather than pump out old wells more efficiently, it wastefully opened new wells. Billions of barrels of oil in the ground are now admixed with water, making future recovery extremely expensive. Because labor was used profligately in the oil fields, hundreds of thousands of people by the 1990s found themselves stuck in the world's largest Arctic swamp. Vast areas are polluted.[88] As Gorbachev found out, the investments required to make the economy more energy efficient, and thereby more durable over the long run, required intolerable short-term sacrifices on the part of the population; by the late 1980s there was almost no room to maneuver.

Precisely this desperate set of choices around energy led to the overly hasty and careless process by which the reactors at Chernobyl, for example, were designed, promoted, and allowed to go on line, as Zhores Medvedev shows.[89] In his masterful analysis of the largest industrial accident in history, Medvedev demonstrates how the crude quality of Soviet industrial welding dictated a vulnerable design, how nuclear power represented a fix for a system that squandered energy against a backdrop of steeply increasing costs for extraction of hydrocarbons and coal, and how a culture of fear and distorted information flow impeded the safe testing of a retrofitted emergency cooling system. Like the dilemma over irrigation and river diversions, the Soviet and Eastern European energy question was not simply about a natural resource; it was about the nature of the entire political and economic system.[90] Once the patrimonial regime had set its goals, the only question was how to attain them, even if all the available choices were fraught with high risk for present and future generations.

Certainly the symbolic use of technology and the arrogant, autocratic style of decision making are crucial parts of the Soviet environmental legacy. Another, however, is the pervasive militarization of the Soviet state from its very inception. Although official Soviet historians and others have long argued that "capitalist encirclement" and foreign intervention "forced" a civil war on a reluctant infant Bolshevik experiment, it is equally possible to find quotes from Lenin proving that he understood that a civil war would almost inexorably follow a Bolshevik seizure of power—and welcoming that prospect.[91] In any event, by 1921 the Bolshevik regime had already acquired a distinctly militarized profile. Equally important, the civil war provided the justification (in all senses of the term) for the imposition of an unrelenting regime of requisitioning on the peasantry, along with the forcible suppression of strikes and of independent unions, all other political parties, elected soviets, and factory councils.

Although the tsarist regime had begun the production of mustard gas in 1915, Soviet-German military cooperation during the 1920s renewed work on chemical weapons under the supervision of the OGPU, or secret police.[92] That work later expanded to the testing and production of biological weapons, one consequence of which was the accidental release of anthrax near the city of Sverdlovsk (Ekaterinburg, population one million) in April 1979, causing 64 officially reported (and, according to one scholarly estimate, 36,000) deaths.[93]

The military-industrial complex represented 30 to 35 percent of the total Soviet budget. However, its shadow over the economy was even greater. The military-industrial complex commandeered up to 70 percent of the metalworking sector for its needs and used 45 percent of the electricity in the country, 50 percent of all metal, and 30 percent of all motor transport. Little of the country's high technology saw its way to the civilian sector; the military-industrial complex monopolized more than 90 percent. Between 50 and 70 percent of all industrial production went to serve military needs. As of January 1, 1990, the number of men under arms in the various military services was 8.5 million, with 4.5 million more in reserves. As noted, the energy needs of this sector were enormous. Products of the 440 active and 85 demobilized atomic power stations (55 more are under construction), spent fuel and wastes now amount to 8,700 tons in about 100 storage sites.[94]

Incalculable areas of land have been poisoned by the Soviet military-industrial complex. More than 90,000 square kilometers in Russia alone, not counting Kazakstan, have been badly polluted by the space program. An estimated 660,000 square kilometers has been used for military maneuvers, including 200,000 in Kazakstan. Perhaps physical compacting of the land is the least of the problems; there is also heavy pollution in these test areas from fuel discharges, uranium, and lead. An additional 60,000 square kilometers was set aside for special military hunting areas.[95]

Owing to the considerable fuel needs of the military (11.8 million tons of reactive fuel in 1987—still far less than the U.S. military's 18.6 million tons),[96] oil and gas fields have been exploited with little concern for the environmental consequences. As a result, enormous areas of the sensitive West Siberian tundra have been badly polluted. At least sixteen regions of the former Soviet Union are badly polluted: the Aral Sea region; areas affected by Chernobyl fallout, extending into Belarus (Gomel') and even Russia (Briansk); the Sea of Azov; the Donbas coal and iron region of Ukraine; the entire republic of Moldova; the Black Sea and its littoral; the Caspian Sea; the Kalmyk Autonomous Republic; the Volga River; the Kola Peninsula; the Urals region; the Kuzbas coal region; Lake Baikal; the Moscow region; the Fergana Valley in Central Asia; and the Semipalatinsk nuclear testing region (now Semei) in eastern Kazakstan. Novaya Zemlya and the Arctic Ocean could be added to this list.[97] It is estimated that only 15 percent of Russia's urbanites live in places that meet official clean-air standards. In the worst-affected areas, such as the city of Sterlitamak, birth defects are so rampant that only 16 percent of births are considered totally normal.[98]

Atmospheric as well as subterranean testing of nuclear weapons has left scars on the human population and landscape. One of the saddest legacies is that of Kazakstan, which endured 450 nuclear tests (119 above ground) between August 29, 1949 and October 19, 1989, until they were stopped under pressure from a powerful grassroots antinuclear movement in the late 1980s. Dangerous radiation exposure left hundreds of thousands of people to cope with birth defects and cancer rates of epidemic proportions. In addition, nearly twenty million hectares of land have become unusable. Eighty nuclear tests have taken place on the fragile Arctic archipelago of Novaya Zemlya, whose mainland and shallow coastal shelf also constituted a "dumping ground for enormous amounts of radioactive and mixed waste": up to 17,000 containers (150,000 cubic meters) of liquid radioactive waste, plus possibly fifteen old or damaged nuclear reactors, some still containing fuel. When a mass die-off of starfish and seals in the White Sea occurred in 1990, many saw it as the result of nuclear dumping.[99] The litany of environmental ills occasioned by the Soviet military-industrial complex would fill a very large book. But perhaps the most arresting point of all is that the military-industrial complex represented the *most efficient* sector of the Soviet economy.

LATE PERESTROIKA:
A NEW BEGINNING STIFLED

Whatever Gorbachev's intentions, perestroika opened the door to new political possibilities. In the aftermath of the elections to the Congress of People's Deputies in March 1989 and right through the summer of 1990, it was still possible to believe that the Soviet Union would lead the way to an enlightened alternative to both Reagan/Thatcher-style capitalism and neo-Stalinism. After all, hadn't the Soviet electorate sent the biggest delegation of world-class intellectuals to a national legislature since the French and American revolutions? Andrei Sakharov, Nikolai Vorontsov, Galina Starovoitova, Roy A. Medvedev, Sergei Zalygin, Roald Sagdeev, and Aleksei Yablokov were only the tip of the iceberg. In the summer following the 1989 elections, Gorbachev's prime minister, Nikolai Ryzhkov, named Nikolai Nikolaevich Vorontsov, an eminent zoologist, to head the USSR State Committee for Environmental Protection. When the state committee was upgraded to a ministry in 1991, Vorontsov became the first non-Communist member of a Soviet government since the spring of 1918. Although saddled with an obstructive and parasitical bureaucracy within his agency which he was politically unable to remove, Vorontsov named able non-Party scientists, such as Aleksandr Bazykin and V. A. Krasilov, to key posts and pushed to reform thoroughly the norms and values of the environmentally hazardous Soviet economy.[100]

The fall of 1990, however, was the start of a cruel and disappointing period for the former Soviet intelligentsia. Hard-liners gained the ascendancy within

Gorbachev's regime, and Vorontsov was almost completely isolated. Foreign Minister Eduard Shevardnadze quit, warning of a crackdown, and soon thereafter Soviet forces imposed repressive measures in the Baltic republics. To his credit, Vorontsov did not give up when things started to unravel. Instead, he tried to inject the perspective of a natural scientist, a biologist, and an expert on organic evolution. This perspective was one that was shaped in great measure by his teachers and mentors from the nature-protection movement of the 1920s through the 1950s, who in their time had also tried to guide policy in a more humane direction on the basis of their own understanding of science. Two examples of the way that Vorontsov's science influenced his positions on political and diplomatic issues were his efforts to keep some kind of federal connection among the successor states to the USSR and his promotion of binational *zapovedniki* on Soviet and later on Russian borders. These undertakings may both be understood as flowing from his conviction that natural history constitutes the original and most enduring common human language, and that the protection of the environment is humanity's most fundamental common concern.

RUSSIA AND THE SUCCESSOR STATES

Despite his heroism during the August 1991 coup, Vorontsov was not kept on as newly independent Russia's environmental minister. Perhaps this was because he had broken a political rule in publicly revealing and criticizing the Soviet army's secret nuclear test on Novaya Zemlya. Vorontsov's colleague at the Institute for Developmental Biology, Aleksei Yablokov, who had become Boris Yeltsin's environmental adviser, was also pushed out by 1993. Viktor Danilov-Danelian, a colorless engineer, was named minister of environmental protection. The tribute-takers had placed one of their own back in the job.

Under a barrage of propaganda emanating as much from the Western leaders and media (particularly the *Wall Street Journal* and the *New York Times*) as from the Russian and post-Soviet press, readers and viewers were led to believe that a fundamental restructuring of the political economies of Russia and the other post-Soviet states had taken place with the fall of Communism.[101] Now, more than a decade later, with large sectors of the Soviet Union's former industrial sector cannibalized to pay for a short-term consumption orgy by the "new Russians" and their post-Soviet counterparts in other republics, there is a growing recognition that despite new labels, the old tribute system has remained in place. If anything, the system's predatory features became more exaggerated as the older unitary hierarchy, enforced by the Communist Party, broke down, and a fierce jockeying for advantage ensued. In many regions, "tribute wars" broke out. Part of the issue in the two bloody wars over Chechnya was the question of who was to control lucrative franchises, such as oil refineries and pipelines.[102] Recent conflicts in Eurasia, especially within the newly independent states (Ukraine, Georgia, Russia, Moldova, and Tajikistan), whether as wars for ethnic independence, gang wars, or peaceful "political" struggles, have pitted warlords, with their own Mafia federations, against each other for the right to loot the contested territories.[103] Although state gangsterism has unquestionably made a relative few very wealthy and very powerful, it has pauperized and debilitated the state in its legitimate, civilian functions: assuring the health, safety, and well-being of the population at large and investing in their future. The immense scale of the post-1991 tribute taking has undermined the state's ability to collect legitimate taxes.

This situation has led to deindustrialization as well as the slashing of funding for science, education, public health, and the environment. One consequence of the decline of investment in industry is that the average age of the industrial plant has increased, and technologically generated accidents rose almost sixfold between 1991 and 1996.[104] Nonpayment of electricity bills has led utilities to shut off power to clients such as the Plisetsk rocket-testing facility in Arkhangelskaya Oblast in 1994, the Murmansk submarine base a year later (the admiral had his troops storm the power station), a strategic-weapons unit in Ivanovskaya Oblast in 2000 (again with a military seizure of the power station), and to the Central Urals copper-smelting refinery in Pervoural'sk in August 1998. This last incident caused a series of accidents, including a dangerous discharge of sulfur dioxide gas, which poisoned crops on five collective farms and provoked asthma attacks in the population. The chief engineer of the smelter led a small private army of Pinkertons in a seizure of that power station. An even more dramatic accident occurred in November 1999 in the same Ekaterinburg (Sverdlovsk) Oblast, when a power shut-off disabled pumps that emptied wastewater from a mineral processing plant's holding reservoir. After the coffer dam burst, the swirling waters washed away a gas line, power lines, and a bridge, and flooded apartments.[105]

Meanwhile, toxic wastes increased from 67.5 million metric tons in 1993 to 108.9 million tons in 1999, despite an unprecedented peacetime *decline* in gross industrial production of 50.9 percent. Yet, because investment in 1999 was only 23.2 percent of that of 1990, reuse and treatment of these wastes declined from 46.5 percent to 31.7 percent of waste generated. Levels of polluted wastewater generation are 74.4 percent of 1990 levels, and only 20 percent of the water treatment capacity of 1990 is in operation.[106] Perhaps the only reason that Vladimir Putin, in a moment of high drama, cast Russia's deciding vote to launch the Kyoto Protocol was the fact that his nation's carbon emissions were relatively low as a result of the unprecedented deindustrialization.

Budget allocations for science continue their downward trends, representing a shrinking percentage of a shrinking budget. Almost 40 percent of the State Hydrometeorological Service's environmental-quality measuring facilities were closed between 1991 and 1997.[107] Perhaps the logical final step was Vladimir Putin's complete elimination of the Ministry for Environmental Protection in 2000. Its functions were taken over by the Ministry for Natural Resources, a move in many ways similar to Stalin's termination of the Interagency State Committee for Nature Protection in 1931. Uzbekistan similarly eliminated its environmental ministry. American, Swedish, Korean, Japanese and other firms have not wasted time gaining access to lucrative resources in the extractive industries (including forests, oil and gas, fishing, and mining) of the former Soviet Union. Was the West's environmental critique of Communism just a ploy?[108]

Continuing to overreach domestically and on the world stage, the leaders of the Soviet Union did not feel that they had the "luxury" to protect their own people or their environment. They left a train of catastrophes in their wake. The current leaders of post-Soviet Eurasia are to an astonishing degree holdovers and products of the previous Communist system. Now they have shed the red flag and have draped themselves in national colors. Most claim to be democrats and supporters of the free market. In reality, they have simply found it to their advantage to establish successor khanates to the former Soviet "Golden Horde."[109]

In geopolitical terms, the disappearance of the Soviet Union seemed to promise a safer planet. Environmentally speaking, however, that conclusion is extremely questionable. The balkanization of Eurasian territory has had the effect of dividing water basins into national segments, often precluding any kind of coordinated management policy. Where the Caspian Sea had effectively been divided between two countries, Iran and the USSR, it is now partitioned five ways, among Kazakstan, Russia, Azerbaijan, Iran, and Turkmenistan, with growing prospects of conflicts over oil and gas. Unpoliceable Mafia clans smuggle plutonium, nuclear-weapons components, and conventional weapons, aided by distribution networks that circle the globe. Finally, the misery that has accompanied the abject dispossession of tens of millions has already contributed to the resurgence of drug-resistant tuberculosis, to outbreaks of cholera, and to a growing AIDS epidemic. Eurasia, like Africa, could well become the site of the world's next pandemic.

COULD THE ENVIRONMENTAL
MOVEMENT CHANGE RUSSIA?

The members of the nature-protection movement of the Soviet Union displayed great courage. The All-Russian Society for the Protection of Nature even survived multiple attempts under Stalin to eliminate it. Where issues of nationality intruded, nature-protection advocates were under double threat. Vladimir Evgen'evich Boreiko's meticulously researched studies on the fate of nature protection in Ukraine paint a bleak picture. All of the voluntary scientific and professional societies of that republic, including those for nature protection, were shut down, in some cases accused of serving as cover for "counterrevolutionary nationalist groups." By Boreiko's count, about 40 percent of the leading nature-protection activists of Ukraine were executed.[110]

Miraculously, as we now know, the scientist-activists, the All-Russian Society for the Protection of Nature, and the *zapovedniki*, although strafed, managed to survive as relative islands of autonomy within the Soviet state, probably owing to their extreme marginality in the eyes of the regime (although the *kraeved* or local-lore societies, which were also deeply involved in nature protection, were closed down by 1937). Against the backdrop of Stalinism, nature reserves acquired an aura of sacred space. In the words of Sergei Zalygin: "The *zapovedniki* remained some kinds of islands of freedom in that concentration-camp world which was later given the name 'the GULAG archipelago.'"[111]

Nature-protection activism became a vehicle, from the 1930s through the 1960s (and beyond), for the defense of a prerevolutionary ideal of science as well as for the cultivation of alternative visions of economic development and resource use, even though activists were ultimately unable to prevent the destruction, authorized by Stalin in August 1951, of the 12.6 million-hectare *zapovednik* system.[112]

Other groups seeking to develop spheres of autonomy from the Soviet state, such as Estonian, Latvian, and Russian nationalists as well as university students, saw that they too could make use of the unpoliced discursive and organizational domain of nature protection.[113] A similar use of "free space" may be seen in the history of Eastern European countries and non-Russian Soviet republics, as Jane Dawson, Barbara Hicks, Katy Láng Pickvance, and Andrew Tickle have shown.[114] However, as Pickvance in particular is keen to emphasize, the larger social implications of such activism were different in Eastern Europe. As my own research has shown, the guild-like and frequently elitist nature of Soviet-era nature-protection movements, by contrast with those of Hungary and Poland, for example, precluded them from serving as enduring and effective nuclei for the defense of broader public interests. As such, they reflected the general inability of groups in the former Soviet Union—especially in Russia—to organize and cooperate across group lines. This failure was perhaps the most poignant and most damaging consequence of the thousand-year, militarized tribute-taking state.

In a cruel irony, the fall of Communism and the transition to "democracy," supported by the vast majority of environmental activists, have created even worse conditions for the growth or even the survival of environmental movements in the post-Soviet political space. "Democrats" and nationalists, who were keen to support environmental activism as part of a broad, multipronged assault on Soviet power, had little need for green politics after they gained control of the successor states. Although environmental problems are just as serious as they were during the late 1980s, the new political realities, plus the exhaustion and cynicism of the general population, have meant that the only available sources of support for post-Soviet environmental groups are foreign foundations and international environmental organizations. Because those who pay the piper call the tune, foreign sponsors imposed their own agendas on Eurasian environmental groups. As a consequence, it is difficult to speak of indigenous environmental activism in the post-Soviet world. Ironically, as foreigners assumed trusteeship over local organizations in an effort to build what they call civil society, they in fact widened the gap between local activists, who now confine themselves largely to grant writing, and a potential mass base.[115] Even so, the Putin regime effectively eliminated the presence of foreign nongovernmental organizations in Russia in 2006.[116] On the basis of the historical record, the equation of environmental groups in the former USSR with an incipient "civil society" is unsupportable. The same is true today. One continues to look in vain for social forces with the potential to take on the tribute state and rebuild the Eurasian political economy from its foundations.

CONCLUSIONS

In the last analysis, the political rationality of Soviet economic practices—owing precisely to their economic *ir*rationality in terms of providing for the long term— fatally undermined the political stability of the system.[117] Its lack of a social vision, its inability to innovate or change, and the determination of its elites to hold on to power at all costs condemned the Soviet Union to implode under the crushing weight of its environmental, health, financial, productivity, and political problems. The political problems were actually the result of the confluence of the system's structural problems. As Arran Gare observes, the Soviet tribute-taking state's complete failure to provide a vision or incentives for its people led to a "loss of meaning . . . which expressed itself, among other things, in the highest incidence of alcoholism in the world."[118] As with tsarism, the long-term, systemic production of such passive and disoriented people made the vast country far easier for the Party to control, but that same process condemned the country to Chernobyl and other environmental disasters, as well as to long-term decay of its infrastructure, resource base, and human capital. Overgrazing, disregard for crop rotation, and an overproduction of tractors has led to the annual loss of 1.5 billion tons of topsoil.[119] Instead of ending up as useful inputs somewhere else, harmful waste products are customarily dumped into the nearest convenient waterway. Between 1981 and 1988, a full 80 percent of the budget for air-pollution control went unspent, and in 1988 Kazakstan fulfilled a mere 1 percent of its environmental-protection investment plan.[120] Even when the quantity of water subject to treatment increased (by 18 percent), as between 1980 and 1990, the amount properly treated *decreased* by 40 percent.[121] Those problems have only worsened since the breakup of the USSR.

Citing the sociologist Mancur Olson, Stefan Hedlund in his provocative study underscores the persistent feelings of insecurity—geopolitical and domestic—at the heart of Russian and Eurasian leaders' rapacious pattern of rule. "If an autocratic ruler has a short-term view, he has an incentive, no matter how gigantic his empire or how exalted his lineage, to seize any asset whose total value exceeds the discounted present value of its tax yield over his short-term horizon. In other words, just as the roving bandit leader who can securely hold a domain has an incentive to make himself king, so any autocrat with a short time horizon has an incentive to become, in effect, a roving bandit."[122]

The "main question," Hedlund asserts, "both in theoretical terms and with respect to the concrete Russian case, is whether a society that has been locked into a situation of destructive roving banditry may actually find a way out. Is it perhaps even the case that there exist 'pathological' institutions, in the form of private mental models, that are immune to public policy?"[123] In other words, how can anyone ever convince the populations of Eurasia, who have been reliving and reproducing historical trauma for a thousand years, that they should begin to believe in the possibility of a more secure existence—the core psychosocial precondition for escaping the lethal clutches of the predatory, militarized tribute state?

Theodore von Laue called attention to this vicious circle forty years ago.[124] Indeed, these persistent feelings of geopolitical and internal insecurity, seared into the consciousness of rulers and ruled alike, have fired the engine of Russia's repetitions. Shattered by the trauma of the Mongol-Tatar conquest—and reinforced by such episodes as the prolonged wars with Poland-Lithuania, the Crimean Tatars, the Ottomans, and the Swedes; the Time of Troubles; a series of anarchic peasant risings; Napoleon's sweep to Moscow; Russia's defeat at the hands of the Japanese in 1905, the humiliating loss to Germany in World War I; Allied intervention during the civil war; Bolshevik perceptions and propaganda about "capitalist encirclement"; the 1927 "War Scare"; Bolshevik leaders' fears during the 1920s of domestic "encirclement" by a "petty bourgeois" peasantry, private entrepreneurs, and non-Party professionals; the Nazi devastation of the European portion of the USSR; the Cold War; and, finally, the split with the Chinese Communists—Russia's rulers were able to gain popular support, or at least acceptance, of an economically punishing, military-oriented, predatory regime that suppressed any dissent and refused to share power. Those times when the regime, inefficiently and at great human cost, succeeded in repelling foreign invasion were tirelessly celebrated so as to bolster the regime's legitimacy during peacetime, when "normal" tribute-taking resumed. A good deal of the problem resides in the fact that Russia's history experientially supports the very kind of traumatized worldview that stands in the way of dismantling the militarized tribute state.

The premature predictions for liberal-democratic transitions by the states of Eurasia (the former Soviet Union) foundered on the reefs of historical legacies and globalization. Today there is a greater need than ever for careful studies of resource politics and economics of the area. Few would disagree that its environmental problems are affecting whole regions and even the entire planet. Because the short-term, nihilistic costing calculus of the predatory tribute-taking state is still in place, and perhaps stronger than ever, a second Chernobyl is simply waiting to happen. Scholars and policy makers alike must deepen their knowledge about these issues and come up with more imaginative ways of reconciling Eurasians' desire to become prosperous, integrated participants in the global economy with the imperative to protect their environmental quality and that of the entire planet. In the process, the global West might even begin to take a look in the mirror, where the outlines of a sinister convergence have become more pronounced of late.

NOTES

I am grateful to Arja Rosenholm, Sari Autio-Sarasmo, and the Aleksanteri Institute for kindly allowing me to republish a reworked version of my article "The Genealogy of the Soviet and Post-Soviet Landscape of Risk," in *Understanding Russian Nature: Representations, Values and Concepts,* ed. Arja Rosenholm and Sari Autio-Sarasmo, Aleksanteri Papers 4/2005 (Helsinki: Aleksanteri Institute, 2005), 209–36.

1. Timothy C. Weiskel, "Toward an Archaeology of Colonialism: Elements in the Ecological Transformation of the Ivory Coast," in *The Ends of the Earth: Perspectives on Modern Environmental History*, ed. Donald Worster (Cambridge: Cambridge University Press, 1988), 141–71.

2. To subscribe to REDfiles, send an e-mail to majordomo@teia.org (Transboundary Environmental Information Agency, Elena Vassilieva, editor). Another useful website is Ecostan News (on environmental issues in Central Asia: www.mit.edu/sts/leep/Ecostan/enindex.html, and www.ecostan.org/Ecostan/enindex.html). For a comprehensive assessment of Russia's current environmental situation, see *Environmental Performance Reviews: Russian Federation* (Paris: Organization for Economic Co-operation and Development, 1999); and N.N. Kliuev, ed., *Rossiia i ee regiony: Vneshnye i vnutrennie ekologicheskie ugrozy* (Moscow: Nauka, 2001). On the successor states to the Soviet Union, see Philip R. Pryde, ed., *Environmental Resources and Constraints in the Former Soviet Republics* (Boulder, CO: Westview Press, 1995).

3. Slash-and-burn cultivation was usually practiced on land covered by birch forest, not evergreens, owing to the difference in productivity. Useful surveys are R.A. French, "Introduction" and "Russians and the Forest," in *Studies in Russian Historical Geography*, vol. 1, ed. J.H. Bater and R.A. French (London: Academic Press, 1983): 13–21, 23–44.

4. V.K. Tepliakov, *Les v zhizni drevnei rusi i moskovii* (Moscow: MLTI, 1992), 11.

5. Tepliakov, *Les v zhizni*, 14.

6. Viktor Nikolaevich Bernadskii, *Novgorod i Novgorodskaia zemlia v XV veke* (Leningrad: Izdatel'stvo Akademii nauk SSSR, 1961). See also Janet Martin, *Treasure of the Land of Darkness: The Fur Trade and its Significance for Medieval Russia* (Cambridge: Cambridge University Press, 1986).

7. Vladimir Evgen'evich Boreiko, *Istoriia okhrany prirody Ukrainy, X vek—1980*, 2nd ed. (Kiev: Kievskii ekologo-kul'turnyi tsentr, 2001), 221.

8. Tepliakov, *Les v zhizni*, 18.

9. Boreiko, *Istoriia okhrany*, 221; Tepliakov, *Les v zhizni*, 27.

10. A.M. Sakharov makes this argument in "Rus' and Its Culture, Thirteenth to Fifteenth Centuries," *Soviet Studies in History* 18, no. 3 (Winter 1979–80): 26–32.

11. See, for example, E.I. Kolycheva, *Agrarnyi stroi Rossii XVI veka* (Moscow: Nauka, 1987), esp. 172–201.

12. Richard Hellie, *Enserfment and Military Change in Muscovy* (Chicago: University of Chicago Press, 1971), 147.

13. Ihor Stebelsky, "Agriculture and Soil Erosion in the European Forest-Steppe," in Bater and French, eds., *Studies*, 1: 48–49.

14. See my discussion of this debate in *A Little Corner of Freedom: Russian Nature Protection from Stalin to Gorbachev* (Berkeley: University of California Press, 1999),

389–94, and in "A Little Reserve Raises Big Questions," *Open Country* 4 (Summer 2002): 8–14.

15. S. V. Kirikov, *Promyslovye zhivotnye, prirodnaia sreda i chelovek* (Moscow: Nauka, 1966); *Chelovek i priroda vostochno-evropeiskoi lesostepi v X–nachale XIX v* (Moscow: Nauka, 1979).

16. Stebelsky, "Agriculture," 54.

17. French, "Russians and the Forest," 32–33.

18. Michael Confino, *Domaines et seigneurs en Russie vers la fin du XVIIIe siècle* (Paris: Institut d'Études Slaves de l'Université de Paris, 1963), 10.

19. Confino, *Domaines,* 123–25.

20. Confino, *Domaines,* 134, 147.

21. Confino, *Domaines,* 164–65. See also Douglas R. Weiner, "The Roots of 'Michurinism': Transformist Biology and Acclimatization as Currents in the Russian Life Sciences," *Annals of Science* 42 (1985): 243–60.

22. Steven L. Hoch, *Serfdom and Social Control: Petrovskoe, a Village in Tambov* (Chicago: University of Chicago Press, 1986), 52, 56, 125.

23. M. A. Tsvetkov, *Izmenenie lesistosti Evropeiskoi Rossii s kontsa XVII stoletiia po 1914 god* (Moscow: Izdatel'stvo Akademii nauk SSSR, 1957), cited in French, "Russians and the Forest," 39–40.

24. Jane Costlow, "Imaginations of Destruction: The 'Forest Question' in Nineteenth-Century Russian Culture," *Russian Review* 62 (January 2003): 91–118, esp. 100.

25. Costlow, "Imaginations of Destruction," 105.

26. Industrial production was only 21 percent of 1913 levels by 1921.

27. Peter I. Holquist, *Making War, Forging Revolution: Russia's Continuum of Crisis, 1914–1921* (Cambridge, MA: Harvard University Press, 2002); Loren R. Graham made this observation in his article "The Formation of Soviet Research Institutes: A Combination of Revolutionary Innovation and International Borrowing," in *Russian and Slavic History,* ed. Don Karl Rowney and G. Edward Orchard (Columbus, OH: Slavica, 1977), 49–75.

28. Alexander Vucinich, *The Empire of Knowledge: The Academy of Sciences of the USSR (1917–1970)* (Berkeley: University of California Press, 1984); Kendall E. Bailes, *Science and Russian Culture in an Age of Revolutions: V.I. Vernadsky and His Scientific School* (Bloomington: Indiana University Press, 1990).

29. Douglas R. Weiner, *Models of Nature: Ecology, Conservation and Cultural Revolution in Soviet Russia,* 2nd ed. (Pittsburgh, PA: Pittsburgh University Press, 2000).

30. Weiner, *Models of Nature.*

31. Weiner, *Models of Nature.*

32. These are the words of Arnosht Kol'man, an arbiter of science for the Moscow Committee of the Communist Party, in his "Sabotazh v nauke," *Bol'shevik* 2 (1931): 75. See Weiner, *Little Corner of Freedom,* 43.

33. Vyacheslav Gerovitch and Anton Struchkov, "Epilogue: Russian Reflections," *Journal of the History of Biology* 25, no. 3 (Fall 1992): 487–95, esp. 488–90.

34. On the 1891 famine, see Richard G. Robbins Jr., *Famine in Russia: 1891–1892* (New York: Columbia University Press, 1975). Robert Conquest has written the definitive work on the 1932–33 famine, *The Harvest of Sorrow: Soviet Collectivization and the Terror-Famine* (New York: Oxford University Press, 1986).

35. R. A. French, "Canals in Prerevolutionary Russia," in Bater and French, eds., *Studies,* 2: 451–81.

36. Paul Josephson, *Totalitarian Science and Technology* (Atlantic Highlands, NJ: Humanities Press, 1996), 78–79.

37. Loren R. Graham, *The Ghost of the Executed Engineer: Technology and the Fall of the Soviet Union* (Cambridge, MA: Harvard University Press, 1993), 52. He relies on the earlier history of the Dnepr Dam by Anne D. Rassweiler, *The Generation of Power: The History of Dneprostroi* (New York: Oxford University Press, 1988).

38. Thomas F. Remington writes: "[The Bolsheviks] cultivated an ideology of technological modernism which linked the accumulation of national power to the liberation of society's resources from underdevelopment. Lenin, in particular, translated the older socialist ideals of justice and equality into formulas of collective power through industrial progress. Industrialism provided the mechanistic images of Lenin's vision of society: a society grown into the state, a state in which, to be sure, power was itself shared with the masses and social choice was disaggregated into millions of discrete but automatic responses. . . . [N]o chaos would be tolerated" (*Building Socialism in Bolshevik Russia: Ideology and Industrial Organization, 1917–1921* [Pittsburgh, PA: University of Pittsburgh Press, 1984], 19).

39. Remington, *Building Socialism,* 143.

40. Jonathan Coopersmith, *The Electrification of Russia, 1880–1926* (Ithaca, NY: Cornell University Press, 1992), 153, 154.

41. On this question, see Ferenc Fehér, Agnes Heller, and György Márkus, *Dictatorship over Needs: An Analysis of Soviet Societies* (Oxford: Basil Blackwell, 1983).

42. Peter Rutland, *The Myth of the Plan* (La Salle, Ill.: Open Court, 1985), 252–53.

43. Remington, *Building Socialism,* 114.

44. Remington, *Building Socialism,* 125; see also V. I. Ponomareva, ed., *Ekologiia i vlast', 1917–1990: Dokumenty* (Moscow: Mezhdunarodnyi fond "Demokratiia," 1999), documents 12 (pp. 34–35), 32 (pp. 84–86), 43 (pp. 103–5), 57 (pp. 127–28), and 91 (pp. 194–96).

45. On the metaphorical Soviet discourse on immortality, see Irene Masing-Delic, *Abolishing Death: A Salvation Myth of Russian Twentieth-Century Literature* (Stanford, CA: Stanford University Press, 1992); Katerina Clark, *The Soviet Novel: History as Ritual* (Chicago: University of Chicago Press, 1985); and Rolf Hellebust, "Aleksei

Gastev and the Metallization of the Revolutionary Body," *Slavic Review* 56, no. 3 (Fall 1997): 500–518.

46. M. Gor'kii, "O temakh," *Pravda*, October 17, 1933, reprinted in *Sobranie sochinenii*, vol. 27 (Moscow: Gosudarstvennoe izdatel'stvo khudozhestvennoi literatury, 1953), 106.

47. Remington, *Building Socialism*, 138.

48. V. Z. Rogovin, "Diskusii po problemam byta i kul'tury v Sovetskoi Rossii dvadt-satykh godov," *Sotsial'nye issledovaniia*, no. 7 (1971): 46–74, esp. 63–65.

49. M. Gor'kii, "Otvet," *Izvestiia*, December 12 and 13, 1929, in *Sobranie sochinenii* 25: 77.

50. Gor'kii, "Otvet," 77.

51. Gor'kii, "O temakh," 100.

52. M. Gor'kii, "O M. M. Prishvine," *Krasnaia nov'*, no. 12 (December 1926), in *Sobranie sochinenii*, 24: 265.

53. M. Gor'kii, "Zasukha budet unichtozhena," *Komsomol'skaia pravda*, September 8, 1931.

54. M. Gor'kii, "O bor'be s prirodoi," *Pravda* and *Izvestiia*, December 12, 1931, in *Sobranie sochinenii*, 26: 198.

55. M. Gor'kii, "Sovetskaia literatura," *Pravda* and *Izvestiia*, August 19, 1934, in *Sobranie sochinenii*, 27: 322.

56. Quoted in Il'ia Shkapa, *Sem' let s Gor'kim* (Moscow: Sovetskii pisatel', 1990), 324.

57. M. Gor'kii et al., eds., *Belomorsko-Baltiiskii Kanal imeni Stalina: Istoriia stroitel'stva* (Moscow: Gosudarstvennoe izdatel'stvo "Istoriia fabrik i zavodov," 1934).

58. "Rech' na slete udarnikov Belomorstroia" originally published as "Prekrasnoe delo sdelano," *Pravda*, September 3, 1933, in *Sobranie sochinenii*, 27: 73.

59. M. Gor'kii, "O kochke i o tochke," *Pravda* and *Izvestiia*, July 10, 1933, in *Sobranie sochinenii*, 27: 43.

60. M. Gorky et al., *Belomor* (New York: Smith and Haas, 1935), 306.

61. Remington, *Building Socialism*, 175.

62. N. F. Kashchenko, "Rol' akklimatizatsii v protsesse pod' ema proizvoditel'nykh sil SSSR," *Iugoklimat: Sbornik po voprosam akklimatizatsii rastenii i zhivotnykh* (Odessa: n.p., 1929), 5. See also Weiner, *Models*, 171–228.

63. M. Ilin, *New Russia's Primer: The Story of the Five-Year Plan*, trans. George S. Counts and Nucia P. Lodge (Boston: Houghton Mifflin Co., 1931), 141 ff., 35.

64. Weiner, *Models*, 171–228; Weiner, *Little Corner of Freedom*, 44–45, 202–5, 228–29, 248, 378–81, 386–87.

65. Vladimir Boreiko, *Belye piatna istorii prirodookhrany: SSSR, Rossiia, Ukraina*, vol. 2 (Kiev: Kievskii ekologo-kul'turnyi tsentr, 1996).

66. I argue this in "Roots of 'Michurinism'" and *Models of Nature*.

67. Stephen J. Pyne, *Vestal Fire: An Environmental History, Told through Fire, of Europe and Europe's Encounter with the World* (Seattle: University of Washington Press, 1997), 521, 525.

68. Mark Bassin, *Imperial Visions: Nationalist Imagination and the Geographical Expansion in the Russian Far East, 1840–1865* (Cambridge: Cambridge University Press, 1999).

69. See Weiner, *Models*, 213–23; Weiner, *Little Corner of Freedom*, 44–61; Boreiko, *Askania-Nova; Tiazhkie versty istorii (1826–1993)* (Kiev: Kievskii ekologo-kul'turnyi tsentr, 1994), 91. On Lysenko and Prezent, see also David Joravsky, *The Lysenko Affair* (Cambridge, MA: Harvard University Press, 1970); Zhores A. Medvedev, *The Rise and Fall of T. D. Lysenko* (Garden City, NY: Doubleday, 1971); and Valery Soyfer, *Lysenko and the Tragedy of Soviet Science*, trans. Leo and Rebecca Gruliow (New Brunswick, NJ: Rutgers University Press, 1994).

70. GA RF (State Archive of the Russian Federation), fond 404, op. 1, d. 53, listy 16–17.

71. Mikhail Vladimirovich Poddubnyi, *Sanitarnaia okhrana okruzhaiushchei sredy v Rossii i SSSR v pervoi polovine XX veka* (Kiev: Kievskii ekologo-kul'turnyi tsentr and Tsentr okhrany dikoi prirody SOES, 1997), 34. Series: Istoriia okhrany prirody, fascicle 16.

72. Poddubnyi, *Sanitarnaia okhrana okruzhaiushchei sredy.*

73. Poddubnyi, *Sanitarnaia okhrana okruzhaiushchei sredy,* 27.

74. Boreiko, *Belye piatna,* 2: 97.

75. Loren R. Graham, "The Fits and Starts of Russian and Soviet Technology," in *Technology, Culture and Development: The Experience of the Soviet Model,* ed. James P. Scanlan (Armonk, NY: M. E. Sharpe, 1992), 3–24.

76. Rutland, *Myth of the Plan,* 107.

77. See especially Arkady Vaksberg, *The Soviet Mafia: A Shocking Exposé of Organized Crime in the USSR* (New York: St. Martin's Press, 1991).

78. Ulrich Beck, *Risk Society: Toward a New Modernity* (London: Sage, 1992); Oleg Nikolevich Ianitskii, *Rossiia: Ekologicheskii vyzov (obshchestvennoe dvizhenie, nauka, politika)* (Novosibirsk: Sibirskii khronograf, 2002), 41.

79. Kliuev, *Rossiia i ee regiony,* 42 ("ostraia ekologicheskaia situatsiia").

80. Ann-Mari Sätre Åhlander, *Environmental Problems in the Shortage Economy: The Legacy of Soviet Environmental Policy* (Aldershot, U.K.: Edward Elgar, 1994), 6–8.

81. Åhlander, *Environmental Problems,* 15.

82. Zhores A. Medvedev, *Nuclear Disaster in the Urals* (New York: Vintage, 1979).

83. Marshall I. Goldman, *The Spoils of Progress: Environmental Pollution in the Soviet Union* (Cambridge, MA: MIT Press, 1972).

84. Joan DeBardeleben, *The Environment and Marxism-Leninism: The Soviet and East German Experience* (Boulder, CO: Westview Press, 1985).

85. Thane Gustafson, *Reform in Soviet Politics: Lessons of Recent Policies on Land and Water* (New York: Cambridge University Press, 1981), and *Crisis amid Plenty: The*

Politics of Soviet Energy under Brezhnev and Gorbachev (Princeton: Princeton University Press, 1989).

86. On the Aral Sea crisis and the problem of cotton-based agriculture in Central Asia, see Tom Bissell, "Eternal Winter: Lessons of the Aral Sea Disaster," *Harper's Magazine*, April 2002, 41–56; Nikolai Ivanovich Chesnokov, *Dikie zhivotnye meniaiut adresa* (Moscow: Mysl', 1989); John C. K. Daly, "Global Implications of Aral Sea Dessication," *Central Asia–Caucasus Analyst* (November 8, 2000); Murray Feshbach and Alfred Friendly Jr., *Ecocide in the USSR: Health and Nature under Siege* (New York: Basic Books, 1992); Michael H. Glantz, ed. *Creeping Environmental Problems and Sustainable Development in the Aral Sea Basin* (Cambridge: Cambridge University Press, 1999); Ulrike Grote, ed., *Central Asian Environments in Transition* (Manila: Asian Development Bank, 1997); "Receding Waters May Expose Soviet Anthrax Dump," *Austin American-Statesman* (June 2, 1999); Philip P. Micklin, ed., "The Aral Crisis," special issue of *Post-Soviet Geography*, no. 5 (1992); Philip R. Pryde, *Environmental Management in the Soviet Union* (Cambridge: Cambridge University Press, 1991); and Erika Weinthal, *State Making and Environmental Cooperation: Linking Domestic and International Politics in Central Asia* (Cambridge, MA: MIT Press, 2002).

87. John K. C. Daly, "Global Implications of Aral Sea Dessication," *Central Asia–Caucasus Analyst* (biweekly briefing), November 8, 2000, www.cacianalyst.org/ Nov_8_2000/Aral_ea_Destruction.htm.

88. John D. Grace, *Russian Oil Supply: Performance and Prospects* (Oxford: Oxford University Press, 2005), chapters 3 and 4.

89. Zhores A. Medvedev, *The Legacy of Chernobyl* (New York: W. W. Norton, 1990).

90. A recent study that focuses on the timber industry similarly refines our picture of the Soviet political economy, pointing out that lower-priority sectors of the economy, such as environmental protection, suffer from lower efficiency and quality of service delivery in addition to (and partly as a consequence of) constricted access to resources. See Åhlander, *Environmental Problems*. For intelligent views of Soviet-style economies from the inside, see Gennady Andreev-Khomiakov, *Bitter Waters: Life and Work in Stalin's Russia, a Memoir* (Boulder, CO: Westview Press, 1997); and Miklós Haraszti, *A Worker in a Worker's State: Piece-Rates in Hungary* (Harmondsworth: Penguin Books, 1977).

91. On Lenin's views, see Sheila Fitzpatrick, "The Civil War as a Formative Experience," in *Bolshevik Culture*, ed. Abbott Gleason, Peter Kenez, and Richard Stites (Bloomington: Indiana University Press, 1985).

92. Vladimir Birstein, *The Perversion of Knowledge: The True Story of Soviet Science* (Boulder, CO: Westview Press, 2001), 121–22.

93. Valerii Ivanovich Bulatov, *Rossiia: ekologiia i armiia* (Novosibirsk: TsERIS, 1999), 62. S. N. Volkov estimates the number of fatalities at thirty-six thousand: see his studies "Spetssluzhby i biologicheskoe oruzhie v dvukh izmereniiakh," in *Mir,*

demokratiia, bezopasnost' 12 (1998): 38–55, and *Ekaterinburg: Chelovek i gorod; Opyt sotsial'noi ekologii i prakticheskoi geourbanistiki* (Ekaterinburg, 1997).

94. Bulatov, *Ekaterinburg*, 20, 23, 51.

95. Bulatov, *Ekaterinburg*, 26, 28–29.

96. Bulatov, *Ekaterinburg*, 29.

97. Philip R. Pryde, "Environmental Implications of Republic Sovereignty," in *Environmental Resources and Constraints in the Former Soviet Republics*, ed. Philip R. Pryde (Boulder, CO: Westview Press, 1995), 12, 14.

98. Boris I. Kochurov, "European Russia," in Pryde, *Environmental Resources*, 50.

99. Anna Scherbakova and Scott Monroe, "The Urals and Siberia," in Pryde, *Environmental Resources*, 74.

100. On Vorontsov, see V. A. Krasilov, ed., E. A. Liapunova, comp., *Evoliutsiia, ekologiia, bioraznoobrazie: Materialy konferentsii pamiati Nikolaia Nikolaevicha Vorontsova (1934–2000)* (Moscow: UNTs DO, 2001), and Evgenii Panov, "Pamiati N. N. Vorontsova," *Okhrana dikoi prirody* 23, no. 4 (2001): 45–46.

101. See Stephen F. Cohen, *Failed Crusade: America and the Tragedy of Post-Communist Russia* (New York: W. W. Norton, 2000); Peter Reddaway and Dmitri Glinski, *The Tragedy of Russia's Reforms: Market Bolshevism against Democracy* (Herndon, VA: United States Institute of Peace Press, 2001); and Stefan Hedlund, *Russia's "Market" Economy: A Bad Case of Predatory Capitalism* (London: University College London Press, 1999).

102. Anatol Lieven, *Chechnya: Tombstone of Russian Power* (New Haven: Yale University Press, 1998), 84–86. That the oil issue is subsidiary does not make the conflict in Chechnya any less of a tribute war in other ways.

103. See Hedlund, *Russia's "Market" Economy;* Martin McCauley, *Bandits, Gangsters and the Mafia: Russia, the Baltic States, and the CIS since 1992* (Harlow, U.K.: Longman Publishers, 2001).

104. Kliuev, *Rossiia i ee regiony*, 47.

105. Kliuev, *Rossiia i ee regiony*, 47.

106. Kliuev, *Rossiia i ee regiony*, 43–44.

107. Kliuev, *Rossiia i ee regiony*, 50. In 1997 science was allotted 2.88 percent of the budget of the Russian Federation. In 2001 the science budget was a mere 1.72 percent.

108. The same question can be asked of ethno-nationalist environmental opposition to Soviet projects, which strangely fell silent once nationalities gained independence from the Soviet Union. The case of the Ignalina nuclear reactor in Lithuania is a good case in point: see Jane Dawson, *Eco-nationalism: Anti-nuclear Activism and National Identity in Russia, Lithuania and Ukraine* (Durham, NC: Duke University Press, 1996).

109. For an acerbic but powerful exposition of this point, see Stephen Kotkin, "Trashcanistan: A Tour through the Wreckage of the Soviet Empire," *New Republic*, April 15, 2002.

110. Boreiko, *Istoriia okhrany,* 1: 50.

111. Sergei Zalygin, "Otkroveniia ot nashego imeni," *Novyi mir* 10 (1992): 215.

112. Weiner, *Little Corner of Freedom,* 63–181.

113. See Robert G. Darst, *Smokestack Diplomacy: Cooperation and Conflict in East-West Environmental Politics* (Cambridge, MA: MIT Press, 2001); Dawson, *Eco-nationalism;* Weiner, *A Little Corner of Freedom;* Oleg Nikolaevich Ianitskii, *Sotsial'nye dvizheniia: 100 interv'iu s liderami* (Moscow: Moskovskii rabochii, 1991).

114. Dawson, *Eco-nationalism;* Andrew Tickle and Ian Welsh, eds., *Environment and Society in Eastern Europe* (Harlow, U.K.: Longman, 1998); Katy Láng Pickvance, *Democracy and Environmental Movements in Eastern Europe: A Comparative Study of Hungary and Russia* (Boulder, CO: Westview Press, 1998); Barbara Hicks, *Environmental Politics in Poland: A Social Movement between Regime and Opposition* (New York: Columbia University Press, 1996).

115. Ianitskii, *Rossiia,* esp. parts 3 and 4. The term *civil society* is an unfortunate one because of its extreme vagueness. Its users seem to assume that the existence of a middle class with independent professional organizations is a guarantor of civility in society and of a functioning democracy. However, the example of Germany during the 1920s and early 1930s, a society with both these features, is instructive. See also the thoughtful discussion by Joseph Bradley, "Subjects into Citizens: Societies, Civil Society, and Autocracy in Tsarist Russia," *American Historical Review* (October 2002): 1094–123.

116. "Putin Signs Restrictive NGO Bill," *Global Policy Forum,* January 17, 2006, www.globalpolicy.org/ngos/state/2006/0117putin.htm.

117. Rutland, *Myth of the Plan,* 63. Rutland prematurely concluded (contra Hillel Ticktin, "Towards a Political Economy of the USSR," *Critique,* no. 1 [1973]: 20–41), that the "continued existence of the Soviet Union is living proof that [political and economic rationality in the Soviet context] are not mutually contradictory." Perhaps he should have waited six years before pronouncing on the issue!

118. Arran Gare, *Beyond European Civilization: Marxism, Process Philosophy, and the Environment* (Bungendore, New South Wales: Ecological Press, 1993), 84.

119. Åhlander, *Environmental Problems,* 18.

120. Åhlander, *Environmental Problems,* 61, 71.

121. Åhlander, *Environmental Problems,* 73.

122. Hedlund, *Russia's "Market" Economy,* 25, citing Mancur Olson, "Why the Transition from Communism Is So Difficult," *Eastern Economic Journal* 21, no. 4 (1995): 445.

123. Hedlund, *Russia's "Market" Economy,* 28.

124. Theodore H. von Laue, *Why Lenin? Why Stalin? A Reappraisal of the Russian Revolution, 1900–1930* (Philadelphia: Lippincott, 1964).

SELECT BIBLIOGRAPHY

Compiled by Michael Adas, William Beinart, Edmund Burke III, Mark Cioc, Kenneth Pomeranz, Mahesh Rangarajan, John F. Richards, Lise Sedrez, and Douglas Weiner

GENERAL WORKS AND SOURCES

Adams, William M. *Against Extinction: The Story of Conservation*. London: Earthscan, 2004.

American Society for Environmental History. www.h-net.org/~environ/ASEH/welcome_NN6.html

————. H-Environment electronic mailing list

Braudel, Fernand. *The Structures of Everyday Life*. New York: Harper and Row, 1981.

Brimblecombe, Peter, and Charles Pfister, eds. *The Silent Countdown: Essays in European Environmental History*. Berlin: Springer-Verlag, 1990.

Christensen, Peter. *The Decline of Iranshahr: Irrigation and Environments in the History of the Middle East, 500 B.C. to A.D. 1500*. Copenhagen: Museum Tusculanum Press, 1993.

Christian, David G. *Maps of Time: An Introduction to Big History*. Berkeley: University of California Press, 2004.

Cronon, William. *Changes in the Land*. New York: Hill and Wang, 1983.

————. *Nature's Metropolis: Chicago and the Great West*. New York: W. W. Norton, 1992.

Crosby, Alfred W. *Ecological Imperialism: The Biological Expansion of Europe, 900–1900*. 2nd ed. Cambridge: Cambridge University Press, 2004.

Davis, Mike. *Late Victorian Holocausts: El Niño Famines and the Making of the Third World*. London: Verso, 2001.

Dean, Warren. *Brazil and the Struggle for Rubber: A Study in Environmental History*. Cambridge: Cambridge University Press, 1987.

Diamond, Jared. *Guns, Germs and Steel*. New York: Vintage, 1998.

———. *Collapse: How Societies Choose to Fail or Succeed*. New York: Viking, 2005.

Drayton, Richard. *Nature's Government: Science, Imperial Britain, and the "Improvement" of the World*. New Haven: Yale University Press, 2000.

Ellis, Richard. *The Empty Ocean*. Washington, DC: Island Press, 2003.

Elvin, Mark. *The Pattern of the Chinese Past*. Stanford, CA: Stanford University Press, 1973.

———. *The Retreat of the Elephants: An Environmental History of China*. New Haven: Yale University Press, 2004.

Elvin, Mark, and Liu Tsui-jung. *Sediments of Time: Environment and Society in Chinese History*. Cambridge: Cambridge University Press, 1998.

Fagan, Brian. *The Long Summer: How Climate Changed Civilization*. New York: Basic Books, 2004.

Forest History Society, Duke University. *Environmental History Bibliography*. www.lib.duke.edu/forest/Research/biblio.html

Gadgil, Madhav, and Ramachandra Guha. *This Fissured Land*. Berkeley: University of California Press, 1993.

Grove, Richard H. *Green Imperialism: Colonial Expansion, Tropical Island Edens and the Origins of Environmentalism, 1600–1860*. Cambridge: Cambridge University Press, 1995.

Grove, Richard, Vinita Damodaran, and Satpal Sangwan, eds. *Nature and the Orient: An Environmental History of India and Southeast Asia*. Delhi: Oxford University Press, 1998.

Guha, Ramachandra. *Environmentalism: A Global History*. Delhi: Oxford University Press, 2000.

Hughes, J. Donald. *Pan's Travails: Environmental Problems of the Ancient Greeks and Romans*. Baltimore: Johns Hopkins University Press, 1994.

———. *An Environmental History of the World: Humankind's Changing Role in the Community of Life*. London: Routledge, 2001.

Mann, Charles C. *1491: New Revelations of the Americas before Columbus*. New York: Alfred A. Knopf, 2005.

Marks, Robert. *Tigers, Rice, Silk and Silt*. Cambridge: Cambridge University Press, 1998.

———. *The Origins of the Modern World: A Global and Ecological Narrative*. Lanham, MD: Rowman & Littlefield, 2002.

Marsh, George Perkins. *Man and Nature*. Cambridge, MA: Harvard University Press, 1965 [1864].

McAdams, Jonathan S., and Thomas O. McShane. *The Myth of Wild Africa: Conservation without Illusion*. Berkeley: University of California Press, 1992.

McCormick, John. *Reclaiming Paradise: The Global Environmental Movement*. Bloomington: Indiana University Press, 1989.

McEvedy, Colin, and Richard Jones. *An Atlas of World Population History*. New York: Facts on File, 1978.

McKibben, Bill. *The End of Nature*. New York: Doubleday, 1999.

McNeill, John R. *Something New under the Sun: An Environmental History of the Twentieth-Century World*. New York: W. W. Norton, 2000.

McNeill, William H. *Plagues and Peoples*. Garden City, NY: Anchor Press, 1976.

Merchant, Carolyn. *The Death of Nature: Women, Ecology, and the Scientific Revolution*. New York: Harper & Row, 1980.

———. *Reinventing Eden: The Fate of Nature in Western Culture*. New York: Routledge, 2003.

Pacey, Arnold. *Technology in World History*. Cambridge, MA: MIT Press, 1991.

Pagden, Anthony. *European Encounters with the New World from Renaissance to Romanticism*. New Haven: Yale University Press, 1993.

Perdue, Peter C. *Exhausting the Earth: State and Peasant in Hunan, 1500–1850*. Cambridge, MA: Harvard University Press, 1987.

Perlin, John. *A Forest Journey: The Role of Wood in the Development of Civilization*. New York: W. W. Norton, 1989.

Pollan, Michael. *Second Nature: A Gardener's Education*. New York: Dell, 1991.

Pomeranz, Kenneth. *The Great Divergence: China, Europe, and the Making of a Modern World Economy*. Princeton: Princeton University Press, 2000.

Pyne, Stephen J. *World Fire: The Culture of Fire on Earth*. New York: Holt, 1995.

Rackham, Oliver, and A. T. Grove. *The Nature of the Mediterranean: An Ecological History*. New Haven: Yale University Press, 2001.

Rajan, S. Ravi. *Modernizing Nature: Forestry and Imperial Eco-development, 1800–1950*. Oxford: Oxford University Press, 2006.

Richards, John F. *The Unending Frontier: An Environmental History of the Early Modern World*. Berkeley: University of California Press, 2003.

Rome, Adam, ed. "Anniversary Forum: What Books Should Be More Widely Read in Environmental History?" *Environmental History* 10, no. 4 (2005): 666–769.

Sieferle, Rolf Peter. *The Subterranean Forest: Energy Systems and the Industrial Revolution*. Cambridge, U.K.: White Horse Press, 2001.

Smil, Vaclav. *Energy in World History*. Boulder, CO: Westview Press, 1994.

Smith, Bruce D. *The Emergence of Agriculture*. New York: Scientific American Library, 1995.

Steinberg, Theodore. *Down to Earth: Nature's Role in American History*. Oxford: Oxford University Press, 2002.

Stine, Jeffrey K., and Joel A. Tarr. "At the Intersection of Histories: Technology and the Environment." *Technology and Culture* 39, no. 4 (October 1998): 601–40.

Tarr, Joel. "Urban History and Environmental History in the United States: Complementary and Overlapping Fields." www.h-net.org/~environ/historiography/usurban.htm, accessed July 8, 2008.

Tucker, Richard P. *Insatiable Appetite: the United States and the Ecological Degradation of the Tropical World*. Berkeley: University of California Press, 2000.

Tucker, Richard P., and J.F. Richards, eds. *Global Deforestation and the Nineteenth-Century World Economy*. Durham, NC: Duke University Press, 1983.

Turner, Billie Lee, et al. *The Earth as Transformed by Human Action*. Cambridge: Cambridge University Press, 1990.

Weiner, Douglas R. "A Death-Defying Attempt to Articulate a Coherent Definition of Environmental History." *Environmental History* 10, no. 3 (2005): 404–20.

White, Richard. *The Middle Ground: Indians, Empires, and Republics in the Great Lakes Region, 1650–1815*. New York: Cambridge University Press, 1991.

Williams, Michael. *Deforesting the Earth: From Prehistory to Global Crisis*. Chicago: University of Chicago Press, 2003.

Wittfogel, Karl. *Oriental Despotism: A Comparative Study of Total Power*. New Haven: Yale University Press, 1957.

World Watch Institute. www.worldwatch.org/North America

Worster, Donald. *The Ends of the Earth: Perspectives on Modern Environmental History*. Cambridge: Cambridge University Press, 1988.

———. *Dust Bowl: The Southern Plains in the 1930s*. Oxford: Oxford University Press, 2004.

Wrigley, E. A. *Continuity, Chance and Change: The Character of the Industrial Revolution in England*. Cambridge: Cambridge University Press, 1988.

PROPERTY RIGHTS IN LAND

Allen, Robert C. *Enclosure and the Yeoman*. Oxford: Clarendon Press, 1992.

Bartlett, Roger P. *Land Commune and Peasant Community in Russia: Communal Forms in Imperial and Early Soviet Society*. New York: St. Martin's Press, 1990.

Berry, Brian J. "Urbanization." In *The Earth as Transformed by Human Action: Global and Regional Changes in the Biosphere over the Past 300 Years,* ed. B.L. Turner. Cambridge: Cambridge University Press, 1990.

Blaikie, Piers M., and H.C. Brookfield. *Land Degradation and Society.* London: Methuen, 1987.

Casey, Edward S. *Getting Back into Place: Toward a Renewed Understanding of the Place-World.* Bloomington: Indiana University Press, 1993.

Chakravarty-Kaul, Minoti. *Common Lands and Customary Law: Institutional Change in North India over the Past Two Centuries.* Delhi: Oxford University Press, 1996.

Cuno, Kenneth M. *The Pasha's Peasants: Land, Society, and Economy in Lower Egypt, 1740–1858.* Cambridge: Cambridge University Press, 1992.

Eaton, Richard. *The Rise of Islam and the Bengal Frontier, 1204–1760.* Berkeley: University of California Press, 1993.

Evenson, Norma. *The Indian Metropolis: A View toward the West.* New Haven: Yale University Press, 1989.

Fischer, David Hackett. *The Great Wave: Price Revolutions and the Rhythm of History.* New York: Oxford University Press, 1996.

Gay, Robert. *Popular Organization and Democracy in Rio de Janeiro: A Tale of Two Favelas.* Philadelphia: Temple University Press, 1994.

Harvey, David. *Justice, Nature, and the Geography of Difference.* Cambridge: Blackwell Publishers, 1996.

Hemming, John. *Red Gold: The Conquest of the Brazilian Indians.* London: Macmillan, 1995.

Hirt, Paul W. *A Conspiracy of Optimism: Management of the National Forests since World War Two.* Lincoln: University of Nebraska Press, 1994.

Hoffman, David L. *Peasant Metropolis: Social Identities in Moscow, 1929–1941.* Ithaca, NY: Cornell University Press, 1994.

Kain, R. J.P., and Elizabeth Baigent. *The Cadastral Map in the Service of the State: A History of Property Mapping.* Chicago: University of Chicago Press, 1992.

Keating, W. Dennis, Norman Krumholz, and David C. Perry. *Cleveland: A Metropolitan Reader.* Kent, OH: Kent State University Press, 1995.

Ladd, Brian. *Urban Planning and Civic Order in Germany, 1860–1914.* Cambridge, MA: Harvard Historical Studies, Harvard University Press, 1990.

Lugalla, Joe. *Crisis, Urbanization, and Urban Poverty in Tanzania: A Study of Urban Poverty and Survival Politics.* Lanham, MD: University Press of America, 1995.

Madanipour, Ali. *Tehran: The Making of a Metropolis.* Chichester: John Wiley, 1998.

Matthews, M.H. *Making Sense of Place: Children's Understanding of Large-Scale Environments.* Lanham, MD: Harvester Wheatsheaf, 1992.

Neeson, J. M. *Commoners: Common Right, Enclosure and Social Change in England, 1700–1820.* Cambridge: Past and Present Publications, 1993.

Netting, Robert M. *Smallholders, Householders: Farm Families and the Ecology of Intensive, Sustainable Agriculture.* Stanford, CA: Stanford University Press, 1993.

Ostrom, Elinor. *Governing the Commons: The Evolution of Institutions for Collective Action.* Cambridge: Cambridge University Press, 1990.

Parker, Linda S. *Native American Estate: The Struggle over Indian and Hawaiian Lands.* Honolulu: University of Hawaii Press, 1989.

Perry, Richard John. *From Time Immemorial: Indigenous Peoples and State Systems.* Austin: University of Texas Press, 1996.

Pyne, Steven J. *World Fire: The Culture of Fire on Earth.* New York: Holt, 1995.

Richards, John F. "Land Transformation." In *The Earth as Transformed by Human Action,* ed. B. L. Turner. Cambridge: Cambridge University Press, 1990.

Rösener, Werner. *The Peasantry of Europe.* Oxford: Blackwell, 1994.

Scherzer, Kenneth A. *The Unbounded Community: Neighborhood Life and Social Structure in New York City, 1830–1875.* Durham, NC: Duke University Press, 1992.

Seabrook, Jeremy. *Life and Labour in a Bombay Slum.* London: Quartet, 1987.

Tsing, Anna Lowenhaupt. *In the Realm of the Diamond Queen: Marginality in an Out-of-the-Way Place.* Princeton: Princeton University Press, 1993.

Winichakul, Thongchai. *Sian Mapped: A History of the Geo-Body of a Nation.* Honolulu: University of Hawaii Press, 1994.

THE MIDDLE EAST

Adams, Robert M. *The Land behind Baghdad: A History of Settlement on the Diyala Plains.* Chicago: Chicago University Press, 1965.

Allan, Tony. *The Middle East Water Question.* London: I. B. Tauris, 2000.

Ashtor, Eliahu. *The Social and Economic History of the Near East in the Middle Ages.* London: Collins, 1976.

Bovill, E. W. *The Golden Trade of the Moors.* London: Oxford University Press, 1958.

Bulliet, Richard. *The Camel and the Wheel.* Cambridge, MA: Harvard University Press, 1975.

Butzer, Karl W. *Early Hydraulic Civilization in Egypt: A Study in Cultural Ecology.* Chicago: University of Chicago Press, 1976.

Coppock, Jane, and Joseph A. Miller, eds. *Transformations of Middle Eastern Natural Environments: Legacies and Lessons.* New Haven: Yale University Press, 1998.

Dolatyar, Mostafa, and Tim S. Gray. *Water Politics in the Middle East.* London: Macmillan, 2000.

Dregne, H. E. *Desertification of Arid Lands*. London: Harwood Academic Publishers, 1986.

Glantz, Michael H. *Drought Follows the Plow: Cultivating Marginal Areas*. Cambridge: Cambridge University Press, 1994.

Glick, Thomas. *Irrigation and Society in Medieval Valencia*. Cambridge, MA: Harvard University Press, 1973.

———. *Irrigation and Hydraulic Technology: Medieval Spain and Its Legacy*. Aldershot, U.K.: Variorum, 1996.

Helfgott, Leonard. *Ties That Bind: A Social History of the Iranian Carpet*. Washington, DC: Smithsonian Institution Press, 1994.

Hillel, Daniel. *Rivers of Eden: The Struggle for Water and the Quest for Peace in the Middle East*. Oxford: Oxford University Press, 1994.

Lewis, Norman. *Nomads and Settlers in Syria and Jordan, 1800–1980*. Cambridge: Cambridge University Press, 1987.

McNeill, John Robert. *The Mountains of the Mediterranean World: An Environmental History*. Cambridge: Cambridge University Press, 1992.

Owen, Roger. *Cotton and the Egyptian Economy, 1820–1914*. Oxford: Oxford University Press, 1969.

———. *The Middle East in the World Economy*. London: Methuen, 1981.

Rackham, Oliver, and A. T. Grove. *The Nature of the Mediterranean: An Ecological History*. New Haven: Yale University Press, 2001.

RAED (Arab Network of NGOs for Development) and Mediterranean Information Office. *Sustainable Mediterranean Newsletter*. www.mio-ecsde.org

Régnier, Phillippe. *Les Saint-Simoniens et Egypte, 1833–1851*. Cairo: Banque de l'Union Européenne, 1989.

Richards, Alan. *Egypt's Agricultural Development, 1800–1980*. Boulder, CO: Westview Press, 1982.

Swearingen, Will D., and Abdellatif Bencherifa, eds. *The North African Environment at Risk*. Boulder, CO: Westview Press, 1996.

Thirgood, J. V. *Man and the Mediterranean Forest*. New York: Academic Press, 1981.

Wagstaff, J. M. *The Evolution of Middle Eastern Landscapes: An Outline to A.D. 1840*. London: Croom Helm, 1985.

Waterbury, John. *Hydropolitics of the Nile Valley*. Syracuse, NY: Syracuse University Press, 1979.

Watson, Andrew. "The Arab Agricultural Revolution, 700–1100." *Journal of Economic History* 34, no. 4 (1974): 8–35.

———. *Agricultural Innovation in the Early Islamic World*. Cambridge: Cambridge University Press, 1983.

Wertime, Theodore A. "The Furnace versus the Goat? The Pyrotechnologic Industries and Mediterranean Deforestation." *Journal of Field Archeology* 10 (1983): 445–52.

Wertime, Theodore A., and James D. Muhly, eds. *The Coming of the Age of Iron.* New Haven: Yale University Press, 1980.

Willcocks, William. *Egyptian Irrigation.* 2 vols. London: E. & F. N. Spon, 1913.

———. *Sixty Years in the East.* Edinburgh: William Blackwood & Sons Ltd., 1935.

CHINA

Benedict, Carol. *Bubonic Plague in Nineteenth-Century China.* Stanford, CA: Stanford University Press, 1996.

Dodgen, Randall. *Controlling the Dragon: Confucian Engineers and the Yellow River in Late Imperial China.* Honolulu: University of Hawaii Press, 2001.

Economy, Elizabeth. *The River Runs Black: The Environmental Challenge to China's Future.* Ithaca, NY: Cornell University Press, 2004.

Ellis, Edward C., and S. M. Wang. "Sustainable Traditional Agriculture in the Tai Lake Region of China." *Agriculture, Ecosystems and Environment* 61 (1997): 177–93.

Elvin, Mark, and Liu Tsui-jung, eds. *Sediments of Time: Environment and Society in Chinese History.* Cambridge: Cambridge University Press, 1998.

Friedman, Edward, Paul Pickowicz, and Mark Selden. *Chinese Village, Socialist State.* New Haven: Yale University Press, 1991.

Goldstein, Joshua. "The Remains of the Everyday: One Hundred Years of Recycling in Beijing." In *Everyday Modernity in China,* ed. Madeleine Yue Dong and Joshua Goldstein. Seattle: University of Washington Press, 2006.

Greer, Charles. *Water Management in the Yellow River Basin of China.* Austin: University of Texas Press, 1979.

He Bochuan. *China on the Edge: The Crisis of Ecology and Development.* San Francisco: China Books and Periodicals, 1991.

Ho Ping-ti. *Studies on the Population of China, 1368–1953.* Cambridge, MA: Harvard University Press, 1959.

Lee, James, and Wang Feng. *One Quarter of Humanity: Malthusian Mythologies and Chinese Realities.* Cambridge, MA: Harvard University Press, 1999.

Lindert, Peter. *Shifting Ground: The Changing Agricultural Soils of China and Indonesia.* Cambridge, MA: MIT Press, 2000.

Menzies, Nicholas. "Strategic Space: Exclusion and Inclusion in Wildland Policies in Late Imperial China." *Modern Asian Studies* 26, no. 4 (1992): 719–33.

Osborne, Anne. "The Local Politics of Land Reclamation in the Lower Yangzi Highlands." *Late Imperial China* 15, no. 1 (1994): 1–46.

————. *China Marches West: The Qing Conquest of Central Eurasia.* Cambridge, MA: Harvard University Press, 2005.

Pietz, David. *Engineering the State: The Huai River and Reconstruction in Nationalist China, 1927–1937.* London: Routledge, 2002.

Pomeranz, Kenneth. *The Making of a Hinterland: State, Society, and Economy in Inland North China, 1853–1937.* Berkeley: University of California Press, 1993.

Rogaski, Ruth. *Hygienic Modernity: Meanings of Health and Disease in Treaty-Port China.* Berkeley: University of California Press, 2004.

Shepherd, John R. *Statecraft and Political Economy on the Taiwan Frontier, 1600–1800.* Stanford, CA: Stanford University Press, 1993.

Skinner, G. William. "Regional Urbanization in Nineteeenth-Century China." In *The City in Late Imperial China*, ed. G. William Skinner. Stanford, CA: Stanford University Press, 1977.

Smil, Vaclav. *China's Environmental Crisis: An Inquiry into the Limits of National Development.* Armonk, NY: M. E. Sharpe, 1993.

————. "Will There Be Enough Chinese Food?" (Review of Lester Brown, *Who Will Feed China?*) *New York Review of Books*, February 1, 1996, 32–34.

————. *China's Past, China's Future: Energy, Food, Environment.* London: Routledge Curzon, 2004.

Thibodeau, John, Philip Williams, and Dai Qing, eds. *The River Dragon Has Come: The Three Gorges Dam and the Fate of China's Yangtze River and its People.* Armonk, NY: M. E. Sharpe, 1998.

Van Slyke, Lyman. *Yangtze: Nature, History, and the River.* Stanford, CA: Stanford Alumni Association, 1988.

EUROPE AND THE RHINE

Aftalion, Fred. *A History of the International Chemical Industry.* Philadelphia: University of Pennsylvania Press, 1991.

Aycoberry, Pierre, and Marc Ferro. *Une histoire du Rhin.* Paris: Éditions Ramsay, 1981.

Blackbourn, David. *The Conquest of Nature: Water, Landscape, and the Making of Modern Germany.* New York: W. W. Norton, 2006.

Brimblecombe, Peter, and C. Pfister. eds. *The Silent Countdown: Essays in Environmental History.* Berlin: Springer-Verlag, 1990.

Brüggemeier, Franz-Josef. "The Ruhr Basin, 1850–1980: A Case of Large-Scale Environmental Pollution." In *The Silent Countdown: Essays in Environmental History*, ed. Peter Brimblecombe and C. Pfister. Berlin: Springer-Verlag, 1990.

Chamberlain, J. P. "The Regime of the International Rivers: Danube and Rhine." PhD diss., Columbia University, 1923.

Cioc, Mark. *The Rhine: An Eco-biography, 1815–2000.* Seattle: University of Washington Press, 2002.

Cowx, Ian G., and Robin L. Welcomme, eds. *Rehabilitation of Rivers for Fish: A Study Undertaken by the European Inland Fisheries Advisory Commission of FAO.* Oxford: Fishing News Books, 1998.

Elkins, T. H., and P. K. Marstrand. "Pollution of the Rhine and Its Tributaries." In *Regional Management of the Rhine: Papers of a Chatham House Study Group,* ed. Royal Institute of International Affairs. London: Chatham House, 1975.

European Society for Environmental History. www.eseh.org

Guillerme, André E. *The Age of Water: The Urban Environment in the North of France, A.D. 300–1800.* College Station: Texas A & M University Press, 1983.

Jansen, P. P., et al. *Principles of River Engineering: The Non-tidal Alluvial River.* London: Pitman, 1979.

Kinzelbach, Ragnar, ed. *Die Tierwelt des Rheins einst und jetzt.* Mainz: Naturhistorisches Museum Mainz, 1985.

Lelek, Anton, and Günter Buhse. *Fische des Rheins: Früher und heute.* Berlin: Springer, 1992.

Löbert, Traude. *Die Oberrheinkorrektion in Baden: Zur Umweltgeschichte des 19. Jahrhunderts.* Karlsruhe: Institut für Wasserbau und Kulturtechnik, 1997.

Maffioli, Cesare F. *Out of Galileo: The Science of Waters, 1628–1718.* Rotterdam: Erasmus, 1994.

Osborn, Matthew. "Sowing the Field of British Environmental History." H-Environment Historiography Series. www.h-net.org/~environ/historiography/british.htm

Schulte-Wülwer-Leidig, Ann. "Ecological Master Plan for the Rhine Catchment." In *The Ecological Basis for River Management,* ed. David M. Harper and Alastair J. D. Ferguson. Chichester: John Wiley & Sons, 1995.

Smith, Norman. *Man and Water: A History of Hydro-technology.* London: Charles Scribner's Sons, 1975.

Tittizer, Thomas, and Falk Krebs, eds. *Ökosystemforschung: Der Rhein und seine Auen: Eine Bilanz.* Berlin: Springer, 1996.

van de Ven, G. P., ed. *Man-Made Lowlands: History of Water Management and Land Reclamation in the Netherlands.* Utrecht: Matrijs, 1993.

van Veen, Johan. *Dredge, Drain, Reclaim: The Art of a Nation.* The Hague: Martinus Nijhoff, 1962.

Wever, Egbert. "The Port of Rotterdam: 'Gateway to Europe'." In *The Rhine Valley: Urban, Harbour and Industrial Development and Environmental Problems; A Regional*

Guide Dedicated to the 28th International Geographical Congress, The Hague, 1996, ed. Heinz Heineberg, Norbert de Lange, and Alois Mayr. Leipzig: Institut für Länderkunde, 41, 13, 1996.

SOUTHEAST ASIA

Adas, Michael. *The Burma Delta: Economic Development and Social Change on an Asian Rice Frontier, 1852–1941.* Madison: University of Wisconsin Press, 1974.

Barker, Randolph, Robert W. Herdt, and Beth Rose. *The Rice Economy of Asia.* Washington, DC: Resources for the Future, 1985.

Bray, Francesca. *The Rice Economies: Technology and Development in Asian Societies.* Oxford: Basil Blackwell, 1986.

Brocheux, Pierre. *The Mekong Delta: Ecology, Economy, and Revolution, 1860–1960.* Madison, WI: Center for Southeast Asian Studies, 1995.

Cheng, Siok-Hwa. *The Rice Industry of Burma, 1852–1940.* Kuala Lumpur: Oxford University Press, 1968.

Feeny, David. *The Political Economy of Productivity: Thai Agricultural Development, 1880–1975.* Vancouver: University of British Columbia Press, 1982.

Furnivall, John. *An Introduction to the Political Economy of Burma.* Rangoon: Burmese Advertising Press, 1931.

Hanks, Lucien. *Rice and Man: Agricultural Ecology in Southeast Asia.* Chicago: Aldine, 1972.

Ingram, James. *Economic Change in Thailand Since 1850.* Stanford, CA: Stanford University Press, 1955.

Ishii, Yoneo, ed. *Thailand: A Rice-Growing Society.* Honolulu: University of Hawaii Press, 1978.

Parnwell, Michael J. G., and Raymond L. Bryant. *Environmental Change in South-East Asia: People, Politics and Sustainable Development.* London: Routledge, 1996.

Pingali, P. L., M. Hossain, and R. V. Gerpacio. *Asian Rice Bowls: The Returning Crisis?* Wallingford, U.K.: CAB International, 1997.

Peluso, Nancy. *Rich Forests, Poor People: Resource Control and Resistance in Java.* Berkeley: University of California Press, 1992.

Richards, John F., and Richard Tucker, eds. *The World Economy and Forest Depletion in the Nineteenth Century.* Durham, NC: Duke University Press, 1983.

Sansom, Robert. *The Economics of Insurgency in the Mekong Delta of Vietnam.* Cambridge, MA: MIT Press, 1970.

Schusky, Ernest L. *Culture and Agriculture: An Ecological Introduction to Traditional and Modern Farming Systems.* New York: Bergin & Garvey, 1989.

Skinner, G. William. *Chinese Society in Thailand: An Analytical History.* Ithaca, NY: Cornell University Press, 1957.

van Schendel, Willem. *Three Deltas: Accumulation and Poverty in Rural Burma, Bengal and South India.* New Delhi: Sage Publications, 1991.

Watts, Michael. *Silent Violence: Food, Famine, and Peasantry in Northern Nigeria.* Berkeley: University of California Press, 1983.

AFRICA

Anderson, David, and Richard Grove, eds. *Conservation in Africa: People, Policies, and Practice.* Cambridge: Cambridge University Press, 1987.

Bayart, Jean-François. *The State in Africa: The Politics of the Belly.* London: Longman, 1993.

Beinart, William. *The Rise of Conservation in South Africa: Settlers, Livestock and the Environment, 1770–1950.* Oxford: Oxford University Press, 2003.

———. "African History and Environmental History." H-Environment Historiography Series. www.h-net.org/~environ/historiography/africaeh.htm, accessed September 18, 2005.

Beinart, William, and Peter Coates. *Environment and History: The Taming of Nature in the USA and South Africa.* London: Routledge, 1995.

Beinart, William, and JoAnn McGregor. *Social History and African Environments.* Oxford: James Currey, 2003.

Carruthers, Jane. *The Kruger National Park: A Social and Political History.* Pietermaritzburg: Natal University Press, 1995.

Chabal, Patrick. *Power in Africa: An Essay in Political Interpretation.* Basingstoke, U.K.: Macmillan, 1994.

Chabal, Patrick, and Jean-Pascal Daloz. *Africa Works: Disorder as Political Instrument.* Oxford: James Currey, 1999.

Connah, Graham. *African Civilizations: Precolonial Cities and States in Tropical Africa.* Cambridge: Cambridge University Press, 1987.

De Waal, Alex. *Famine That Kills: Darfur, Sudan, 1984–5.* Oxford: Clarendon Press, 1989.

———. *Famine Crimes: Politics and the Disaster Relief Industry in Africa.* Oxford: James Currey, 1997.

Fairhead, James, and Melissa Leach. *Misreading the African Landscape: Society and Ecology in a Forest-Savannah Mosaic.* Cambridge: Cambridge University Press, 1996.

———. *Reframing Deforestation: Global Analysis and Local Realities: Studies in West Africa.* London: Routledge, 1998.

Feierman, Steven. "Struggles for Control: The Social Roots of Health and Healing in Modern Africa." *African Studies Review* 28, nos. 2–3 (1985): 73–147.

———. *Peasant Intellectuals: Anthropology and History in Tanzania.* Madison: University of Wisconsin Press, 1990.

Feierman, Steven, and J. Janzen, eds. *The Social Basis of Health and Healing in Africa.* Berkeley: University of California Press, 1992.

Giblin, James. "Trypanosomiasis Control in African History: An Evaded Issue?" *Journal of African History* 31, no. 1 (1990): 59–80.

Guha, Ramachandra, and Joan Martínez-Alier. *Varieties of Environmentalism: Essays North and South.* London: Earthscan, 1997.

Hardin, Graham. "The Tragedy of the Commons." *Science* 162 (1968): 1243–48.

Harms, Robert. *Games against Nature: An Eco-cultural History of the Nunu of Equatorial Africa.* Cambridge: Cambridge University Press, 1987.

Iliffe, John. *Africans: The History of a Continent.* Cambridge: Cambridge University Press, 1995.

Juma, Calestous. *The Gene Hunters: Biotechnology and the Scramble for Seeds.* London: Zed Books, 1989.

Kiriro, Amos, and Calestous Juma, eds. *Gaining Ground: Institutional Innovations in Land-Use Management in Kenya.* Nairobi: Acts Press, 1991.

Kjekshus, Helge. *Ecology, Control and Economic Development in East African History.* London: Heinemann, 1977.

Kreike, Emmanuel. *Re-creating Eden: Land Use, Environment, and Society in Southern Angola and Northern Namibia.* Portsmouth, NH: Heinemann, 2004.

Leach, Melissa, and Robin Mearns, eds. *The Lie of the Land: Challenging Received Wisdom on the African Environment.* Oxford: James Currey, 1996.

MacKenzie, John. *The Empire of Nature: Hunting, Conservation and British Imperialism.* Manchester: Manchester University Press, 1988.

Maddox, Gregory H. "Africa and Environmental History." *Environmental History,* April 1999. www.looksmartusa.com/p/articles/mi_qa3854/is_199904/ai_n883342

Mamdani, Mahmood. *Citizen and Subject: Contemporary Africa and the Legacy of Late Colonialism.* London: James Currey, 1996.

Mandala, Elias C. *Work and Control in a Peasant Economy: A History of the Lower Tchiri Valley in Malawi, 1859–1960.* Madison: University of Wisconsin Press, 1990.

McCann, James C. *Green Land, Brown Land, Black Land: An Environmental History of Africa, 1800–1999.* London: Heinemann, 1999.

———. *Maize and Grace: Africa's Encounter with a New World Crop, 1500–2000.* Cambridge, MA: Harvard University Press, 2005.

―――. "Causation and Climate in African History." H-Environment Historiography Series. www.h-net.org/~environ/historiography/africa.htm, 2005.

Moore, Henrietta, and Megan Vaughan. *Cutting Down Trees: Gender, Nutrition, and Agricultural Change in the Northern Province of Zambia, 1890–1990*. London: James Currey, 1994.

Ranger, Terence O. *The Recovery of African Initiative in Tanzanian History*. Dar es Salaam: University College, 1969.

―――. "Whose Heritage? The Case of the Matobo National Park." *Journal of Southern African Studies* 15 (1989): 217–49.

―――. *Voices from the Rocks: Nature, Culture and History in the Matopos Hills of Zimbabwe*. Oxford: James Currey, 1999.

Richards, Audrey. *Land, Labour and Diet in Northern Rhodesia: An Economic Study of the Bemba Tribe*. London: International Africa Institute, 1939.

Richards, Paul. "Ecological Change and African Land Use." *African Studies Review* 26, no. 2 (1983): 1–72.

―――. *Indigenous Agricultural Revolution: Ecology and Food Production in West Africa*. London: Unwin, 1985.

Schoenbrun, David L. *A Green Place, a Good Place: Agrarian Change, Gender, and Social Identity in the Great Lakes Region to the Fifteenth Century*. Portsmouth, NH: Heinemann, 1998.

Scoones, I., ed. *Living with Uncertainty: New Directions in Pastoral Development in Africa*. London: Intermediate Technology Publications, 1995.

Showers, Kate B. "Soil Erosion in the Kingdom of Lesotho: Origins and Colonial Response." *Journal of Southern African Studies* 15, no. 2 (1989): 263–86.

Steyn, Phia. "The Greening of Our Past? An Assessment of South African Environmental Historiography." H-Environment Historiography Series. www.h-net.org/~environ/historiography/safrica.htm, 2005.

Sutton, J. E. G. "Irrigation and Soil Conservation in African Agricultural History." *Journal of African History* 25, no. 1 (1984): 25–42.

Tiffen, Mary, Michael Mortimore, and Francis Gichuki. *More People, Less Erosion: Environmental Recovery in Kenya*. Chichester: John Wiley, 1994.

Vansina, Jan. *Paths in the Rainforests: Toward a History of Political Tradition in Equatorial Africa*. Madison: University of Wisconsin Press, 1990.

Vaughan, Megan. *The Story of an African Famine: Gender and Famine in Twentieth-Century Malawi*. Cambridge: Cambridge University Press, 1987.

Wilson, Francis, and Mamphela Ramphele. *Uprooting Poverty: The South African Challenge*. Cape Town: David Philip, 1989.

Agarwal, Anil, Ravi Chopra, and Kalpana Sharma, eds. *The State of India's Environment: A Citizen's Report*. Delhi: Centre for Science and Environment, 1982.

Arnold, David. *The Tropics and the Travelling Gaze: India, Landscape and Science*. Delhi: Permanent Black, 2006.

Arnold, David, and Ramachandra Guha, eds. *Nature, Culture and Imperialism: Essays on the Environmental History of South Asia*. Delhi: Oxford University Press, 1995.

Buchy, Marlene. *Teak and Arecanut: Colonial State, Forests and People in the Western Ghats, 1800–1947*. Pondicherry: French Institute, 1996.

Deloche, Jean. *Transport and Communications in India, Prior to Steam Locomotion*. Vol. 1: *Land Transport*. Delhi: Oxford University Press, 1993.

Greenough, Paul, and Anna Lowenhaupt Tsing, eds. *Southern Projects in Nature*. Delhi: Orient Longman, 2005.

Guha, Ramachandra. *The Unquiet Woods: Ecological Change and Peasant Resistance in the Western Himalaya*. Delhi: Oxford University Press, 1989.

Guha, Sumit. *Environment and Ethnicity in India, 1200–1991*. Cambridge: Cambridge University Press, 1999.

John Richards Collection, Duke University. *Environment of South and Southeast Asia Bibliography*. www.lib.duke.edu/forest/Research/databases.html

Karunaratna, Nihal. *Forest Conservation in Sri Lanka from British Colonial Times, 1818–1912*. Colombo: Trumpet Publishers, 1987.

Lewis, Michael. *Inventing Global Ecology: Tracking the Biodiversity Ideal in India, 1947–95*. Delhi: Orient Longman, 2003.

Ludden, David. *An Agrarian History of South Asia*. Cambridge: Cambridge University Press, 1999.

Mackenzie, John M. *The Empire of Nature, Hunting, Parks and British Imperialism*. Manchester: Manchester University Press, 1988.

Rangarajan, Mahesh. *Fencing the Forest: Conservation and Ecological Change in India's Central Provinces, 1860–1914*. Delhi: Oxford University Press, 1996.

———. *India's Wildlife History: An Introduction*. Delhi: Permanent Black, 2001.

Saberwal, Vasant Kabir. *Pastoral Politics, Shepherds, Bureaucrats and Conservation in the Western Himalaya*. Delhi: Oxford University Press, 1998.

Satya, Laxman D. *Cotton and Famine in Berar, 1850–1900*. New Delhi: Manohar, 1997.

Shiva, Vandana. *Staying Alive: Women, Ecology and Survival in India*. London: Zed Books, 1989.

Skaria, Ajay. *Hybrid Histories: Forests, Frontiers and Wildness*. Delhi: Oxford University Press, 1998.

Sukumar, Raman. *The Living Elephants: Evolutionary Ecology, Behaviour and Conservation*. Delhi: Oxford University Press, 2003.

Whitcombe, Elizabeth. *Agrarian Conditions in Northern India: The United Provinces under British Rule, 1860–1900*. Berkeley: University of California Press, 1972.

LATIN AMERICA

Alston, Lee J., Gary D. Libecap, and Bernardo Mueller. *Titles, Conflict, and Land Use: The Development of Property Rights and Land Reform on the Brazilian Amazon Frontier*. Ann Arbor: University of Michigan Press, 1999.

Balée, William. "Indigenous History and Amazonian Biodiversity." In *Changing Tropical Forests: Historical Perspectives on Today's Challenges in Central and South America*, ed. Harold K. Steen and Richard P. Tucker. Durham, NC: Forest History Society, 1992.

Brannstrom, Christian. "Rethinking the 'Atlantic Forest' of Brazil: New Evidence for Land Cover and Land Value in Western São Paulo, 1900–1930." *Journal of Historical Geography* 28, no. 3 (2002): 420–39.

Browder, John O., and Brian J. Godfrey. *Rainforest Cities: Urbanization, Development, and Globalization of the Brazilian Amazon*. New York: Columbia University Press, 1997.

Cañizares-Esguerra, Jorge. *How to Write the History of the New World: Histories, Epistemologies, and Identities in the Eighteenth-Century Atlantic World*. Stanford, CA: Stanford University Press, 2001.

Castro Herrera, Guillermo. "The Environmental Crisis and the Tasks of History in Latin America." *Environment and History* 3 (1997): 1–18

———. "Environmental History (Made) in Latin America." H-Environment Historiography Series. www.stanford.edu/group/LAEH/index.html, accessed July 8, 2008.

Cleary, David. "Towards an Environmental History of the Amazon: From Prehistory to the Nineteenth Century." *Latin American Research Review* 36, no. 2 (2001): 65–96.

Collinson, Helen. *Green Guerrillas: Environmental Conflicts and Initiatives in Latin America and the Caribbean*. London: Latin American Bureau, 1996.

Crosby, Alfred W. *The Columbian Exchange: Biological and Cultural Consequences of 1492*. Westport, CT: Greenwood Press, 1973.

———. *Ecological Imperialism: The Biological Expansion of Europe, 900–1900*. Cambridge: Cambridge University Press, 1986.

Dean, Warren. *Brazil and the Struggle for Rubber: A Study in Environmental History*. Cambridge: Cambridge University Press, 1987.

———. *With Broadax and Firebrand: The Destruction of the Brazilian Atlantic Forest*. Berkeley: University of California Press, 1997.

Durham, William. *Scarcity and Survival in Central America: Ecological Origins of the Soccer War.* Stanford, CA: Stanford University Press, 1979.

Evans, Sterling. *The Green Republic: A Conservation History of Costa Rica.* Austin: University of Texas Press, 1999.

Farris, Nancy M. *Maya Society under Colonial Rule: The Collective Enterprise of Survival.* Princeton: Princeton University Press, 1984.

Galeano, Eduardo H. *Open Veins of Latin America: Five Centuries of the Pillage of a Continent.* Trans. Cedric Belfrage. New York: Monthly Review Press, 1973.

Gootenberg, Paul Eliot. *Between Silver and Guano: Commercial Policy and the State in Post-independence Peru.* Princeton: Princeton University Press, 1989.

Guy, Donna J., and Thomas E Sheridan. *Contested Ground: Comparative Frontiers on the Northern and Southern Edges of the Spanish Empire.* Tucson: University of Arizona Press, 1998.

Keck, Margaret E. "Social Equity and Environmental Politics in Brazil: Lessons from the Rubber Tappers of Acre." *Comparative Politics* 27, no. 4 (1995): 409–24.

Mann, Charles C. *1491: New Revelations of the Americas before Columbus.* New York: Alfred A. Knopf, 2005.

Martínez-Alier, Joan, and Manuel González de Molina Navarro. *Historia y ecología.* Madrid: Marcial Pons, 1993.

McCook, Stuart George. *States of Nature: Science, Agriculture, and Environment in the Spanish Caribbean, 1760–1940.* Austin: University of Texas Press, 2002.

Melville, Elinor Gordon Ker. *A Plague of Sheep: Environmental Consequences of the Conquest of Mexico.* Cambridge: Cambridge University Press, 1994.

Miller, Shawn W. *Fruitless Trees: Portuguese Conservation and Brazil's Colonial Timber.* Stanford, CA: Stanford University Press, 2000.

Onis, Juan de. *The Green Cathedral: Sustainable Development of Amazonia.* New York: Oxford University Press, 1992.

Place, Susan E. *Tropical Rainforests: Latin American Nature and Society in Transition.* Wilmington, DE: Scholarly Resources, 1993.

Roberts, J. Timmons, and Nikki Demetria Thanos. *Trouble in Paradise: Globalization and Environmental Crises in Latin America.* London: Routledge, 2003.

Russell-Wood, A. J. R. "Technology and Society: The Impact of Gold Mining on the Institution of Slavery in Portuguese America." *Journal of Economic History* 37 (1977): 59–83.

Sauer, Carl Ortwin. *The Early Spanish Main.* Berkeley: University of California Press, 1966.

Sedrez, Lise. "The Use of the Internet as a Source for Environmental History." *Environmental Green Journal.* http://egj.lib.uidaho.edu/egj08/sedrez1.html, 1998.

———. "Historia ambiental de América Latina: Orígenes, principales interrogantes y lagunas." In *Repensando la naturaleza: Encuentros y desencuentros disciplinarios en torno a lo ambiental,* ed. Germán Palácio Márquez and Astrid Ulloa. Bogotá: Universidad Nacional de Colombia–Sede Leticia, 2002.

Sedrez, Lise, John D. Wirth, and José Augusto Drummond. *Online Bibliography on Environmental History of Latin America.* California State University at Long Beach, www.csulb.edu/laeh

Simon, Joel. *Endangered Mexico: An Environment on the Edge.* San Francisco: Sierra Club Books, 1997.

Simonian, Lane. *Defending the Land of the Jaguar: A History of Conservation in Mexico.* Austin: University of Texas Press, 1995.

Slatta, Richard W. *Gauchos and the Vanishing Frontier.* Lincoln: University of Nebraska Press, 1983.

Steen, Harold K., and Richard P. Tucker, eds. *Changing Tropical Forests: Historical Perspectives on Today's Challenges in Central and South America.* Durham, NC: Forest History Society, 1992.

RUSSIA

Åhlander, Ann-Mari Sätre. *Environmental Problems in the Shortage Economy: The Legacy of Soviet Environmental Policy.* Aldershot, U.K.: Edward Elgar, 1994.

Anderson, David G. *Identity and Ecology in Arctic Siberia: The Number One Reindeer Brigade.* Oxford: Oxford University Press, 2000.

Bailes, Kendall E. *Science and Russian Culture in an Age of Revolutions: V.I. Vernadsky and His Scientific School.* Bloomington: Indiana University Press, 1990.

Balzer, Marjorie. *The Tenacity of Ethnicity: A Siberian Saga in Global Perspective.* Princeton: Princeton University Press, 1999.

Bassin, Mark. *Imperial Visions: Nationalist Imagination and the Geographical Expansion in the Russian Far East, 1840–1865.* Cambridge: Cambridge University Press, 1999.

Bater, James H., and R. A. French, eds. *Studies in Russian Historical Geography.* 2 vols. London: Academic Press, 1983.

Bonhomme, Brian. *Forests, Peasants, and Revolutionaries: Forest Conservation and Organization in Soviet Russia, 1917–1929.* New York: Columbia University Press—East European Monographs, 2005.

Conquest, Robert. *The Harvest of Sorrow: Soviet Collectivization and the Terror-Famine.* New York: Oxford University Press, 1986.

Darst, Robert. *Smokestack Diplomacy: Cooperation and Conflict in East-West Environmental Politics.* Cambridge, MA: MIT Press, 2001.

Dawson, Jane. *Eco-nationalism: Anti-nuclear Activism and National Identity in Russia, Lithuania and Ukraine.* Durham, NC: Duke University Press, 1996.

DeBardeleben, Joan. *The Environment and Marxism-Leninism: The Soviet and East German Experience.* Boulder, CO: Westview Press, 1985.

Feshbach, Murray, and Alfred Friendly Jr. *Ecocide in the USSR: Health and Nature under Siege.* New York: Basic Books, 1992.

Glantz, Michael H., ed. *Creeping Environmental Problems and Sustainable Development in the Aral Sea Basin.* Cambridge: Cambridge University Press, 1999.

Goldman, Marshall I. *The Spoils of Progress: Environmental Pollution in the Soviet Union.* Cambridge, MA: MIT Press, 1972.

Graham, Loren R. *The Ghost of the Executed Engineer: Technology and the Fall of the Soviet Union.* Cambridge, MA: Harvard University Press, 1993.

Grote, Ulrike, ed. *Central Asian Environments in Transition.* Manila: Asian Development Bank, 1997.

Gustafson, Thane. *Reform in Soviet Politics: The Lessons of Recent Policies on Land and Water.* Cambridge: Cambridge University Press, 1981.

———. *Crisis amid Plenty: The Politics of Soviet Energy under Brezhnev and Gorbachev.* Princeton: Princeton University Press, 1989.

Jancar-Webster, Barbara. *Environmental Management in the Soviet Union and Yugoslavia: Structure and Regulation in Federal Communist States.* Durham, NC: Duke University Press, 1987.

Josephson, Paul. *Totalitarian Science and Technology.* Atlantic Highlands, NJ: Humanities Press, 1996.

Komarov, Boris [Ze'ev Vol'fson]. *The Destruction of Nature in the Soviet Union.* Armonk, NY: M.E. Sharpe, 1980.

Lemeshev, Mikhail. *Bureaucrats in Power: Ecological Collapse.* Moscow: Progress Publishers, 1990.

Medvedev, Zhores A. *Nuclear Disaster in the Urals.* Trans. George Saunders. New York: W.W. Norton, 1979.

———. *The Legacy of Chernobyl.* New York: W.W. Norton, 1990.

Micklin, Philip. *The Water Management Crisis in Central Asia.* Pittsburgh, PA: University of Pittsburgh Center for Russian and East European Studies, 1991.

Moon, David. *The Russian Peasantry, 1600–1930.* Harlow, U.K.: Longman Publishers, 1999.

Oldfield, Jonathan D. *Russian Nature: Exploring the Environmental Consequences of Societal Change.* Aldershot, U.K.: Ashgate, 2005.

Organization for Economic Co-operation and Development. *Environmental Performance Reviews: Russian Federation.* Paris: OECD, 1999.

Pallot, Judith, and D. J. B. Shaw. *Landscape and Settlement in Romanov Russia, 1615–1917.* Oxford: Oxford University Press, 1990.

Peterson, D. J. *Troubled Lands: The Legacy of Soviet Environmental Destruction.* Boulder, CO: Westview Press, 1993.

Pickvance, Katy Láng. *Democracy and Environmental Movements in Eastern Europe: A Comparative Study of Hungary and Russia.* Boulder, CO: Westview Press, 1998.

Pryde, Philip R. *Conservation in the Soviet Union.* Cambridge: Cambridge University Press, 1972.

————. *Environmental Management in the Soviet Union.* Cambridge: Cambridge University Press, 1991.

————, ed. *Environmental Resources and Constraints in the Former Soviet Republics.* Boulder, CO: Westview Press, 1995.

Rosenholm, Arja, and Sari Autio-Sarasmo, eds. *Understanding Russian Nature: Representations, Values, Concepts.* Helsinki: Aleksanteri Institute, 2005.

Shaw, D. J. B. *Russia in the Modern World: A New Geography.* Oxford: Blackwell, 1999.

Shtilmark, Feliks Robertovich. *History of the Russian Zapovedniks, 1895–1995.* Trans. G. H. Harper. Edinburgh: Russian Nature Press, 2003.

Singleton, Fred, ed. *Environmental Problems in the Soviet Union and Eastern Europe.* Boulder, CO: Lynne Riener Publishers, 1987.

Sunderland, Willard. *Taming the Wild Field: Colonization and Empire on the Russian Steppe.* Ithaca, NY: Cornell University Press, 2004.

Tickle, Andrew, and Ian Welsh, eds. *Environment and Society in Eastern Europe.* Harlow, U.K.: Longman, 1998.

Transboundary Environmental Information Agency. *Russian Environmental Digest.* www.teia.org/publications

Weiner, Douglas R. *A Little Corner of Freedom: Russian Nature Protection from Stalin to Gorbachev.* Berkeley: University of California Press, 1999.

————. *Models of Nature: Ecology, Conservation and Cultural Revolution in Soviet Russia.* 2nd ed. Pittsburgh, PA: Pittsburgh University Press, 2000.

Yanitsky (Ianitskii), Oleg Nikolaevich. *Russian Environmentalism: Leading Figures, Facts, Opinions.* Moscow: Mezhdunarodnyje Otnoshenija Publishing House, 1993.

————. *Russian Greens in a Risk Society: A Structural Analysis.* Helsinki: Kikimora Publications [Series B], 2000.

Yemelyanenkov, Alexander. *The Sredmash Archipelago.* Trans. Andrei Starkov, Juri Legin, Dmitry Klenin, and Oleg Bagaev. Moscow: International Physicians for the Prevention of Nuclear War—SLMK, 2000.

Ziegler, Charles E. *Environmental Policy in the U.S.S.R.* Amherst, MA: University of Massachusetts Press, 1987.

CONTRIBUTORS

MICHAEL ADAS is the Abraham E. Voorhees Professor of History at Rutgers University. His most recent book is *Dominance by Design: Technological Imperatives and America's Civilizing Mission* (Cambridge, MA: Harvard/Belknap Press, 2006).

WILLIAM BEINART is Professor of Race Relations at the University of Oxford and is the author of *The Rise of Conservation in South Africa* (Oxford: Oxford University Press, 2003).

EDMUND BURKE III is Professor of History at the University of California, Santa Cruz, and is the author of *The Ethnographic State: France, Islam and Morocco, 1890–1925* (Princeton: Princeton University Press, forthcoming).

MARK CIOC is a Professor of History at the University of California, Santa Cruz, and is the author of *The Rhine: An Eco-biography* (Seattle: University of Washington Press, 2002). He is currently the editor of *Environmental History*.

KENNETH POMERANZ is Chancellor's Professor of History at the University of California, Irvine. He is the author of *The Great Divergence: China, Europe and the Making of the Modern World Economy* (Princeton: Princeton University Press, 2000), among other works.

MAHESH RANGARAJAN is Visiting Professor of History, Jadavpur University, Kolkata, India, and a political commentator. He is the author of *India's Wildlife History: An Introduction* (Delhi: Permanent Black, 2003).

JOHN F. RICHARDS was Professor of History at Duke University and the author of *The Unending Frontier: Environmental History of the Early Modern World* (Berkeley: University of California Press, 2003) and other books and articles.

LISE SEDREZ is Professor of Latin American History at the California State University at Long Beach. She is the editor of the *Online Bibliography on Latin American Environmental History* (www.csulb.edu/projects/laeh).

DOUGLAS R. WEINER is Professor of History at the University of Arizona, past president of the American Society for Environmental History, and the author of *A Little Corner of Freedom: Russian Nature Protection from Stalin to Gorbachev* (Berkeley: University of California Press, 1999).

INDEX

AIDS, 25, 303
air pollution: cleanup, 12, 13; coal revolution and, 44; Russia, 292, 293, 299, 306; Southeast Asia, 199
Akbar, 234
Algeria, 97, 99, 105
Alsace, 171, 176, 184
Amazon, 257, 263, 265
Ambedkar, Bhimrao, 244
American Society for Environmental History, 260–61
Americas: agriculture emerging, 36; colonizers' depopulating effects, 40, 211, 238; dates on peopling of, 35; discovery, 93; environmentally disruptive colonization, 41, 211, 213, 218, 238, 259; export orientation, 128, 259; Great Dying, 40; irrigation, 88; migration to cities, 66; pre-Columbian land use intensification, 7; religions imported to, 10; silver, 92, 93; species extinction by indigenous peoples, 220; wheat frontiers, 23. *See also* Latin America; North America
Anatolia, 94–95, 103–4. *See also* Turkey
animals: African history, 223–24; domestication, 37, 277; endangered species, 12–13; India, 232–33, 240, 243; labor, 37, 43; Middle Eastern horse breeding, 95; North African grazing concerns, 106; Russia, 277, 278, 280; species extinctions, 213, 220, 240; species transmission, 11. *See also* cattle; elephants; fish; hunting; wildlife management
aquaculture, China, 148
Arabia: modernization, 97; Saudi petroleum, 50; wind systems in climate, 82
Arabic, ancient world united with, 86
Arabs: nomads, 89, 90; water management, 85, 87
Aral Sea, desiccation of, 295–97
arsenic dumping, 181–82

Asia: agrarian age, 39, 40; "oriental despotism," 89, 121, 139, 184; spice trade, 92, 94; urban dwellers, 66, 69. *See also* Central Asia; East Asia; Middle East; South Asia; Southeast Asia
Aswan Dam, Egypt, 24, 84, 99–103, 109
Atlantic: fishing, 12, 156n21; rain forest, 262
Aurangzeb, 233
Australia: environmentally disruptive colonization, 213; indigenous peoples and species extinction, 220; wheat frontiers, 23
Austria: Rhine, 165. *See also* Vienna
authoritarianism, 13, 27, 278

Bacon, Francis, 9
Baden, Rhine, 170, 171
Baltic–White Sea Canal (Belomorstroi), 26, 284, 285, 289
Bandopadhyay, Bibhutibhushan, 244–45
Banerjee, Prathama, 244
barley, 105, 116n93
Bascottah, Ramachander, 233
Bassin, Mark, 291
Bavaria, Rhine, 171
Bazykin, Aleksandr, 300
Beck, Ulrich, 293
Beijing, 123, 125–26, 130, 140, 148
Beinart, William, 9, 24–25, 211–28
Belgium, Rhine, 165, 170, 171
Belgorod defense line, 280
Bemba, ashbed cultivation, 219
Bengal, 10, 39
Big Bang, 34
"big history," 16
biodiversity: India, 229–30; Russia, 278. *See also* animals; biodiversity reduction; plants; wildlife management
biodiversity reduction: Africa wildlife recovery from, 223; global, 54; Rhine, 23, 166, 176, 177–78, 183–84, 186; Russia, 295, 300; Southeast Asia rice

frontiers, 198, 203; today's river engineering and, 185. *See also* species extinctions

"biological old regime," 11–12

biological weapons, 296, 298

biomass fuels, 34, 41–42, 54; for metallurgy, 90, 281; for silk production, 94; transition to fossil fuels from, 42, 44, 95–96. *See also* wood supply

birth-control policies, China, 153, 164n130

birth defects, from pollution in Russia, 299, 300

birth maximization, peasant, 38

Bismarck, Otto von, 171

Black Death, 39, 92

Bolotov, Ivan, 282

Bolsheviks, 283, 285, 286–87, 298, 310n38

Boreiko, Vladimir, 293, 304

Borsch, Steven, 91

Bowring, John, 195

Brailovsky, Antonio Elio, 264

Brandis, Dietrich, 237

Braudel, Fernand, 11

Brazil: famines, 107; forest clearance, 23; rebellion, 255; Tupi Indians, 56

Brezhnev, Leonid, 290–91, 296

Britain: Africa, 212–13, 231; air pollution and cleanup, 12, 44; energy, 42, 43, 44, 46–49; farmers, 29n14; labor hours, 11; Middle East, 101, 102, 104; peasant communal institutions, 62; plague, 91; Rhine Navigation Commission, 171; South Asia, 14, 16, 25, 63, 65, 89, 98, 229–46; Southeast Asia, 15, 192, 194–97

Bronze Age, 90

Burke, Edmund, III, 7, 9, 16, 20, 21, 33–53, 81–117

Burma: British, 15, 192, 194–97; military juntas, 204; rice, 194–97, 200, 202, 204

Byzantines, Sasanid struggle with, 85

Caland, Pieter, 174

Calcutta, India, 77–78n39

California model of agriculture, 106, 107, 116n98

"California school," global or comparative history, 16

Cambridge School, 16

canals, 169–70, 184; China's Grand Canal, 39, 88, 122–26, 129–30, 134, 158n59; French engineering, 99, 175–76; India, 230, 231, 240–41, 246; Middle East, 84–85, 94, 97, 98, 100, 101, 104; Rhine, 174, 175–76, 185; Russia, 26, 284, 285, 289, 295, 296; Southeast Asia river deltas, 195, 202; today's engineering, 185

Cañizarres-Esguerra, Jorge, 266

capitalism, 8; agricultural, 71; developmentalist project vs., 9–10; Europe, 5–6, 8; global, 192, 277; Latin America, 268; Southeast Asia, 192–93; urban land markets, 64. *See also* global economy

Caribbean: slave trade and sugar production, 92. *See also* Cuba

caste, India, 231, 233–34, 235, 244, 253n63

Castelli, Benedetto, 168

Castro Herrera, Guillermo, 257–58, 260, 261

Catherine the Great, 96

cattle: Africa, 62, 213, 218; India, 233

Central Asia: agrarian age, 38–39; cotton, 295; nomads, 124, 280; water management, 86, 295–97

centralization, state, 55–60, 71, 150–51

Chao Phraya River, 192; rice in basin, 192–200, 204

charcoal. *See* biomass fuels

chawls (Mumbai tenement buildings), 67, 77n41

Chechnya, 302

Chekhov, Anton, 282

chemical agricultural usages, 106, 107, 202

chemical energy, 35

chemical pollution: Rhine, 23, 167, 180–83; Russia, 294

chemical weapons, 298

Chernobyl, 294, 295, 298, 306, 307

Chevalier, Michel, 98–99

chieftaincy, Africa, 216, 223

China, 15–16, 118–64, 124*map;* agrarian empire, 40; agriculture, 36, 39, 119, 121, 125, 126, 130, 133–42, 148–53, 162n103, 233; cities, 123, 125–26, 130, 140, 148, 151; "commercialism without capitalism," 8; Communist Party (CCP), 22, 132, 133, 135, 136–53; Cultural Revolution, 142, 150, 159n59; developmentalism, 22, 118–36, 142, 143, 150–53; economics, 92–93, 118–19, 121–23, 125, 127, 137, 147–50, 151, 153; elephants, 234; energy access, 44; energy consumption, 45, 148–49; "fractal" nature of Chinese state and society, 149; Grand Canal, 39, 88, 122–26, 129–30, 134, 158n59; Han, 6, 45, 154n2; "hydraulic society," 89, 121, 184; industrialization, 8, 119, 129, 131, 134, 135, 136, 151; internal colonization, 39, 92–93, 123–24; irrigation, 88, 134–44, 149; labor, 28n4, 121, 128–29, 136–39, 141, 145, 158–59n59; land markets, 69–70, 71; Ming dynasty, 22, 40, 62, 92, 121, 123–27; Mongol Yuan, 92, 123; "moral meteorology," 11; Nationalist Party (Guomindang/GMD), 133, 134–35, 137, 144, 159n59; peasant land rights, 62–63, 137; People's Liberation Army (PLA), 138, 146; People's Republic, 22, 135, 136–53; petroleum-poor and coal-rich, 47, 142, 147; population growth, 40, 127, 128, 129, 141, 147; proletarianization rate, 28n4; silver, 11, 30n20, 92; Song dynasty, 39; statecraft, 7, 22, 119, 122–42, 149–53; Taiping Rebellion, 130–31, 152; Tiananmen incident (1989), 138, 139; water management, 22, 121–52, 158–59n59; xenophobia, 123. *See also* Qing dynasty; Yangzi River area; Yellow River area

Chinese, Southeast Asian river delta, 15, 196

Christensen, Peter, 91, 108

Christianity, 96, 278

Cioc, Mark, 9, 12, 14, 22–23, 165–90

cities: Africa, 66, 69, 77n48, 222; agriculture near, 29n14; air pollution, 12, 13, 44, 299; automobile culture, 67–68; China, 123, 125–26, 130, 140, 148, 151; as complex energy machines, 37; energy demand, 95; green space per inhabitant, 64; housing, 55, 65–70, 77–78nn39,41; India, 66–69, 77–78nn39,41, 233; land markets, 58, 64–70; Latin America, 26, 69, 268; Middle East, 69, 87, 95; migration to, 64, 65–70, 136; population growth, 26, 64, 65–69, 95; property rights, 55, 65, 66–70; Rhine, 166, 167, 178; rise of, 64, 95; Russia, 278, 279, 280, 293, 299; Southeast Asia, 193, 199; squatters, 65, 68–69; upper-class and elite flight, 67–68; wastewater into rivers, 166, 167, 199; water supply, 137–38, 140; zoning, 65, 72

"civilizing" projects: of European colonizers, 193; within states, 15, 143

class: cities, 67–68; civil society, 315n115. *See also* caste; gentry; lower class; serfdom; slavery

Cleary, David, 263

climate, Middle East, 82

coal, 35, 42, 50; age of (1800–1914), 42–46, 95–96, 102; China, 47, 142, 147; consumption of, 44–46, 47; Europe, 42–44, 49, 95, 96; Rhine and,

23, 166, 178; water pollution caused by, 44, 178–79

Cold War, 89, 216, 296

collectivization, Russia, 69–70, 284, 286, 288

colonization, 231; by Bantu-speaking black Africans, 219; China's internal, 39, 92–93, 123–24; ecological "archaeology of colonialism," 276; environmentally disruptive, 25, 41, 211, 213, 218, 238, 259; Latin America, 259. *See also* European colonizers; imperialism

Colson, Elizabeth, 222

Columbian exchange, 20, 264, 269

commercialization, 5, 8, 10–12, 19, 128. *See also* markets

commodity perspective: environmental history, 266–67. *See also* economics

Common Market, Rhine Navigation Commission and, 168, 186

Communists: Chinese, 22, 132, 133, 135, 136–53; Russia, 26–27, 283–96, 300–307; Vietnam, 197

community identity, and property rights, 41, 55, 60–64, 67, 72

Confino, Michael, 281

Conklin, Barbara, 265

Connah, Graham, 219

conservationism: African chieftains, 223; China soil, 139, 144–45; colonizers', 106, 214, 223; India, 242; Latin America, 266; Russia, 280, 283–84, 292. *See also* environmentalism; parks; wildlife management

consumption, 33, 44–45, 50; China, 45, 119–20, 122, 148–49; energy, 32n35, 41, 44–49, 46*fig*, 48*table*, 49*fig*, 53n32, 95, 148–49; Latin America, 268

cooperative governance: European economics, 168, 186; Rhine, 14, 179–80, 185. *See also* multinational environmental management

Coopersmith, Jonathan, 285

Costlow, Jane, 282

cotton: Central Asia, 295, 297; China, 128; Egypt, 100–101

Cotton, John, 144

Cronon, William, 257, 262

Crosby, Alfred, 14, 211, 218, 238, 257, 264

Cuba, land markets, 71

cults: Indian Muslim, 10–11; Middle Eastern, 30n18; Zimbabwean territorial, 220

Cunha, Euclides da, 255

Curzon, Lord, 243, 253n68

Damodar Valley Authority (DVA), 244

dams, 184, 231; Africa, 222; China, 135, 138–46, 149, 150; India, 231, 240, 244; Middle East, 21–22, 24, 84, 97, 99–106, 109; Rhine, 175, 176, 177; Russia, 284–85, 290. *See also* hydropower

Danilov-Danelian, Viktor, 301

Darwin, Charles, 266

Dawson, Jane, 304

Dean, Warren, 257, 262, 263, 264

DeBardeleben, Joan, 294

declensionist narratives, Latin American, 26, 261–63

deep history, 4; Middle East, 81–91, 108–9. *See also* energy regimes (deep history)

deforestation, 13, 20, 33, 57, 58–59; China, 129, 132, 145–46, 152, 161–62n97; cults associated with, 10–11; early modern, 41–42; fire and, 37, 58, 59; French colonizers' concern with, 106, 214; indigenous, 220; Latin America, 265, 267; Middle East, 89–90, 94, 97; Russia, 282; Southeast Asia rice frontiers, 198–99, 203; U.S., 31n27; Western Europe, 95

deltas. *See* river valleys and deltas

deserts, Middle East, 81–82

determinism, 211, 255, 276

developmentalist project, 4, 7–16, 19, 83; China, 22, 118–36, 142, 143, 150–53; concrete manifestations, 10; engineers central to, 98–99; liberal, 7, 10, 13–14, 27, 119–23; Middle East, 94–100, 103, 104, 108, 109–10; populist, 132–33, 135–36, 137; pursuit of "material benefit," 119–20; Rhine, 14, 22–23, 165–90; Russian interactions, 27; second colonial occupation in Africa, 216; Third World countries, 107–8. *See also* modernization

dike construction, Southeast Asia river deltas, 195, 201–3

diseases: Africa, 213, 222; AIDS, 25, 303; from air pollution, 44; Black Death, 39, 92; colonizer science treating, 25, 213; colonizers spreading, 24, 40, 57, 211, 213, 218; epizootic rinderpest, 218; Great Dying, 40; India, 253n67; Mesopotamia, 91; from perennial irrigation, 102; plague, 5, 91; Russia, 296, 303; Southeast Asia rice frontiers, 199; trypanosomiasis, 213, 214, 221–22

domestication, animal, 37, 277

droughts: China, 132; and famines, 216; high-input agriculture and, 107; Middle East, 103–4; North Africa, 105, 106

Duisberg, Carl, 182

Durham, William, 263

Dust Bowl, 107, 223, 244

early modern period, 4, 10–12, 41–43, 62, 63; agriculture, 11, 38, 41; land use intensification, 55, 71. *See also* colonization; imperialism

East Africa: famines, 107; wind systems in climate, 82

East Asia: military and fiscal revolution, 109; per capita primary-product demand, 147. *See also* China; Japan

Eastern Europe: agriculture, 39; export orientation, 128; industrialization, 8; land markets, 69–70, 71; spheres of autonomy from the Soviet state, 304–5. *See also* Russia

East India Company, 242

ecological devastation, 33; Africa, 24, 211, 213; China, 11, 132; cleanup, 12–13; developmentalist project and, 11–14; Latin America, 259; outside the realm of human causality, 51n12; Rhine, 23, 176–86; Russia, 13, 281, 293–99, 306, 307. *See also* biodiversity reduction; environmental degradation; species extinctions

ecology: caste and, 231, 233–34; "imperial" vs. "Arcadian" view, 241; India, 229–30, 241–43; local knowledge, 9, 215–23; range ecology, 215–16; Rhine, 166–67, 172–84; Russian defiance of, 291. *See also* animals; biodiversity; ecological devastation; environmentalism; nature; plants

economics: China, 92–93, 118–19, 121–23, 125, 127, 137, 147–50, 151, 153; developmentalist project, 8, 10, 13; economic environmental history, 266–67; energy costs, 17–19, 18*fig*, 32n34; environmental sustainability with benefits in, 9; European cooperative, 168, 186; French Revolution and, 170–71; human welfare indicators, 8, 147; inequality, 13, 137; organic and inorganic, 16; Rhine projects, 178–84, 186; Russia, 279, 283–97, 300, 302, 305; state-owned land, 60; water pollution, 178–84. *See also* capitalism; markets; taxes; trade

Edison, Thomas A., 45

Egypt: agriculture, 36, 84, 108; British, 101, 102; cotton, 100–101; engineering schools, 99–100; "hydraulic society," 89, 184; land markets, 63; Muhammad Ali, 7, 9, 21–22, 97, 99, 100–101; Nasser, 21, 99, 102; pharaohs, 100;

water management, 21–22, 24, 84, 99–103, 109. *See also* Nile River area

Eisenstein, Sergei, 286

electricity, 45, 98; China's hydropowered, 142–47; Egypt, 102; Mumbai slums, 68; nuclear power–generated, 49; Russia, 284–86, 302

elephants: Africa, 217, 220, 234; China, 234; India, 232, 234; in warfare, 234, 250n30

Elvin, Mark, 8

eminent domain, 55

Emmerich, Rudolph, 179

Emscher Cooperative, 179, 185

Emscher River, 178–80, 182, 185

endangered species, 12–13. *See also* species extinctions

energy, 33–53; and agricultural transformations, 20, 36–38; animal power, 37; chemical, 35; classic view of significance of, 16–17; consumption, 32n35, 41, 44–49, 46*fig*, 48*table*, 49*fig*, 53n32, 95, 148–49; defined, 34; fire, 34, 35, 37; forms in the universe, 34–35; global per capita, 32n35; Industrial Revolution, 33, 35, 43, 44, 49, 50, 96, 98; mechanical (kinetic), 35; modern use, 17–19, 18*fig*, 32n34; Rhine grid, 166; Russia, 284–85, 297–98, 299, 302; solar, 34–37; steam, 43, 45, 98; technology for efficient use, 12, 17, 32n37, 37, 43, 297; thermal, 35; urban demand, 95; "useful work," 32n34; wind, 40. *See also* biomass fuels; electricity; fossil fuels; hydropower; nuclear power

energy regimes (deep history), 33–53; age of fossil fuels (1800 C.E. to present), 35, 36*table*, 37, 42–50, 95–96, 98; age of solar energy (10,000 B.C.E. to 1800 C.E.), 34–37, 36*table*, 40

Enfantin, Barthélemy Prosper, 98

engineering: century of engineers, 98; China, 118, 134–35, 137, 139, 142, 149; French model, 98–99; India, 98, 240–41, 244; Middle East, 98–109; Renaissance-Enlightenment, 23, 168–69, 170, 172, 176, 185; Rhine, 22–23, 168–70, 172–78, 185; river manipulation, 168–70, 172–78, 185; Russia, 284, 287; schools, 98, 99–100, 168–69; Southeast Asia river deltas, 201. *See also* canals; dams; irrigation

England. *See* Britain; London

Enlightenment, 5, 9, 96, 211, 241; Rhine engineering, 23, 169, 170, 172, 176, 185

environmental adaptations, 200, 201

environmental degradation: Africa, 214–20; China, 144; early modern, 41–42; global warming, 13–14, 24, 204–5; Latin America, 262; limits of restoration, 184–86; Middle East, 89–90, 94–95, 97, 103, 108–10; Rhine, 23, 166–67, 172, 178–86. *See also* deforestation; ecological devastation; pollution

environmental disaster, 13, 182. *See also* ecological devastation

environmental history, 255–56; Africa, 25, 211–24; Americas, 218; apocalyptic, 24, 213; energy regimes and, 33–53; India, 229–54; and industrialization, 13, 16–19, 33; "liberal project," 120; Middle East, 81–108; Russia, 26–28, 276–315; Southeast Asia river deltas, 15, 23–24, 191–205; U.S., 265, 269; world history and, 3–32. *See also* animals; ecology; environmental degradation; environmental management; Latin American environmental history; plants

environmentalism: China's dams and, 142; French colonizers', 106; Latin America, 268; of poor, 9, 216, 222; Soviet nature protection/*zapovedniki*, 280, 283, 284, 291, 292, 300–305. *See also* conservationism; ecology; sustainability

environmental-justice movements, 26

environmental management: Africa, 213,
215–20; China, 118–42, 151–53; India,
230–31; multinational (Rhine), 14,
168, 170–72, 179–80, 185, 186; Russian
tribute-taking, 26–27, 276–315. *See
also* land management; water management; wildlife management
epizootic rinderpest, 218
erosion: Lesotho, 214, 220; Rhine, 175,
176; Tibet, 146; Yellow River area,
129, 144
Ethiopian highlands, agriculture emerging, 36
Euphrates, 83–84, 85, 103–4
Eurasia: balkanization, 303; complex
societies and cities emerging, 36–37,
41; fall of Communism, 304–7; industrialization, 14. *See also* Asia; Eastern
Europe; Russia
Europe, 7; agrarian age, 39, 40; agriculture, 29n14, 39; capitalism, 5–6, 8;
common property, 62; energy uses, 43,
45, 47, 95; forest coverage, 12; frontier
exploitation, 41; Hapsburg, 40, 88, 93,
170; imperialism, 43, 96, 192, 211, 229;
market for North African agriculture,
106; "neo-Europes," 191; Ottoman
competition with, 93, 94; population
growth, 40; Rhine, 14, 22–23, 165–90;
river engineering, 168–70; science,
5–6, 10; state power, 5–6, 41; suburbanization, 67–68; urban migration,
66. *See also* Eastern Europe; European
colonizers; Western Europe
European colonizers, 15–16, 92, 264–65;
Africa, 24–25, 97, 99, 105–7, 212–23,
231; Americas, 40, 41, 211, 213, 218, 238,
259, 265; diseases spread by, 24, 40, 57,
211, 213, 218; diseases treated by science
of, 25, 213; slaveholders producing for,
10; Southeast Asia, 15, 192–202; subjects' vs. overseas subjects' rights, 16.
See also Britain; France

European Union, 168, 186
Evenson, Norma, 67
exports: American orientation, 128, 259;
European orientation, 128; food, 107,
192, 194–98, 201, 204, 259; textile, 10
extinctions. *See* species extinctions

fables, Africa, 222–23
Fairhead, James, 214, 220
famines: Africa, 102–3, 107, 216;
droughts and, 107; Russia, 282,
284, 286; Southeast Asia, 196
Faraday, Michael, 45
Feierman, Steven, 221
fertilizers, 108, 130, 156n21, 202
Feynman, Richard, 34
fire: and deforestation, 37, 58, 59; as
energy, 34, 35, 37; Madeira cleared by,
213; North African environment well
adapted to, 106; Russians using and
fighting against, 280, 290–91, 308n3; in
source of civilization, 34; technology
using, 37, 58, 59. *See also* biomass fuels
fish, Rhine, 167, 172, 173, 176–77, 186
fishing: China, 148, 156n21; globally
stretched to limits, 148; Japan, 12,
156n21; Mediterranean, 103; oceanic,
12, 41, 156n21; Rhine, 172, 176–77,
184; Southeast Asia, 203; state regulation of, 60; Uzbek basin, 295
flooding/flood control/floodplain:
Africa, 216; China, 121, 124–46, 152,
162n97; India, 229; Middle East,
83–85, 88, 91, 102, 103; Rhine, 166–67,
168, 175, 178, 183–86; Russia, 295
Florez-Malagon, Alberto Guillermo, 261
Foguelman, Dina, 264
food: Central Asia, 295; entitlements,
216; exports, 107, 192, 194–98, 201,
204, 259; Middle East security, 109;
Southeast Asia, 192, 194–98, 201, 203,
204. *See also* famines; grains
Ford, John, 221–22

forests, 5, 12, 13, 16, 58–59; Africa, 24, 214, 217, 220; ashbed cultivation, 219; China's reforestation, 131, 139; coal energy sparing, 43; French Forest Code (1827), 106; at heart of power, 30n17; India, 25, 230–32, 237–40, 243–46, 253n69; Latin America, 265, 267; Russia, 277, 278, 280, 281, 282, 308n3; U.S., 12, 31n27, 237. *See also* deforestation

fossil fuels: age of (1800 C.E. to present), 35, 36*table*, 37, 42–50, 98; age of coal (1800–1914), 42–46, 95–96, 102; age of petroleum and natural gas (1880–present), 42, 45, 47, 96, 102; China, 142; revolution to, 20, 34, 42–44, 95–96, 98, 109; sustainable strategy, 50. *See also* coal; natural gas; petroleum

France: Africa, 105–8, 214; agrarian age, 40; banks, 99; chemical industry, 181; coal, 49; engineering model, 98; Forest Code (1827), 106; French Revolution, 22, 62, 168, 170; Middle East, 21, 97, 98–99, 100, 101; Napoleon, 169, 170; nuclear power, 47–49; Rhine, 165, 166, 168, 170, 171, 175–76, 181, 184; Southeast Asia, 15, 192, 195–202

Frank, Zephyr, 267

frontier narrative: Latin American environmental history, 265; Southeast Asian environmental history, 23–24, 191–205

frontiers, 23, 191; Bengal, 10; Southeast Asian rice, 23–24, 191–205; state exploitation of, 41, 56–57

Furtado, Celso, 266–67

Gadgil, Madhav, 231
Galeano, Eduardo, 261–62
Gallini, Stefania, 258, 261, 262
Gandhi, Mohandas, 244
Ganges valley, rice cultivation, 39, 232
Garden, Don, 256

Gare, Arran, 305–6

gases: greenhouse, 204; methane, 204. *See also* natural gas

Gastev, Aleksei, 287–88

gender. *See* women

genetics, Soviets and, 291

gentry, Russia, 279, 280, 281–82

geography, 291; coal distribution, 44; "geographical determinism," 255–56; historical, 256–57, 268; India's heterogeneous, 229

"geo-optimism," 288

Gerbi, Antonio, 265

Germany: chemical industry, 181–82; China influenced by, 134; civil society, 315n115; Duisburg-Ruhrort, 166; Federal Republic, 171; land reform, 62; Napoleonic creations, 170; Nazi, 171; Rhine, 165, 166, 170, 171, 175–76, 181, 185; World War I economy, 283

Gibson, Alexander, 242

Gichuki, Francis, 221

Glick, Thomas, 87

Gligo, Nicolò, 262

global domination. *See* imperialism

global economy, 92–94, 97; Africa, 216–17, 218; China, 92–93, 119, 128, 147–53; Great Depression, 105, 197, 203; Middle East, 93–94, 97, 98–99, 110; Russia, 293, 297; Southeast Asia, 192–97, 201, 203, 204. *See also* capitalism; trade

global history/comparative history, 16

global warming, 13–14, 24, 204–5

gold, African trade, 88, 93

Golden Horde, 278

Goldman, Marshall, 294

Gol'tsman, Iakov, 285

Gorbachev, Mikhail Sergeevich, 297, 300–301

Gorky, Maxim, 26, 287, 288–89

Goudsblom, Johan, 34

Graham, Laura, 265

income per capita, China, 137, 147, 151, 153

India, 229–54; agriculture, 36, 233, 235, 236, 238, 240, 244; British, 14, 25, 63, 65, 89, 98, 229–46; heterogeneity, 229–30, 236, 238, 246; "hydraulic society," 184; independence (1947), 230; industrialization, 8; intelligentsia, 244; irrigation, 25, 88–89, 98, 240, 241, 246, 253n63; Islam, 10–11, 232–33; land use intensification, 5, 25, 233, 235; Mughal, 10, 40, 232–34, 235; peasant land rights, 63, 236; petroleum-poor and coal-rich, 47; population growth, 40, 229, 235; precolonial, 10–11, 230–35, 238, 246; urban housing, 66–69, 77–78nn39,41

Indian Ocean zone: climate, 82; Europeans exploiting, 41

Indians (from India), in Southeast Asian river delta, 15, 196–97

Indians (indigenous Americans), 40, 211, 220, 238, 265

indigenous peoples: Africa, 214–23; Americas, 40, 211, 220, 238, 265; as colonizers and migrants, 219; diseases from colonizers, 24, 40, 57, 211, 213, 218; extermination of animal species aided by, 220; local knowledge, 9, 215–23; property rights, 41, 55, 56–57, 58; South Asia, 10–11, 230–35, 238, 246

Indonesia, 56

industrialization, 8, 14–15; China, 8, 119, 129, 131, 134, 135, 136, 151; in environmental history, 13, 16–19, 33; Latin America, 259, 268; and Rhine pollution, 23, 166, 167, 178–84, 185; Russia, 8, 69–70, 281, 284, 285, 299, 302, 303, 310n38; and Southeast Asia river pollution, 199; urban land markets, 64. *See also* Industrial Revolution

Industrial Revolution: and energy, 33, 35, 43, 44, 49, 50, 96, 98; and land use in Latin America, 259

Indus valley, 36, 240

inequality: economic, 13, 137; environmental, 13, 26

intellectual environmental history, 26, 265–66

intellectual property rights, 215

intelligentsia: India, 244; Russia, 300–301

international organizations: and environmental problems, 14, 305. *See also* multinational environmental management

Iran/Persia, 97; agriculture, 85–88, 91, 108; engineers, 100; irrigation, 85–88, 93; Mongols, 90; pastoralists, 94–95; water supply, 104; wind systems in climate, 82

Iraq: agriculture, 85, 90, 93, 104, 108; water management, 83, 85, 90, 93, 103–4. *See also* Mesopotamia

iron industry, biomass demands, 90, 281

Irrawaddy river, 192; rice frontier in delta, 193–200, 204

irrigation: Africa, 222; China, 88, 134–44, 149; engineers, 99; "hydraulic societies," 89, 121, 184; Iberia, 87–89; India, 25, 88–89, 98, 240, 241, 246, 253n63; Middle East, 21–22, 84–89, 99, 100–104; North Africa, 104, 106–7; perennial, 21, 101–2; *qanat* systems, 85–88, 104; Southeast Asia rice frontiers, 195, 200, 201; U.S., 231

Isfahan, expansion of, 95

Islam: cults, 10–11, 30n18; India, 10–11, 232–33; Middle East "medieval Islamic green revolution," 38, 83, 86–88

Istanbul, population, 95

Italy, river management, 168–70, 171

Ivan IV ("the Terrible"), 278–79, 286

ivory, Africa, 217, 220

Leopold, Aldo, 170
liberalism: Chinese, 119–23; classical, 120; developmentalist, 7, 10, 13–14, 27–28, 119–23; French Revolution and, 170–71; Rhine project and, 168
"liberal project," 120–23, 147
Libya, 104
Lieberman, Victor, 5
Liechtenstein, Rhine, 165
life expectancy: China, 151; human welfare indicators, 147
life on earth, emergence of, 35
Lindert, Peter, 144–45, 152, 161–62n97
local knowledge: Africa, 9, 215–23; India, 234
logging. *See* deforestation; wood supply
London, air pollution and air cleanup, 12, 44
"long nineteenth century" (roughly 1800–1918), 98
lower class: urban housing, 55, 65–70, 77–78nn39,41. *See also* peasants; poor; serfdom
Lunacharskii, Anatolii Vasil'evich, 283
Luxembourg, Rhine, 165
Lysenko, Trofim Denisovich, 290, 291
Lysenkoists, Russian, 27

MacKenzie, John, 213
Madeira, foundation of, 213
Maffioli, Caesare, 88
Mafia, Eurasian, 293, 303
Maghreb: agriculture, 104–8. *See also* Algeria; Morocco; Tunisia
Malawi, Tchiri Valley, 216
Malthus, Thomas, 20, 50
Mamdani, Mahmood, 224
Manchus, 6, 62, 130
Mandala, Elias, 216
Maoism, 136, 139, 141, 145, 152
Mao Zedong, 138
mapping, cadastral, 57
Marichal, Carlos, 267

markets: developmentalist project, 10–11, 119; sumptuary laws, 192. *See also* global economy; land markets; trade
Marks, Robert, 8
Marsh, George Perkins, 106
Martínez-Alier, Joan, 257
Martius, Carl von, 266
Marxism, 8, 230; Russia, 27, 285–86, 294. *See also* Communists
Maurice, Byzantine emperor, 277
Maxwell, David, 220
Mayaram, Shail, 237
McCann, James, 218
McCook, Stuart, 263–64, 266
McNeill, John, 4, 13, 16
mechanical (kinetic) energy, 35
mechanization: early modern, 43. *See also* technology
Mediterranean: economic and political hub, 98–99; fish stocks, 103; Middle East dry farming areas, 81–82
Medvedev, Roy A., 300
Medvedev, Zhores, 298
Mekong, 192; rice in delta, 193, 195–200, 202, 204
Meléndez, Silvia, 261
Melville, Elinor, 263, 264
Menzies, Nicholas, 129
Meratus Dayaks, South Kalimantan, 56
Mercator projection, 178
Mesopotamia: agriculture, 36; diseases, 91; environmental history, 108–9; "hydraulic societies," 89; Mongols, 90; water management, 84–85, 88, 91. *See also* Iran/Persia; Iraq; Syria; Turkey
methane gas, rice paddies, 204
Mexico: Mexico City population growth, 64; water management, 88
Middle East, 16, 81–117; agrarian age, 38–39; agriculture, 21–22, 36, 38, 81–97, 100–104, 108; deep history, 81–91, 108–9; developmentalist project, 94–100, 103, 104, 108, 109–10;

292, 300–305; Soviet transformation of, 284, 285, 287–90, 292–93, 295; Soviet war on, 26–27, 288–93. *See also* animals; biodiversity; ecology; plants; wildlife management

navigation. *See* ships; transport

Nehru, Jawaharlal, 8, 244

Nekrasov, Nikolai, 282

"neo-Europes," 191

Neolithic period, 35–36, 45

Netherlands: cadastral mapping, 57; chemical industry, 181, 183; per capita energy use, 32n35; Rhine, 165, 166, 171, 173–74, 176, 181, 183, 184, 186; Rotterdam's Europoort, 166, 174; water management, 88

Netting, Robert, 61

Niagara Falls, hydropower, 45

niche pattern, environmental adaptation, 200

Nicholas II, tsar, 282

Nile River area, 83–84; dam, 21–22, 24, 84, 99–103, 109; floodplain, 83–84, 102, 103; irrigation system, 21, 84, 91, 101

Nobiling, Eduard Adolph, 174–75

nomads, 6; Central Asia, 124, 280; Middle East, 7, 82, 90, 94–95, 97, 104; South Asia, 25, 232, 235; states vs., 6–7, 15, 25, 56, 232, 235–36; sustainable way of life, 106. *See also* hunter-gatherers

North Africa: agrarian age, 38–39, 40; dry farming and pastoralism, 104–8; land markets, 63. *See also* Egypt; Maghreb; Middle East

North America: energy consumption, 46–47; myth of the ecological Indian, 9; suburbanization, 67–68. *See also* Mexico; United States

nuclear power, 35, 47–49; Rhine cooling reactors, 166; Russia/Chernobyl, 277, 294, 295, 298–301, 303, 306, 307; waste, 294, 299, 300; weapons, 299–300, 303

"Occidentalism," 25–26, 242

oceans, 30n24; fishing, 12, 41, 156n21; transport, 40, 43, 93. *See also* Atlantic; Indian Ocean zone

oil. *See* petroleum

Olson, Mancur, 306

opium, China, 128, 157n39

"oriental despotism," 89, 121, 139, 184

Orientalism, 242

Ottomans, 7, 21, 30n18, 93–96; agrarian state, 40, 93; developmentalist project, 94, 96; Egyptian engineers, 99; Europe's competition with, 93, 94; gunpowder use, 117n105; Sultan Mahmud II, 96; *tanzimat* reforms, 21, 96–97, 104; water management, 93–94

Pacey, Arnold, 88

Pádua, José, 266

Palácio, Germán, 260

Paleolithic era, 35

Panchen Lama, death of, 139

parks: Africa, 213, 223; Russian reserves, 283–84; U.S., 284

pastoralists. *See* nomads

peasants: birth maximization by, 38; China, 62–63, 123, 125, 132–33, 136–37; community property rights, 41, 55, 60–64; cost of labor, 9; Egypt, 101, 102; emancipation, 62; enclosure, 62; India, 63, 230, 232–33, 236, 241; land markets, 60–64, 69–70; migration to cities, 69–70, 136; North Africa, 107; Russia, 279–82, 284, 286, 291

perestroika, 300–301

Perlin, John, 90

Persia. *See* Iran/Persia; Iraq

pesticides, synthetic, 106, 107

Peter I ("the Great"), 96, 280–81, 284

petroleum, 35, 42; age of (1880–present), 42, 45, 47, 96, 102; China, 47, 142; Middle East, 50, 96, 102, 109; Russia, 297, 299

Petruchevsky, Oleg, 90
photosynthesis, 35
Pickvance, Katy Láng, 304
Pinchot, Gifford, 237
Pittsburgh, air cleanup, 12, 13
plague, 5, 91
planning, Soviet, 283, 286, 288–93, 296
plants: photosynthesis, 35; species trans-
    mission, 11. *See also* agriculture;
    forests; parks
politics: developmentalist, 119–20, 123;
    early modern management, 41;
    "hydraulic societies," 89, 121, 184;
    land management, 65, 66, 67, 69,
    72–73; "oriental despotism," 89, 121,
    139, 184; perestroika, 300–301; Rhine,
    170, 171–72; Russian tribute-taking,
    26–27, 276–315; urban, 65, 66, 67, 69;
    water management, 89, 103–4. *See also*
    international organizations; Marxism;
    rebellions; states
Pollan, Michael, 202
pollution: acid rain, 44; chemical, 23, 167,
    180–83, 294; Latin America, 268;
    nuclear wastes, 294, 299, 300; Russia,
    292, 293–94, 296, 297, 299–300, 302–3,
    306; Southeast Asia, 199, 201; thermal,
    167, 182–83. *See also* air pollution; envi-
    ronmental degradation; water pollution
Pomeranz, Kenneth, 3–32, 92, 118–64
poor: China, 119, 124, 136–37, 152–53,
    154n10; energy use, 53n32; environ-
    mentalism of, 9, 216, 222; peasants, 61,
    107; science and state as allies of, 24–25,
    222; urban, 65–69. *See also* lower class
poorer countries, focus on, 4
population, 5, 6, 11, 12, 20, 56–57; Africa,
    218, 219; agrarian age, 38–40, 39*fig*,
    40*fig*; birth-control policies, 153,
    164n130; China, 40, 127, 128, 129, 141,
    147; colonizers' depopulating effects,
    40, 211, 238; and energy consumption,
    41, 50, 53n32; India, 40, 229, 235; and

Middle East agriculture, 21, 22, 87;
    and Moroccan agriculture, 107; path
    to modernity, 91–92; peasant commu-
    nities, 61; Rhine watershed, 166;
    Russian famine casualties, 284;
    Southeast Asia rice frontiers, 199, 200;
    urban, 26, 64, 65–69, 95. *See also* land
    use intensification; migration
populism, developmental, 132–33,
    135–36, 137
Potemkin, Mikhail Petrovich, 292
Potosí silver mines, 11
Pratap, Ajay, 238
Prezent, Isai Izrailovich, 291
Procopius, 277
progress: idea of, 98; Rhine degradation
    and, 167
property rights, 54–78; China, 62–63,
    137, 145; common, 41, 55, 60–64, 137,
    220–21; indigenous peoples, 41, 55,
    56–57, 58; informal, 68–70; intellec-
    tual, 215; Latin America, 267; national
    boundaries, 55, 56; peasant communi-
    ties, 41, 55, 60–64, 137, 236; private,
    10, 20–21, 55, 57–58, 61–62, 70, 71,
    102; Russia, 278; state, 20–21, 41,
    55–60, 71–72, 237; urban, 55, 65,
    66–70. *See also* land management
prostitution, China, 157n39
Prussia, Rhine, 165, 170, 171, 174–75,
    179, 180–81, 182, 184
Putin, Vladimir, 303, 305
Pyne, Stephen J., 34, 290–91

qanat irrigation systems, 85–88, 104
Qing dynasty, 5, 92–93, 153; agrarian age,
    40; developmentalism, 22, 121–35, 151;
    Manchus, 6, 62, 130; taxes, 150; water
    management, 22, 121–35, 138, 140

Radium Institute, Vernadskii's, 283
railroads: China, 131; Egypt, 101; French
    engineering, 99; India, 237; Rhine

competition, 171; Russia, 284, 285, 290, 291; steam-powered, 43, 45

rainfall: China, 121; Middle East, 82, 104. *See also* droughts; monsoons

Rangarajan, Mahesh, 6–7, 9, 15, 16, 25–26, 229–54

Ranger, Terence, 212, 220

Rawls, John, 7

Ray, Satyajit, 245

rebellions: Africa, 216; Brazil, 255; Burmese nativist, 197; over environmental issues, 216, 238; India, 235, 238–40; Taiping Rebellion, 130–31, 152

religions: Christianity, 96, 278; Hinduism, 88; "world," 10–11. *See also* cults; Islam

Remington, Thomas, 285, 286–87, 290, 310n38

Renaissance: Italian, 168–70; Rhine engineering, 23, 168–69, 172, 176, 185; science, 9

Repin, Il'ya, 282

Reza Shah, 100

Rhine, 165–67; Action Plan on Flood Defence, 186; Alpine and non-Alpine parts, 172–73; Amsterdam-Rijn canal (1931–38), 174; biodiversity reduction, 23, 166, 176, 177–78, 183–84, 186; channel straightening, 167, 176, 185; cooperative governance, 14, 179–80, 185; ecology, 166–67, 172–78; engineering, 22–23, 168–70, 172–78, 185; environmental degradation, 23, 166–67, 172, 178–84; first rectification project (1817), 169; floodplain destruction, 166–67, 186; Grand Canal d'Alsace, 176; Honsell-Rehbock Project (1906–36), 175; limits of restoration, 184–86; Magistrat du Rhin, 170; Merwede Project (1850–1916), 173–74; Meuse widening and canalization (1918–42), 174; Navigation Commission, 14, 168, 170–72, 184, 186; Nederrijn widening

and canalization (1954–69), 174; Nieuwe Waterweg Project (1860–72), 174; Rhine Protection Commission, 172, 182–83; river-edge habitats, 177; Salmon 2000 project, 186; self-cleansing capacity believed in, 180–82, 185; Stork Plan, 186; Tulla Project (1817–76), 175

rice: China, 39, 127, 130; India, 39, 232; Southeast Asia frontiers, 15, 23–24, 191–205

Richards, John, 4, 5, 16, 20–21, 41, 54–78

Richards, Paul, 215, 221–22

rivers, 172; manipulated by engineering, 168–70, 172–78, 185; Rhine, 14, 22–23, 165–90; Russia, 294–95; Southeast Asia, 192

river valleys and deltas: India, 36, 39, 232, 240; Middle East, 81–85, 100–104; Russia, 277; Southeast Asia, 15, 23–24, 191–205, 194*map*. *See also* Nile River area; Rhine; Yangzi River area; Yellow River area

Rodgers, W. A., 215

Romans, 89, 90, 105

Rösener, Werner, 62

Russia, 15–16, 26–28, 276–315; agrarian age, 40; agriculture, 69–70, 277, 279, 280–82, 294, 295–97, 306; Black Sea expansionism, 96; China and, 131, 134; ecological devastation, 13, 281, 293–99; environmental history, 26–28, 276–315; fall of Communism, 304–7; militarized regimes, 26, 27, 279, 280, 296, 298–301; *mir*, 62; Napoleon invasion (1812), 169; nature protection, 280, 283, 284, 291, 292, 300–305; revolution (1905), 282; Stolypin reforms (1909), 62; Time of Troubles (1599–1613), 279; tribute-taking state, 26–27, 276–315; tsarist, 26–27, 96, 278–84, 286, 293, 298, 306; utopianism, 26, 285–87. *See also* Soviet Union

Soluri, John, 26, 267

Song dynasty, 39

South Africa: jackals partially eradicated, 223; Pondoland revolt (1960), 216; water distribution, 222

South Asia: agrarian age, 38–39; Britain, 14, 16, 25, 63, 65, 89, 98, 229–46; energy access, 44; environmental problems, 25–26; financial institutions, 8; monopsonies on local textiles for export, 10; states vs. nomads, 6–7, 25; Tipu Sultan's Mysore, 7; water management, 86, 88. *See also* India

Southeast Asia: absence of land and labor markets, 28n4; environmental history of river deltas, 15, 191–205; European colonizers, 15, 192–202; land use intensification, 5, 23–24; rice deltas, 194*map;* rice frontiers, 23–24, 191–205; water management, 23–24, 88, 202. *See also* Burma; Thailand/ Siam; Vietnam

Soviet Union, 26–27, 276, 283–306; energy policy, 297–98; "hydraulic society," 89; industrialization, 8, 69–70, 284, 285, 299, 302, 303, 310n38; land markets, 69–70, 71; nature protection/*zapovedniki*, 283, 284, 291, 292, 300–305; production quotas, 10; science, 27, 283, 291–93, 300–301, 303, 304, 314n107; society, 283, 286–88, 291, 293, 305–6; transformation of nature, 284, 285, 287–90, 292–93, 295; war on nature, 26–27, 288–93. *See also* Russia

Spain: agrarian age, 38–39, 40; Americas, 213, 259; Hapsburgs, 88; Umayyads, 87; water management, 87, 88; wool production, 95

species extinctions, 33; colonizers contributing to, 213, 240; indigenous people contributing to, 220. *See also* endangered species

species transmission, through trade and missionary work, 11

spice trade, 92, 94

Stalin, Joseph, 284–87, 289–93, 295, 303, 304

Stanchiniskii, Vladimir Vladimirovich, 291

standardization, Soviet celebration of, 27, 287–88

Starovoitova, Galina, 300

states: Africa, 24–25; antimarket policies, 61; centralizing, 55–60, 71, 150–51; China's statecraft, 7, 22, 119, 122–42, 149–53; "civilizing" projects within, 15, 143; defined, 19; early modern expansion of powers, 10–11, 92; environmental history and formation of, 4; Europe, 5–6, 41; French model of engineering in service of, 98; frontiers exploited by, 41, 56–57; "hydraulic societies," 89, 121, 184; India, 10, 40, 63, 229–46; land management, 20–21, 41, 55–60, 71–72, 230–44; Latin America, 259; "liberal project," 120; Middle East deep history, 109; and naturalism, 266; vs. nomads, 6–7, 15, 25, 56, 232, 235–36; Ottoman *tanzimat* reforms, 21, 96–97, 104; poor peoples' allies, 24–25, 222; promarket policies, 61; property rights, 20–21, 41, 55–60, 71–72, 237; river engineering central to, 168–69; Russian tribute-taking, 26–27, 276–315; territoriality defining membership, 56. *See also* environmental management; politics

steam energy, 43, 45, 98

steppes, Russia, 280, 281, 293

suburbanization, 67–68

Suez Canal, 97, 98, 99, 100

sugar islands, ecological devastation, 11

sugar revolution (1650–1800), 92

Sultan Mahmud II (1807–39), 96

Sun Yat-sen, 131, 135, 138

sustainability: in forest use, 59; fossil fuel strategy, 50; local solutions, 9; nomadic life, 106; *qanat* technology, 86

Sutter, Paul, 269

Sutton, J. E. G., 219

Switzerland: chemical industry, 181; Rhine, 165, 171, 181

Syria: agriculture, 108; dams, 103–4

Tabaqa Dam, 103

Taiping Rebellion, 130–31, 152

Taiwan, 147

Tanzania, early colonial rule, 213

tanzimat reforms, Ottoman, 21, 96–97, 104

Tatars, Russia and, 276, 278, 280

taxes: China, 119, 125, 130, 136, 150–51, 153; India, 234; land maps and, 57; Russia, 279, 302, 306

Taylor, Frederick, 287

technocrats: China, 118, 122–23, 133–34, 142, 149, 153; Russia, 285. *See also* engineering

technology: advanced technological society, 47; agricultural, 22, 41; early modern, 41; energy efficiency, 12, 17, 32n37, 37, 43, 297; fire-using, 37, 58, 59; Industrial Revolution, 35, 43; and Middle East environment, 81; military, 41, 96, 296; and population growth, 38–39; Russia, 27, 284–85, 293, 297, 298, 299, 302; state and entrepreneurial edges, 38; water-saving, 148. *See also* energy; engineering; industrialization; irrigation; railroads; weapons

"Tekhintern," 142

Tesla, Nicola, 45

Thailand/Siam: Chao Phraya River basin, 192–200, 204; European pressures, 15, 192–97; independence, 15; Rama IV, 195; rice, 195–97, 200, 201, 202, 204; Thonburi (Bangkok), 193

thermal energy, 35

thermal pollution, 167, 182–83

Third River project, Iraq, 104

Thirgood, J. V., 90

Three Gorges Dam, 135, 138, 142, 143, 149, 150

Tiananmen incident (1989), 138, 139

Tianjin, water supply, 140

Tibet: deforestation, 146; erosion problem, 146; Han immigration to, 153; water supply, 143; Yamdrok Tso project, 138, 149

Tickle, Andrew, 304

Tiffen, Mary, 221

Tigris, 83–84, 104

Tilly, Charles, 19

timber. *See* wood supply

Tokugawa Japan, 5, 7, 40, 63

Tokyo, air cleanup, 12

Tolstoy, Leo, 282

Topik, Steve, 267

topographers, Latin American environmental historians, 264

tourism, on state-owned lands, 60

township and village enterprises (TVEs), China, 141–42, 150–52

trade: agrarian age, 38; China, 11, 128; early modern long-distance, 10–12, 41; French Revolution policies, 170; fur, 278; gold, 88, 93; India, 234; ivory, 220; Latin America, 259–60, 267; medieval Islamic, 86, 88; Rhine, 170, 172, 186; slave, 92, 217; species transmission through, 11; spice, 92, 94. *See also* exports; markets

"tragedy of the commons," 215, 220–21

transport: Chinese grain shipments, 123, 125, 130; Chinese infrastructure, 151; energy consumption, 45, 46; global, 93; Rhine, 166, 175, 184; sailing ships, 40, 43; Southeast Asia rice frontiers, 201; steam-powered, 43; wind energy, 40. *See also* canals; railroads; rivers; ships

trypanosomiasis, 213, 214, 221–22
tsetse fly, 213
Tsvetkov, M. A., 282
Tulla, Johann Gottfried, 169, 170, 175
Tunisia, 77n48, 100, 105
Turkey: agriculture, 108; Anatolian pastoralists, 94–95; Istanbul, 95; modernization, 97; water management, 86, 103–4

Ukraine: Belgorod-Don shelterbelt, 293; conflicts, 302; famine, 284; forests, 278; foxes, 290; nature protection, 304
United Nations, Red de Formación Ambiental, 258
United States, 244; agricultural outputs dwindling, 108; air cleanup in Pittsburgh, 12, 13; California model of agriculture, 106, 107, 116n98; China influenced by, 134; coal gas, 43; Dust Bowl, 107, 223, 244; energy consumption, 53n32; environmental history, 265, 269; farmers on central plains, 107; forests, 12, 31n27, 237; frontier, 191; Indo-American relationships, 244, 253–54n73; in Iraq, 104; irrigation systems, 231; Niagara Falls hydropower, 45; nuclear power, 49; Ogalala Aquifer, 140; salinization and siltation, 116n98; water management, 88
urban areas. See cities
utopianism, Russian, 26, 285–87
Uzbekistan, 295–96, 303

Vaughan, Megan, 216
Venice, water management, 88
Vernadskii, Vladimir Ivanovich, 283
Vienna: Ottoman siege, 117n105; settlement, 22
Vienna Congress, Rhine Navigation Commission, 168, 170–72, 186
Vietnam: French, 15, 192, 195–97, 199–202; Mekong, 192, 193, 195–200,

202, 204; Revolution and two colonial wars, 204; rice, 193–204
village communities, 234. See also peasants; township and village enterprises (TVEs)
Vorontsov, Nikolai, 300–301
Vyshinskii, Andrei Ianuar'evich, 292

Wang Shaoguang, 150
war on nature, Russian, 26–27, 288–93
wars: Eurasian, 5; financing, 5, 8; Russia, 278–81, 282, 283, 290, 298, 302, 306–7; Sino-Japanese, 133, 135. See also World War II
wastewater: into Rhine, 166, 167, 178–80; Russia, 292, 293, 302–3, 306; into Southeast Asia rivers, 199
water management: Africa, 86, 87–88, 222; China, 22, 121–52, 158–59n59; conservation measures, 140; Middle East, 21–22, 24, 83–109; Russia, 295–96; Southeast Asia, 23–24, 88, 195, 201–3; Spain, 87; technology, 85–88, 104. See also canals; dams; erosion; flooding/flood control/floodplain; hydropower; irrigation; rainfall; rivers; wastewater; water wastage
water pollution: chemical, 23, 167, 180–83; chloride, 182–83; from coal, 44, 178–79; economics of, 178–84; Rhine, 23, 167, 178–85; Russia, 292, 293, 296; Southeast Asia, 199; thermal, 167, 182–83; urban wastewater, 166, 167, 199
water quality: China, 141, 146–47; Russia, 293–94. See also water pollution
water shortages, China, 146–47, 148–49
water transport. See canals; rivers; ships

water wastage, China agriculture, 140,
148–49, 160n73
Watson, Andrew, 38, 86–87
weapons: biological, 296, 298; chemical,
298; gunpowder, 40, 109, 117n105;
nuclear, 299–300, 303; Russia, 296,
298, 299–300, 303; state regulation
of, 60
Weigelt, Curt, 130
Weiner, Douglas R., 13, 26–28,
276–315
Wells, H. G., 286
Wertime, Theodore, 90
West, 307; in China, 131; East/West
dichotomy, 242, 245; liberal versions
of developmentalism, 27–28, 120;
meat supply, 148; "Occidentalist,"
25–26, 242. See also Americas;
Enlightenment; Europe;
Renaissance
West Africa: agriculture, 36, 215; Bantu-
speaking people spreading out from,
219; gold, 93; indigenous empires, 217,
218–19; palm oil, 220; slavery and
slave trade, 217
Western Europe, 97; Black Death, 92;
coal, 42–44, 49, 95, 96; export orientation, 128; nuclear power, 47–49, 166.
See also Britain; France; Germany;
Iberia; Netherlands; Rhine;
Switzerland
Westinghouse, 45
Westphalia, Rhine, 170, 180–81, 182, 184
wetland reclamation, China, 152
wheat, 23, 105
White, Richard, 265
wildlife management: India, 230–33, 243,
253nn68,69; state rights, 60. See also
animals; biodiversity; hunting; parks;
plants
Williams, Michael, 237
wind energy, 40
wind systems, Middle East climate, 82

Wittfogel, Karl, 89, 121, 184
women: African cultivators, 216; Chinese
labor, 128; role in environmental
change, 241
Wong, R. Bin, 149
wood energy. See biomass fuels
wood supply: for building, 42–43;
China, 131; for energy, 41–42, 44, 90;
foresters' concerns, 59; Middle East,
94, 95, 96, 97; Rhine and, 172. See also
forests
wool production, 95
World Bank, 103
world history, and environmental
history, 3–32
"world" religions, 10–11
World War I, Russia, 282, 283
World War II: Rhine Navigation
Commission, 171; Yellow River
works, 138
Worldwatch Institute, 47, 49fig
Worster, Donald, 241, 257
Wrigley, E. A., 16

Yablokov, Aleksei, 300, 301
Yamdrok Tso project, Tibet, 138, 149
Yan Fu, 7
Yangzi River area, 10, 137; agriculture,
127, 128, 129, 130; Central Asian
nomads, 124; dams, 135, 138–44, 149,
150; deforestation, 145–46, 152,
161–62n97; flooding/flood control,
125–27, 138, 152; Grand Canal, 125;
labor, 28n4, 129, 137–38; local elite
power, 124, 125–27, 130–31, 137, 152;
population, 127, 128, 129; transport,
123, 125, 130; wealth subsidizing
other regions, 22, 125, 126, 127,
128, 130
Yanitsky, Oleg, 293
Yellow River area, 137, 140–41; agriculture, 36, 126, 133; deforestation, 129;
erosion, 129, 144; flooding/flood

control, 121, 125, 129–32, 135, 141, 145–46; Grand Canal and, 125, 129–31; hydropower, 143–44; labor, 137–38, 158n59; salinization, 132, 133; Sanmenxia Dam and reservoir, 138, 145–46; water shortages, 146

Text:	10.25/14 Fournier
Display:	Fournier
Cartographer/Illustrator:	Bill Nelson
Indexer:	Barbara Roos
Compositor:	International Typesetting and Composition
Printer and Binder:	Maple-Vail Book Manufacturing Group